D0984672

Yale Studies of the City 1

NINETEENTH-CENTURY CITIES

Essays in the New Urban History
edited by
Stephan Thernstrom
and
Richard Sennett

Yale University Press,
New Haven and London, 1969

Copyright © 1969 by Yale University.
All rights reserved. This book may not be
reproduced, in whole or in part, in any form
(except by reviewers for the public press),
without written permission from the publishers.
Library of Congress catalog card number: 73–89905
Standard book number (clothbound): 300–01150–4
Standard book number (paperbound): 300–01151–2
Designed by Sally Sullivan,
set in Baskerville type,
and printed in the United States of America by
The Carl Purington Rollins Printing-Office
of the Yale University Press.
Distributed in Great Britain, Europe, Asia, and
Africa by Yale University Press Ltd., London; in
Canada by McGill-Queen's University Press, Montreal;
and in Mexico by Centro Interamericano de Libros
Académicos, Mexico City.

CONTENTS

HT 119
.Y3
1968

PREFACE

Stephan Thernstrom and Richard Sennett

The "new economic history" was christened but a few years ago; already the leading practitioners of that arcane art have transformed our image of significant segments of the past. It may be premature to claim that a complementary "new urban history" has emerged as yet, but it is clear that the burgeoning field of urban history is now in a state of creative ferment. New questions are being raised, new sources are being exploited, new methods of analysis are being employed by a generation of younger scholars. This volume, a collection of papers originally prepared for the Yale Conference on the Nineteenth-Century Industrial City held in November 1968, offers a number of new insights into the social dimensions of urbanization and opens up a great many more questions that deserve further exploration. It provides a taste of some of the advanced research now going on in urban history and perhaps a foreshadowing of the direction in which the field will develop in the future.

The conference from which this volume grew came about because of the discovery of the two editors that a number of urban researchers around the country were working on broadly similar problems in broadly similar ways but with little awareness of each other. To varying degrees they shared three related traits: (1) an interest in linking sociological theory to historical data, moving back and forth across the boundaries separating the traditional disciplines; (2) an understanding of the uses of quantitative materials; (3) an eagerness to broaden the scope of urban studies to embrace the social experience of ordinary, unexceptional people. When we began planning the meeting we knew of several scholars working in this vein.

We were frankly surprised, however, to find that our list of conference invitees soon grew to triple the length originally anticipated, and still more happily surprised to find that no less than twenty papers materialized to provide the basis for two days of profitable discussion. A few of these papers were either too preliminary to merit inclusion here or were committed for publication elsewhere, but this volume contains most of them, along with a new essay by Norman Birnbaum to provide an overview of the whole.

The papers vary considerably in focus, method, and style. The cities treated range from small communities like Springfield and Paterson to giants like Philadelphia, Chicago, Boston and London. Four of the essays move outside the United States and supply comparative material from other societies—Canada, England, France, and Colombia. Some are based upon examination of the entire population of a city, or of a sample representative of the entire population; others focus upon particular social groups—the glassblowers of Carmaux, the manufacturers of Paterson. Some contributors emphasize methodological difficulties as much as substantive findings. A few of these essays are austerely statistical, whereas others focus on dimensions of urban life that are less amenable to quantitative analysis.

For all of these differences, however, the papers presented here have a common purpose. They all aim at deepening our understanding of the lives of men and women living in dense urban settlements undergoing explosive growth and structural transformation. Two essays explore the critically important and much neglected matter of family structure; a third paper prepared for the conference—Herbert Gutman's and Laurence Glasco's pioneering investigation of Negro family patterns—

could not be included here, alas, but is scheduled for separate publication. A second group of essays examines questions of political and social control and the role of urban elites in that process. A third group focuses upon residential and ecological patterns. The longest section of the book treats several facets of class structure and the mobility process. A number of the other essays also have some bearing on the question of social mobility and class, for the various forms of mobility are the source of much of the dynamic of urban change, but these six papers confront the question directly. Taken together, these essays give a good sense of both the diversity and the common threads that are now visible in this rapidly developing area of scholarly concern.

Few of our contributors would claim that these essays are the last word on the subject. All too often, indeed, they are practically the first word that has ever been written on it. Most of our authors plunged into their subjects at a time when there was little or no literature to guide them, and many are still in the process of working out the larger implications of their findings. These papers are first reports on unexplored areas of urban social life and should be read as such.

It should also be noted that this volume is a genuinely interdisciplinary effort, in which contributors are attempting to transcend established disciplinary categories. Half have had their advanced training in history; the rest are products of the other social sciences or of interdisciplinary programs. Half now teach in history departments, half in other social science departments. Crossing traditional boundaries entails certain risks. Some of these essays perhaps pay too little attention to the full historical context to appeal to the historian, and some may seem primitive in technique by the standards of the sociologist sophisticated in quantitative analysis. But we are convinced that the gains that come from venturing into unexplored territory more than compensate for the losses.

To the historian the gain is that whole dimensions of the past that had either been neglected entirely or treated superficially may be brought into clearer focus. Historians writing about nineteenth-century cities have perforce made assumptions about the character and structure of social life—about the division of the community into social classes, the rigidity or permeability of those classes, the processes that governed the flow of people into and out of the city, the functions of the family and the values it inculcated in its children, etc. But many of these assumptions, it would seem from the essays in this volume, are wrong, or at best half true. The judicious use of concepts and techniques developed in such disciplines as sociology and economics, and the exploitation of sources historians in the past have left relatively untouched because of uncertainty about how to make use of them, can provide a sounder and a richer understanding of urban social life.

The effect of researches such as these on the sociological study of the city is to emphasize the dynamic character of the urban form itself. For it has been all too common in sociological investigations of city life to treat the city as a fixed set of social elements. The classic urban theorists of the Chicago school, such as Robert Park and Louis Wirth, recognized this to be a problem in their own work, but until recently a body of historical data that could be used in the reconstruction of a theory of cities as historically alive and changing institutions has not been available. Historical information of a kind that speaks to questions of social theory has been lacking, and to bridge that impasse is the intent of the authors of these essays. Some of this research has already forced a recasting of older social theory; the essays on urban elites offer a challenge to certain elements of Pareto's ranking of elites, and the essays on urban families challenge elements of Parsonian theory of the nuclear family.

The opportunity to assemble a group of scholars for the conference meetings from which this volume has come was the result of the generosity and effort of Yale's Office of Urban Studies and Programs. Associate Provost Joel L. Fleishman provided encouragement and useful advice at every opportunity; Conference Coordinator A. Tappan Wilder and his assistant Richard Moore spent an enormous amount of time and energy providing a congenial setting and conference structure in which the participants could work. We are deeply indebted to them for making possible the opportunity for the scholars in this field to meet and learn from one another.

The following scholars gathered in New Haven in November 1968 to participate in the Yale Conference on Nineteenth-Century Cities:

Wendell Bell, Chairman
Department of Sociology
Yale University

Norman Birnbaum
Department of Sociology
Amherst College

Stuart Blumin
Department of History
Skidmore College

A. Guido Dobbert
Department of History
Youngstown University

Robert Doherty
Department of History
University of Pittsburgh

Robert Fogelson
Department of City
   Planning
Massachusetts Institute of
   Technology

Michael H. Frisch
Department of History
Princeton University

Herbert Gans
The Center for Urban
    Education
New York

Howard M. Gitelman
Department of Economics
William and Mary College

Laurence Glasco
Department of History
University of Buffalo

Clyde Griffen
Department of History
Vassar College

Herbert G. Gutman
Department of History
University of Rochester

Theodore Hershberg
Department of History
University of Pennsylvania

Michael Holt
Department of History
Yale University

Daniel Horowitz
Committee on American
    Civilization
Harvard University

Frederic C. Jaher
Department of History
University of Illinois

Michael B. Katz
Ontario Institute for
    Studies in Education

Peter R. Knights
College of
    Communications
University of Illinois

Howard R. Lamar,
    Chairman
Department of History
Yale University

Eric E. Lampard
Department of History
University of Wisconsin

John Larkin
Department of History
Brandeis University

Marvin Lazerson
Department of History
Harvard University

Lynn Lees
Department of History
Mount Holyoke College

Virginia McGlaughlin
Bronx
New York

William McFeely
Department of History
Yale University

Anthony Maingot
Department of Sociology
Yale University

Stephen Mick
Department of Sociology
Yale University

Richard Morse
Department of History
Yale University

Rollin G. Osterweis
Department of History
Yale University

George W. Pierson
Department of History
Yale University

Leo F. Schnore
Center for Demography
    and Ecology
University of Wisconsin

Joan W. Scott
Department of History
University of Chicago

Richard Sennett
Department of Sociology
Yale University

Allan Spear
Department of History
University of Minnesota

Maynard Swanson
Department of History
Yale University

Stephan Thernstrom
Department of History
Brandeis University

Charles Tilly
Center for Advanced Study
    in Behavioral Sciences
Palo Alto

Sam Bass Warner, Jr.
Department of History
University of Michigan

PART ONE: URBAN CLASS AND MOBILITY PATTERNS

THE GLASSWORKERS OF CARMAUX, 1850–1900[1]
Joan W. Scott

In December 1893, when the lists of "dangerous anarchists and revolutionaries" in the Department of the Tarn
were being revised, the Police Commissioner of Carmaux
wrote to the Prefect concerning one of the workers on the
lists.

> This man, as a result of hard work and economy has
> purchased a small piece of land which he cultivates
> himself. His vineyard is a veritable garden, and he
> shows it with pride to all who visit him. When the vine-
> yard is fully developed in two years, he says, it will pro-
> duce twenty *barriques* of wine. N——— likes to say
> too, "there are those who eat their money at the cab-
> arets; I don't go to them and this is what I have achieved
> instead." In light of these circumstances, if N——— is
> an anarchist, it seems to me he ought not to be classified
> as a dangerous one.[2]

The Police Commissioner assumed that attachment to
the city, particularly ownership of some land, was a mod-
erating influence on urban residents. He echoed the outlook of generations of Carmaux's officials who had con-
gratulated themselves on the semirural lives of the town's
miners. After 1856, they watched uneasily for signs of disorder among the glassworkers—an itinerant artisan population that had no material stake in the city.

The Commissioner's assumption, in one variant or another, runs through much of the contemporary literature
on urbanization. Working-class unrest in the early stages
of industrialization is attributed to the dislocations experienced in the move from rural to urban areas, in the
change from self-disciplined domestic labor to standard-

ized norms of factory work, in the loss of traditional social institutions (family, religion) and the lack of any replacement for them. This is essentially the view of American sociologists like Kerr, Smelser, and Hauser,[3] and of social historians like Louis Chevalier. For Chevalier, working classes and "dangerous classes" began to merge in nineteenth-century Paris, as lonely men arrived and floundered in the chaos of the large city.[4] For Lorwin, early working-class protest in Western Europe comes from economic dislocations, and he sees the occupations most prone to radicalism as those that are least stable and most isolated from "normal" social life.[5] Thernstrom attributes the absence of organized working-class protest in Newburyport, Massachusetts, to a high incidence of property mobility.[6] An extension and refinement of the argument goes beyond the Police Commissioner's equation of land-ownership and stability, maintaining instead that some form of "integration" into city life is a prerequisite for "normal" or stable conditions. Usually the argument goes the other way—the absence of integrative institutions is seen as a factor leading to working-class unrest.

Much of this position is based on an explicit or implicit idealization of rural life. The city is unfavorably contrasted with the more perfect country, which provides stability and calm in its organization of life. Of course, there have been many studies that dispute the existence of the rural ideal. But even leaving these aside, what if one examined the city in terms of its own organization of life? Perhaps then the entire argument could be reversed and working-class protest and unrest attributed to the kind of integration a city does provide for its residents.

Certainly, in the case of Carmaux, generations of police were misled because they held to the truth of their simple assumption. The semirural miners were always a source of greater trouble than the glassworkers. Despite their roots in Carmaux and its countryside, they held strikes, rioted, and even pillaged the Marquis' château. The glassworkers, until the 1890s, were markedly absent from any sort of protest. In fact, incidences of militant working-class action grow in Carmaux as miners and glassworkers become increasingly attached to the city.

The view of the city as somewhat coherently organized (however different this organization is from "the country") is implicit in many discussions of working-class consciousness. Marx attributed the growth of such consciousness, in part, to the communication afforded workers by proximity in the factory and in the working-class neighborhood. Like Marx, Georges Duveau and E. P. Thompson see shared living and working experiences that contrast sharply with the life of others in the city as contributing to workers' consciousness. (Thompson, of course, insists that an entire cultural tradition and shared historical experience, as well as economic and political factors, formed the consciousness of England's workers.)[7] More recently, Thernstrom has expanded the discussion by arguing that geographic stability is an important factor in the development of class consciousness and the organization of collective action.[8]

I would take Thernstrom one step farther and add that along with geographic stability, and perhaps preceding it, was an identification of the city with one's means of livelihood, a sense that one's future, one's work, was defined by a particular place. Throughout the nineteenth century, French glassworkers found security in the fact that they possessed a skill. They could practice it in any glass bottle establishment. The miners of Carmaux were only partly miners; they also cultivated their land. Only at the end of the nineteenth century did both groups come to iden-

tify their occupations with Carmaux. Then they saw their
economic well-being linked not only to their labor and
to the factory or mine, but to the city itself. At this point,
workers in individual factories and particular trades
(some already organized in trade unions) joined in militant actions with workers from different occupations.
Their occupational roots in the city (and in some cases
actual ownership of property as well), rather than mod-
erating workers' behavior, seems to have provided the
basis for collective action broader than that which occurred within specific trade unions. It was precisely those
workers with a sense of integration into the city (or a
desire to belong to it) and not rootless, wandering marginal migrants, who exhibited the greatest sense of working-class consciousness in the nineteenth century. At least
this seems to have been the case in Carmaux.

Carmaux is a small city in the Department of the Tarn
in southwestern France. In 1851, it had a population of
2,678; in 1901 there were 10,956 inhabitants. Mining was
Carmaux's chief industry in the nineteenth century, as it
is today. It flourished as a glass bottle-blowing center before the Revolution and again after the 1860s. Both the
mines and glassworks were owned by the family of the
Marquis de Solages until 1856, when a merchant from
Toulouse bought the glassworks.

The first part of this paper deals with glassmaking
before 1856. The second, third, and fourth parts analyze
the effects of changes brought by expansion and technological innovation from 1856 to 1900. In the second half
of the nineteenth century, glassblowing in Carmaux (and
throughout France) lost its position as a specialized craft
and became, at best, a semiskilled industry. Even the term
that designated a glassworker in census and civil records
changed from *verrier* (1850s–80) to *ouvrier verrier* after

1880. (Miners were referred to usually as *ouvriers mineurs;* auxilliary workers at the glassworks were designated *ouvrier à la verrerie.*) By 1901, most large establishments replaced skilled blowers with semiautomatic blowing machines, and an apprenticeship of fifteen years was reduced to several days. The glassworkers of Carmaux provide a case study in the effects on artisans of the decline and disappearance of their craft and of the effects on Carmaux of the "settling" of formerly itinerant glassblowers after 1885.[9]

In an elaborate entry in his parish register, the curé of Carmaux detailed the baptism of the Verrerie on April 20, 1754. Assisted by two other priests, the curé in surplice and violet hat raised the cross and began his tour, chanting the *Vene Creator* as he walked. When he arrived at the furnace he sang a psalm and then lit its first fire. As the flames soared, his voice rang out the *Te Deum.* The curé then proceeded to a house adjacent to the glassworks which was to lodge the workers. Two days later, a solemn mass was sung asking God's blessing for the new enterprise of the Chevalier de Solages.[10]

This account, and the numerous other more conventional entries in the parish registers of Carmaux and its neighboring commune of Blaye from 1712 to 1789, provide a wealth of information about the first glassworkers of Carmaux. From the priest's description alone, we get a sense of the importance of the occasion. The physical structure of the Verrerie can be deduced as well. A central building, attached to the château of the Chevalier, housed a single furnace. In accordance with medieval custom, lodging was provided for the *verriers.*

The curé's entries for baptisms, deaths, and marriages enlarge the picture. All *verriers* are referred to as *Sieur.*

Only doctors, lawyers, and nobility received higher esteem in the register; their names were always prefixed by *Monsieur*. Bourgeois, *controlleur, merchand,* and *maître verrier* (or *souffleur*—the two were usually synonymous) ranked equally in receiving the appellation, *Sieur*. Most other craftsmen—carpenter, blacksmith, mason, shoemaker, tailor, miller—even sheriffs, as well as workers of every other sort (miners, common laborers) and peasants were referred to merely by name. None of the earliest *verriers* came from Carmaux or from its neighboring departments. Two came from Sauvigny, one from Normandy, one from Nevers, and another from Verdun. They tended to marry daughters of glassworkers or of others in their social status (merchants and bourgeois). That social intercourse took place primarily among equals, and especially among those in the same occupation, is further indicated by witnesses at glassworkers' weddings, and by the godparents chosen for their children.

Though the Verrerie Royale de Solages differed from other glassworks in the region in its use of coal rather than wood as fuel, its organization of work and the status of its workers was characteristic of mid-eighteenth-century glass manufactories. In its origins, glassblowing was a trade restricted to nobles. It was, in fact, the only one they could engage in without derogating themselves. By 1754, though nobles retained sole rights to direct verreries, the blowers themselves were not necessarily of noble blood. They were a group apart, however. They received special privileges from the Crown. They were literate. Their sons inherited the right to practice the craft; their daughters were wooed by young men wishing to enter it.

A young man (generally the son of a glassblower) usually began his training as a bottle carrier—bringing the finished bottle to its baths of cold and hot water, and then to the *arrangeur* who stacked and sorted them. By the age of thirteen, he became a *gamin,* preparing the molten glass at the end of a long tube. After several years, a *gamin* became a *grand garçon,* shaping the hot glass and beginning the blowing process. By twenty-five or twenty-eight years of age, the young man was qualified to blow finished bottles as a *souffleur* or *ouvrier en bouteilles.* He then headed an *équipe* of workers, consisting of himself and his three apprentices. The number of *équipes* depended on the number of *places* at a *four,* that is the number of openings from which one could draw molten glass. At Carmaux in the eighteenth century, there were four places at the furnace, indicating four *équipes* and one relay or relief group, whose members replaced ill or disabled *verriers.* In 1758, the sixteen workers and their assistants—moldmakers, blacksmiths, errand boys, stackers, etc.—were manufacturing 200,000 bottles a year.[11]

Although the privileged status of glassblowing came to an end well before the Revolution, the organization of work at the Verrerie Royale de Solages continued essentially unchanged until the middle of the nineteenth century. The production records and pay lists for 1810 to 1817 and 1830 to 1840 indicate no major changes. *Gamins* and *grand garçons* still served five years each, and the length of time from *porteur* to *souffleur* was still about fifteen to twenty years. By the age of twenty-five, the son of a *verrier* was qualified as a *souffleur.*

The situation was different, however, for sons of those working at the Verrerie in jobs not directly connected with bottleblowing. Smelters, blacksmiths, and warehouse managers were skilled auxiliary personnel, and they ranked second only to *souffleurs* in the wage scale. *Souffleurs* earned two or three times as much as anyone else, but the three auxiliary positions were higher paid than either the master of the relay or any *grand garçon* or *gamin*. Moldmakers, potters, those who prepared the constituent materials of the glass, those who tended the furnaces, the numerous workers who stacked and arranged and transported bottles constituted almost as large a (sometimes larger) work force as the *verriers*. By the first decade of the nineteenth century, with expanded production demanding more workers, the sons of auxiliary personnel at the glassworks, and particularly of the most skilled, began entering glassblowing. For them, advance was more difficult, involving many more steps. They began early doing odd jobs in the shops, serving the *verriers*, carrying water, grinding and cleaning sand. The move from *porteur de cour* to *porteur de relai* (from the outer yards to an *équipe*) came after three years for one Valery, *fils*. And he was sixteen when he began the work usually given to eight- to ten-year-olds. Similarly, Raymond Maurel, son of a tanner who had worked at the Verrerie at least since 1810, worked as a laborer for nineteen years before qualifying as a *gamin*. In the same period of time, however, the son of the master smelter the highest paid position after the *souffleur*) moved from laborer to relief *souffleur*.

This kind of mobility was possible usually for only one of a craftsman's sons, though all his sons worked at the Verrerie in some capacity. That family connections for glassworkers and associated employees predominated is indicated by pay lists which refer to a person's place in his family rather than to his name. Thus, Boyer, *père;* Boyer, *fils aîné;* Boyer, *fils cadet;* Boyer, *le petit,* referred to the family of master smelter Joseph Boyer whose oldest son, Joseph, eventually became a master glassblower. Boyer served at the Verrerie for at least thirty years (from 1810

to 1840) and his descendants continued to serve until the
end of the century. In the decade 1830–40, though the
time was somewhat lessened, the pattern remained the
same: only one son of a craftsman usually became a *souffleur*. The blacksmith, Paliès, appears on pay lists first
in 1835. His oldest son is listed as "his father's assistant"
and then, five years later, simply as "blacksmith." A
younger son is a mason; the youngest begins as a *gamin*
in 1838. Unlike earlier workers, Paliès had his entire family enlisted at the Verrerie. His wife and daughter worked
preparing the clay and sand for the potters who made the
molds. (Women are mentioned for the first time in 1835.
They are always wives and daughters of associated personnel or widows of glassblowers.)

For the earlier generation of associated personnel
(1810), a long stay for the father seems to have been a
prerequisite for his son's entry into glassblowing. As production expanded, however (from 274,812 bottles a year
in 1817 to 401,572 in 1831), workers seem to have been
admitted more rapidly. Though, in principle, a *verrier's*
apprenticeship lasted an average of fifteen years, few
grand garçons actually became *souffleurs* after five years
in Carmaux. From 1810 to 1840 there were only four positions opened as master glassblowers, and the masters'
terms generally lasted twenty to twenty-five years. In fact,
three of the masters in 1810–17 had themselves been, or
were sons of, *verriers* who had been working in Carmaux
since 1760—the first decade of the Verrerie. Since sons of
masters were given priority in succeeding to their fathers'
places (and often a son was kept on as *souffleur* sharing a
place with his father), there were few openings for a
grand garçon when he completed his apprenticeship.
Some, like one Gerlant, remained a *grand garçon* for fourteen years (thereby blocking the mobility of the *gamin*

behind him) and eventually became a master. Most, however, left Carmaux for a larger or newer verrerie.[12] In the late eighteenth and early nineteenth centuries a glass-blower's prosperity depended on national rather than local conditions. And he had a sense of himself as a member of a national (even international, since glassworkers often came from and went to Belgium and Italy) corporation.

In the period 1810–17, there were thirty-six families working at the Verrerie. In 1835, only thirteen of them were still present. Almost two-thirds had either left the Verrerie or Carmaux itself. (Since we have no census data for these years, the nature of departure is impossible to determine.) One explanation for such mobility lies in the duration of work at the Verrerie. The *campagne,* or term of production, lasted anywhere from six to eight months (from September or October until June or July). At the end of this time, all production was suspended and the furnace repaired (summers were generally chosen since the heat made work at the furnace impossible anyway). Many workers, except those engaged in repairs and the *verriers* (who were frequently under contract not to leave during the *four mort*), left the Verrerie in the slack period.

Of the thirteen families who remained, five had fathers who worked as smelters, blacksmiths, or in the storerooms as supervisors in 1810 and sons who were glassblowers in 1835. Three were established families of glassblowers or had members at some stage of apprenticeship in 1810 and were still in Carmaux as glassblowers in 1835. The other five remained in their original occupations.[13] Master glassworkers and those with high-ranking craft or supervisory positions seem to have been most stable. The same families of blacksmiths, smelters, and store super-

visors served the Verrerie for generations. Their stability
seems to have achieved further mobility for at least one
son—in the form of entry into the glass trade. The son's
continued success, however, often was assured only by his
leaving Carmaux. At least one and frequently two sons
of a glassblower, on the other hand, most often (though
not necessarily) inherited their father's position and, with
it, the right to geographical stability as well.

Their origins, the status and relatively high pay of their
occupation, and their tenure in the community brought
additional rewards to those glassblowers who became masters and settled in Carmaux. They usually were able to
buy land and hold political office in the town. The first
electoral list, based on property qualifications (compiled
in March 1790), included seven *ouvrier en bouteilles*. On
November 15, 1790, Jacques Chappa, *père* (who had arrived in Carmaux from Verdun in 1760), was elected a
notable and a municipal officer. In 1796, as the oldest
citizen in Carmaux, he was made honorary president of
the *Bureau Provisoire*. His son, Jacques, also a glassworker who had been an executive commissioner of the
Directory in 1795, was made president of the Bureau as
well as of the Municipal Council. From 1834 to 1848 at
least one glassblower (who also listed himself as a *propriétaire*) served on the Municipal Council, whose members consisted predominantly of landowners, professionals, and merchants.[14]

Records of landownership indicate that large holdings
were acquired by the families of glassworkers at the end
of the eighteenth and in the early nineteenth century.
In fact, though few *verriers* owned land in the early nineteenth century (only three or four who actually settled
in Carmaux did), their holdings were far more extensive
than those of the *verriers* in a later period. The early

glassworkers qualify as substantial *propriétaires* (and
often list their occupation as *propriétaire-cultivateur*
rather than, or in addition to *verrier*); the later ones generally owned little more than a house and tiny garden.
Those in the late nineteenth century who had large holdings were invariably descendants of settled *verrier* fami-
lies.Boyer and Alary (the fathers were smelter and storekeeper, respectively, in 1810, the sons, *verriers* in 1835)
are prime examples. Neither family began as glassblowers, but their high-paying jobs at the Verrerie enabled
them to acquire land and to participate in politics. The
succeeding generations of Alarys and Boyers entered
glassmaking, remained in Carmaux, and continued to
expand their holdings.[15]

The Verrerie de Solages seems to have prospered into
the 1840s, manufacturing anywhere from 200,000 to
600,000 bottles a year. In 1838, the work force consisted
of forty-nine people. Nineteen were directly involved in
bottle blowing, the other thirty ranged from smelters,
blacksmiths, and store supervisors to messengers and common laborers (including women). The workshop still ad-
joined the Solages' château, but workers no longer lived
on the grounds. Most resided in Carmaux or Blaye in
houses they rented or (in a very few cases) owned. In the
1840s production declined badly. After 1845, there are
no entries for bottles produced. The company was running at a deficit, and the amount paid in salaries to "Mes-
sieurs les ouvriers en bouteilles" dropped from 3,097
livres for the second six months of 1844, to 100 *livres* in
1845, to "rien" in 1849. In early 1856, production seems
to have climbed. The *verriers* received a large salary, but
the company was more heavily in debt than it had been
before. (The debt was largely to itself since coal—the primary expense of the Verrerie—was bought from the Sol-

ages mining company. Though the Verrerie and coal mines were kept on separate accounts, they were considered a single company by Solages.)[16]

For a century from 1754 to 1854, the Verrerie de Solages functioned as a specialized craft. Its organization, the number of its employees, the status of its workers, its methods of management and administration in 1854 would not have been strange to the first *verriers* from the north in 1754. In 1856, Solages sold the Verrerie to M. Rességuier, a bottle merchant from Toulouse, and in less than a generation, glassmaking in Carmaux was fundamentally changed.

From 1856 to 1883 Rességuier expanded the glassworks. In 1862 he moved the Verrerie from the Solages' château to the site of the new railway station, and by 1875 there were six furnaces in operation and 200 workers employed. Glassworkers from all over France were recruited to Carmaux's Verrerie Ste. Clothilde. Most came as practiced artisans from other establishments. A few were locally recruited and the first in their families to enter glassblowing. In fact, the figures seem to indicate that in the first ten years of the Verrerie, the need for labor enabled sons of local *propriétaires,* especially, to become glassworkers. As the years passed and the Verrerie expanded, however, workers tended increasingly to come from glassblowing centers outside the Tarn. Thus in the decade 1853–62, one-third of the glassblowers who married in Carmaux came from the Tarn, and 50% came from beyond its neighboring departments. Sixteen percent were sons of glassblowers, whereas 33% were sons of peasants (listed as *propriétaire* or *cultivateur*). In 1873–82, however, only 17.1% of the *verriers* married came from the Tarn, 28.5% came from the Tarn and surrounding departments (this movement might be attributed to a normal regional migratory pattern), whereas 71.4% were from farther away. Of these, most were from the Loire and Rhône, sons of glassworkers in the large centers of Rive-de-Gier and Givors. Of the glassworkers married in 1873–82, 31% were sons of glassworkers.

These figures, based solely on marriage acts, give only a rough approximation of the origins of Carmaux's glassworkers, and they tend to overrepresent the younger, single men. In fact, most glassworkers were married when they arrived in Carmaux, and they came in large family groups. In the census listings a father and all his sons over thirteen (frequently a grandfather as well) are listed as "verriers," and often several young boarders also listed as "verrier" traveled with the family.[17] Toussaint Rauzier arrived from the Gard in 1866 with three sons, aged twenty-two, twenty-one, and eleven; all were glassworkers. In addition, three boarders, all in their twenties, were glassworkers.

Few of the glassworkers who came to Carmaux remained very long. The censuses reveal an extremely high turnover. Most families are present for only one census, indicating a stay of less than five years. (The finished family reconstitution will enable greater precision in determining length of stay and differences, if any, between those who did remain and those who left.) The movement might, in part, be explained by the fact that glassworkers died at a relatively young age. The average age of death of active males over fifteen was forty-two years, nine months in 1873–82, and thirty-three years, two months in 1883–92. But the departure of their families still needs explanation, since most had sons at the Verrerie. And many more *verriers* and their families left Carmaux than died.[18] The length of the *campagne* was no longer an operative factor since, with more than one furnace in operation, there was no need to stop all· work for repairs. Rather, repairs were rotated so that only one furnace was *mort* at a time, and work was continuous throughout the year.[19]

There are indications that frequent moves were typical for glassblowers all over France (at least for those who eventually came to Carmaux). The listings of place of birth in the censuses of 1872 and 1876 are revealing in this connection. The family of Jean Claude Peuginot, *verrier,* was first listed in the Carmaux census of 1876. Peuginot and his wife were both born in the Jura and were probably married there since their first three children were also born in the Jura. (These three, all sons, were *verriers* in 1876.) Their fourth child was born in the Marne, their fifth in the Saône-et-Loire. The next child was born in the Haute Marne, the next in the Loire, another in Saône-et-Loire, and the last in the Tarn (Carmaux). The oldest son, Hippolyte, came with the family to Carmaux, where he worked as a glassblower. He married the daughter of a miner in 1879, left to work elsewhere, then returned. His first two children were born in the Nord, the other three after his return to Carmaux.[20]

Since their stay was short, glassworkers rarely bought property. Instead, they rented lodgings in the streets surrounding the Verrerie. All the censuses for Carmaux I examined reveal the same geographic concentration of glassworkers.[21] Although miners lived scattered throughout the commune, the names of almost all glassworkers could be found on two or three successive pages in the census book. The Rue de la Gare and the Rue de la Verrerie, especially, were inhabited almost exclusively by glassworkers and their families. The nature of their work dictated these living arrangements. They worked long and late hours, and in the winter a long walk would have been detrimental to the already weakened physique of the glassblower.[22] In addition, rotation of *équipes* and the system of replacements (by which a substitute was awakened to take the place of a *verrier* who reported sick) were simplified by having all workers living near the shops.

The glassworkers' living arrangements, in turn, created a sense of themselves as a self-contained, separate community within the city. The glassworkers were isolated because they had no roots in the area and by their inability to speak the *patois,* the local dialect spoken by peasants and by the miners who constituted the bulk of Carmaux's population. But they saw themselves as not only different from, but superior to other workers. Aware of their noble ancestors (there are constant references to "les gentilhommes verriers"), they were still "aristocrats," performing a specialized craft that was closed to most residents of Carmaux. In the eyes of the town, as well as in their own eyes, they were a step above other workers. By virtue of their salaries alone, the glassworkers were superior. A *souffleur* at the Verrerie in 1882 earned approximately 250 francs monthly, and he worked eleven hours a day. A miner in the same period worked eight hours and earned 85 francs a month. Master smelters, mechanics, and blacksmiths earned more than *grand garçons* (125 francs a month) and *gamins* (100 francs) and considerably more than their counterparts in the mines. *Grand garçons* and *gamins* (though paid per bottle, so the rate fluctuated) earned 40 to 50 francs more a month than all categories of miners. The *verriers* and their skilled assistants earned salaries equivalent to the *employes,* the supervisory personnel at the mines.[23] Their high salaries made them better customers, and the delicacy of their physical condition demanded finer foods and more drink. Whereas miners maintained their own gardens, living largely self-sufficiently like the peasants, the glassworkers were completely dependent on local shops for their food.[24]

Glassworkers occupied the same position of respect within their communities as at work. *Souffleurs* (the term *maître* was dropped by the 1860s, and functional terms rather than honorific ones were used, perhaps an indication of the beginning of the end of specialized terminology and of the distinction of the craft) received greatest respect. Their apprentices were seen as privileged, whereas auxiliary workers, though paid more than apprentices, never attained quite the status of the *verrier*. Glassworkers still tended to marry daughters of glassworkers or of other artisans, though increasingly they married miners' daughters.[25] Sons of miners had most difficulty entering the glass trade. (In 1873–82 only 5% of *verriers* married were sons of miners, though close to 20% of their wives were miners' daughters.) This sense of separateness probably made frequent moves less difficult. A *verrier* was easily accepted in a new glassworker community and was accorded the status commensurate with his work. There is evidence, too, that glassworkers traveled not only in family groupings, but in larger groups made up of families from the same town—giving the impression to one writer of a nomadic tribe.[26]

The feeling of belonging to a national corporation rather than to a particular town reinforced the geographic and social isolation of glassworkers from miners and other workers in Carmaux. The relatively small size of the town (6,160 in 1876, 6,905 in 1881) created some inevitable social contacts in cafés and shops and at the Friday market. Yet the smallness of the town did not itself create a common denominator of working-class consciousness. If they were conscious of themselves as artisans, glassworkers seemed to exhibit little sense of identity with any other group in Carmaux.

A police report in 1882 contrasted the working populations of Carmaux in an interesting fashion. Having described the successful attempts of the miners in forming a union as motivated purely by economic needs, the Commissioner found them "animated by good sentiments [and] far from approving the anarchist manifestations which have occurred in certain working class centers." Though the miner who was also a *petit-propriétaire* was a disappearing figure, the Commissioner of Police echoed the statements of his predecessors: the miners were a stable element in Carmaux's population. The glassworkers on the other hand did not share "the moderation and wisdom of the miners, but their number is not great enough to cause fear of serious complications."[27]

What is interesting about the report is its inaccuracy. From 1854 to 1884, the records of arrests for political activities list only miners. They struck frequently, engaged in militant mass actions, and even pillaged the Marquis de Solages' château during the general strike of 1869. By 1883, they had successfully organized a union. Though the issues in the strikes varied, they were frequently direct or indirect responses to the introduction of new techniques designed to modernize and industrialize the mines. Though Rességuier, too, improved and expanded his operation, there were no strikes of glassworkers in this period until an attempt failed in 1882. Neither is there any evidence of glassworker support for miners. The glassworkers seem to have passed through the town without creating a disturbance worthy of note in newspapers or police and prefect reports.

One possible explanation for the differences in miner and glassworker activity might lie in the different work they performed. One could argue that while the numerous miners began to be "proletarianized" in this period (the policy of the company was designed to change the semipeasant miners into full-fledged workers)[28] and engaged in militant action, the fewer artisan glassworkers clung to traditional, conservative, guildlike organizations.[29] A nice explanation perhaps and partially accurate for the miners, but it really doesn't work for the glassworkers. If glassworkers thought of themselves as artisans, they formed no organizations in this period, and they undertook no actions designed to protect the standards and quality of their craft. The open market created by an expanding bottle industry provided jobs for everyone, and if standards dropped at one manufactory, a dissatisfied glassworker could always move on.

Geographic mobility, in fact, seems to have been a key factor in preventing the creation of any glassworker organizations in this period (whether guildlike or "modern"). Stephan Thernstrom's argument that "considerable stability of the working class at least within a given city . . . would seem to be a minimal necessity if mere complaints are to be translated effectively into class grievances and to inspire collective protest" seems accurate in the case of the glassworkers of Carmaux.[30] Whereas 85% of the miners were recruited within a twelve-mile radius from Carmaux, and most of them were born in the commune itself, most glassworkers came from faraway departments and remained in the town for fewer than five years. As the policy of the Compagnie des Mines succeeded, and miners increasingly became city dwellers, they came to depend more completely on their wages.[31] Such dependence, coupled with closer contacts among miners within the city, were crucial spurs to trade-union organization.

Glassworkers, on the other hand, did not identify their fortunes with any particular establishment or any particular town. Their prosperity rested on the skills they possessed. The future of their sons would be insured by the transfer of these skills.

There were other advantages than collective action in the stability of the miners. As integrated members of a city of Carmaux's size, their activities seemed less suspicious—even to a Police Commissioner. For the police report of 1882 confirms the fact of the glassworkers' isolation. Undoubtedly, the Commissioner trusted the miners in part because he knew them personally, or was at least familiar with their language and style of life. The glassworkers, on the other hand, were foreigners, speaking with strange accents and rarely residing long enough to establish themselves in the town.

The Commissioner's discussion of political ideologies would have some future merit. The miners rarely became anarchists, though the most militant were socialists by the 1890s. Although some of the glassworkers' leaders became socialists, too, anarchism was the prevailing tendency among this group. Perhaps their isolation and geographic mobility, coupled with a sense of membership in a national community of glassworkers, contributed to this. The projection of their own experience—the ease with which new social relationships were established, independent of existing local institutions—into a political vision would not have been difficult.

"In entering the heart of the establishment and its workshops, I realized immediately that they had undergone a transformation so complete, and enlargements so considerable that there was no comparison I could establish between what existed when I last visited in 1865, and what exists today"[32]. So wrote M. de Planet, the inspector for the Exposition Décennale de l'Industrie à Toulouse, in his report of November 1883. A year later, he would have been even more amazed. In addition to the spacious halls and large buildings, the workshops and storage rooms, a new process of production had been introduced. The old *fours à pots* were replaced by *fours à cuve* (or *fours à bassin*). In the *fours à pots,* crucibles full of the raw materials were placed in the furnace at noon. At midnight, the melted glass was ready for the blowers. This system divided the work day in two. For twelve hours the furnace was heated, bottles blown the preceeding day were annealed, and crucibles were prepared and filled. In the next twelve hours, bottles were blown.[33] With *fours à cuve,* the melting process was continuous. Flames of gas (derived from coal) controlled the fusion of primary materials which were injected mechanically into the furnace and emerged as molten glass at various openings. With this system, the day was divided into three eight-hour shifts and bottles were blown during every shift. The number of bottles blown far surpassed the additional numbers of workers needed to staff the Verrerie. The decade 1884–95 also saw the introduction of other mechanical devices that improved production efficiency and cut the need for manpower.

The eight-hour shifts permitted by the *fours à cuve* changed the glassworkers style of life as well as the organization of his work. Though the work day was considerably reduced, the pace of work quickened. A *souffleur* was expected to produce more bottles per hour than previously. If he did not, his salary was lowered since he was paid per bottle blown. A kind of leveling took place with the intoduction of eight-hour shifts. No special time of day was accorded the glassworker. He was ex-

pected to work in the heat of the afternoon as well as at
night. Like the miner, he was assigned a shift arbitrarily.
Apparently, too, the nature of skills required had changed
as well. Although the system of production by *équipes*
consisting of master, two apprentices, and bottle carrier,
and supported by a host of skilled and unskilled auxiliary
personnel was the same as in the eighteenth century,
modifications of these arrangements had occurred. In the
union statutes of 1892, the duration of each stage of apprenticeship was one to two years.[34] Thus, beginning as
a *gamin* at age fourteen, a young man would be ready to
assume the position of *souffleur* by age eighteen or twenty.
Once an apprenticeship of fifteen years had been required; now it was at most five years. The influx of
younger, less skilled men threatened to upset the traditional age and skill hierarchy of the glassworks.[35]

But the most far-reaching and indeed the most disturbing effects of the new technology was overproduction
of bottles. As the Verrerie increased production to 33,000
bottles a day, the demand for bottles was suddenly and
dramatically reduced by the phylloxera, the disease which
attacked grapevines and crippled wine production in the
Midi. Whereas in 1883, the Tarn had 49,386 hectares of
vine planted, in 1888 there were only 27,901 hectares.
The harvest in 1883 was 1,150,255 hectoliters; five years
later it was 100,047 hectoliters.[36] Glassworkers who had
prospered as their industry expanded, who had found
security (and frequently advancement) in geographic mobility, whose skill had been in great demand, began to
find their jobs and salaries threatened and the future of
their sons uncertain. Their response, individual and collective, was to attempt to control the conditions of their
work and of their lives.

One of the most remarkable changes observable in the

demographic data is an increasing tendency to settle in Carmaux after 1885. With a bottle surplus throughout France, the security of one's job depended on holding it. Moving to a new place entailed the risk of unemployment; a glassworker might have to travel long and far to find a verrerie with openings. Claudius Saintoyen and his father, both *verriers*, arrived in Carmaux in 1893 hoping to find employment. When none was available, they wrote to several places and finally received word of openings at Chalons-sur-Saône. "Unfortunately," the police report on them concluded, "having no resources, they were obliged to go there on foot."[37]

Whereas the number of glassworkers from outside the Tarn increased from 1854 to 1882, their numbers began to decline after 1883. Between 1873 and 1882, only 17.1% of glassworkers married were born in the Tarn. In the period 1893–1902, 46.3% of those married were born in the Tarn. Partial checking of the family reconstitution sheets indicates that this, in part, can be attributed to sons of glassworkers who arrived in the '70s and '80s and who settled in Carmaux rather than move on. (It indicates also an increase in *verriers* whose fathers were not glassworkers and who were locally recruited. This opening of glassblowing to a different sector of Carmaux's population will be discussed below.) The Peuginot family is again illustrative. Having worked in at least seven different departments over the course of twenty years, Jean Claude Peuginot apparently decided to settle in Carmaux. His oldest son, however, left soon after his marriage and sought work in the Nord. Perhaps because his family was still there, Hippolyte (born 1854) returned to Carmaux in 1886, where he remained for the rest of his life. His two sons, both of whom became glassworkers, never left the city of their birth. One was married in

Carmaux in 1907, the other in 1911. The second Peuginot son (born 1856) followed Hippolyte's pattern. After his marriage in 1881, he departed for Saône-et-Loire, but he, too, returned ten years later. His sons, both *verriers,* settled and married in Carmaux. A younger Peuginot, François Clement (born 1871), fifteen years younger than his older brothers, began work at the Verrerie in 1886. He never left the town. He was married in Carmaux in 1905, all his children were born there, and there, too, he died. The first generation of Peuginots moved on the average of once every three years. The oldest sons of the next generation began to repeat their father's pattern. They apparently found it unsatisfactory and began to settle in the late 1880s. The third generation of the family evinced a decided absence of geographic mobility.[38]

Although the turnover was still high, more and more families arriving in Carmaux after 1885 followed the Peuginot pattern. Many began to save and buy small plots of land—a house, a garden, perhaps a piece of a vineyard. In the ten years from 1890 to 1900, four times as many glassworkers bought land as had in the preceeding decade.[39] (The glassworker population in 1890–1900 was about double that of 1880–90.)

At the same time that they began, perhaps unconsciously, to modify their own lives, the glassworkers organized a trade union in 1890 in a deliberate collective attempt to retain control of their craft and of their positions within it. In this effort they encountered the formidable opposition of their employer whose interest was efficiency and profit, best attained (in his definition of the situation) by maximizing his own control over all areas of production. In battle with their *patron,* the glassworkers of Carmaux became increasingly militant. The police report of 1882 described them as Republicans, whose

rootlessness made them less careful and less moderate
than the miners.[40] Thirteen years later, at the height of
socialist activity (by miners and glassworkers) in Carmaux, glassworker leaders were categorized as dangerous
anarchists and die-hard revolutionaries.[41]

Although wages were the specific focus of the two
strikes before 1895, the glassworkers of Carmaux devoted
much of their time at local meetings and national con-
gresses to the search for a way to limit their numbers.
Many of the solutions offered envisioned the *syndicat* as
a locally based (though nationally affiliated) organization,
which would protect its members from wage cuts and
other such maneuvers of their employer and which would
prevent outside workers (from other glassworks in France)
from entering their establishment. The *syndicat* was conceived of as a fortress within whose walls worked a stable
population of glassblowers. This notion was based on,
and perhaps hastened, the settling process already indi-
vidually begun. The speeches and articles of glassworker
leaders developed a new theme: the longing of the glassworker to live in his *pays natale*. Marien Baudot, whose
family had moved more than once before its arrival in
Carmaux in 1888, spoke of the desire of all men for a
small house and garden, of their identification with the
"petites verreviers disparus" in the towns of their birth.[42]
Philippe Claussé of Toulouse offered the national congress in 1891 an elaborate plan to stop the "avalanche of
young workers," who, rapidly trained, created a surplus
of personnel that permitted wage cuts and the firing of
older workers. To "control our work" he advocated a
limit on the number of apprentices in each establishment.
He insisted that apprentices be promoted to *souffleurs*
only as existing places were vacated. And that "nomina-
tions [for employment] be made exclusively in the local-

ity where the student had consummated his apprenticeship."[43] Even the question of wages was defined in terms
of the control of conditions of work. The general strike of
1891 demanded a unified salary schedule for glassworkers
in all of France. With a single salary, it was felt, workers
would have no monetary incentive to move to other glassworks, and would remain settled in one place.

Settling, or the desire to settle, seems to have been a
crucial factor in the militance of the *verriers* of Carmaux.
As the stable population of glassworkers increased, greater
continuity of organization became possible. Twelve glassworkers had been listed among the twenty-six founding
members of the Socialist party-inspired Cercle des Travailleurs in 1882. Only half of them still lived in Carmaux
in 1890. Those who founded the union in 1890, on the
other hand, remained in Carmaux (or, after 1895, in Albi)
for at least the next twenty years.[44]

In fact, another element in their militance seems to
have stemmed from the glassworkers' intention to establish themselves as citizens of Carmaux. Of the forty-two
leaders of glassworker trade union and political activity,
thirty-one arrived in Carmaux between 1886 and 1895.
(The other eleven came in the twenty years from 1866 to
1885). Of these leaders, 30% had fathers who were glassworkers, and a number of them (a number disproportionate to the representative experience of Carmaux's
glassworkers) had never left the city of their birth until
they came to Carmaux. This was especially true of the
five from Montlucon who arrived in 1888–89. All had
been fired during a strike and then hired by Rességuier.[45]
Much of the activity of the '90s has been attributed to the
agitation of the group from Montluçon. But the fact of
their prior militance does not seem a sufficient explanation, since it does not account for their success in securing

a following in Carmaux, nor does it explain how or why the other thirty-six leaders arrived at their positions. If anything, the experience of the leaders seems to have heightened their preoccupation with security and control of their jobs—a preoccupation they nonetheless shared with most glassworkers in Carmaux.

The existence and activities of the glassworkers' union gained a certain security for workers at the Verrerie Ste. Clothilde. And it also provided them social and political integration into Carmaux. As the glassworkers determined to remain in the city, their fate became increasingly tied to it. Not only must they direct their demands to a particular *patron,* but local questions of housing and schools, of taxation and food prices must be resolved through Carmaux's political administration.[46] The miners too became an increasingly urban population in the 1890s and, after 1892, most newcomers to the mines were sons of local miners.[47] Unlike their fathers they had but one source of income—their salaries from the mines. If the produce from a small garden cut the cost of food, it was most likely a garden attached to a rented house, or one shared by several mining families.[48] Like the glassworkers, the miners began to seek political solutions to their problems. The effect of their settling in the city and of the consciousness engendered by each militant *syndicat,* was to unite the glassworkers and miners into a distinctively working-class community.

In part, the political unity of glassworkers and miners was a direct response to a common enemy. The Marquis de Solages, owner of the mine, joined the Administrative Council of the Verrerie in 1890, institutionalizing an alliance that had existed informally before. Though Rességuier was a Republican and Solages a Monarchist, they stood together on most municipal issues. Throughout the 1870s and '80s, administrators of the glassworkers and a head engineer at the mine served on the Municipal Council, on juries, and on administrative bodies. No workers were represented until 1888. But miner-glassworker unity had roots, too, in the fact that unlike earlier generations, their security was tied to their living in Carmaux.

There is striking evidence in newspapers, police reports, and personal documents that a working-class community existed in the 1890s in Carmaux. Miners and glassworkers supported one another's strikes and demonstrated together. In addition to the unions, study groups and social *cercles* emerged. Even purely personal events —marriages, birth, and death—began to be altered. Civil marriage, baptisms,[49] and particularly funerals became occasions for political manifestations and the refusal of the church's blessing was seen by some as the beginning of a peculiarly working-class phenomenon. Secular rather than religious schools were demanded by committees of workers and, in 1892, the worker's socialist slate captured the Hôtel de Ville. The election of miner militant Jean Baptiste Calvignac as mayor of the city symbolized the soldity of Carmaux's working class. By capturing municipal government, the workers could now secure political representation for themselves as a class.[50] For *patrons*, administrators, and police, as well as for the class-conscious miners and glassworkers, Carmaux had indeed become "a state within a state."[51]

The workers' achievement of political power in the city was, in part, a function of the strength of their unions. Certainly at the glassworks the *syndicat* had gained a measure of power. In 1893, there are reports of glassworkers in search of jobs being sent away by Rességuier in compliance with the union's demands that no strangers be hired.[52] The 1894 minutes of the union deal with the problem in terms that imply a certain control. The question of how to keep away glassworkers from Rességuier's plant in neighboring Bosquet d'Orb, when their furnace was closed or worked slackened, was assumed to be the union's to answer. The discussions of how to issue special cards to new or temporary workers did not raise the problem of the union's right to issue the cards—it had that right and must merely resolve the mechanics of admitting new workers.[53]

In part, the union's power rested on its organization, which was based on the organization of work at the Verrerie. The *souffleur,* as master of his team, traditionally had the right to hire and fire, to punish and to promote his apprentices. If *souffleurs* belonged to the union, they could force their assistants to belong by threatening to dismiss them if they refused. The union, in fact, was based on the *souffleurs,* most of whom belonged to and led it. (There was a separate union of auxiliary personnel founded in 1891.) It was organized according to *équipes,* with a union member responsible for each place at the furnace during each eight-hour shift. The statutes of the *syndicat des Verriers,* like the rules of the medieval corporation (and in much the same language—a language strikingly absent from the miners' union statutes) regulated the terms of apprenticeship as well as the internal operation of the union. If a *gamin* or *grand garçon* violated the rules of the workshop by blowing a bottle, for example, then the union fined him or increased his term as an apprentice. If the same worker refused to pay his union dues or failed to attend a meeting to which he had been summoned, he was either fined, had his apprenticeship term increased, or was refused work by his own and every other *souffleur* in the Verrerie. The rules

of work and of the trade union were intertwined in the
statutes and practices of the Chambre syndical des verriers
de Carmaux.[54]

Though the union was permitted a certain control in
the Verrerie, the areas of its authority were never clear-
cut. From its foundation in 1890 to its demise after the
strike of 1895, the *syndicat* was engaged in a continual
struggle for power with Rességuier. The union demanded
that it be allowed to determine which bottles were to be
rejected (for imperfections); Rességuier countered that it
was his right. The union insisted on setting the numbers
of workers needed at the Verrerie; Rességuier, as director, felt he had the right to decide how many to employ.
The union organized a *caisse de prevoyance* (to be used
as a strike fund as well as to aid sick workers and their
families); Rességuier maintained that all glassworkers
must contribute to his fund. When the union asked that
they be paid for rejected bottles that were sold as seconds,
or that such rejects be broken, Rességuier drew the line.
With a huge stock of unsold bottles, he seized an opportunity to suspend production temporarily. His actions,
as much as the militance of his workers, launched the
strike of 1895, which not only rid the director of his
oversupply of bottles, but of the troublesome union as
well.

The strike of 1895 was, in a sense, the final battle for
control by the glassworkers of Carmaux. The strike began
because Rességuier intervened in an area normally left to
his workers. He fired glassworker Marien Baudot, leader
of the union, because he failed to come to work. Ordinarily, glassworkers worked as they chose at the Verrerie.
If they decided not to work on a particular day, they
need only inform the man who set up and notified the
teams about which shift they were to work. This man

then called in a replacement. There were no penalties, except the voluntarily incurred one of loss of wages. It was clear that Rességuier fired Baudot for political reasons. He not only led the union, but recently he had been elected a municipal councillor on the Socialist ticket. Rességuier fired Baudot, too, because, according to his chief engineer, the union's attempts over the last year to regulate "the recruitment of glassworking personnel, of auxiliaries at the furnaces, as well as certain practices of work" had become "intolerable," since "the Director wished to regulate them himself."[55]

The union called a strike over the firing of Baudot. Rességuier then locked his workers out of the Verrerie. The strike, with the overwhelming support of miners and many shopkeepers in the town,[56] began on July 31, 1895, and did not end until November 26. Work could not be resumed, however, until January 1, 1896.

When the Verrerie Ste. Clothilde reopened, twenty-two glassworkers were not rehired. These men had formed and led the union, had been most active in the strike and in the National Federation of Glassworkers. They, and a number of their supporters from Carmaux, set up a cooperative glassworks in Albi, a town ten miles southeast of Carmaux. The choice of Albi as the site for the new verrerie created a great deal of hard feeling in Carmaux. Initially the cooperative was to have been built directly across from Rességuier's—a symbol of the strength of his working-class opposition. But Albi was a more practical choice, closer to sources of power and to the railroad. When the decision to go to Albi was announced, the miners decried the betrayal of the working-class community in Carmaux, claiming that fraternity had been sacrificed to economy.[57] Although the glass-

workers at Albi continued to identify with Carmaux (they
organized and attended meetings there and many even
went back to be married), the political power of Carmaux's workers did diminish. Calvignac served as mayor
until his resignation in 1929, but with little active support from the new glassworkers in the city. After the *verriers* departed in 1895, miners were the only actively militant workers left in Carmaux.

With the help of Jean Jaurès and a number of other
prominent socialists and cooperators, the Verrerie Ouvrière d'Albi, with the motto of Fourier, "Capital, Travail,
Talent," emblazoned on its walls, began production at the
end of 1896. The buildings and furnaces were built by
some two-hundred glassworkers from Carmaux and other
dedicated militants who left more lucrative jobs to construct the cooperative owned, as Jaurès put it, by all the
workers of France.

For a number of years the Verrerie Ouvrière faltered,
operating at a deficit and paying barely anything to its employees. The glassworkers' wives and daughters became
frequent visitors to the convent in Albi which distributed
food to the poor. The nuns referred to them always as *les
aristocrates,* remarking on their dignity and pride.[58] The
sacrifice, it was hoped, though terrible at first, would be
of short duration, with greater rewards in the future. By
1900, the Verrerie Ouvrière was competing successfully
with its rival at Carmaux. Three furnaces were operating
in 1899, and in 1913, with four furnaces built, the cooperative produced 900,000 bottles a year. (The Verrerie
Ouvrière is still in operation today, organized as a cooperative on the principles of 1896. It is now, in effect, a
subsidiary of the St. Gobain monopoly, which contracts
for its products. The Verrerie at Carmaux closed in 1930.)
Despite political struggles between Guesdists and anar-

chists which plagued the Verrerie Ouvrière for years, its success was important in the development of working-class institutions in the Tarn and in France.[59] It was a success too, in more personal and immediate terms for its founders.

The number of shares of stock in the Verrerie Ouvrière was limited from the beginning. They were owned by representatives of labor and socialism, most of whom resided in Paris, and by the leading militants of Carmaux. The *actionnaires* were a closed group; no new shares were issued nor were shares split among workers at the Verrerie Ouvrière. The former trade-union leaders of Carmaux (like Aucouturier, Baudot, Charpentier) became administrators at Albi. Few practiced their craft as *souffleurs*, and as the years went by they became more at home in their offices than in the shops. Although, initially, skilled workers blew bottles at the Verrerie Ouvrière, the work force increasingly was recruited locally, among the miners, common laborers, and peasant populations in the area.[60] The regulations for the factory at Albi were more severe than Rességuier's ever had been. In part, this was a result of the extreme pressure under which the cooperators operated—they could not afford to indulge the luxuries of skilled artisans. In addition, the administrators had to deal with a number of anarchists who wanted the Verrerie to be a place in which workers enjoyed complete freedom, to work or not to work, to fulfill themselves as they chose. But the rules were also addressed to a new kind of worker, one who had not experienced factory routine or the discipline of this particular kind of work. Aimed at enforcing the principles of "community, solidarity and political liberty which ought to guide socialists," they were also an attempt to introduce workers to the organization of work in a factory. Drunkenness, quarrels, and disturbances were prohibited. Theft of tools and materials brought immediate dismissal. Lateness was punished, and unexcused absence was not tolerated; even insults to superiors brought the possibility of loss of one's job.[61]

At Carmaux, a similar change in the work force occurred more rapidly. Although some 17% of glassworkers married in 1903–12 were sons of glassworkers, more than 20% were sons of miners, and more than 12% were sons of peasants or common laborers. In the same period 69.7% of glassworkers married had been born in the Tarn —an increase of 40% over the 1883–92 decade. Even more dramatic is the contrast between 1891–95 and 1896–1900. Before the strike, 32.4% of glassworkers married were born in the Tarn; after the strike, the number in this group had risen to 51.5%. (Similarly, their wives were increasingly of local origin: 68.9% in 1891–95 and 82.8% in 1896–1900.) This probably indicates a more rapid turnover in Carmaux's glassworking population than in Albi's—most of the young skilled workers went to the Verrerie Ouvrière, there to perpetuate their craft under conditions they could control. In Carmaux, on the other hand, the places of the skilled artisans were filled with sons of the unskilled. Although the craft of glassmaking itself was in decline, the new recruits did not experience downward occupational mobility. For many of them, the departure of the more skilled opened hitherto closed positions. The sense that their work represented an improvement over that of their fathers may have been partly responsible for the inability of the generation of Carmaux's glassworkers after 1896 to form a union.

Despite repeated urgings by the militants at Albi and offers of help from the socialist miners in the town, the new glassworkers of Carmaux never resurrected their union. There were several attempts, all thwarted by Rességuier. But the lack of a union could only partly be attributed to the strength of the director's opposition. The articles of the Albi militants addressed to their comrades at the Verrerie Ste. Clothilde blamed the glassworkers' passivity. At a special public meeting in Carmaux of the National Congress of Glassworkers (held in Albi in 1906), Griffuelhes, the secretary of the Confédération Générale du Travail, and several other prominent national leaders, spoke of the "shame" of Carmaux's glassworkers' failure to organize. It was the *verriers'* duty, he told an audience consisting overwhelmingly of miners, to "revive the memory" of the struggles of their brothers in Albi.[62] Although the defeat of Jaurès, as Deputy from the Tarn, by Solages in 1898 can be explained by many factors,[63] among them was certainly the loss of glassworker support in Carmaux. Few glassworkers wished to join a union, even when the introduction of the Boucher machine— the automatic blower—threatened the last skilled positions in 1900. In October 1900, shortly after the machine had been installed, an attempt to organize the glassworkers of Carmaux drew 134 of 900 workers—hardly equivalent to the almost unanimous support for a *syndicat* in 1890.[64] A meeting on December 24 to support this effort drew 600 people, most of them miners. The representatives of glassworkers were Baudot and Aucouturier of Albi.[65] The issue for the new *verriers* of Carmaux was not preserving status or control of their craft. They were workers interested in their jobs, in their wages, in the houses and gardens their savings might enable them to buy.[66]

At Albi, too, the craft of the *souffleur* was in decline, though Rességuier's monopoly of the Boucher machine prevented full mechanization until 1918. But, increasingly, the most skilled workers were absorbed into administrative posts (a few left for other glassworks or other jobs, often as a result of ideological divisions), and there was no question about the futures of their children. Almost to a man, the sons and daughters of the militant glassworkers who founded the Verrerie Ouvrière left not only glassmaking but the working class. Although many retained their fathers' Socialist party loyalties, they became teachers, civil servants, or white-collar workers in the growing bureaucracies of Carmaux and Albi. Most famous, but not least representative, was the daughter of leading mili-

Table 1. Syndicats of Glassblowers and Auxiliaries

Year	No. Syndicats	No. Members
Before 1884	6	549
1884	9	717
1885	10	777
1886	10	777
1887	11	892
1888	11	892
1889	14	1084
1890	22	1064
1891	43	4799
1892	43	5701
1893	44	6778
1894	45	7352
1895	40	7143
1896	33	4064
1897	22	1925
1900	23	2913

Source: Associations Professionales Ouvrières, T. III, 518-19. The figures combine glassworkers and auxiliaries *(similaires)* but they are nonetheless an indication of overall trends. *Similaires* tended to have much smaller unions, whereas the *verriers* usually organized an entire shop into their union. In Carmaux in 1892, for example, the *verriers* had 430 members, the *similaires*, 80. A. D. Tarn, XIII M 11 4.

tant Michel Aucouturier, who became Mme. Vincent
Auriol, whose husband was a President during the Fourth
Republic.

There is evidence to indicate that the changes occurring in Carmaux were representative of French glassworkers generally. The statistics for union membership
from 1884 to 1900 seem to corroborate the Carmaux
data.[67]

From 1890 to 1891, the number of union members
increased more than four times, the number of *syndicats*
doubled. After 1895, there is a sudden drop in both categories, and by 1897 membership has fallen to the level of
1890. Carmaux's glassworkers organized in 1890. By 1891
almost every glassblower in the Verrerie had adhered to
the union. In 1895, the great strike of *verriers* cut the
union's strength. No union existed at the Verrerie Ste.
Clothilde from 1896 to 1900. And though the Verrerie
Ouvrière was unionized by its administrators, reports indicate that some workers were often reluctant to affiliate.

In a sense, 1891–95 represented the last stand of artisan
glassworkers in France. When mechanization and overproduction of bottles threatened their jobs, they organized to control entry into the trade (rather than to
prevent the introduction of machines). Their ideology
and rhetoric was "modern," it echoed the socialist, syndi-
calist, and anarchist programs of the day. Glassworkers
were anti-capitalist rather than anti-industrial; and, for
many, the union offered personal security rather than a
means of preserving their craft.

As bottleblowing demanded less skill, French *verriers*
began to look elsewhere for their sons' futures and, if
Carmaux is typical, they sent them to school and into
white-collar jobs available in the expanding bureaucracies of the city. Given the nature of the glassworker

population turnover in the late 1890s, it is misleading to talk of technological changes as deflating the status of specific artisans. Instead, after fighting to retain their places within the craft, many glassblowers seem to have moved (or sent their sons) into equally high, if not higher status positions. They were displaced, but not downgraded. Their places were filled by newcomers to the industry who considered themselves fortunate to be able to acquire the few skills needed by a twentieth-century *verrier*.[68] The different men who experienced different aspects of the process that industrialized glass bottleblowing reacted to it differently. The artisans seem to have used their militance to preserve their economic position as well as to defend their jobs. The first generation of men who staffed fully mechanized bottle factories were markedly unmilitant, probably because industrialization of the trade had upgraded or, at least, not downgraded their positions.

And what of their tie to Carmaux? The artisans' consciousness certainly seems to have been shaped, in part, by the link they perceived between their jobs and the city. The first generation of semiskilled glassworkers must have perceived a similar link, especially since most came from Carmaux or its environs. Of course, as long-time residents of the city, they may not have seen it as anything but the place in which they happened to live. They may have taken for granted that one sought work where he lived. (In this connection it is important to note that *settled* glassworkers—those who were from long-established families in Carmaux—were generally absent from militant ranks.) In addition, though, their mobility may have been a factor influencing their perception since, for them, the city provided a means of improving their situations. For the *settling* miners and glassworkers of the

1880s and '90s, on the other hand, moving to Carmaux
signified a certain insecurity. To the miners, it meant the
loss of the land that supplemented their incomes and provided an alternative employment. To the glassworkers, it
meant the end of the security provided by simply pos-
sessing a skill. The new glassworkers, for the most part,
were recruited among residents of Carmaux. Only 6%
of those married in the years 1903–12 had fathers living
and working in rural areas. More than 60% were sons of
men who resided and worked in the city of Carmaux. In
other words, they were *settled* Carmausins, moving a step
upward within the working class.

I do not want to push the settled/settling contrast too
far. Class consciousness and collective action stemmed
from many other factors, such as changes in techniques,
economic security or insecurity, occupational mobility,
tradition, etc. The settled miners, sons of miners, carried
on their fathers' militant tradition in Carmaux. Certainly, their lack of mobility and the experience of generations of their families in the mines contributed to their
sense of membership in a class. Settled workers (among
them many sons of miners) who moved into the more
lucrative glassmaking trade did not become radicals—at
least the first generation of semiskilled glassworkers did
not. Undoubtedly, their mobility, their sense of personal
success made them less conscious of themselves as members of a class.

The class-consciousness of glassworkers and miners in
the 1890s, however, was informed by their perception that
Carmaux was crucial to their specific jobs. The changing
nature of their work forced their economic and social
integration into the city. Perhaps because of the nature
and newness of the connection between city and job, they

were concerned about it, as well as aware of it. They manifested their concern by directing their collective action beyond their jobs to the city itself, seeking through strikes, demonstrations, and political organizations the power to control their work, and the arrangements of their lives as well.

1. I am grateful to Charles Tilly, J. Harvey Smith, and Donald M. Scott for reading and criticizing an earlier version of this paper. A Research Training Fellowship from the Social Science Research Council provided technical training and financial assistance.

2. Archives Départementales du Tarn (A.D. Tarn hereafter), IV M 2 75. (A *barrique* is a large wine barrel which holds 225 liters.)

3. Clark Kerr, *Industrialism and Industrial Man* (Cambridge, Mass., 1960); Neil Smelser, *Social Change in the Industrial Revolution* (Chicago, 1959); Philip Hauser, "The Social, Economic and Technological Problems of Rapid Urbanization," in Bert Hoselitz and Wilbert Moore, eds., *Industrialization and Society* (The Hague, 1963).

4. Louis Chevalier, *Classes laborieuses et classes dangereuses* (Paris, 1958). One of the drawbacks of Chevalier's analysis is his reliance on literary sources as a reflection of reality. He accepts the confusing of *classes laborieuses* with *classes dangereuses* by bourgeoise writers as a portrayal of the fact that this has happened, rather than using the literary evidence to show why the writers see things as they do. He demonstrates that urbanization has resulted in geographical segregation of workers and bourgeoisie, it has forced workers to live where criminals live, it has, in short, fused the classes (dangerous and laboring) for anyone looking at them from outside; but has it, in fact, made workers criminals? This Chevalier does not show.

5. Val Lorwin, "Working Class Politics and Economic Development in Western Europe," *American Historical Review*, (1958).

6. Stephan Thernstrom, *Poverty and Progress; Social Mobility in a Nineteenth Century City* (Cambridge, Mass., 1964).

7. Georges Duveau, *La Vie Ouvrière en France sous le Second Empire* (Paris, 1946); E. P. Thompson, *The Making of the English Working Class* (New York, 1963).

8. Stephan Thernstrom, "Working Class Social Mobility in Industrial America," in Melvin Richter, ed., *Social Theory and Social History: An Approach to General Education* (Cambridge, Mass., forthcoming).

9. Much of this study is based on demographic data. Manuscript censuses and records of birth, death, and marriage have permitted me to determine who was affected by changes in glassmaking, who participated in political protest, and frequently even the nature of their participation. Family reconstitution (which at the time of this writing is only partially complete) has enabled me to trace several marriage patterns, family size, age at marriage and at death, geographic and occupational mobility. More traditional historical sources—newspapers, national and local police and administrative archives, personal papers, trade-union con-

gresses, company records, and land records—have been used as well. But
the demographic data has enriched and vastly deepened the quality of
my understanding. This paper is a summary of work in progress. It is
based on some crude statistical calculations, some tentative insights,
and it is not meant to be at all conclusive. One of the major foundations
of the finished study, the family reconstitution, which will provide the
most specific evidence about the length of a glassworker's stay in
Carmaux, his social and geographic origins, etc., is not yet in finished
form.

10. The Parish Registers of Carmaux and Blaye are in the Archives
Municipal at the Mairie of the town of Carmaux.

11. St. Quernin, *Les Verriers de Languedoc, 1290–1790* (1906).

12. There is some evidence to indicate that *souffleurs* assisted masters
in the *èquipes,* even though they had no official designation. The statistics and information of the Verrerie Royale de Solages are based on the
Archives Solages which are on microfilm at the Archives Départementales
du Tarn in Albi. The materials used were in Cartons 12 and 16.

13. A. D. Tarn, Archives Solages, Cartons 12 and 16.

14. These lists, plus a great deal of documentation from the Archives
Municipales de Carmaux, have been published by the city's present
mayor, Jean Vareilles, in the *Revue du Tarn,* No. 41 (March, 1966). The
later lists, from 1834 on, are in the A. D. Tarn, II M 7 197.

15. Land records are in the Matrices du Cadastre in the city halls of
Carmaux and Blaye. There are also volumes in the A. D. Tarn which
contain records of all transactions of property—land, houses, household,
furnishings, etc. These indicate the terms of sale, mortgage, etc. Aside
from economic records, they provide interesting information about the
style of life of those involved in the transactions. See below, note 24.

16. A. D. Tarn, Archives Solages, Carton 12.

17. Manuscript censuses for Carmaux were available for 1851, 1856,
1861, 1866, 1872, 1876, 1881, 1886, 1891, 1896, 1901. Most of the demographic materials referred to are based on these censuses, which listed
occupation, age, and position in the family. In 1872 and 1876, department
of birth was also included. The other censuses distinguish only between
Frenchmen and foreigners. There is some difficulty in distinguishing the
position in the Verrerie of someone designated "verrier" in the census.
For a time, everyone who worked there, whether on an *équipe* or as auxiliary personnel, was listed as "verrier." After about 1881, however, the
designation became more precise. Those who were glassblowers were
listed as "ouvrier verrier," those who were assistants were listed as
"ouvrier à la Verrerie." The civil records, especially marriage acts, enable greater precision for the earlier period.

18. In any case, average age of death is not a precise indicator of
mortality rates since it takes into account neither the overall age structure of the population nor the number of deaths in relation to the total
population. (For purposes of this study, the glassworkers are considered
a total population.) A better measure is the age-specific death rate, which
is the ratio between the number of deaths in an age category and the
total number in that age-group. My calculations of the age-specific death
rate for the glassworkers of Carmaux will be based on the as yet un-
finished family reconstitution. For a discussion of the problems involved
in the calculation of death rates, see Réné Baehrel, "La Mortalité sous
l'ancien régime. Remarques inquiètes," *Annales E.S.C.*, 12e Année, No. 1
(January–March 1957), pp. 85–98. See also Louis Henry, and Baehrel's
reply to him, in *Annales*, No. 4 (October–December 1957), pp. 628–38.

19. Léon Seilhac, *La Grève de Carmaux* (Paris, 1897), pp. 8–10.

20. The rapid turnover of the glassworking population may be just
another example of the high working-class geographic mobility that historians are beginning to discover was characteristic in the nineteenth
century. It still needs explanation, however, in particular cases like
Carmaux.

21. Censuses of 1856, 1861, 1866, 1872, 1876, 1881, 1886, 1891, 1896, 1901.

22. Respiratory infections were particularly dangerous, and tuber-
culosis, especially, plagued the glassworker. In addition, the use of the
same blowing tube by several blowers increased the spread of all ill-
nesses, and epidemics were frequent among the workers at the Verrerie.
For a long discussion of the health problems of glassworkers, see the report of Louis Renoux to the Exposition of 1900, in Renoux's private
archives.

23. A. D. Tarn, Archives Solages, Carton 16; and A. D. Tarn, IV M 2
68. (Police report of 1882 comparing the economic condition of miners
and glassworkers in Carmaux.)

24. Seilhac, p. 50. An act of sale in 1896, by the wife of a glassworker
in Carmaux, is indicative of the style of life of glassworkers—and provides a contrast with that of miners and peasants in Carmaux. There
were closets and beds of oak and varnished chairs instead of the un-
finished, cheaper wood of the peasants and miners. Chairs were unusual
in a miners' house—benches were used instead. A cooking stove (instead
of the hearth) and high-quality linens, and, especially, a sewing machine,
indicated an urban style of life. But the presence of a pig, the numbers
of unused linens, were reminiscent of the more primitive rural life.
See, Registre Transcriptions d'Albi, No. 818. I am grateful to Rolande
Trempé for finding this document and for the comparisons she indicated
based on her study of Carmaux's miners.

25. Since many more single male glassworkers than daughters of glass-workers came to Carmaux, it was inevitable that glassworkers began marrying the daughters of miners and other workers in the city.

26. Maurice Talmeyr, "Chez Les Verriers," *Revue des Deux Mondes,* 1 février, 1898.

27. A. D. Tarn, IV M 2 68, "Rapport sur la situation économique des ouvriers verriers," 22 décembre, 1882.

28. Rolande Trempé, "Les Mineurs de Carmaux de 1848 à 1883" (unpublished diplôme, Université de Toulouse, 1954).

29. In 1882, there were some 2,000 miners and fewer than 400 glass-workers in Carmaux. The differences in the size of the two populations did not change appreciably in the period we are considering.

30. Thernstrom, "Working Class Social Mobility," p. 4.

31. The report of 1882 (see note 27 above), unlike earlier police reports, noted that the *mineur-propriétaire* was fast disappearing in Carmaux.

32. The report of M. Planet is at the Musée Social in Paris, Carton

4727.
33. Seilhac, pp. 6–25.

34. A. D. Tarn, bibliothèque, C 437 26.

35. Marriage acts are especially useful since they indicate precisely the occupation of the groom (as well as of everyone else associated with the wedding). In 1892–93 there are a great number of *souffleurs* aged nineteen to twenty-one.

36. Rolande Trempé, "Les Mineurs de Carmaux," p. 225.

37. A.D. Tarn, IV M 2 74.

38. Census and civil records were the basis of the reconstruction of the Peuginot family.

39. Matrices cadastral de Carmaux, 1830–1913.

40. A. D. Tarn, IV M 2 68.

41. A. D. Tarn, IV M 2 75.

42. *Le Reveil des Verriers,* October 29, 1893.

43. IIe Congrès National de la Fédération du Verre (Lyon, 1891), p. 68.

44. A. D. Tarn, IV M 6 10.

45. Seilhac, pp. 6–25.

46. Charles Tilly's suggestive discussion of the use of violence and disruption by "political actors in France" to win "their memberships in the national community" might have relevance for Carmaux. Certainly one effect of the glassworkers' militant behavior was to win them a recognized position in the community. See Charles Tilly, "The Changing Place of Collective Violence" (unpublished paper, February 1968), p. 35.

47. Trempé, pp. 197, 201.

48. Most of the increase in Carmaux's population resulted from the influx of miners from surrounding rural areas to the city.

49. The notices of these occasions are in *La Voix des Travailleurs* 1891–95, passim.

50. Harvey Goldberg, *The Life of Jean Jaurès* (Madison, Wis., 1962), pp. 102 ff., details the effects of Calvignac's election. By 1895, there were sixty-three Socialist municipalities in France. It would be interesting to study these cities for similarities to Carmaux.

51. A. D. Tarn, IV M 2 74.

52. A. D. Tarn, IV M 2 74.

53. The handwritten minutes of the *Syndicat* for 1894 were in the library of the son of militant Louis Renoux, and are on microfilm in my possession.

54. The statutes are in A. D. Tarn, XIII M 2 4.

55. The letter of M. Sirven is at the Musée Social in the collection of the strike of 1895. See also articles in *La Voix des Travailleurs,* 1895–96, passim.

56. The lists of donors to the strike fund, printed in *La Voix des Travailleurs* throughout the strike, contain a surprising number of local merchants.

57. The debates are carried in *La Voix des Travailleurs,* 1895–96.

58. Talmeyr, "Chez Les Verriers."

59. Léon Seilhac, *La Verrerie Ouvrière d'Albi* (Paris, 1898).

60. By peasants I mean those who are listed as "propriétaires," "agriculteur," "paysan," cultivateur" in the census.

61. Seilhac, *La Verrerie*.

62. A. D. Tarn, IV M 4 25, Rapport sur le 5e Congrés de la Fédération

Nationale des Verriers, 18 Septembre, 1906.
63. Goldberg, pp. 228–31.

64. A. D. Tarn, IV M 2 95, Rapport No. 99.

65. A. D. Tarn, IV M 2 95 24 and 28 Novembre, 1900, Rapports Nos. 131, 134.

66. The land records show a remarkable increase in the number of glassworkers buying tiny plots in Carmaux after 1900.

67. I don't think it is necessary to justify a case study by pointing to its representativeness. It seems to me that such studies are valuable for the insights they offer into particular historical processes, for the information they offer indirectly about a society or a period of time, and for the questions they raise about other similar cases.

68. The Lynds' discussion of the effects of industrialization on glassworkers in *Middletown* seems to neglect the possibility of turnover in the workers who experience the changes; Robert M., and Helen Lynd, *Middletown: A Study in American Culture* (New York, 1929).

WORKERS DIVIDED: The Effect of Craft and Ethnic
Differences in Poughkeepsie, New York, 1850–1880

Clyde Griffen

The recent interest among historians in quantitative
studies of geographical and social mobility has one common source: these studies seek a more reliable description
of the experience of most Americans than can be gleaned
from the impressions of an articulate minority, whether
fellow citizens or foreign observers. Their usefulness has
been most obvious to historians concerned with the extent to which America really was a land of opportunity,
especially for immigrants. But these studies also contribute to a related interest: explanation of the general
absence in nineteenth-century American cities of a working-class consciousness and class conflict.

This last contribution is less direct but no less important. The historian still must proceed by inference,
making assumptions about how inarticulate men viewed
their circumstances. But a more precise picture of those
circumstances can vastly increase the plausibility of the
inference, as Stephan Thernstrom's pioneering study
of unskilled laborers in Newburyport, Massachusetts,
shows.[1] The failure of Newburyport laborers to reject
the ideology of the dominant class makes much more
sense after Thernstrom's demonstration of the frequency
of modest improvement among those who stayed in the
city and of the frequency of departure among the less successful.

The use of quantitative evidence for this purpose is
fraught with pitfalls as well as promise, particularly in
studies of the entire labor force of a city. In dealing with
data on hundreds or thousands of individuals, the need

for simplification in classification and analysis becomes acute. To mention only the most obvious problem, the study of social mobility requires some division of workers by levels of skill and responsibility and the assignment of hundreds of occupational designations to these levels. Unfortunately, the character of these occupations changes over time, occasionally from decade to decade. Unless assignments to skill-level are made and changed accordingly, the experience of important groups of workers will be distorted.

Even if the assignments are sensitive to changes in the character of occupations, the effect of these changes will not be apparent unless separate analyses of mobility are made for different occupations. City-wide aggregates of persistence in the community, change in degree of skill, and extent of property ownership show the general prospects for advancement for the whole population studied, but they obscure the immense variation in the prospects of particular groups of workers. Investigation of this variation is essential to an understanding of why American workers did not develop a strong sense of class solidarity.

In the many cities in mid-nineteenth-century America that were diversified in economic activity and in ethnic composition, dissimilarity in the opportunities of workers in different occupations at the same skill-level discouraged development of a common interest. Even in one-industry towns, which were more nearly polarized into employers and workers in the same kind of enterprises, there often was substantial diversity in circumstances among trades and services employing an important minority of workers outside the major industry.[2]

Workers' perceptions of their situation depended primarily upon personal experience and gossip. Gossip emphasized the immediate and specific. In the absence of unfamiliar or threatening events affecting large numbers in the community, men judged from the familiar—from the character and circumstances of the coopers or carpenters, the Irish or Germans whom they encountered in their daily lives. In diversified urban economies workers were unlikely to generalize adversities in their trade into defects of the economic system as a whole.

Similarly, they judged their prospects for advancement more by the instances of success in their own trade than by cases of "rags to riches" in unrelated occupations. As Thernstrom suggests, had Newburyport laborers judged their progress by the models of success exemplified in Horatio Alger novels, they would have despaired. But their frame of reference was the experience of their own kind in their community.

Until late in the nineteenth century the frame of reference of most urban workers was localized by the scale and nature of business enterprise. Few occupations had acquired the degree of standardization and impersonality that characterized mass production subsequently. Specialization and mechanization increased rapidly in many trades, but even in these trades most men still worked in small shops and factories.[3] The unevenness in the timing and impact of skill-dilution—differing within and between trades and from city to city—tended to separate the interests of workingmen.[4] Skill-dilution also made it easier for employers to hire less skilled immigrants, exaggerating differences in interest within the labor force.

These differences must be taken into account in estimating the likelihood that workers within a trade might make common cause in dealing with their employers or develop a common interest with workers in other occupations. Quantitative studies based on federal or state cen-

suses can bring these differences to the historian's attention and help him evaluate their probable effects. Such
studies can determine the ethnic composition, age distribution, and proportion of the propertied and self-employed in each occupation and how these traits of the
work force change over time. More important, they can
discover the rate of turnover and the opportunities for
advancement among workers with any combination of
these traits. They can, for example, suggest the comparative prospects for exploitation or advancement of the
young and the alien within the same occupation in different periods of time or between occupations in the same
period. Supplemented by investigation of patterns of
residence and voluntary association, they can suggest the
extent to which attitudes fostered by men's occupations
were reinforced or counteracted by their experience away
from work.

Quantitative study of the labor force of one small city,
Poughkeepsie, New York, between 1850 and 1880 illustrates some important kinds of diversity among workingmen and their probable effect on attitudes. The primary
source of information is the manuscript population schedules of the federal census, supplemented by annual city
directories.[5] The results presented here are based on a
complete tabulation of persistence in the city's labor force
after each of three censuses, 1850, 1860, and 1870. Persistence is defined as the reappearance of workers listed
in one census in the next census; nonpersistence, as
failure to appear in the next census. Male labor force here
is defined as all employed male workers and all unemployed males sixteen years old or more.

Analysis of intra- and inter-generational occupational
mobility among those who did persist will be essential to
a full picture of the character of opportunities in Pough-

keepsie during these years.[6] But the results of comparing the traits of those who remained and those who left the city between censuses suggest how useful the study of persistence alone can be in describing the experience of workers in the various occupations.

These results yield a picture of remarkable dissimilarity between twenty-three major occupations, including professionals and proprietors. Some trades declined in size of work force; some increased steadily; others went through both marked contraction and expansion during the period. The Irish and German immigrants who entered in large numbers at the beginning of the period found opportunities in some fields but not in others. And the opportunities changed from decade to decade. A few consistent patterns appear for most occupations, notably the tendency for the proportion of the foreign-born and their children to increase dramatically during periods of rapid expansion. These patterns, however, were not likely to foster class-consciousness.

For perspective on the results of this investigation and on their relevance to other cities in the same years, some characteristics of Poughkeepsie are essential. In 1830 the village numbered 5,023 inhabitants. By 1850 it ranked with Newburyport as one of the sixty cities in America with 10,000 or more people, and four years later it secured a transfer to municipal status from the State. Doubling again in size between 1850 and 1870, Poughkeepsie was the sixty-fifth largest city in the nation in the latter year. Unlike Newburyport, it had continued to grow in these years. Despite the ambitious visions of local promoters, however, that rapid growth ceased with the panic of 1873.[7]

Since Poughkeepsie did not become a large city, it shares some of the limitations of Newburyport for a study of the experience of urban workers. However, the marked shifts in the city's fortunes within this period are advantageous in that they permit a study of the effects of fluctuations in urban growth on various groups in the labor force. In these thirty years, Poughkeepsie first experienced a large increase in the proportion of foreign-born workers, German as well as Irish, with a very high rate of turnover in the population as a whole. Subsequent decades saw first a rapid expansion of jobs in many trades

Table 1. Number of Workers at each Census and Percentage Increase between Censuses

	1850 N	Change in %	1860 N	Change in %	1870 N	Change in %	1880 N
Lawyer	53	+ 19	63	+ 6	67	+19	80
Doctor	25	+ 16	29	+ 17	34	+ 6	36
Merchant *	152		117	+ 66	194	+11	214
Grocer *			58	+ 24	72	+11	80
Clerk	120	+ 78	217	+ 61	349	+18	412
Baker	30	+ 20	36	+ 47	53	+13	60
Butcher	42	– 26	31	+ 90	59	+47	87
Shoemaker	128	0	128	– 10	115	–26	85
Tailor	74	+ 18	87	+ 15	100	0	100
Cabinetmaker	45	– 20	36	– 44	20	– 5	19
Cooper	34	+382	123	+ 16	143	– 5	136
Carriagemaker	36	+136	85	– 16	71	–32	48
Machinist	57	0	57	+ 74	99	+ 2	101
Molder	23	+ 30	30	+ 33	41	0	41
Carpenter	159	+ 24	197	+ 53	301	–26	222
Brickmason	75	– 8	69	+125	155	–46	83
Painter	58	+ 29	75	+ 73	130	– 2	127
Blacksmith	62	+ 15	71	+ 32	94	– 6	88
Teamster/Carter	52	+ 38	72	+ 69	123	–17	102
Boatman	63	+ 52	96	– 19	78	+ 5	82
Gardener	43	+ 72	74	+ 45	107	–10	96
Laborer	818	– 28	587	+ 75	1030	–10	927

* In the 1850 census, grocers were listed as merchants.

followed by a sharp decline in rate of growth for some and contraction in others (see Table 1). These fluctuations make it easier to see how trades adapted to good and bad times.

Before 1830 Poughkeepsie had been primarily a trading and shipping center for its agricultural hinterland. Early in the century a number of small factories developed along the Fallkill River; a few of them made a successful transition to steam power later. The number and size of factories increased after 1850. By 1880 the city had ten establishments with more than one hundred workers each, but in five of these—shoe, carpet, silk, shirt, and skirt factories—at least half the employees were women. Of these five, all but the carpet factory opened after 1869. The proportion of the male labor force employed by factories of this size was little more than one-tenth. Employment for skilled male workers was limited primarily to the mower and reaper works, the dye wood mill, and the glass factory.[8]

Most male workers in manufacturing worked in smaller shops or factories. Among furnaces, foundries, cooperages, carriage shops, pottery, wheelbarrow, and chair factories, the major firms employed between fifteen and fifty men. By 1860 the proportion of the male labor force in manufacturing was 34% compared with 12% in the building trades, 9% in transportation, 8% in trade and finance, 6% clerical, 6% professional, and 15% unskilled labor.[9] Despite the small scale of many of the factories, the growth of manufacturing helped spur the rapid increase in population and altered the character of the community.

Perhaps the most unpleasant sign that Poughkeepsie had lost the simplicity of village life was the increasing contamination of private wells by private sewage disposal. The city invested nearly $2,000,000 in public water and sewage systems, stimulating a postwar boom in the construction trades. Construction of a city railroad, a cross-county railroad, and the beginnings of a railroad bridge over the Hudson River encouraged speculation in real estate and extension of residential districts into previously rural areas within the city's boundaries.

Change was everywhere apparent, not least in the ethnic composition of the population. Enough Irish had come to the village by 1837 to warrant a resident Catholic pastor, but the construction of the Hudson River Railroad in the late '40s brought an unprecedented influx. By the census of 1850 the Irish constituted 21%, the Germans 8%, and the English and Scotch 6% of the male labor force. By 1880 these groups and their native-born sons together accounted for one half (see Table 2).

Table 2. *Composition of the Labor Force by Nationality Group*

	Native		Irish		German		English-Scotch	
Census	NB	NBNP	FB	NBFP	FB	NBFP	FB	NBFP
1850	64		21		8		6	
1860	60		20		12		6	
1870	65	55	18	5	11	3	4	2
1880	72	51	14	11	9	7	4	3

NB stands for native-born, NBNP for native-born of native parentage, FB for foreign-born, and NBFP for native-born of foreign parentage. Members of nationality groups other than the three above constituted no more than 2% of the labor force at any census; they are not included in the table.

Comparison of rates of persistence in the city shows significant differences between the native and the foreign-born and, among the latter, between the Irish, Germans, and English and Scotch[10] (see Table 3). Between 1850 and 1860 the rate of persistence among the foreign-born, especially the Irish, English, and Scotch of every age-

Table 3. *Rates of Persistence among the Native-born and Foreign-born*

	Native-born	Irish	German	English-Scotch
1850–60	34	21	29	24
1860–70	44	45	44	38
1870–80	36	40	44	32

group, was lower than for the native-born. During the period of rapid growth after 1860, however, the Irish and the Germans remained as frequently as the native-born. In the decade after 1870, with business depression, the Irish and Germans stayed on at a slightly higher rate. The English and Scotch show the greatest turnover of any nationality, not much more than one-third remaining even during the decade of rapid growth. The persistence of the Germans and the Irish after 1860 and 1870 suggest that when jobs were available they had a much stronger propensity to settle than the English and Scotch.

In Newburyport the foreign-born were overwhelmingly Irish, tending to polarize the community. In Poughkeepsie greater diversity in ethnic composition seems to have been accompanied by a somewhat more hospitable attitude toward the foreign-born. Perhaps because of the large number of families of Dutch descent in the city, the Germans were viewed with particular favor. In 1864 one newspaper described the increasingly numerous Germans in Poughkeepsie as "poor, but industrious and frugal." In 1868 it commented that "the Germans record themselves all over the world as industrious, law-loving, and law-abiding citizens. As a class, they are as intellectual and as well-posted in the history of foreign government as any other people who come from the other side of the Atlantic."[11]

The Irish aroused some antagonism. The city's historian observed in 1905 that "several gangs of Irishmen

known locally as Corkonians, Fardowners, Whaledock-
ers, etc., used to indulge occasionally in street fights, and
they did not always get along well with the English and
German residents."[12] But the community was willing to
accommodate even the Irish in ways that Newburyport
did not. Beginning in 1873, Poughkeepsie experimented
with an arrangement whereby two Catholic schools were
leased and maintained by the Board of Education but
continued to be staffed by Catholic priests, nuns, and lay-
men. Even before then the Protestant-dominated school
system must have seemed less threatening to the Irish
than it did in Newburyport, for there was no significant
difference between the major nationality groups in the
percentage of children reported in the census as attending
school.[13]

Keeping their children in school rather than putting
them to work did not prevent the foreign-born from
making rapid advances by comparison with the native-
born in amount of property accumulated. The percentage
of native-born heads of household reporting amounts of
real and personal property combined of $1,000 or more
changed only slightly between 1860 and 1870, from 43%
to 45%, whereas the percentage for German heads of
household rose from 26% to 42% and for the Irish, from
22% to 35%. The increase in the proportion of the
foreign-born reporting property of $10,000 or more is
less striking, but impressive for comparative newcomers.
While the percentage of native-born heads of household
with that amount increased from 10% to 16% between
1860 and 1870, the percentage for the Germans rose from
2% to 7% and for the Irish from 1% to 3%.

The increase in substantial amounts of property owned
by alien newcomers indicates that a large minority not
only remained in Poughkeepsie for a decade or more, but

prospered there. Men like the German boss butcher Jacob Blankenhorn and the Irish cooperage owner William Moore, reporting real estate valued at $30,000 and $12,000 respectively in 1870, had acquired a stake in the community and, presumably, an interest in its well-being. But the continued presence of the most successful newcomers probably had less influence on the attitudes of the foreign-born toward their new home than stability among the much larger number with modest stakes, usually a house and lot.

The most visible evidence supporting the ideology of success for the industrious was the achievement by members of all nationalities of ownership of real estate and their persistence in Poughkeepsie in large and similar proportions. The highest rates of persistence of the propertied for all nationalities appear between the censuses of 1860 and 1870. The next decade saw lowered rates, but despite the hard times after the panic of 1873, more than half of the propertied of all nationalities remained in the city (see Table 4).

By contrast, those without property left the city much more frequently. Whether possession of real estate was a primary influence on decisions to stay or to move cannot finally be determined. The act of investment may reflect prior intention to settle permanently. What does seem clear is that persistence has a stronger association with ownership of real estate than with any other variable available in quantifiable sources.[14] For the most part, owners were heads of household, married, and more than thirty years of age, but none of these traits is as useful as property in predicting persistence.

These traits do indicate, in conformity with migration theory, the general tendency of the middle aged with family responsibilities to stay where they are rather than

Table 4. Rates of Persistence among Owners and Nonowners of Real Estate, by Nativity
(Age 30–59 Only)

	Native-born		Irish		German		English-Scotch	
	Owner	Nonowner	Owner	Nonowner	Owner	Nonowner	Owner	Nonowner
1850–60	49	40	31	23	58	35	41	23
1860–70	64	43	60	41	67	39	63	32
1870–80	54	35	59	39	60	41	58	22

risk the uncertainties of a new situation.[15] As Table 5 shows, there is a much lower rate of persistence among those less than thirty years of age than among those between thirty and fifty-nine years of age. Single boarders especially tended to be transients. Whether prompted by

Table 5. Rates of Persistence by Age-Group and Nativity

(All employed males and males sixteen years or more)

	Less than 20 years	20—29 years	30—59 years	60 years or more
Census Nativity				
1850—60				
Native-born	28	31	40	23
Irish	14	20	24	12
German	20	21	37	14
English and Scotch	15	21	26	21
1860—70				
Native-born	38	39	52	27
Irish	40	36	51	27
German	34	44	48	22
English and Scotch	25	40	41	26
1870—80				
Native-born	32	32	41	27
Irish	16	29	46	22
German	31	36	48	40
English and Scotch	29	24	36	28

lack of opportunities in Poughkeepsie or better opportunities elsewhere, those without a stake or responsibility —the young, the single, and those without property— —moved on most frequently, regardless of nationality. The very people in the community who best could afford to risk conflict or mount protest *if* they perceived injustice in the practices of their employer, trade, or the community were the first to go elsewhere.

Those groups who benefited most from the status quo also remained in Poughkeepsie with the greatest frequency. The city's professional, financial, and commercial men continued overwhelmingly to be the native-born of native parentage and very stable. As Table 6 shows, more

Table 6. Rates of Persistence of Workers in Twenty-two Occupations

	1850—60	1860—70	1870—80
Lawyer	43	54	58
Doctor	56	52	59
Merchant	59	60	45
Grocer		55	49
Clerk	34	42	33
Baker	17	36	34
Butcher	40	35	44
Shoemaker	42	50	38
Tailor	42	49	45
Cabinetmaker	51	42	50
Cooper	44	41	45
Carriagemaker	19	46	38
Machinist	37	49	38
Molder	30	50	46
Carpenter	36	46	40
Brickmason	39	46	37
Painter	36	45	41
Blacksmith	35	35	40
Teamster	47	44	46
Boatman	35	41	28
Gardener	26	35	34
Laborer	25	45	30

than half of the lawyers, doctors, merchants and dealers, and grocers who were recorded in the censuses of 1850, 1860, and 1870 appeared in the next census, except for the lawyers of 1850 and the merchants and grocers of

1870.[16] The latter suggest a higher rate of business failure during the depression, especially among younger proprietors.[17] The proportion of older men in each of these occupations increased by 1880.

A substantial number of the city's lawyers, merchants, bank officers, and bank stockholders belonged to families prominent in Poughkeepsie for at least two generations. Others had come to the city from smaller towns in Dutchess County or neighboring counties in the Hudson valley. Some of the larger manufacturing enterprises begun during this period were led by newcomers, almost all native-born. Investment in them by city residents suggests a willingness to accommodate talented outsiders if only to promote more business for the city.

The Germans and, to a small extent, the Irish early became a significant proportion of the city's dealers in products of crafts in which they were well-represented, like shoemaking, tailoring, cigarmaking, and butchering. But not until 1880 did they comprise as much as one-fifth of the merchants and dealers in dry goods, lumber and coal, and other lines where proprietorship did not grow out of prior skill in a craft.

Among the grocers, many of whom served neighborhoods where their countrymen were numerous, the foreign-born accounted for one-fourth of the total as early as 1860 and nearly one-half by 1870. The Irish predominated. The rate of persistence for the foreign-born and their sons in the grocery business during the decade of depression was significantly higher than for the native-born of native parentage. Only 41% of the grocers with native parents in 1870 remained in Poughkeepsie in 1880, reducing this group for the first time to less than two-fifths of all grocers, whereas 59% of those with Irish parents and 64% of those with German parents remained.

Promotional works and histories written in these years as well as the city's newspapers saw the stability of its proprietors and professionals as reason for self-congratulation. They took pains to spell out the long and useful careers of these men, making special note of those born in Poughkeepsie. At the same time, there were enough successful newcomers, including foreigners, to confirm in leading citizens the sense that their community held great opportunities for the enterprising.

By contrast with the proprietors and professionals, skilled craftsmen moved in and out of the city very frequently. Of the fourteen trades in Table 6, in only one—cabinetmaking between 1850 and 1860—did as many as half the workers remain between censuses. In only two, however—the bakers and the molders between 1850 and 1860—did the proportion of workers staying fall below one-third. The rate of departure among journeymen and apprentices was higher than the table suggests. Since the census does not consistently distinguish between employers in these crafts and workers in their shops or crews, boss carpenters, masons, bakers, and butchers, and the owners of cooperages and of cabinetmaking, blacksmith, carriage, and machine shops, have been grouped with their workers.

The rate of turnover among apprentices and some journeymen can be inferred from the usual difference in persistence between workers in a trade who were less than thirty years of age and those between thirty and forty-nine years (see Table 7). Two-thirds or more of the younger workers in nine of the fourteen crafts in 1850 departed during the next decade, whereas that rate of turnover for the middle aged is found only in three crafts. A similar pattern in persistence by age-group characterizes these crafts between 1870 and 1880, a decade with business de-

Table 7. Rates of Persistence among the Young and the Middle-aged Workers in Thirteen Skilled Trades

| | 1850—60 | | 1860—70 | | 1870—80 | |
	Below 30 years	*30—49 years*	*Below 30 years*	*30—49 years*	*Below 30 years*	*30—49 years*
Baker	0	40	43	27	34	24
Butcher	41	45	27	33	59	33
Shoemaker	29	53	50	55	22	44
Tailor	35	49	47	55	47	41
Cabinetmaker	46	63	42	44	33	86
Cooper	40	50	35	50	38	52
Carriagemaker	17	25	38	64	31	45
Machinist	29	46	30	60	37	37
Molder	33	29	59	45	48	36
Carpenter	27	40	47	52	33	44
Brickmason	13	45	50	40	38	35
Painter	32	38	42	47	34	50
Blacksmith	44	32	33	40	23	38

pression. The period of expansion in Poughkeepsie between 1860 and 1870 is the exception. Young and middle aged alike persisted at a high rate, more than two-fifths of both groups surviving in most trades. Even in that decade the middle aged tended to remain with somewhat greater frequency than the young.

In times of contraction or slower growth in a trade, the proportion of the aged usually increased. Insofar as age settles men in their ways, this pattern supported the status quo in times of trouble. The much greater geographical mobility of the young in response to changed opportunities diminished the likelihood of major changes in the habits of the trades.

The present analysis underestimates both the extent of continuity in the work force of the trades and of the transiency among workers who remained in Poughkeepsie less than a decade. By limiting estimates of persistence to the proportion of workers in one census who reappear in the next, it obscures the stabilizing influence of that important minority who spent most of their working lives in Poughkeepsie. At the other extreme, the census itself fails to capture the large number of workers who entered and left the city between enumerations.

In comparatively stable trades, this limitation of the census does not distort the pattern of geographical mobility seriously. Tracing members of an expanding trade like the plumbers and gas fitters year by year through city directories yields few cases of men who do not appear in any census.[18] But the census presents a very misleading picture of trades with a rapid turnover.

The census shows shoemakers with a higher rate of persistence than most craftsmen from 1850 to 1870 and somewhat less than the average after 1870. This apparent stability reflects the minority of shoemakers and boot and shoe dealers who spent most of their working lives in Poughkeepsie. But of the total of 439 persons listed as shoemakers in city directories between 1843 and 1880, about half practiced their trade in the city for less than five years, and only half appeared in any federal census during the period.[19]

Generally, transiency was greatest in trades already affected by skill-dilution with diminishing opportunities for employment. Men lingering in these crafts tended to move from place to place in the hope of finding a locality where their skill was still in demand. Among the unskilled, transiency was a permanent condition with profound consequences for their likelihood of influencing the conditions in which they worked and lived.

Day laborers alone constituted more than 15% of the entire male labor force in Poughkeepsie at each census during the period. Their low status, irregular and menial employment at low wages, and generally less desirable places of residence might have given them a common interest. Their numbers might have given that interest some influence. But the rate of turnover among them made coalescence unlikely.

Furthermore, there were important differences in patterns of behavior among laborers, especially between the native and the foreign-born. For the Irish laborers in Newburyport, possession of their own home and land seems to have had great importance. To achieve ownership, they were willing to put children to work at an early age and reduce an already low standard of consumption. In Poughkeepsie the Irish record of investment in real estate is just as impressive despite the strong tendency of native-born and foreign-born alike until late in the period to keep their children in school.[20]

In 1850 the proportion of the propertied among native-born day laborers exceeded that among foreign-born day laborers, only recently arrived in great numbers (see Table 8). After that census, that situation was reversed by the Irish who accounted for between 56% and 61% of all day laborers at each enumeration. The propertied never constituted more than one-fifth of native-born, German, or, except in 1870, English and Scotch laborers. But in 1860 nearly one-half and in 1870 nearly one-third of the Irish laborers reported real estate. For all nationalities the proportion of the propertied persisting was much higher than among those without property.

The volatility of Irish laborers without real estate contrasts with the extraordinary stability among their propertied kinsmen. Of the latter, 61% in 1860 and 57% in 1870 remained until the next census, a higher rate of persistence than characterized the propertied in many skilled crafts during the decade of depression. The contrast

Table 8. *Percentage of Day Laborers Owning Real Estate and Rates of Persistence for Owners and Nonowners, by Nativity*

Census	Native-born	Irish	German	English-Scotch
Owners (1850)	8	5	5	0
Owners Persisting	38	22	67	
Nonowners Persisting	29	21	25	5
Owners (1860)	13	32	16	18
Owners Persisting	63	61	57	33
Nonowners Persisting	32	42	46	24
Owners (1870)	7	24	15	25
Owners Persisting	42	57	63	29
Nonowners Persisting	27	23	37	14

The percentage of native-born day laborers owning property in 1870 is depressed by the large number of native-born sons of foreign parents, especially Irish, appearing for the first time in that census as workers or as males of sixteen years or more.

underscores the desire of the Irish to be settled. This desire was frustrated for the majority of day laborers by the frequent contractions in demand for their labor in any one community. As Thernstrom concludes, most of these laborers drifted helplessly. For them the American city, even the smaller city, was a kind of Darwinian jungle.

For skilled workers, departure from the city even during business depression seems more often to be a deliberate move to a known opportunity elsewhere. Systematic tracing of departures is impossible, but the local newspaper frequently reported movements of individual craftsmen and some semiskilled workers. The source probably is biased in favor of those finding better opportunities. There are enough reports of failures or simply of transfers to comparable jobs elsewhere, however, to take seriously the impression given of conscious choice between specific alternatives.

In the late seventies, a number of Irish and native-born engineers, train dispatchers, conductors, and telegraph operators with the Hudson River Railroad accepted similar positions with railroads in the northeast, middle and far west, and Canada and with the elevated railways of New York City. Some Irish and native-born masons, policemen, and clerks found employment with the New York customs house, metropolitan police force, and Sing Sing prison. A cooper became superintendent of a Long Island woodworking manufactory; a German jeweler returned to his former position with a New York City firm; the son of an English cabinetmaker moved to a larger establishment in that trade in New York City; and a shoe-factory worker entered a machine shop in Newburgh down the river. Several changed occupations. A carpenter became superintendent of an artificial-stone manufactory in Denver, Colorado, and a printer entered the confectionery business in Albany.[21]

Within the skilled crafts, the varying rates of persistence, proportion of the propertied, and number of the foreign-born and their children indicate that opportunities for the employment of the young and the alien differed between trades. So did the likelihood of accumulating property. A man's perception of his chances for advancement in a given trade were not likely to be shaped by general notions of opportunity in America, but by the current gossip he heard in his community and what he could see for himself of the condition of firms and workers there.

Perhaps the most visible sign of the relative prosperity of a trade was the real estate that workers owned. Table 9 shows the distribution of property among workers in sixteen occupations on the city tax list for 1865. Trades varied significantly in amounts of property accumulated by workers and in the concentration of cases at each level. Among carriagemakers and machinists, there were one or two rich owners of factories or foundries. The majority

Table 9. Distribution of Assessments of Real Estate by Occupation from the 1865 Tax List, Compared with Percentages of Those Reporting No Real Estate in those Occupations in the 1860 and 1870 Censuses.

| | Tax list: Number of cases | | | | Census: Percentage Reporting No Real Estate | |
	$ 1 to 499	$500 to 999	$1000 to 4999	$5000 or more	1860	1870
Baker	1	2	4	1	83	85
Butcher	2	1	4	1	65	81
Shoemaker	13	8	16	1	73	65
Tailor	5	7	3		77	66
Cabinetmaker	6	4	2		72	60
Cooper	5	12	7		83	83
Carriagemaker	4	4	4	2	87	77
Machinist	8	8	1	1	81	79
Molder	3	1	2		90	80
Carpenter	25	21	14		74	75
Brickmason	7	12	9		64	69
Painter	6	9	1		84	89
Blacksmith	5	5	7		85	78
Teamster	26	14	1		64	69
Boatman	5				91	91
Gardener	13	3	4		73	77

There is general correspondence between the numbers in each occupation reporting real estate in the census and assessed on the tax list. The latter has been chosen for distribution of amounts because of its uniform standard of evaluation, although the assessments are less than market value and less than the amounts reported in the census.

of the propertied owned modest amounts. Most trades, however, show a more even distribution by property level. The median case usually falls in the modest $500 to $999 level, but a fair number of workers are assessed for $1,000 or more.

Estimates of the relative prosperity of the trades change as soon as the proportion of those reporting no real estate is considered. In a few cases, as Table 9 indicates, the impression given by the tax list is confirmed by the census. A few machinists did well, most did not. But the very low proportion of bakers and butchers owning property reverses the impression given by the tax list.

Examining individual trades in detail reveals the complexity of circumstances affecting mobility as well as perception of opportunity. Without this close examination, the behavior of workers in many trades seems inexplicable. The history of the coopers in Poughkeepsie during these years is a case in point. Twenty-four coopers appear on the tax list. Seven were assessed for $1,000 or more, a proportion similar to many other crafts. But the census reveals that less than one-fifth of the coopers in any decade reported real estate, a lower proportion than in most crafts (see Table 10). This fact is all the more striking because coopers were more numerous in Poughkeepsie than any other craftsmen except those in the building trades. And most of their production was "tight work"— barrels and kegs for liquids—traditionally the most skilled work in the craft.

Spurred by demand from local breweries, coopering experienced a greater expansion in one decade than any trade in the city. The number of workers quadrupled between 1850 and 1860. Almost two-thirds of the work force in 1865 was employed by five firms. But at least fifty of the city's coopers in 1865 were self-employed,

Table 10. Composition of the Coopers' Work Force

	1850	1860	1870	1880
Increase in Work Force		+382	+16	−5
Native-born	68	49	71	72
Rate of persistence	43	37		
Native-born of native parentage			64	58
Rate of persistence			44	
Irish	9	26	15	13
Rate of persistence	33	34	43	
German	18	24	20	25
Rate of persistence	66	62	55	
English and Scotch	3	1	1	4
Rate of persistence	0	0	100	
Less than 30 years of age	29	40	33	29
30 to 49 years of age	65	49	45	39
50 years of age or more	6	11	22	32

In this table, and all others on individual occupations, native-born sons of foreign parentage have been included with the nationality of their parents for the censuses of 1870 and 1880. This group first became a significant proportion of the labor force in 1870, when the sons of the Irish and the German immigrants of the late 1840s and 1850s began to appear in large numbers in the census among the employed. Fortunately, the census of 1870 did note whether parents were native or foreign born, and since the vast majority of the native born who had foreign parentage were sons, it is possible to identify easily the nationality of the parents in all but a very few cases.

working alone or with one or two assistants. The owners of the five major firms account for all but two of the assessments of $1,000 or more; owners of small shops explain most of the seventeen valuations of less than that amount (Table 9). Clearly, if the prospect for substantial property ownership was a major consideration for workers entering the trade, then coopering was not inviting.

Nor did the prospect improve. Only one of the small shops of 1865, the German Faust brothers, subsequently became a large cooperage, employing thirty-five men by 1880. The number of small shops declined; by 1880, more than four-fifths of the coopers worked for four firms. And the decline in opportunities for self-employment was accompanied by a decline in wages for the trade as a whole. In 1865 the wage rates reported by major cooperages were roughly comparable to those in most trades. By 1875 the average was little better than for day laborers and substantially less than in most crafts.[22] Opportunities for even modest prosperity could not account for men remaining in the trade during the last decade of the period. Yet the rate of persistence among coopers without property rose from 37% between 1860 and 1870 to 44% between 1870 and 1880, the first decade in which the trade showed a decline in total number of workers.

If the prospects for acquiring property cannot explain entry into coopering during its great expansion in Poughkeepsie, they are totally irrelevant in explaining the persistence of many coopers as the trade declined. One clue to an explanation is the changing composition of the work force by national origin. At the beginning of the period, nearly one-third of the coopers were foreign-born, with Germans predominating. During the great expansion in the next decade, the Germans and Irish advanced to half of the total. The Irish temporarily became more numerous, a pattern repeated in other trades during times of rapid expansion.

For the immigrants who entered Poughkeepsie near the beginning of the period, coopering was the only skilled craft during the first decade to hire them in large numbers. For them the trade was an opportunity for employment at a time when jobs were scarce. As growth leveled off after 1860, the proportion of Irish dropped sharply, never to recover. The Germans declined somewhat in proportion of the total in 1870 but not in absolute number. They held their own largely in small shops soon fated to disappear. Of the twenty-four coopers on the 1865 tax list, eight were German, all assessed for less than $1,000. By 1880 most of these shops were gone; but the Germans and their native-born sons nevertheless comprised one-fifth of all coopers, largely through the expansion of the Faust Brothers cooperage.

Among the native-born it seems probable that persistence in the trade before 1870 was partly a matter of reasonable wages as late as the 1860s and partly of pride in a craft that once had been so important to the life of small communities everywhere. During the decline after 1870, many native-born coopers remained because they saw no more favorable alternatives. The steady decrease in the proportion of young workers and the increase of workers fifty years or older after 1860 support the idea that older workers in the trade tended to be trapped by their inability to adapt easily to other kinds of skilled work. With the exception of largely mechanized sash and blind factories, all the woodworking trades declined in number of workers during this period. So there was no easy escape to related trades in Poughkeepsie.

The experience of the coopers points up the critical importance of the state of the particular trade—its expansion, stability, or decline—in determining opportunities for employment, self-employment, and even limited prosperity. This was especially true for the foreign-born and their children who by 1880 comprised half of the city's working force. The history of coopering also suggests that for the foreign-born, achievement of proprietorship in a trade increased their chances for preserving employment opportunities first gained in time of rapid expansion. The Germans were more successful in this respect than the Irish.

The very success of the Germans, however, may have hindered organization of workers in the trade in Poughkeepsie. In the state census for 1865, cooperages with foreign-born proprietors reported lower average wages than the larger establishments with native-born proprietors. There had been a society of coopers in Poughkeepsie earlier, and in 1864 the newspaper reported an attempt—apparently unsuccessful—to revive it. No union existed in the city when the State Bureau of Labor Statistics surveyed conditions in the trade in 1888. And that report suggests that in most cities in the state which had coopers' unions, the majority of nonunion men were German. Jobs for the foreign-born in many trades, particularly in small cities like Poughkeepsie, entailed a willingness to work for lower wage than native-born workers. In large cities, foreign-born craftsmen might be sufficiently numerous to form unions of their own. But in a community like Poughkeepsie, securing the jobs that meant survival in trades dominated by the native-born apparently came at the cost of craft solidarity.[23]

Increase in the proportion of the foreign-born and their children in the skilled trades was selective, early and rapid in some, negligible in others (see Table 11). Three-fourths of the machinists, carriagemakers, carpenters, and painters remained native-born of native parentage as late as 1870. The English accounted for most of the foreign-born machinists and carriagemakers throughout the period. An owner of a large shop in each trade was English. The few Irish and German workers who appeared in each census usually did not remain in the next. In the two building trades the Irish made the most headway, but

Table 11. Percentage of the Foreign-born (and for 1870 and 1880 the Foreign-born and their Native-born Sons) in Twenty-two Occupations

	1850	1860	1870	1880
Lawyer	0	2	4	7
Doctor	12	24	9	22
Merchant	23	15	11	17
Grocer		24	46	61
Clerk	9	7	27	33
Baker	43	50	79	83
Butcher	31	45	49	71
Shoemaker	37	53	61	67
Tailor	65	82	82	82
Cabinetmaker	27	44	45	63
Cooper	32	51	36	42
Carriagemaker	22	16	23	37
Machinist	16	14	25	36
Molder	30	27	63	61
Carpenter	18	24	27	26
Brickmason	39	41	63	66
Painter	16	20	26	34
Blacksmith	40	46	53	58
Teamster	19	43	39	48
Boatman	11	10	15	34
Gardener	72	68	75	74
Laborer	68	79	71	73

only a few were listed as boss carpenters or painters in the city business directory.

By contrast, the foreign-born, primarily the Germans, quickly became prominent as workers and shop owners in the food and apparel trades. In some cases, such as tailoring, their dominance seems to have resulted from their driving out native-born workers. In other cases, such as butchering, it was due to rapid expansion of the trade rather than displacement of native-born workers. In both cases, small proprietorships could be established without much capital. Whereas some of the shops of the foreign-born catered largely to neighborhoods where many of their countrymen lived, a significant proportion located and prospered in the heart of the business district on Main Street close to fashionable and largely native-born residential areas.

In 1870 seven of the sixteen merchant tailors and clothiers on upper Main Street were German, two of these reporting real estate of $19,000 and $11,000. Most of these proprietors employed between one and three tailors for custom work at low wages. The rate of $25.00 per month seems to have been standard in German shops in Poughkeepsie in 1865 compared to an average rate of between $35.00 and $40.00 per month in the leading cooperages that year.

But the proportion of self-employed among foreign-born tailors was high, and the proportion of the propertied advanced steadily (see Table 12). Although much larger amounts of property are reported by German tailors, the Irish propensity for investing in real estate appears again in the proportion of the propertied to all workers in each nationality. The Irish were highest among tailors in both 1860 and 1870, with half reporting

Table 12. Composition of the Tailors' Work Force

	1850	1860	1870	1880
Native-born	35	18	21	30
Rate of persistence	35	63		
Native-born of native parentage			18	18
Rate of persistence			44	
Irish	18	15	19	13
Rate of persistence	23	62	42	
German	23	43	48	50
Rate of persistence	65	41	46	
English and Scotch	23	16	9	
Rate of persistence	47	50	78	
Real-estate Owners	5	23	34	

property in the latter year as compared to about two-fifths
of the Germans and less than one-fifth of the native-born.

The remarkable expansion of German workers in the
trade and the corresponding decline in the proportion of
English and native-born poses the question of direct competition between workers of different nationalities. Were
the English and native-born driven from the field as unsuccessful competitors, or does their declining importance
reflect a difference between the nationalities in numbers
of new workers entering the trade? Comparison of rates
of persistence suggests that in the first decade sharp competition for work may have occurred. The Germans survived at a much higher rate than the native-born and
achieved most of their increase in tailoring during that
one decade. The difference in persistence probably reflects the willingness of the Germans as well as the Irish
to work for less compensation. Whether this undercutting
of the wages of native labor led to as much ill-feeling between the nationalities in Poughkeepsie as it did elsewhere in New York State during the 1840s and '50s is
unclear, but there is some evidence of economic nativism
in the city.[24]

After 1860, the rates of persistence for both the native-
born and the English tailors compare favorably with
those for the Germans. The failure of the Irish to maintain in 1880 the proportion they had achieved by 1870
reflects a decline in new workers of that national deriva-
tion rather than any significant difference in rate of departure. Opportunities for the sons of the Irish to enter
the trade probably were less than for the sons of the
native-born, Germans, and English. Only one of the
thirty-two merchant tailors and clothiers of 1870 was
Irish, and another was a Canadian of Irish descent.

In some trades in which the foreign-born became a majority of the work force, their apparent improvement in status over unskilled labor is misleading. The fact that the Irish and their children came to comprise one-fourth of the city's bakers suggests upward mobility. Examination of that trade, however, reveals that the majority of those listed as bakers received low wages for long hours. Most of the city's bakeries were small shops run by the proprietor alone with one or two helpers. But one shop, frequently referred to as the cracker factory, employed more than one-third of the workers in the trade in 1865. Bartlett and Sons reported paying ten men and ten boys average wage of $15 per month. Assuming that the boys received between $8 and $10 each, common rates that year, the adult workers were the most underpaid in the skilled crafts.

The proportion of all bakers less than thirty years of age was consistently higher than in any other trade, being three-fifths of the total (see Table 13). The turnover among the young was great and, contrary to the usual pattern, even greater among the middle aged. Only one-

Table 13. *Composition of the Bakers' Work Force*

	1850	1860	1870	1880
Native-born	57	50	34	50
Rate of persistence	24	33		
Native-born of native parentage			21	17
Rate of persistence			45	
Irish	13	8	13	27
Rate of persistence	25	66	29	
German	20	22	51	47
Rate of persistence	0	50	33	
English and Scotch	7	19	11	3
Rate of persistence	0	14	17	
Real-Estate Owners	13	17	15	
Less than 30 years of age	60	58	60	65

fourth of the middle aged in 1860 and again in 1870 persisted to the next census. By 1870 the foreign-born and
their sons comprised four-fifths of the work force. Half of
the bakers were German. They fared best, owning most of
the small shops in town. With no proprietorships in the
trade, the Irish fared worst. Most of them worked at the
cracker factory. They probably were semiskilled at best
and seldom remained long in Poughkeepsie.[25]

If the Irish entry into a craft like baking represents
less of a gain than might be supposed, similar doubts
must be raised about the improvement in status of the
many native-born sons of foreign parents listed as clerks
in the censuses of 1870 and 1880. By 1870 they accounted
for one-fifth of the city's clerks, who at every census in
this period were almost entirely native born.

Unfortunately, the census does not consistently differentiate between clerks in offices and clerks in retail stores
or, among the latter, between types of firms. There are,
however, enough cases where "clerk in grocery store,"
"Druggist's clerk," etc., is specified to suggest differences
between nationality groups in proportions of those holding more responsible positions. A higher proportion of
the Irish sons were grocery clerks, undoubtedly reflecting
the predominance of the Irish in the provision business
and especially in neighborhood groceries. Although
grocery clerks might do some keeping of accounts and
wait on customers, much of their time was spent handling
produce, filling shelves, and other comparatively menial
work. By contrast, a clerk in a furniture store was likely
to be a salesman, and a clerk in an insurance office a
scribe. Their status and their opportunities for advancement were greater.

In general, the Irish and their American-born children
advanced more slowly into skilled and clerical work than

the English and Germans and had more difficulty holding their own in these employments during contractions
in the work force. Although the proportion of American
sons of Irish parents listed in skilled trades increased as
compared to their fathers, one-third of this group were
listed as laborers in 1870 compared to less than one-tenth
of the American-born sons of American and of German
parentage. Furthermore, the Irish and their native-born
sons together failed in several trades to sustain the proportion of all workers which the Irish-born alone constituted earlier. Among blacksmiths and masons, the decline was small; the Irish maintained their predominance
in bricklaying and remained second only to the native-
born sons of native parents in smithing.

In six occupations with a large number of workers, the
Irish did increase in proportion to the total during the
hard times after 1870. That Irish advance then should
have been limited to grocers, bakers, molders, boatmen,
gardeners, and laborers suggests the difficulty the Irish
encountered in moving beyond unskilled and semiskilled occupations. Gardeners and boatmen were mostly
semiskilled workers.[26] The frequency with which individuals listed in both occupations in census and directory
appear in other years as "laborers" suggests their status.
A large proportion of the gardeners were older men employed by the well-to-do native-born and not infrequently listed as boarders at their employers' addresses. The
young predominated consistently among boatmen. Like
most workers associated with the river trade, the boatmen had been overwhelmingly native-born. Only in this
unskilled or semiskilled work did the Irish make any
headway in waterfront occupations and then only after
1870 when river traffic was declining.

By contrast, the steady and sharp increase of Irish

molders to half of the total in 1880 *was* a major advance
if judged by compensation. Wage rates reported in the
six wards of the city in that trade in 1875 were the same
as or only slightly less than the rates for machinists and
masons and generally slightly higher than for carpenters,
painters, blacksmiths, and printers. The rate of persistence among Irish molders was high, more than half persisting after both the 1860 and 1870 censuses. But the
work was hot and dirty, the skill-level for most molders
already reduced, and the opportunities for self-employment slight. None of the city's foundries was owned by
an Irishman.

The one trade in which the Irish came to predominate
with good wages, status, *and* opportunity for self-employment and acquisition of substantial real estate was
bricklaying. About one-third of all masons reported real
estate in 1860 and 1870, and among the Irish 45% were
propertied in 1870. In the latter year the officers of the
bricklayers' union in the city were Irish and so were a
majority of the boss masons.[27]

Once again, the expansion of the proportion of Irish
in a skilled trade coincided with a period of rapid growth.
The masons more than doubled in number during the
postwar building boom and so did the proportion of
Irish. The same pattern appears among Irish painters.
The great exception appears in those trades in which
native-born workers constituted four-fifths or more at the
beginning of the period and the native-born sons of native parentage three-fourths or more by 1880. In these
trades the increase in the proportion of the foreign-born
and their sons was gradual even during rapid expansion
of the work force.

A different pattern appears in trades suffering steady
and permanent decline in the city during these years,

notably shoemaking and cabinetmaking. There the proportion of the foreign-born increased, but the number of workers represented generally remained about the same or decreased. In both trades the rate of persistence of native-born workers stayed about the same or declined slightly after 1870; in both, the foreign-born and their sons remained at a somewhat higher rate than the native-born sons of native parentage in the last decade. During the decline, the proportion of older and propertied workers increased steadily.

The growth of mass production made both crafts obsolete except for the limited market for fine custom work. Cabinetmaking declined as a craft as soon as wood turning became automatic. Improvements in the stocking lathe made that machine capable of reproducing even the curlicues in vogue in furniture in that era. By 1865 the cabinetmakers already had been reduced to less than three-quarters of their number in Poughkeepsie in 1850. But as late as 1865 two firms continued to employ about ten workers each at an average rate of $43, a good rate for that year in the city's crafts. The proportion of the propertied reflects that favorable return, but also leads to the suspicion that this rate helped price these firms out of the market (see Table 14).

Table 14. Percentage of Cabinetmakers Owning Real Estate

	1850	1860	1870	1880
Owning Real Estate	11	28	40	
Rate of persistence of owners	40	50	75	
Rate of persistence of nonowners	53	38	33	
Less than 30 years of age	58	33	30	21
30 to 49 years of age	36	50	35	32
50 years of age or more	7	17	35	47

Both firms had disappeared by 1880. The production of the nineteen cabinetmakers remaining was so insignificant that the first historian of the county failed to mention furniture and coffin making in an otherwise remarkably comprehensive discussion of small manufacturing in Poughkeepsie. Competition from machine work in large factories elsewhere gradually turned a once flourishing craft into a small remnant, nearly one-half of whom were fifty years of age or older in 1880. There was no protest from the workers, simply a gradual loss of men through a rate of turnover similar to other crafts and through failure to replace those leaving.[28]

In the case of shoemaking, the competition from factory production which finally replaced the craft became visible in Poughkeepsie itself with the establishment of the Whitehouse Shoe Factory in 1870. With about four hundred workers, the factory became the largest single employer in the city. No public opposition emerged from the ninety shoemakers—excluding twenty-five boot and shoe dealers some of whom were themselves shoemakers—still in the city in that year. The only noticeable response was a higher rate of departure of shoemakers from the city during the next decade.

Very few skilled shoemakers entered the factory. Half of its employees were women. A large proportion of the men were young, including many native-born sons of foreign parentage in their teens. In 1880 sixty of the latter were of Irish parentage. For them factory employment was an improvement in status and certainly in security in the form of regular work. The remarkable stability of the 101 male shoe-factory workers listed in the city directory that year indicates the importance of that security. More than half of them appear in the directory ten years later; of that half, more than two-thirds were still employed in the shoe factory.

With one major exception, the behavior of the shoe-makers during the trade's decline was similar to that of the cabinetmakers. An important minority moved into work related to their crafts, either as dealers or repairers. The Irish dealers were least successful. Three of the four in 1870 had shops on lower Main Street patronized large-ly by their countrymen. Generally, they did repairs and, in addition to their own production, kept some manu-factured shoes in stock. Only one of the Irish dealers re-ported a large amount of property in 1870.

The picture given by the census obscures the painful consequence of obsolescence for shoemakers and for other skilled workers in declining trades who drifted from place to place in search of employment. Through its failure to capture that half of all shoemakers listed in the city di-rectory who entered and left Poughkeepsie between enu-merations, the census exaggerates the proportion of the stable and propertied (see Table 15).

Table 15. Composition of the Shoemakers' Work Force and Real Estate Ownership (Includes Boot and Shoe Dealers)

	1850	1860	1870	1880
Rate of persistence	42	50	38	
Native-born	63	47	41	45
Native-born of native parentage			39	33
Irish	12	13	20	21
German	21	34	30	34
English and Scotch	4	5	9	8
Real-estate owners	16	27	35	
Rate of persistence of owners	62	69	63	
Rate of persistence of nonowners	38	43	25	
Less than 30 years of age	40	25	16	14
30 to 49 years of age	45	46	51	38
50 years of age or more	16	28	33	48

The census also distorts the patterns among nationality groups. In the census, the native-born and the Germans persist in most years at a higher rate than the Irish and the English, reflecting an important minority of successful dealers and craftsmen who spent their working careers in the city. Directory tracing, by contrast, yields a much higher frequency of departure among the native-born and Germans (71% and 89%) within the five-year period in which they were first listed than among the Irish and English (50% and 46%).

The transiency among shoemakers, greatest in the 1850s, reflects dislocations that began before the factory system in shoe manufacture. Development of mass production of shoes under the putting-out system in New England and the garret workshops of Philadelphia and New York City squeezed out the small shoemaker except for the custom trade. In addition, the decline of village population in Dutchess County, with the shift from grain to dairy farming, brought a swarm of village shoemakers to the city, usually as the first stop in a migration westward.

The shoemakers' plight is a useful reminder of the unhappy experience of many workers at one time or another in Poughkeepsie and in other cities like it, notwithstanding a general increase in job opportunities for immigrants as well as the native-born. Apart from three trades in permanent decline, three of the remaining eleven crafts examined here experienced a reduction in size of work force of at least one-fourth during one decade in this period.

Besides these temporary contractions in individual trades, stability in employment varied markedly between decades in most occupations. A high rate of turnover characterized the labor force as a whole between 1850 and 1860 and again in the decade after 1870. For the foreign-born the first decade was the worst. Among the Irish who came in such numbers to build the Hudson River Railroad, both the character of their first employment and the sudden drying up of job opportunities with its completion hardly suggested the promised land. As one student at the Poughkeepsie Collegiate School noted in his diary in 1849, "We saw the blasts go off on the Railroad. . . . Dont they have to scatter. A piece weighing about 200 pounds was thrown about a quarter of a mile. Dont the paddies have to work."[29]

By 1850 half of the male inmates at the city poorhouse were Irish. Judged only by the census, the turnover among the sons of Erin was immense, less than one-fourth of those listed in 1850 remaining in 1860. Even the native-born left more frequently, corresponding to the greater geographical mobility in the nation as a whole during that decade than in any other during this period.[30]

Throughout these years, sudden termination of employment for many workers resulted from failure of individual firms and especially from frequent destruction of shops and factories by fire. When the Whitehouse Shoe Factory burned down in 1879, the newspaper reported that "the employees have commenced to leave town by the dozen, every boat and train carrying them away, and some have already obtained employment elsewhere."[31]

Natural disaster only compounded the peculiarity of circumstances for workers in different occupations in the same decade. Job opportunities expanded in some trades and contracted in others. In some the foreign-born and their children made headway; in others they lost ground or continued to be a small minority of the work force. In some middle-aged and older workers predominated; in others the majority were young and turned over rapidly.

Hardly a promising environment for development of a common interest among workers or for coalescence at any given time around a common set of grievances.

Given such diversity in occupational experience, proximity in place of residence among workers with similar circumstances might have been a countervailing influence for developing a common interest. No such concentration developed in Poughkeepsie during this period. Regardless of occupation or level of skill, workers tended to settle in neighborhoods with large numbers of their countrymen. Although the coopers clustered on a few streets, workers in most occupations scattered.

Occasionally members of the same trade lived in the same house, but far more often men in unrelated trades with different conditions shared a dwelling. Table 16 shows the combinations of occupations in all dwellings with two or more male workers on one short street in 1865. Because Perry Street lay in Ward II, which had a

Table 16. *Occupations of Workers Sharing the Same Dwelling on Perry Street, 1865*

House Number		House Number	
5	Edge Tool Maker Carpenter—Boarder Cooper—Boarder	6	Tailor Tinsmith—Boarder
13	Baggagemaster—Irish Cabinetmaker—Irish	14	Physician—German Cooper—German
15	Two Cartmen—German Blacksmith—German	17	Engineer—German Coachman—Irish
24	Two Coopers—Irish Flagman (Railroad)—German	26	Physician—German Cigarmaker—German
28	Varnisher Cooper	29	Merchant Tailor—English Chairmaker Laborer—German
32	Shoemaker—German Laborer—German	34	Mason—Irish Molder Soldier—German

more balanced ethnic composition than any ward in the city, the frequency of workers of different national origin in the same house is atypical for the city as a whole. But the mixture of occupations is typical.

The proportion of skilled workers and proprietors on Perry and other residential streets near the main business thoroughfare tended to be higher than on outlying streets. But even in neighborhoods farthest from the central business district, day laborers or semiskilled workers rarely exceeded one-half of the residents. Only in that proportion of Ward I in which the Irish became an overwhelming majority did day laborers predominate on a number of contiguous streets. Even there the major thoroughfare remained mixed in nationality, occupation, and skill-level.

In the one area in Poughkeepsie most closely approximating a ghetto, residents continued to be exposed to workers in different circumstances. Furthermore, the majority of transient Irish day laborers on the side streets were interspersed with a remarkably stable minority of propertied Irish laborers. On the street with the highest concentration of unskilled workers in the city, one-fourth of the laborers listed in the 1865 directory remained on that street twenty-five years later. The example of more successful neighbors lent some credibility to the hopes of the more transient Irish for a secure and settled existence.

The high rate of persistence of property owners of every nationality throughout the city and their strong tendency to stay at the same address was a stabilizing influence hard to overestimate. Although home ownership was more frequent on some streets, notably in the more fashionable and predominantly native-born areas, comparison of the 1865 tax list with the city directory for that year shows at least a significant minority of owners on every street in the city. The same pattern appears on an 1876 map of the owners of all lots.

The majority of the population did not own their dwellings. Newspaper notices each spring, the season for renewal or termination of rentals, suggest frequent movement within the city among renters. Hard times increased this movement. The newspaper reported in 1876 that "there is already an unusual demand for small tenement houses, . . . and many families who have hitherto occupied a house alone are renting out apartments." Even in 1879, it noted that "the words 'To Let,' increase in number daily about the city, and it seems as if there will be more moving this year than for many years before."[32]

The result was a constant reshuffling of the majority of residents on most streets. To be sure, much of this reshuffling among the Irish and the Germans took place within and between areas of the city with large concentrations of their countrymen. But the general effect was to increase the exposure of most citizens to workers in other occupations. If this exposure had any influence, it probably increased their sense of the diversity and peculiarity of opportunities in different occupations. When change of dwelling involved a move of half a mile or more, as it frequently did even among the foreign-born, it tended to limit association with the previous neighborhood and whatever mutuality of interest might have developed among its residents.

The mobility of Americans even within the same city widened their acquaintance with and increased their adaptability to different situations and people. But one result was to throw individuals back on themselves, their families, and voluntary associations for any sense of stability and security in the midst of so much change. Turnover within occupations and neighborhoods heightened that individualism, that eye for personal opportunity, which the national faith exalted. Hunger for the familiar maintained a more developed sense of community among the foreign-born for some time. But that community cut across economic classes. Voluntary associations like the Germania Singing Society, St. Peter's (Irish Catholic) Temperance Association, and the German Odd Fellows lodge brought together the skilled and unskilled, the prosperous and the poor.

The exposure of poorer workers of each nationality to the others in the river-front wards might, hypothetically, have developed some sense of common interest. But the patterns of change of residence within these wards indicate that proximity to countrymen remained more attractive than proximity to workers in similar circumstances. The same pattern appears elsewhere in the city. The Irish and Germans who appeared in predominantly native-born wards in 1850 show a strong tendency to move westward by 1860 to the river-front wards where most of their countrymen lived. After 1870 this pattern changed as apparel factories employing large numbers of the foreign-born and their children opened up on the eastern edge of the city. But even in 1880 a large number of Irish shoe-factory workers continued to live in the older neighborhoods despite the distance from the factory.

A major exception to this pattern began to develop among some of the more prosperous Germans who bought houses in predominantly native-born neighborhoods. The assimilation of the most successful of the recent foreign-born into the city's social as well as economic elite had commenced. For the Irish, progress was slower. But even before 1892 when immigrants from Central and Southern Europe entered the city in large numbers, the Irish had both increased their proportion of the city's proprietors and bosses in the crafts and their dispersion in place of residence.

However modest, prolonged, and uneven the improvement in condition for the foreign-born and their children after the great influx in the '40s and '50s, it held promise enough to prevent their rejection of the national faith that success came to the industrious. It apparently discouraged any social conflict more serious than brief, sporadic disputes between workers and employers in individual trades and occasional hassles between groups of different nationality. Nativist fears of competition from foreign workers brought some workers in different crafts together in the United Order of American Mechanics. Limitation of immigration remained their primary concern, however.

Labor organization for the purpose of altering wages and working conditions aroused no more than temporary interest when more than one craft was involved. In the late 1860s, the city's trade unions flirted briefly with cooperation in the eight-hour movement, but the cooperation seems to have been short-lived. Craft unionism rather than reform unionism offered the best opportunity for labor organization in so divided a work force. But even craft unionism had rough going in a small city where most shops and factories remained small, and foreign-born workers were numerous. Only two building trades unions, the carpenters and the masons, had a continuous existence. Even they were not listed in the city directory until after 1885.[33]

The high rate of persistence among the more successful in every occupation and nationality group reduced the likelihood of protest against the status quo. And in the absence of events capable of polarizing so diversified a community, the successful easily justified for most citizens their sense of Poughkeepsie's promise for their own advancement. For the city's largely native-born economic elite, the success in their midst of some of the foreign-born confirmed their sense of the soundness and opportunity of their city. For the many small cities in America with comparably diversified economies and populations, local experience confirmed the national faith that merit sooner or later was rewarded by success.

1. Stephan Thernstrom, *Poverty and Progress: Social Mobility in a Nineteenth Century City* (Cambridge, Mass., 1964), especially Chap. 6.

2. For illustration in one New England textile mill town, Lawrence, Mass., see Donald B. Cole, *Immigrant City* (Chapel Hill, 1963), Chap. 7, and on the effects of Lawrence's ethnic diversity, Chap. 4; the best description of the diversity in circumstances and opportunities between occupations in this period is Robert Ernst, *Immigrant Life in New York City, 1825–1863* (New York, 1949), Chap. 6–9.

3. For a brief description of the character of the American labor force, 1862–72, see David Montgomery, *Beyond Equality* (New York, 1967), Chap. 1; on the influence of the depression of the 1870s in spurring rapid adoption of mass-production methods, see Alfred Chandler's essay in David T. Gilchrist and W. David Lewis, eds., *Economic Change in the Civil War Era* (Greenville, Del., 1965), pp. 150–51; and on the frequency of small-shop manufacturing and the continuing social and economic heterogeneity of as large a city as Philadelphia as late as 1860, see Sam Bass Warner, Jr., *The Private City* (Philadelphia, 1968), Chaps. 3–4.

4. On the differences between firms in the same industry in the timing of adoption of successful technological innovations, see W. Paul Strassman, *Risk and Technological Innovation* (Ithaca, 1956) which analyzes American manufacturing methods in the iron and steel, textile, machine tool, and electrical industries in the nineteenth century. A similar impression of the unevenness in mechanization and specialization in many more industries prior to 1864 is given by the older, disorganized *History of American Manufactures* by J. B. Bishop (Philadelphia, 1864). Because of his detailed descriptions of differences between firms in the same industry, Bishop remains more useful in this respect than Victor S. Clark, *History of Manufactures in the United States* (New York, 1929).

5. Individual records have been compiled for the nearly 20,000 males in Poughkeepsie during this period who were gainfully employed or at least sixteen years of age. The compilation was underwritten by a Ford Foundation Public Affairs grant to Vassar College and by grants-in-aid from the college's Research Committe. The collaboration of my wife, Sarah D. Griffen, in organizing and analyzing the data has been continuous and invaluable.

6. The investigation, yet to be done, of intra- and inter-generational occupational mobility will remove one important limitation of the present analysis of persistence. The latter does not distinguish between workers keeping the same occupation at the next census and those shifting to other lines of work. In most trades, especially among workers thirty years of age or older, persistence in the same occupation was the rule. But in a few, primarily those with younger, less stable work forces, shifts in occupation were more common.

7. Between 1860 and 1870, the growth rate for Poughkeepsie was 36%; for Newburyport, a loss of 6%. The rate for that decade for forty-nine cities in the northeast with more than 10,000 inhabitants ranged from Newburyport, the only instance of loss, to Jersey City, the only community to more than double its population. Poughkeepsie was almost the median case, twenty-five cities having a lower rate of growth. J. G. Williamson and J. A. Swanson, "The Growth of Cities in the American Northeast, 1820–1870," *Explorations in Entrepreneurial History, 4,* No. 1 (Supplement, 1966), 78–79.

8. James H. Smith, *History of Dutchess County* (Syracuse, 1882), pp. 387–96, and the enumeration of firms with product valued at more than $500 annually in the manuscript schedules of the New York State censuses for 1865 and 1875.

9. The following tabulation of the number of business enterprises in operation in 1843 and 1873 in Poughkeepsie presents a similar picture:

	Retail	Wholesale	Manufacture	Craft	Service	Total
1843	186		45	119	43	393
1873	396	10	123	89	158	776

R. G. and A. R. Hutchinson and Mabel Newcomer, "A Study in Business Mortality: Length of Life of Business Enterprises in Poughkeepsie, New York, 1843–1936," *American Economic Review, 28* (September 1938), 509.

10. Since the initial collation of the four censuses for persistence, increasing familiarity with Poughkeepsie families has led to discovery of some additional cases. When the study is completed, there undoubtedly will be some increase in the rates of persistence presented here.

11. Poughkeepsie *Daily Eagle,* January 18, 1864; July 27, 1868.

12. Edmund Platt, *The Eagle's History of Poughkeepsie* (Poughkeepsie, 1905), p. 150.

13. Percentage of children in the census ages 10 to 14 reported as enrolled in school:

	Native-born	German	Irish
1860	89	78	83
1870	82	87	69
1880	82	77	83

Unfortunately, Board of Education reports on attendance compared to enrollment before the Poughkeepsie Plan went into effect are not classified by nationality. In the first year of the Plan, the Board reported that approximately 94% of those children "belonging" to the two Plan schools attended daily compared to only 75% of those "belonging" to the other ten public schools in the city. City of Poughkeepsie, *Annual Report of the Board of Education* (1874).

14. Nor does the amount of property significantly affect this relationship. Those assessed for less than $1,000 real estate on the 1865 tax list appear with slightly greater frequency than those with higher valuations in the city directories for 1870, 1874, and 1881. The difference reflects the tendency for the richer to be older on the average and their correspondingly higher mortality.

15. These aggregates do obscure the frequency of exodus among middle-aged and even propertied heads of household in occupations afflicted by contraction in demand for workers.

16. Only a few men listed as "merchants" in the census for Poughkeepsie were engaged in importing and exporting; some were wholesalers, but the majority were retailers. Since the census frequently does not record the nature of their business, merchants have been grouped with other retailers listed as "dealers." Among the dealers, a minority who tended to come from and continue to participate in a craft have been grouped with those crafts. The same individuals will be recorded in different censuses as tailors, merchant tailors, and clothiers, or as shoemakers and as boot and shoe dealers, suggesting continued pride in craft as well as the mixture of production and retailing in their business.

17. The city's historian asserts that "although many local businessmen lost heavily as a result of the panic, there were few failures." Platt, *Eagle's History*, p. 225. The assertion seems warranted for the larger and older firms, but not for many smaller ventures which first appear in the 1860s or early 1870s.

18. The only major exception occurs in the first year of depression, 1873–74, when the directory reports seventeen new entries in the trade, fourteen of whom were not listed the following year. This unusual turnover is less important for analysis of the plumbers and gas fitters than for investigation of migration in time of depression.

19. The analysis of the shoemakers in this paper is drawn largely from a thorough study of that craft in Poughkeepsie by Edna C. Macmahon. The project as a whole has benefitted greatly from her knowledge of nineteenth-century crafts.

20. The small proportion of workers among children less than fifteen years of age prior to 1880 probably reflects limited opportunities for employment. The shoe, shirt, silk, skirt, and glass factories that opened between 1870 and 1880 employed a large number of the very workers listed in the 1880 census.

21. *Daily Eagle* for 1876: January 14; March 13, 28; May 1. For 1879: January 15; April 7; July 2, 9, 16, 31; August 9, 13, 14; September 10; October 21, 27, 28; December 25.

22. The New York State Census recorded average wages in the city's cooperages ranging from $37.50 to $40.00 per month compared to a

range for day laborers—assuming regular employment—of $32.50 to $45.00 and for carpenters from $58.50 to $78.00 in the six wards of the city. The ranges for masons and machinists were still higher.

23. *Daily Eagle,* January 26, 1864; *Sixth Annual Report of the Bureau of Statistics of the State of New York for the Year 1888* (Albany), pp. 291–95.

24. Robert Ernst, "Economic Nativism in New York City During the 1840's," *New York History, 29* (1948), 170–86; Douglas T. Miller, *Jacksonian Aristocracy* (New York, 1967), pp. 100–01; Poughkeepsie *American* for 1846: July 11, August 29, September 12, December 19; and for 1847: January 16, April 17, July 24. Political nativism in Dutchess County was largely confined to the years 1845–48 and directed against the Irish, but a chief concern had been protection of native labor from the competition of immigrants. One offshoot of this nativist outburst survived between 1850 and 1880, a local council of the Order of United American Mechanics. In the first year of depression, 1874–75, two new councils were formed. *Daily Eagle* for 1874: January 9, 31; February 10; and July 3, 4.

25. Conditions for workers in that trade did not improve for some years. The life of bakers in New York State was described as "mere slavery" in *Report of the Bureau of Statistics of Labor* (1886), p. 485.

26. A few horticulturists, nurserymen, and seedsmen were reported as "gardeners" in the census, and a few ship captains and pilots as "boatmen," but these more skilled workers normally were differentiated in the enumeration.

27. *Daily Eagle,* April 27, 30, 1870; see also November 7, 1868 and May 8, 1869.

28. On the fate of the dwindling number of woodworkers in New York State who persisted in their crafts after machine work had drastically reduced the market for their services, see Jared Van Wagenen, Jr., *The Golden Age of Homespun* (New York, 1963), Chaps. 12–16, a nostalgic and anecdotal but very useful account.

29. *Year Book of the Dutchess County Historical Society, 36* (1951), 47.

30. Advisory Commission on Intergovernmental Relations, *Urban and Rural America* (Washington, D.C., 1968), p. 14.

31. *Daily Eagle,* July 26, 1879. The failure of one cooperage in 1870 put thirty men out of work; destruction of another by fire in 1876 cost twenty-nine coopers their tools as well as their jobs. Ten, mostly Irish, had not insured their tools. Both cooperages reopened later, but these incidents illustrate the sudden and sometimes lengthy disruptions that hurt workers in many trades. Ibid., April 14, 1870; April 24, 1876.

32. Ibid., April 5, 1876; February 24, 1879.

33. Ibid., July 1, 15, August 15, and December 15, 1868; January 1, 1869.

THE REALITY OF THE RAGS-TO-RICHES "MYTH": The Case of the Paterson, New Jersey, Locomotive, Iron, and Machinery Manufacturers, 1830–1880.

Herbert G. Gutman

In recent decades, historians have vigorously disputed the validity of the belief that nineteenth-century American industrialists rose from "rags to riches." A popular literature has been subjected to critical textual analysis, and the promises of popular ideology have been measured by empirical head-counting that involves the collection of data about the social origins of "business leaders." These studies share a common conclusion: very few workers—day laborers, unskilled workers, and skilled artisans—became successful manufacturers. After studying nearly two hundred leaders of the largest early twentieth-century corporations, William Miller convincingly concluded that to look for men of "working class or foreign origins" among the most powerful financiers, public utility and railroad executives, and mining and manufacturing corporation officials was "to look almost in vain." Fully 95% came from families of upper- or middle-class status. Not more than 3% started as poor immigrant boys or even as poor American farm boys. Andrew Carnegie was an important American in 1900, but hardly any men of his economic class or social position shared with him a common career pattern.[1]

Other studies, not as careful in their selection of a representative sample of manufacturers, have tended to validate Miller's findings about the 1900–10 elite for earlier periods of industrialization. Miller's study carefully explained its limits: his data described " 'career men'—bureaucrats that is . . . all office-holders, many of them [having] *never* organized a business of any kind." The work of C. Wright Mills and his critics Reinhard Bendix and Frank W. Howton ranged over all of American history in an effort to define the changing composition of the "American business elite." Mills drew evidence from biographical sketches of business leaders in the *Dictionary of American Biography*.[2] Bendix and Howton worked primarily from biographical sketches in the *National Cyclopedia of American Biography* to challenge—provocatively but not convincingly—Mill's conclusion that "in the nineteenth century the business elite was composed of significantly more men from the lower classes than was the case previously or than has been the case since."[3] Both Mills and his critics agreed, however, that the "American business elite" always drew its membership predominantly from men born with high status and sired by well-to-do fathers. But Mills and his critics quarreled about the changing social composition of the "business elite" over time. Overall, for the *DAB* entries examined on business leaders born before 1907, Mills found that 9.8% were the sons of skilled craftsmen or semiskilled and unskilled workers. The percentage varied from generation to generation but was highest (13.2%) among those industrialists, merchants, and financiers born between 1820 and 1849. Using mostly *NCAB* biographies, Bendix and Howton found little change over time in the *percentage* of those industrialists who came from working-class families. The *rates* were consistently low: 2% for those born between 1801 and 1830, 1% for those born between 1831 and 1860, and 2% for those born between 1861 and 1890.

Percentages may be useful for comparative purposes over time, but they are dangerous statistical abstractions and may tell little about a particular moment in history.

How representative, for example, was the Bendix and Howton sample for the pre-Civil War generations? They found information about only fifty-six fathers of "business leaders" born between 1801 and 1830 and 225 born between 1831 and 1860. Translating their findings into absolute numbers, we learn from this sample that only three out of 281 business leaders born between 1801 and 1860 came from working-class families.[4] Even cursory knowledge of the history of American manufacturing before 1890 should raise numerous questions about a sampling technique that yields so narrow a base for a historical generalization.

The most detailed study of the early post-Civil War "industrial elite" has been conducted by Frances W. Gregory and Irene D. Neu, who generally confirmed the earlier findings.[5] Gregory and Neu examined the careers of 303 leaders of the railroad, textile (mostly cotton), and steel industries in the 1870s by studying the place of birth, the occupation of the father, the religious affiliation, the educational level attained, and the age on first starting work of the executives of seventy-seven large firms. These included the treasurer and agent of thirty textile mills mostly capitalized at more than one million dollars; the president, vice-president, and general manager (or superintendent) of thirty steel mills; and the president, vice-president, and general manager of the seventeen largest railroads. Their careful findings about the occupations of 194 fathers showed that 8% (sixteen men) were the sons of "workers." Not one railroad leader rose from the "lower depths"; 15% of the textile manufacturers (ten of sixty-seven) did, along with 11% of the steel manufacturers (six of fifty-seven). In contrast, 64% of the entire group came from business or professional backgrounds; one of every four was born on a farm; 3% were the sons

of "public officials." The authors asked and answered a
critical question: "Was the typical industrial leader of
the 1870s, then, a 'new man,' an escapee from the slums
of Europe or from the paternal farm? Did he rise by his
own efforts from a boyhood of poverty? Was he as innocent of education and of formal training as has often been
alleged? He seems to have been none of these things."
Combining variables, they described the archetypal industrial leader of the 1870s. He was American by birth,
of a New England father, a Protestant in his religion,
and distinctly upper class in origin:

> Urban in early environment, he was . . . born and bred
> in an atmosphere in which business and a relatively
> high social standing were intimately associated with his
> family life. Only at about eighteen did he take his first
> regular job, preparing to rise from it, moreover, not by
> a rigorous apprenticeship begun when he was virtually
> a child, but by an academic education well above the
> average for the times.

For the men they studied, Gregory and Neu found little
evidence that "the top-level businessman" of the 1870s
was "but a generation removed from poverty and anonymity."[6]

More recently, Stephan Thernstrom has brought significant and original insight to the patterns of social mobility in mid-nineteenth-century industrializing America.
*Poverty and Progress: Social Mobility in a Nineteenth
Century City* breaks with older studies of social mobility
by focusing in close detail on one community: it treats the
career patterns of nearly three hundred unskilled day laborers in Newburyport, Massachusetts, between 1850
and 1880.[7] Thernstrom finds among them a good deal of
geographic mobility out of the city, but for those immi-

grant and native workers and their sons who remained, substantial material improvement ("property mobility" or the acquisition of personal and real estate) and occupational mobility (from unskilled to semiskilled and skilled work). Their most common form of social advancement was "upward mobility *within* the working class." Thernstrom finds no evidence of spectacular upward mobility: "In the substantial sample of workers and their sons studied for the 1850–1880 period not a single instance of mobility into the ranks of management or even into a foremanship position was discovered." Many workers and their sons improved in these thirty years, some even as small shopkeepers and white-collar workers. But not one met the test of the rags-to-riches ideology. "Few of these men and few of their children," Thernstrom concludes, "rose very far on the social scale; most of the upward occupational shifts they made left them manual workers still, and their property mobility, though strikingly widespread, rarely involved the accumulation of anything approaching real wealth."

The findings of Thernstrom, Gregory and Neu, and Miller, among others, are the work of serious scholars, careful in their methods, deep in their research, and modest in their conclusions. But there is question about the larger inferences to be drawn from these studies about the social origins of the industrial manufacturing class in the decades of prime American industrialization. Hundreds, even thousands, of successful manufacturers—often members of particular elites in their particular communities but rarely memorialized on the national level—did not meet the criteria for admission to the *Dictionary of American Biography* or the *National Cyclopedia of American Biography*. Gregory and Neu reveal in detail the social origins of "the industrial elite" of the

1870s, but draw heavily in their narrow sample on a well-developed industry (cotton textile manufacturing) and an industry that attracted as its leaders lawyers, merchants, and financiers (the railroads). Thernstrom tells much that is new and significant about the life style and aspirations of mid-nineteenth-century workers, but Newburyport had developed as a manufacturing city before 1850; and although the composition of its population changed between 1855 and 1880, the city underwent little development in the years studied.

What of the manufacturers who founded new firms that involved small outlays of capital at the start? What of the workers, skilled as well as unskilled, who lived in rapidly expanding cities? In these pages, we shall examine a select group of successful local manufacturers in one such city—the locomotive, machinery, tool, and iron manufacturers of Paterson, New Jersey, between 1830 and 1880. Were they as a group a lesser mirror image of the archetypal industrialist described by Gregory and Neu? If there were workers among them, were they unusual and atypical? Information is available only on their occupational careers and their places of birth, but it is sufficient to test the reality of the promise of rags to riches in one important industrial city.

In explaining why Paterson, New Jersey, became a prime nineteenth-century American industrial city, economic and social historians usually have stressed its development as a center of textile, particularly silk, manufacture. And with good reason. By 1890, Paterson was the Lyons of America. But the silk industry came quite late in the city's development: not until the Civil War and the decade following did the silk mills and the city become so closely entwined. Yet Paterson had been an industrial city of importance before that time. Its magnificent waterfalls promised potential waterpower, and it early attracted the attention of Alexander Hamilton and other industrial enthusiasts. The story of the ill-fated Society for Establishing Useful Manufacturers in the 1790s is well known. But after it failed, irregular and usually unsuccessful efforts at cotton manufacture shaped the city's industrial history until 1837 and remained important (although not essential) after that time. However, such uneven enterprise (only one of nearly twenty cotton "mills" survived intact the depression in the late 1830s) did not explain Paterson's solid growth as an industrial city between 1830 and 1880. Early textile manufacturing mattered mainly because it attracted machinists to the city to repair and build cotton and other textile machinery. These men and others who followed them after 1840 were in the city at the start of a great boom in the manufacture of transportation equipment, machinery, and ironware of all kinds. Between 1830 and 1880, they sparked the development of Paterson's locomotive, iron goods, machinery, and machine-tool industries—changes that in turn spurred the city's growth. In 1850, eleven thousand persons lived in Paterson, and about 1,450 worked in these industries. Ten years later, the city counted nearly twenty thousand residents, and one of every ten was an "iron worker." A great industrial spurt occurred between 1860 and 1873, partly the result of the rapid rise of large silk and other textile mills but also a consequence of the expansion of older industries. By 1870, the population had risen to 33,581, and the locomotive, iron, and machinery industries employed 5,300 workers on the eve of the 1873 depression. About 15% of the city's entire population worked in these industries. The invigorated and new textile mills recruited large numbers of women and children to their factories so that adult male workers in the

Paterson manufacturing industries after the Civil War found jobs primarily as iron workers and machine, tool, and locomotive makers.

Although the Paterson iron and machine industries have not yet found their historian, a quick glance suggests their importance to the city's development and even to the national economy. In the mid-1850s, Paterson had four locomotive factories: Rogers, Ketchum & Grosvenor (probably the second largest such factory in the country, outdistanced only by the Philadelphia Baldwin Locomotive Works); the New Jersey Locomotive and Machine Company; the Danforth Locomotive and Machine Works; and William Swinburne's Locomotive Works. Swinburne's enterprise failed in 1857–58, but the three that survived had an annual capacity of 135 locomotives in 1859. Eighteen years later, their combined capacity had risen to 554, sixty-four more than the Baldwin Works. In 1837–38, Rogers, Ketchum & Grosvenor (renamed the Rogers Locomotive Works in 1858 after Rogers' death) completed its first five locomotives. In the great burst of railroad construction between 1869 and 1873, the factories filled orders for no less than 1,683 locomotives. Overall, between 1837 and 1879, Paterson locomotive workers built 5,167 locomotives and contributed much to the "transportation revolution."

The growth of the Paterson iron, tool, and machinery manufacturers may have been less spectacular than the locomotive manufacture but was just as substantial in different ways. Textile machinery and tools formed an important part of the local manufactured product. The market for Paterson firms after 1850 reached across the continent and even stretched around the globe. The J. C. Todd Machine Works (later Todd & Rafferty) marketed its hemp and twine machinery as far away as England

and even in Russia, Latin America, and Asia in the late
1850s. After 1857, the Paterson Iron Works, which specialized in rolling large bars of iron, built heavy forgings
used by transoceanic steamship and even sent iron shafts
across the continent on order to the Pacific Mail Steamship Company. The Watson Manufacturing Company
exported its millwright work and machinery to Mexico
and South America, and gained wide attention for its
turbine wheels and Corliss steam engines. The huge
bevel wheels it constructed helped make the Higgins Carpet Factory one of New York City's great manufacturing
establishments. The manufacture of structural iron later
allowed the Watson firm to contract to build iron bridges
in and near New York City, and its finished iron found
place in the city's Museum of Natural History, Metropolitan Museum of Art, Equitable Building, and Lenox
Library. In the 1870s and 1880s, the Passaic Rolling Mill
also found important customers in the great metropolis
nearby: the iron beams that built New York's first elevated trains came from it as did the iron for such projects
as the Harlem River bridge, the *New York Post* building,
and the massive Seventh Regiment Armory. Finished iron
from the Passaic Rolling Mill also helped build the new
state capitol in Albany, a widely acclaimed drawbridge
over the Mississippi River at St. Paul, an elevated cable
car in Hoboken, and the 1876 Centennial Exposition
buildings in Philadelphia. These examples are cited
merely to illustrate the importance of the Paterson locomotive, iron, and machine factories in the development of
industry and transportation and in the building of Victorian American cities.

What were the social origins and career patterns of the
men who founded and developed these particular firms
between 1830 and 1880? These men or their firms per-

severed in the turbulent early decades of industrialization. In 1880, some of the pioneer manufacturers were dead, others at the height of their careers, and a few still relatively new to enterprise. Many had failed in comparison to the number that succeeded. Although the printed sources tell little about those who started unsuccessful manufacturing enterprises, there is no reason to doubt that these men differed in social origin from their more favored contemporaries. For the group that succeeded, useful biographical information has been found for nearly all of them. What follows therefore is *not a sample* but a description of the social origins of the most successful Paterson iron, locomotive, and machinery manufacturers.[8]

Scientific American, groping for a simple sociological generalization about these men, praised Paterson's early enterprisers in these words: "In the eastern States [New England], flourishing cities have been built up by corporations of wealthy capitalists. . . . In Paterson, it was different. With few exceptions, almost every manufacturer started, financially, at zero, enlarging his establishment as the quicksilver expanded in his purse." *Scientific American* was not guilty of mouthing abstract rhetoric or just putting forth a paean of traditional tribute to an invisible hero, the "self-made man." Instead, it accurately described the successful locomotive, iron, and machinery manufacturers of the era, and what it wrote applied as well to the group in 1840 and 1880 as in 1859.

One Paterson manufacturer started as a clerk. A second, the son of a farmer, made his way first in railroad construction before turning to iron manufacture. Two others had fathers who were manufacturers. George Van Riper took over a bobbin-pin factory in 1866 that had been started by his grandfather in 1795 as a small shop and then run by his father for thirty-five years. Patrick Maguinnis was the son of an Irish cotton manufacturer who left Dublin after the failure of revolutionary anti-British agitation and manufactured cotton and velveteen first in Baltimore and then in Hudson, New York.

But the social origin of these four manufacturers was not characteristic of the thirty-odd men studied. The typical successful Paterson manufacturer arrived in the city as a skilled ironworker or a skilled craftsman or as a young man who learned his skill by apprenticing in a Paterson machinery works. Individual proprietorship or copartnership allowed him to escape from dependence and start his own firm. Only a small number of Paterson apprentices became manufacturers between 1830 and 1880, but most successful Paterson iron, machinery, and locomotive manufacturers started their careers as workers, apprenticed to learn a skill, and then opened small shops or factories of their own.

With only a few important exceptions, the men who were either Paterson-born or migrants to Paterson before 1830 played an insignificant role in the subsequent development of these industries. In 1825, the Rev. Dr. Samuel Fischer counted seventy-seven ironworkers in eleven blacksmith shops, two millwright shops, and a single iron foundry. Some repaired and built textile machinery. Trumbull lists at least ten machine shops that lasted only a few years. Biographical information is lacking for the men who started these faulted firms, but information is available for four men who pioneered in the development of the Paterson machinery and locomotive industries: John Clark, his son John Clark, Jr., Thomas Rogers, and Charles Danforth. Not one was native to the city. John Clark, Sr., settled there first. Born in Paisley, Scotland, the elder Clark, then aged twenty-one, migrated to Paterson in 1794 with his wife and two children to build machinery for the S. E. U. M. After the society failed, Clark, first with his partner and then alone, used a portion of the idle mill to manufacture textile machinery. One son, John, Jr., followed in his footsteps, and in the early 1820s took two partners, Abram Godwin (a local resident, Godwin's father had served on George Washington's military staff) and Thomas Rogers. A hotel and storekeeper and the father of Parke Godwin, noted later as a journalist and as editor of the *New York Evening Post,* Abram Godwin supplied Clark with capital. Rogers' contribution was of another order.

Born in 1792 in Groton, Connecticut, and, according to Trumbull, descended from a Mayflower Pilgrim, Thomas Rogers apprenticed himself at the age of sixteen to a Connecticut house carpenter. He settled in Paterson as a journeyman house carpenter and built several dwelling houses before a cotton-duck manufacturer hired him to construct wooden loom patterns. Soon Rogers was building wooden looms for John Clark, Sr. After the elder Clark retired, Rogers joined with Godwin and young Clark to expand the firm. The three partners bought an empty cotton mill, purchased a small foundry and a molding shop, and managed, for the first time in Paterson, a machine shop with all branches of the trade under "one roof." The partners prospered in the 1820s, but in 1831 Rogers left the firm to start his own machine works, the Jefferson Works, and to spin cotton yarn. Rogers' early triumphs as a machine builder attracted the attention of Morris Ketchum and Jasper Grosvenor, two New York City merchant capitalists and financiers active as railroad developers. A partnership was founded, called Rogers, Ketchum & Grosvenor. A house carpenter turned skilled machinist and then machine manufacturer thus had as

business associates two men whom *Scientific American*
called "men of abundant means and decided financial
ability."

Charles Danforth replaced Rogers in the machine
works of Clark and Godwin. The evidence concerning
Danforth's background is unclear. Trumbull records
that his father was a Norton, Massachusetts, "cotton
manufacturer," but a more detailed biographical sketch
in *The History of Bergen and Passaic Counties* notes that
Danforth's father was "engaged in agricultural pursuits"
and that in 1811, then fourteen, Danforth worked as a
throstle-piercer before engaging as an ordinary seaman.
After the War of 1812, he taught school near Rochester,
New York, and in 1824 superintended a cotton carding
room in a Matteawan, New York, factory. Hired to help
set up a new cotton mill in Hohokus, New Jersey, he invented an improved spinning frame and settled in Paterson in 1828 to manufacture it as a partner with Godwin
and Clark. Financial troubles in the late 1830s caused the
dissolution of the partnership, and in 1840 Danforth
bought out the entire machine-shop interest and in 1848
formed Charles Danforth and Company. His partner
was John Edwards, his foreman. Born in England, Edwards moved to Paterson as a young man and worked in a
hotel; he later apprenticed to John Clark and became his
foreman, keeping the same supervisory position under
Rogers and Danforth. Danforth so valued Edwards' abili-
ties that he gave him a one-tenth interest in the firm.

The career of another workman, William Swinburne,
illustrates this same mobility through the possession of
technological skills. Born in Brooklyn in 1805, Swinburne
first worked as a carpenter before moving to Matteawan as
a machine patternmaker. Swinburne then came to Paterson to work as a patternmaker for Rogers and soon found

himself draftsman, patternmaker, and superintendent of the new locomotive shops. Here he worked with Watts Cooke, Sr., from County Armagh, Ireland. By trade, Watts Cooke also was a carpenter. He migrated to Montreal in 1822, helped construct Notre Dame Cathedral there, moved to Albany, New York, stayed five years to learn the skill of patternmaking at an Albany furnace, worked for the Matteawan Machine Company, and settled finally in Paterson in 1839. When Swinburne took over the locomotive shops, he hired as his assistant one of Cooke's four sons—the seventeen-year-old John Cooke, an apprentice patternmaker.

In 1845, both Swinburne and young Cooke left Rogers, Ketchum & Grosvenor to become its competitors. Swinburne first joined former iron molder Samuel Smith and cotton manufacturers Patrick Maguinnis and James Jackson to make textile machinery and cotton cloth, but the completion of the Erie Railroad's eastern division directed their attention to locomotives. In 1851–52, when it incorporated as the New Jersey Locomotive and Machine Company (later renamed the Grant Locomotive Works), Swinburne quit for unexplained reasons and started his own company, the Swinburne Locomotive Works. It was the first large Paterson manufacturer to depend entirely on steam power, and Swinburne soon employed between two and three hundred hands. He prospered until the 1857 depression caused severe financial difficulties that persuaded him to sell this plant to the Bank of New Jersey. Soon his factory was nothing more than an Erie Railroad repair shop.

John Cooke found more fortune than Swinburne. In 1852, Edwin Prall, Danforth's chief bookkeeper, urged his employer to add locomotive manufacturing to his enterprise and suggested John Cooke, then earning $1,800 a year as superintendent of the Rogers locomotive shops, as a partner. When the Danforth works was incorporated in 1865, Danforth, Cooke, and Prall became the principal stockholders. Prall's background differed from that of Cooke, Rogers, Swinburne, and even Danforth. He was born on Staten Island ("of good Knickerbocker-Moravian stock," noted Trumbull) and although orphaned as a child, grew up in a family immersed in entrepreneurial aspirations, surrounded by enterprising relatives. He worked first for a New York City cousin who imported drugs, then for an uncle who manufactured cotton in Haverstraw, New York, and finally for another uncle who was Danforth's bookkeeper. Prall took over when his uncle died.

John Cooke and his brothers, the sons of an immigrant patternmaker, assumed important roles in the Danforth locomotive shops. Brother William Cooke became chief draftsman, and Watts, Jr., joined the firm under unusual circumstances. Then nineteen years old, he was a bound apprentice to Thomas Rogers and was in Cincinnati installing three engines when John Cooke shifted from Rogers to Danforth. Rogers let him buy the "balance" of this time as an apprentice, and young Cooke became foreman of the Danforth locomotive erecting shops—aged nineteen. Two years later (1854), a customer, the Delaware, Lackawanna & Western Railroad, hired him as Master Mechanic, and Watts Cooke did not return to Paterson until 1868. Significantly, a fellow apprentice at Rogers, James Ayres, took Cooke's place as foreman of the Danforth locomotive erecting shops and held that position for nearly thirty years.

As a group, the developers of the Paterson locomotive industry, except for Ketchum and Grosvenor (and they lived in New York City), experienced enormous occupa-

tional mobility in their lives. In one generation—often
in a few years—men jumped class lines and rose rapidly
in prestige and status. One can argue about Danforth, but
Prall had been an orphan and a clerk as a boy, and the
others—Clark, Rogers, Swinburne, Watts Cooke, Sr., his
sons William, John, and Watts, Jr.—had all started in
life as skilled artisans and risen to become factory foreman or superintendents and owners of large, new manufacturing enterprises. The triumphs of these men were
only part of the Paterson story. Their locomotive factories
became workshops that trained machinists and other
skilled ironworkers. Most did not all stay within the firm.
They struck out on their own as small manufacturers to
be swept up and tested by the surge of industrial development after 1843. A few became manufacturers of great
wealth; most succeeded in a more modest fashion. All
were closely identified with the development of Paterson's iron and machinery and tool industries between
1843 and 1880—a process shaped by the efforts of self-
made men entirely different in social origin from the
archetypal members of Gregory and Neu's "industrial
elite" in the 1870s. None came from professional, mercantile, or manufacturing backgrounds. Only one was
born in New England, and almost all of them were British
immigrants. These were not "princes" prepared by training and education to become "kings" of industry. Instead,
they rose from the lower classes and achieved substantial
material rewards in their lifetimes. For those of their contemporaries who sought "proof" about the promise of
rags to riches, these men served as model, day-to-day evidence.

Paterson's two most successful machinery works were
started by apprentice machinists, one who labored as a

child in a cotton factory and the other who grew up on a
farm and worked first as a carpenter. William Watson
and Joseph Todd learned their machinist skills in the
Paterson machine and locomotive shops. In 1844, Joseph
Todd and a partner opened a small machine shop in the
rear of a cotton mill, a common practice. They started
with two lathes (one borrowed), and a few years later one
Phillip Rafferty joined them. (The sources tell only that
Rafferty was employed to build a blacksmith shop in an
early textile mill in 1837.) Senior partner Joseph Todd
was born on a New Jersey farm and at sixteen apprenticed as a carpenter to his uncle. Three years later, he left
for New York City, and then went to Paterson to help
construct a Methodist church. He stayed on to work at
Godwin, Clark & Company and Rogers, Ketchum &
Grosvenor as a machine patternmaker. His successful development of a hemp-spinning machine led him, at
twenty-seven, to start his own small machine shop. In
1860, the firm employed 135 workers, and a decade later
as many as 350 hands. Its successes rested on the manufacture of the twine machinery, but it also made steam
engines and boilers and later manufactured jute bagging.

William Watson was even more successful than Todd.
Watson and his younger brother spent their childhood in
Lancashire, England, and followed their father to Belleville, New Jersey. At the age of ten he helped his father
in a print works. When the family moved to Paterson, the
young Watson brothers labored in textile mills. Then
William Watson apprenticed to a machinist, studied
draftsmanship, and became a foreman. After a few years,
Watson left Paterson, worked in a Newburgh mill, and
helped run a New York City screw factory. In 1845, then
twenty-six, he opened his own Paterson machine shop,
employing ten men in millwrighting work, tool manufac-

ture, and later in structural iron. The firm counted sixty employees in 1860 and no less than eleven hundred men and boys in 1873.

Few other manufacturers were as successful as Todd and Watson between 1840 and 1880, but the career patterns of eight lesser manufacturers and the seven machinists who formed a copartnership called the Machinists' Association paralleled the paths followed by Todd and Watson. Examples from among them show a quite distinct pattern. Samuel Smith left Ireland as a youth and worked for a time for a Nova Scotia clergyman before settling with his family in Paterson and apprenticing as a molder at Rogers, Ketchum & Grosvenor. In later years, he and a copartner started a foundry, opened a machine shop, and manufactured steam boilers.

Benjamin Buckley and a partner began manufacturing spindles and flyers for textile machinery in 1844. Born in Oldham, England, in 1808, Buckley came to the United States in 1831, first worked in a Paterson cotton mill, then for Rogers and finally for Danforth. When he opened a small factory of his own he employed six hands. Buckley later failed as a cotton manufacturer, but his spindle works survived more than forty years. He employed twenty workers in 1859 and ran the enterprise with the help of his sons. Buckley also was president of the Passaic County National Bank in the early 1870s.

Three years after Buckley settled in Paterson, John Daggers arrived from Lancashire, England. Born in 1819, he apprenticed at the Rogers factory and then traveled south to construct cotton machinery in Alabama and Georgia. Later he returned to Paterson to manufacture bobbin pins. George Addy and Robert Atherton arrived in Paterson in the late 1840s. Addy, a third-generation Yorkshire blacksmith, borrowed passage fare to cross the

Atlantic in 1849, worked two years for Danforth, then for Rogers, and in 1851 started manufacturing bolts and screws. Addy's firm expanded over the years, and in the 1880s made bolts and screws, smut machines, moving machines, and straw cutters. He also earned income from successful urban real-estate investment. Robert Atherton did not rise as rapidly as Addy. Atherton grew up in Westchester County, New York, finished primary school there, moved to New York City, and settled in Paterson in 1848. He labored first in a cotton mill, apprenticed to a roller manufacturer and then to Buckley, failed in a partnership with Samuel Watson (William Watson's son), worked a number of years as a "general machinist," superintended a silk-machinery manufactory, and in 1878 started a machine works with his sons that soon occupied about seven thousand square feet in a cotton mill and employed nearly fifty workers in the manufacture of silk machinery.

Atherton's later success depended in good part on the development of the Paterson silk industry after the Civil War. So did the fortunes of some other Paterson machinists. Among the first to benefit were seven machinists (the *Scientific American* called them "practical mechanics"), most of them former Danforth employees, who formed a copartnership in 1851 called the Machinists' Association. Nothing is known of them as individuals except that each contributed two hundred dollars to start the firm. By 1859, with most of their orders coming from southern textile mills, the firm was assessed at $25,000, clear of all obligations. The Machinists' Association shifted from the manufacture of general textile machinery to silk machinery and soon thereafter employed more than one hundred men. By 1876, its machinery had been bought by more than two hundred manufacturers.

When he started, Benjamin Eastwood had no partners. In 1872–73, with an investment of $1,500 and three employees, he began manufacturing silk machinery. Two years later he moved to larger quarters in the rear of a silk mill and hired ten or twelve workers. In 1878, he built his own mill, employed between fifty and sixty men, and was ready to become the city's major manufacturer of silk machinery. Eastwood's career illustrates extensive geographic and occupational mobility. Born in Lancashire, Eastwood benefited from a "common school education" and training in a machine shop before his departure for the United States in 1863. He worked for a time in Paterson, then briefly in Milwaukee, and again in Paterson. A gold-mining venture in Mecklenberg County, North Carolina, took him south to build engines and machinery and to serve as a mine superintendent for two and a half years. The company failed, and Eastwood returned to Paterson to work again as a machinist. He started a small shop but left it to travel to Venezuela as a "mechanical engineer." Illness ("fever") sent him back to Paterson for the fourth time but only to spend a year in a locomotive shop. He then went to a New York City "experimental shop" that hoped to develop ways to use motive power more efficiently on canals. Eastwood remained in New York City for eighteen months. He returned to Paterson again, worked for a year in a sewing-machine factory that soon left the city, and in 1872 or 1873, ten years after he arrived in the country and after having traveled to Milwaukee, North Carolina, Venezuela, and New York City, opened his small silk-machinery factory.

Two other British-born machinists, John Royle and James Jackson, also manufactured textile machinery, but they started at it quite late in life. Royle was born in

Chester, England, migrated to Paterson with his parents in 1830, worked in a cotton mill as a ten-year-old, and became an apprentice machinist. Illness forced an early retirement, but he later supervised the construction of turbine water wheels manufactured by Watson. He remained with Watson until 1860, rented a small machine shop that failed quickly, worked again for Watson manufacturing flax machinery for two years, left to wander through the West for a time seeking "opportunity," and finally returned to Paterson in 1863 and started manufacturing textile machinery "on a very limited scale." Royle developed a quality high-speed routing machine and other valued textile machinery, and the firm expanded rapidly after 1878. Jackson's career was somewhat different. Born in Caton, England, he was the son of a silk dresser and the grandson of a master carder. He did not migrate to the United States until he was forty. At thirteen, he apprenticed to a machinist, and at twenty-one he started a ten-year stint as master mechanic and superintendent of a Caton cotton mill; then he superintended another twelve years at an Oldham mill. Migrating to the United States in 1869, he spent several months in Philadelphia before settling in Paterson to work as a machinist at the Rogers Locomotive Works. In 1873 he started making Jacquard silk machinery. A year later, he expanded to a larger mill and, like Royle, took his sons into the manufacturing business.

Machine and tool shops owned by men like Eastwood, Royle, and Jackson depended on one or another branch of the textile industry for customers, but Paterson's two large iron works resulted from sparks set off by the railroad boom after 1840. Neither the Paterson Iron Works nor the Passaic Rolling Mill Company was started by apprentices or artisans, but men who had begun their careers as workers soon controlled them. The Paterson Iron Works began in 1853 because of the efforts of two New Hampshire capitalists, cotton manufacturers in the Granite State drawn to Paterson by the developing locomotive industry. They hoped to manufacture axles, tires, and shapes for locomotives and heavy engines. A year later, Franklin Beckwith, a railroad contractor, bought an interest in the firm, and by 1861 he had purchased the interest of the New Hampshire men and a local manufacturer. Beckwith dominated the firm until his death in 1875, when his sons took over the enterprise. Beckwith's career differed from those who ran successful machine shops. Born in Saratoga, New York, one of nine sons of a farmer, he worked on the family farm until aged nineteen and received, at best, a common-school education. An older brother who had become chief engineer and contractor in building the Boston & Albany Railroad hired him as a foreman. Beckwith soon became a contractor himself. He settled in Troy, but in 1845 was drawn to Pennsylvania to try iron smelting. Five years later, he was principal contractor on the Delaware division of the Erie Railroad. When the Erie Railroad acquired the old Paterson & Hudson River road, Beckwith went to New Jersey to rebuild its track and its railroad bridges. Paterson attracted his attention, and this farmer turned railroad construction foreman and contractor became an iron manufacturer. In 1860, his firm employed forty workers and built seven thousand railroad tires and forgings for seventeen hundred locomotives.

Sherman Jaqua, one of the men from whom Beckwith purchased an interest in the Paterson Iron Works in 1861 for about $20,000, did not they rest quietly. Soon after, Jaqua received a charter for a new Paterson ironworks that would specialize in making rolled bar iron from scrap. Called the Idaho Iron Company, it failed, and Jaqua sold his machinery to a California company. In 1868, the Cooke brothers, spurred by Watts Cooke, Jr., who returned from Scranton and brought with him some investment capital supplied by the Delaware, Lackawanna & Western Railroad, purchased what remained of the Jaqua property, renamed the firm the Passaic Rolling Mill Company, and in three months turned out rolled iron bar. The firm specialized in making structural iron beams, angels, and teels, and shifted to bridge iron in 1876. William Cooke quit his brothers in 1873 to work in New York City, but W. O. Fayerweather purchased his interest. Watts Cooke, Jr., who had purchased his apprentice contract from Thomas Rogers in 1852, came back to Paterson sixteen years later as president of the Passaic Rolling Mill Company. W. O. Fayerweather, who had left Paterson as a young man to work as an errand boy in the great metropolis nearby, returned in 1873 as treasurer and partner of one of the northeast's most important iron factories. Like Watts Cooke, Jr., Fayerweather had returned home. Both men traveled different routes, but they followed tracks that moved steadily upward.

Pertinent biographical information to complete this collective portrait is lacking for a number of other Paterson manufacturers of machinery, tools, and textile supplies. Similarly, the social origins of certain small manufacturers of wire hoop, copper and brass castings, files, and weaver's supplies are not recorded. Nevertheless, scattered evidence tells that some of these men and other small manufacturers had careers no different from the dominant pattern uncovered for most Paterson manufacturers. C. C. E. Van Alstine's unusual success resulted from his inventive genius. Van Alstine started as a ma-

chinist in Paterson in 1872, worked for a company for a
year, took odd jobs repairing optical glasses and sewing
machines, and finally invented a machine press that
punched "the eye of a lingo" (an important weaving implement) and shaped its head at the same time. Van Alstine became a manufacturer and quickly improved his
position. Starting in the mid-seventies with four workers,
he employed between 175 and 200 in a few years. Other
skilled workers and craftsmen began the trek upward in
less spectacular ways. When James Walder started manufacturing reeds and heddles in 1866, he hired two men
and rented factory floor space. He moved several times
(always to rented premises) before purchasing a small
building and enlarging it to a 20 by 200 foot plant. In the
early 1880s, Walder was Paterson's most important reed
and heddle manufacturer. Eight other firms followed
Walder's path between 1855 and 1880, and the evidence
suggests that all were started and developed by skilled
workers who opened small shops as individuals or with a
partner. Although the data about these men (Charles
Moseley, Christian Kohlhaus, James Dunkerley, Robert Brooks, Robert Taylor, Robert McCullough, and
Thomas Wrigley and his brother John) is slight, there is
enough information to tell that all started as skilled workers, usually machinists, and rose to become manufacturers
in a single generation.

Much remains to be written about the Paterson iron,
locomotive, and machinery manufacturers who started in
life as workers, but their social status, their political role
(many held public office), and their labor policies cannot
be briefly summarized.[9] What matters for purposes of
this study is the fact that the rags-to-riches promise was
not a mere myth in Paterson, New Jersey, between 1830

and 1880. So many successful manufacturers who had begun as workers walked the streets of that city then that it is not hard to believe that others less successful or just starting out on the lower rungs of the occupational mobility ladder could be convinced by personal knowledge that "hard work" resulted in spectacular material and social improvement. Thernstrom has argued convincingly that small improvements in material circumstances counted for much in explaining the social stability of Newburyport between 1850 and 1880. What role did the frequent examples of spectacular upward mobility in developing industrial Paterson play vis-à-vis its social structure? Whether the social origin of the Paterson manufacturers was typical of other manufacturers of that era cannot yet be known, but their career pattern was quite different from the one uncovered by other students of the nineteenth-century American "business elite."

Detailed research, however, has not yet been done on the manufacturers of other new industrial cities such as Buffalo, Pittsburgh, Cincinnati, and Chicago. Developing industrial cities and new manufacturing industries offered unusual opportunities to skilled craftsmen and mechanics in the early phases of American industrialization. Such was the case in Paterson, and surely such opportunities existed in other cities. Who took advantage of such opportunities, however, is still a subject for careful inquiry. The detailed examination of other local industrial "elites" will make it possible to learn whether the Paterson manufacturers were a mutant group or mere examples of a pattern of occupational mobility common to early industrializing America. Whatever the final findings, such community-oriented studies will shed unusually important light on one of the many dark corners of the mid-nineteenth-century American economic and social structure.

1. William Miller, "American Historians and the Business Elite," in William Miller, ed., *Men in Business. Essays on the Historical Role of the Entrepreneur* (New York, 1962), pp. 309–28.

2. C. Wright Mills, "The American Business Elite: A Collective Portrait," in Irving Horowitz, ed., *Power, Politics and People. The Collected Essays of C. Wright Mills* (New York, 1962), pp. 110–39.

3. Reinhard Bendix and Frank W. Howton, "Social Mobility and the American Business Elite," in Reinhard Bendix and Seymour Martin Lipset, eds., *Social Mobility in Industrial Society* (Berkeley, 1959), pp. 114–43.

4. Bendix and Howton also report the findings of Susanne Keller in her unpublished dissertation, "The Social Origins and Career Lines of Three Generations of American Business Leaders." Of 254 business leaders born about 1820, Keller found that only eight (3%) had fathers who labored as "wage earners and office workers [clerks?]."

5. Frances W. Gregory and Irene D. Neu, "The American Industrial Elite in the 1870's: Their Social Origins," in Miller, *Men in Business*, pp. 193–211.

6. See Miller, ed., *Men in Business*, p. 149.

7. Stephan Thernstrom, *Poverty and Progress: Social Mobility in a Nineteenth Century City* (Cambridge, 1964), passim but especially pp. 114, 161–65, 213, 223.

8. Several sources supply the salient data, but the most important is L. R. Trumbull, *A History of Industrial Paterson, Being a Compendium of the Establishment, Growth, and Present Status in Paterson, N.J., of the Silk, Cotton, Flax, Locomotive, Iron and Miscellaneous Industries; Together with Outlines of State, County and Local History, Corporate Records, Biographical Sketches, Incidents of Manufacture, Interesting Facts and Valuable Statistics*. Published in Paterson in 1882, the Trumbull volume is just what its title suggests: an ill-digested but rich and invaluable collection of local firm histories interspersed with biographical accounts of early Paterson industrialists. Supplementary biographical information is found in Charles Shriner, *Paterson, New Jersey. Its Advantages for Manufacturing and Residence: Its Industries, Prominent Men, Banks, Schools, Churches, etc., Published Under the Auspices of the [Paterson] Board of Trade* (Paterson, 1890); Edward B. Haines, ed., *Paterson, New Jersey, 1792–1892. [The] Centennial Edition of the Paterson Evening News* (Paterson, 1892); William Nelson and Charles Shriner, *History of Paterson and Its Environs. The Silk City* (New York and Chicago, 1920). These books share a common weakness in celebrating uncritically the triumphs of local enterprise, but it is unwise to dismiss them as no more than primitive public relations works. Buried among adjectives of pious praise are rich morsels of data that tell much about

these local "heroes" and their firms. Additional information has been culled from Paterson city directories published in 1859, 1871–72, and 1880–81, and from a detailed survey of Paterson manufactures that appeared in the first volume of *Scientific American* in 1859 under the dates October 29 and November 5, 12, and 19.

9. Some evidence of the social and political role played by the Paterson manufacturers in the 1870s is found in H. G. Gutman, "Class, Status, and Community Power in Nineteenth-Century American Industrial Cities—Paterson, New Jersey: A Case Study," in Frederic C. Jaher, ed., *The Age of Industrialism in America: Essays in Social Structure and Cultural Values* (New York, 1968), pp. 263–87.

IMMIGRANTS AND WASPS: Ethnic Differences in Occupational Mobility in Boston, 1890–1940*

Stephan Thernstrom

One of the great themes of American history is the story of how millions of immigrants from distant shores entered the society and made their way there, becoming new men and women—Americans—in the process. American folklore is rich with metaphors to characterize the immigrant's experience in the New World: he was beckoned by the golden door, drawn into the melting pot, and eventually found his way into the American mainstream. The historical and sociological literature devoted to some aspect of immigration and immigrant assimilation is rich, even superabundant. And yet there are some large gaps, some important questions for which more than impressionistic answers have yet to be given.

We know that more often than not newcomers to America came with little in the way of capital or skills valuable in an urban industrial society, and that immigrants tended accordingly to begin at the bottom. We know that all groups experienced some social mobility in time, and produced men who attained wealth, power, and recognition in the larger society. We know, likewise, that the initial heavy concentration of most immigrants in the central city was eventually reduced, and that a process of residential dispersion began to operate. But there has been surprisingly little systematic study of the rate, timing, and channels of mobility experienced by newcomers to America. If immigrants typically began their careers at a lower point on the occupational scale than native-born Americans, did they at least experience comparable upward mobility in the course of their careers, or did they fall farther behind with the passing of time? Did the children of the foreign-born, second-generation Americans, characteristically make far greater progress than their fathers, as legend would have it, or were they too sorely handicapped in the occupational competition? To what extent did differences in the cultural background of particular immigrant groups, or in the character of the economy and the labor market at the time they first arrived, speed or slow their progress? Did all groups, whatever their national background, have essentially similar forms and channels of mobility, or may we contrast "typically Irish" with "typically Italian" or "typically East European" patterns?

The nearest thing we have to an answer to such questions as these comes from studies like E. P. Hutchinson's *Immigrants and Their Children,* studies that assess the occupational or residential distribution of particular groups—"the Irish," "the foreign-born," or whatever— at two or more points in time, and take the net shift that occurred in the interim as a measure of group social mobility.[1] This procedure can be illuminating, but it provides only a shaky foundation for inferences about the mobility achievements of the *individuals* who comprise the group in question. Something like the ecological fallacy, though technically distinct from it, operates here. There can be considerable change in the composition of a group over even a relatively short period of time, due to deaths, retirement from the labor market, and continuing migration into or out of the unit under scrutiny; the group of Irish immigrants listed in the U.S. Census of 1890 were not simply the Irish-born recorded in the Census of 1880 now ten years older. And groups may vary sharply in the degree to which their composition is altered by these variables. Some immigrant groups came to

these shores in one large wave; in other cases, like that of
the Irish, the group was diluted by the continued entry of
newcomers over a long period of time. Likewise, some
nationalities had a high propensity to return to the
mother country, some did not; this and other circumstances gave some groups unusual age distributions,
which in turn affected their socioeconomic level. Similarly, fortuitous shifts in the resources and skills immigrants
from particular countries brought with them can produce misleading changes in indexes of the type employed
by Hutchinson and others. Thus the influx of Jewish professionals and businessmen fleeing Hitler in the 1930s
raised the position of the "born in Germany" group by
the time of Census of 1940; it would obviously be foolish
to interpret the rising index as evidence that many of the
individual German immigrants who had been living in
the country prior to 1933 had been dramatically successful in climbing the social ladder in the depression years.[2]

To obtain an accurate estimate of the social trajectory
followed by men of various ethnic origins after they
reached these shores it is essential to trace the experiences
of representative individuals. This paper, part of a larger
investigation of social mobility in Boston in the period
1880–1968, describes the results of one such trace. If it
avoids some of the pitfalls inherent in the methods used
by earlier investigators, however, it has glaring flaws of
its own. What was true of Boston may well not have been
true of other communities, for one thing, though in fact
another part of the full study demonstrates that overall
mobility rates and patterns in Boston strongly resembled
those in such cities as Indianapolis, San Jose, and Norristown, Pennsylvania. Another difficulty is that the
random samples employed were not large enough to provide reassuringly large cell numbers in tables assessing

the influence of ethnic background. Our information
about the ethnic origins of sample members is incomplete. The sources used indicated parental nativity as well
as nativity for only two of the age cohorts studied; second-generation immigrants could not be distinguished
from old-stock Americans except in those cases. The results, therefore, can only be suggestive.

Career Mobility: Natives vs. Foreign-born

Initially let us ask how being born in this country or
abroad influenced the occupational rank of Boston residents when they first entered the labor market and at the
time of their last job.[3] Table 1 provides this information
for four groups of men, born respectively in the 1850s, in
the years 1860 to 1879, in the 1880s, and in the first decade
of the twentieth century. Those in the first cohort were
already launched on their careers in 1880, the date of our
first occupational information; those in the last cohort
were in midcareer during the Great Depression of the
1930s, and some were still at work in Boston in the post-
World War II period. (Another group of men, born in
the city in 1930, was included in the Boston Mobility
Study, but no discussion of native-immigrant differences
in mobility patterns in this cohort is possible, obviously,
because all of its members were native-born Americans.)
The available evidence spans most of the period of greatest concern to the student of immigration, from the massive wave of Irish immigration of the mid-nineteenth century to the last great influx of newcomers arriving before
World War I and the restrictive legislation that followed
effectively closed the golden door, but it does not permit
exploration of the extent to which differences in national

Table 1. Career Mobility between Blue-Collar and White-Collar Jobs at Start and End of Career, by Nativity

Birth Cohort	Starting White Collar in %	Ending White Collar in %	Blue-Collar Starters Climbing* in %	White-Collar Starters Skidding in %	Number
1850-59					
U.S.-born	51	62	33	11	241
Foreign-born	18	24	13	25	68
1860-79					
U.S.-born	55	56	22	16	614
Foreign-born	50	60	33	14	42
1880-89					
U.S.-born	51	61	32	13	215
Foreign-born	23	39	28	23	206
1900-09					
U.S.-born	40	47	23	17	146
Foreign-born	23	31	14	14	35

* Note that this is the percentage *not* of the entire group but of those who *started* their careers in manual jobs. The skidding rate in the next column is likewise expressed not as a percentage of the entire cohort but of those who started work wearing white collars. For this reason, one cannot subtract the skidding rate from the climbing rate and add the result to the figure in column one to arrive at the percentage ending white collar (column two). Unless skidding and climbing rates are computed on this basis—taking not the entire group but only those who began their careers in a position from which the move in question was possible—comparisons between groups are difficult to make. A higher percentage of the total foreign-born groups, for instance, would likely move upward for the simple reason that a much larger fraction of the native born started as white-collar workers and hence were by definition not able to move to a higher class. By computing the rate in the manner done here we control for the initial distribution of the group and see subsequent differences in mobility more clearly.

origin remain important determinants of occupational status today.[4] For a variety of reasons immigrants to this country in the period since World War I have deviated from the earlier pattern; our concern here is with the relatively uneducated and impoverished newcomers of the classic period of American immigration as they struggled to make a living in late nineteenth- and early twentieth-century Boston.

The striking initial advantage of native-born Americans in the competition for secure and well-paid jobs is perfectly clear in Table 1. (A rather crude index of occupational rank—holding a nonmanual as opposed to a blue-collar job—is employed here.[5] Where analysis by more refined categories suggests different conclusions it will be indicated.) In three of four possible instances, foreign-born youths were much less likely to start their careers in a white-collar calling. (The one exception to this, the cohort of those born in the 1860s and 1870s, is only a seeming exception, as will be explained shortly.) Only two out of ten young men born outside the United States began work using their heads rather than hands; approximately five out of ten native youths did so.

If much of the immigrant's handicap, however, was due to his sheer lack of familiarity with American ways and the English language, it might be expected that the gap between native and foreigner would narrow in time, and that their final occupational ranks would be more similar than their starting points. Thus the familiar folklore figure, the struggling immigrant lad who starts as a newsboy or perhaps as the operator of a sewing machine in a sweat shop, but whose superior ambition and drive win him business success once he has learned the ropes. These struggling immigrant lads, it appears from the third column of Table 1, were not very common in Boston. We see there what proportion of the native-born and foreign-born men who first worked in a manual job climbed to a white-collar position after that. The only cohort in which immigrant youths climbed faster than their native peers, and hence narrowed the gap in the course of their careers, was the one whose exceptional character will be analyzed below. In the other three groups, immigrants starting out in blue-collar jobs later ascended to nonmanual posts distinctly less often than native youths. They were even farther behind at the end of the race than they had been at the starting gun.

What is more, the select 20% of immigrant youths who did gain an initial foothold in the white-collar world did not display any greater ability to retain their hard-won positions than the 50% of native sons whose first job was nonmanual. The fourth column of the table discloses, indeed, that in two of the four groups immigrant white-collar workers were roughly twice as likely as natives to skid downward into a blue-collar post as their careers unfolded; in the other two, natives and immigrants were on a par. On every count, therefore, the foreign-born were at a disadvantage. They started their careers at the bottom more often than native Americans, and the margin of their handicap actually widened rather than narrowed with each passing year. At the time of their final jobs they were much more heavily concentrated in working-class callings than the native-born.

The 1860–79 cohort was the one clear exception to this pattern, and its special position is readily explained. The foreign-born in this instance, who fared about as well as the natives, were living in Boston before they were twenty years of age. The median age of the cohort at the time of the Census of 1880, when they appeared in the sample, was only ten. The foreign-born youths in this cohort, therefore, had mostly left their homelands and arrived in Boston when they were still young children. Legally they were foreign-born, but in terms of experience they can more properly be classified as *second-generation* immigrants. They were exposed to immigrant ways at home, as all second-generation immigrants were, but they were involved in American culture as well early in their formative years, attending American schools and so forth. It has sometimes been suggested that individuals who are born abroad but enter the host society before the age of twelve should be classified as second- rather than first-generation immigrants. It is quite possible that the ability of these technically foreign-born youths of the 1860–79 group to compete on an equal basis with native-born Americans merely indicates that de facto second-generation immigrants did not face the same barriers to mobility as men who spent their formative years in a quite different kind of society.

Career Mobility for Three Ethnic Generations

Full exploration of this issue requires information by which we can distinguish men reared in a foreign culture from those (wherever born) reared in the United States by foreign parents and from native men whose parents were also native to the American scene. There is no way of knowing the exact age at which the foreign-born in our samples came to these shores—for the 1860–79 cohort we can give a rough approximation, for the others not even that—but for two of the cohorts we do at least know not only the country of birth but the father's country of birth for each individual. Thus we can examine differences in the career patterns of men born abroad, native-born youths whose fathers were born abroad, and men who were at least third-generation Americans. To depend upon birthplace information, as we must, leaves unresolved the problem that not only those classified second generation in the 1860–79 cohort but also those technically born abroad and hence classed first generation were for all practical purposes second-generation immigrants, having resided in the U.S. during their formative years. An undetermined number of foreign-born men in the other cohorts as well were truly second generation in this sense too. But the breakdown by ethnic generation that appears in Table 2 is still an advance over the simple native-foreign dichotomy, even with this unavoidable flaw in the classification procedure. We can only note that the problem exists, that its general effect will be to blur and minimize somewhat the differences between first- and second-generation newcomers, and that this blurring will be strongest in the figures for the 1860–79 cohort.

The distinctiveness of the career patterns of second-generation immigrants in late nineteenth- and early twentieth-century Boston stands out strikingly in Table 2. It is frustrating that the information required to distinguish ethnic generations was available in the U.S. Census of 1880 but not in the sources from which the later samples were drawn, so that the occupational trajectories of only two cohorts—men in their twenties in 1880, and youths under twenty at the time of the census—can be analyzed here. The pattern visible in the table, however, is sufficiently clear to suggest the possibility that it prevailed in later years as well.

Looking first at the cohort of men born in the pre-Civil War decade, we can see that both immigrants and the children of immigrants were overwhelmingly concen-

Table 2. Career Mobility between First and Last Jobs, by Ethnic Generation

Birth Cohort and Generation	Starting White Collar in %	Ending White Collar in %	Blue-Collar Starters Climbing in %	White-Collar Starters Skidding in %	N
1850-59					
1st Generation	18	24	13	25	68
2nd Generation	25	44	34	25	98
WASP	69	74	32	7	141
1860-79					
1st Generation	49	59	33	15	41
2nd Generation	45	47	21	22	401
WASP	75	74	26	10	210

trated on the lower rungs of the occupational ladder at the time they first entered the labor market, and that native-born sons of native-born parents were largely clustered on the upper rungs. Second-generation youths were slightly more likely than those born abroad to start their careers wearing a white collar, but the glaring disparity was between young men whose fathers had always lived in the United States and those from immigrant families, whether or not they themselves had been born in this country.

The initial disadvantage of both first- and second-generation immigrants was enormous. Was it diminished during the course of their careers? Our previous comparison of immigrants with the native-born revealed that the gap between them had actually grown wider by the end of the race; the foreign-born were less often upwardly mobile and more often downwardly mobile than the natives. Now that it is possible, however, to break the crude category "native-born" into two more revealing classes—the native-born whose fathers were immigrants, and the native-born of native-born stock—a new pattern appears. Both first- and second-generation youths typically started at the bottom, but the second-generation youths were far more successful at climbing later into more highly paid and respectable callings. They did not actually narrow the gap between them and WASP youths, but at least they rose at the same rate, a rate nearly three times as high as that for the immigrant generation.[6] To have been of recent immigrant stock was a major handicap when one entered the occupational race; whether one was actually born abroad or not was irrelevant. But it was highly relevant to what happened after the starting gun was sounded. First-generation immigrants were far more likely to remain blue-collar workers for life; the second generation found the white-collar world as accessible as it was to those youths of old American stock who also began their careers in a manual job.

If the second generation was like the third in its propensity to rise, however, it was notably less able to carve out a secure niche in the middle-class world after arriving there. A mere 7% of the WASP youths who began in a nonmanual calling were manual workmen at the time of their last job; fully a quarter of both the first- and the second-generation immigrants in the cohort were downwardly mobile in this manner.

The second generation was located midway between the immigrants and the WASPs, but the experience of the second generation in finding a place in the American occupational structure was not what could have been predicted by averaging the records of the first and the third generation. We might have anticipated that native-born Americans of foreign stock would have started their careers well ahead of immigrant youths but well behind WASPs, that they would have risen more often than the first but less often than the third generation, and that their rate of downward mobility would likewise be at a midpoint between that of raw immigrants and long-time Americans. Instead, the second generation found their first jobs in the white-collar world no more often than the immigrants. During the course of their careers, however, they were uniquely restless and mobile, shifting across the manual/nonmanual line with greater frequency than either the first or the third generation. They rose from a lowly start as often as WASPs; they fell downward after a good start as often as new immigrants. In this respect one could say that their attainments were midway between those of more established and more recently arrived groups, but they arrived at this middle position by being exceptionally mobile *in both directions,* by being men whose first jobs, whether white collar or blue collar, were least likely to be their final jobs.

This conclusion stands out even more sharply when we examine more complex mobility matrices that display not only movement between white-collar and blue-collar occupations but also movement within these broad occupational classes—for instance, the shift from unskilled to skilled laborer or from clerk to manager. Presentation of the detailed tables plotting shifts between five occupational strata—high white collar, low white collar, skilled, semiskilled, and unskilled—would burden the text unnecessarily here. Suffice it to say that the association between the strata of first and last job, as measured by the statistic gamma, was exceedingly close (.88) for WASPs and rather close (.70) for immigrants, but notably weaker (.40) for the second generation.[7]

Further evidence of the distinctiveness of the second generation may be gained from a closer look at the experiences of these young men in a particular decade, that of the 1880s (Table 3). In this decade, as over their entire careers, second-generation youths moved across the white-collar–blue-collar line much more frequently than either immigrants or WASPs. Nearly one in four shifted from a working-class to a middle-class job or vice versa, as opposed to one in twelve first-generation and one in ten third-generation men. In addition, the likelihood that they would continue to hold a job in the same occupational stratum for these ten years was unusually low. The figures for continuity within each of the five strata disclose a nearly identical pattern for first-generation immigrants and old-stock Americans, but a distinctly different one for the second generation, who at every occupational level were less stable. Overall, more than four out of ten

Table 3. *Career Mobility and Continuity in the Decade 1880-90 by Ethnic Generation*

	Generation		
Interclass mobility	*1st*	*2nd*	*WASP*
% of manual starters climbing	7	20	15
% of white-collar starters skidding	12	29	8
% of total group changing class during the decade	8	23	10
Continuity rates by stratum			
high white collar	90	75	89
low white collar	75	63	72
skilled	91	66	81
semiskilled	68	48	68
unskilled	77	36	57
All	81	58	75
Association between stratum of 1880 and 1890 job (gamma)	.87	.54	.87
Number	211	113	210

of them moved to a job in a different stratum during the decade, as opposed to only one in four immigrants and one in five WASPs. The association between 1880 and 1890 jobs was identically strong for the first and third generation; the value of gamma was .87 for each group, but only .54 for the second generation.

These generalizations are based on the record of the older of the two cohorts. The career patterns of the younger of these groups, it has been noted, are somewhat more difficult to interpret, because a large fraction of these youths were living in Boston by the time they were ten years old, and those of them technically born abroad could more properly be considered second generation in their contact with American culture. If we keep this complication in mind, the data for the 1860–79 cohort in Table 2 are fully consistent with the argument advanced above. Again both first- and second-generation immigrants started out much more heavily concentrated in working-class callings than WASPs. (That a much higher fraction of them entered a white-collar job at the outset than in the previous cohort does not signify a general dimunition in the handicaps of men of foreign stock, but only the accident that these young men happen to have lived in Boston longer and were thus selected by the migration process.[8] No such clear dimunition in the initial disadvantage of the foreign-born is evident in the records of the later cohorts included in Table 1.) In the case of the 1860–79 cohort, however, all three generations had somewhat similar rates of upward movement after the first job, with the immigrants actually the most successful. Since most of these technically first-generation men were actually second-generation, this is not surprising. If we were to class them with the second generation and recompute the second-generation rate accordingly, the second and the third generations would be equally mobile upwardly, as with the earlier cohort. After a poor beginning, men of foreign stock rose to middle-class positions about as rapidly as WASPs; the gap between them did not narrow, but neither did it grow wider. The other key generalization—that the second-generation men who began their careers in nonmanual posts had unusual difficulty in keeping their painfully acquired footholds in the middle class—is also confirmed by the experience of the younger cohort. Indeed, second-generation youths were even more prone to fall back into the working class than the foreign-born in this group, though the difference is not large enough to be statistically significant. The main point is that men of foreign stock, wherever they were born, were downwardly mobile in the course of their careers considerably more often than old-stock Americans. Three-quarters of the latter ended their working lives on the upper side of the white-collar–blue-collar line, a proportion much higher than that for newcomers in either cohort.

The measure of occupational mobility employed in much of this analysis—movement between manual and nonmanual callings—is, of course, a crude one. It might be thought that these findings are due to that crudity. For example, the skidding syndrome manifested by men of foreign stock could have stemmed from the fact that such men were disproportionately concentrated in menial white-collar posts from which downward movements was common, whereas third-generation Americans were disproportionately clustered in the upper echelons of the nonmanual category. Utilizing more detailed occupational categories, however, allows us to rule out that line of argument. The group differences under consideration here did not evaporate when finer measures of status were employed; they remained clear-cut.

Indeed, more refined tabulations (not given here), which take into account upward and downward movement from stratum to stratum as well as shifts between the blue-collar and white-collar classes, give a heightened sense of the difficulties confronted by newcomers and their children. Not only did men of first- or second-generation immigrant stock who started their careers as white-collar employees of some kind lose those jobs and drop into the working class much more frequently than WASP youths; a much smaller fraction of those of them who remained in nonmanual posts were able to move upward into highly paid professional, proprietary, or managerial positions. Two out of ten third-generation white-collar starters climbed to the high nonmanual stratum in the course of their careers, whereas only one fell into a blue-collar job. For the first- and second-generation immigrants who started their careers wearing white collars, the proportions were reversed; the chance of skidding subsequently into a laboring job was twice the chance of climbing further.

The overall conclusion suggested by the evidence relating career patterns to nativity and parental nativity is that native-born Americans had a distinct advantage in the competition for jobs on the higher rungs of the occupational ladder, and that native-born Americans whose fathers were also native-born had a still greater advantage. Both immigrants and the native-born children of immigrants were far more likely both to begin and to end their careers working with their hands and wearing blue collars. Not only did the foreign-born start more often at the bottom; they were less often upwardly mobile after their first job, and those who started well were more prone to lose their middle-class positions and end up in a manual job. The critical second generation, however, was somewhat more favorably placed, though not as favorably as the melting pot folklore would have it. Having a foreign-born father, even though you yourself were born in this country, was a distinct handicap. It meant that you were much more likely than the son of a native-born father to enter the labor market at the manual level, and it meant that if you did find a white-collar job at the outset, you were twice as likely to skid as to climb further. But unlike men actually born abroad, second-generation immigrants who began as manual laborers had relatively good prospects for subsequent upward mobility into clerical, sales, and petty proprietary positions; they were not left further and further behind the WASP with each passing year.

The Influence of Class Origins

It is possible that the foregoing has given an excessively
bleak picture of the handicaps of men of foreign birth or
parentage. It is, of course, a truism that an individual's
occupational attainments have something to do with the
attainments of his father. Students of occupational mobility, indeed, have devoted far more attention to the study
of intergenerational mobility, to the measurement of the
extent of "occupational inheritance" between father and
son, than to any other facet of the mobility process. The
larger study of which this paper is a part demonstrates,
not surprisingly, that the occupational rank of fathers in
Boston had a distinct influence upon the career patterns
of their children.

Consider the possibility that the great majority of the
fathers of Boston's first- and second-generation immigrants were manual laborers, while the fathers of old-
stock Americans were disproportionately concentrated in
business and professional callings. This, rather than any
other characteristic of immigrant and second-generation
youths, might well explain their inability to compete on
equal terms with WASPs. The correlation we have observed between ethnic background and career mobility,
that is to say, may be spurious, the result of differences
in class origins that happen to be correlated with ethnic
background. It is necessary, therefore, to examine the influence of national origins upon career mobility while
controlling for inherited class position by holding constant the father's occupational rank.

Table 4 provides at least a crude control of this kind,
displaying patterns of career mobility for working-class
and middle-class sons separately. The occupations of the
fathers of many of the men in the sample are unknown,

Table 4. Class Origins, Ethnicity, and Career Mobility

Birth Cohort and Generation	Starting White Collar in %	Ending White Collar in %	Blue-Collar Starters Climbing in %	White-Collar Starters Skidding in %	N
1850-79					
Sons of Blue-Collar Fathers					
2nd generation	35	39	21	27	375
WASP	58	53	8	13	112
1880-89					
1st generation	23	29	21	43	31
2nd generation	43	56	36	17	68
1850-79					
Sons of White-Collar Fathers					
2nd generation	67	77	27	16	95
WASP	89	90	50	5	174

alas, for the fathers were not employed in Boston and thus were not listed in local records. This was especially true of first-generation immigrant youths, whose fathers often remained in Europe, but it was true of all groups to some degree. The two cohorts initially distinguished in the sample drawn from the 1880 census have been combined for this reason, and even then there were too few first-generation immigrants to justify inclusion. But at least some of the relationships observed previously may be reexamined with the influence of class origins held constant.

It is clear from the first column of Table 4 that the initial handicap of men of foreign birth or stock cannot be explained away by differences in social origins. In the first cohort, one in three second-generation immigrants from working-class families began their careers wearing white collars, but nearly six in ten WASP youths with blue-collar fathers, a glaring difference. The data for the 1880–89 cohort do not supply the information needed to distinguish second-generation immigrants from WASPs, but we can see that foreign-born men of working-class origins were very heavily concentrated on the bottom rungs of the occupational ladder at the time of their first job, whereas native-born men of similar origins were twice as successful at entering white-collar jobs. It is reasonable to surmise that if it had been possible to break down the native-born group into second-generation and old-stock Americans, the figure for the second generation would have been well under the 43% overall figure, and that for WASPs up in the 55% to 60% range of the other cohort.

The influence of ethnic background upon the level at which young men began their careers was just as potent within families headed by middle-class fathers. Some immigrants found business, professional, and other white-collar jobs for themselves in late nineteenth-century Boston; that there was an emerging immigrant middle class at all was a significant fact. But by one crucial criterion the position of that immigrant middle class was terribly weak, Table 4 reveals. A key index of a man's status is his ability to ensure that his children attain a comparably high status themselves, and by that measure the immigrant middle class was highly vulnerable. Nine out of ten of the WASP youths from white-collar families started work wearing white collars themselves; only one in ten dropped below the occupational level they had "inherited," so to speak, from their fathers. The comparable downward mobility figure for middle-class sons who were second-generation immigrants was more than three times as high; 33% became manual laborers of some kind at the outset of their careers, a proportion closer to that for WASP youths of working-class origins (42%) than to that for middle-class WASPs (11%).

The handicap of not only the first-generation but the second-generation immigrants as well at the time they first entered the labor market, therefore, was real, not spurious. Controlling for the broad occupational class in which the fathers of these men were situated does not make the handicap disappear. Nor, it should be added, does a more refined occupational control, distinguishing fathers by five occupational strata. It is true that middle-class sons of WASP stock more often had fathers in the upper white-collar stratum, fathers who were professionals or the owners or managers of large enterprises, whereas second-generation middle-class youths frequently came from households headed by salesmen, clerks, or petty proprietors. This partly explains the superior head start of the former group, but only partly. In detailed tables broken down by specific stratum so as to control for this influence (not given here), the generational differences noted above still stand out.

On the other hand, as we can observe from the other columns of Table 4, there was in the case of middle-class sons some tendency for these differences to narrow during the course of these young men's careers. Whereas WASP middle-class sons typically started their careers at a higher level than their first- and second-generation competitors, and ended their working lives with some margin of superiority still, the margin had shrunk. Nine out of ten WASP middle-class sons in the first two cohorts began work wearing white collars, and nine out of ten ended their careers in a nonmanual calling; a few individuals moved up from lower beginnings, and a few skidded after a good start, but the overall concentration in the white collar class remained virtually unchanged. Second-generation youths moved from 67% to 77% representation in white-collar callings, still behind their WASP competitors, but less so.

This narrowing of the gap, however, was in part the result of a "ceiling effect"; WASP middle-class sons began with such a high concentration in the nonmanual category that there was little room for further improvement. If we examine not the question of access to white-collar jobs in general but access to upper-echelon professional, managerial, and proprietary posts, the advantage of WASP youths remained substantial; 46% of them ended their careers in the high nonmanual stratum, but less than a third of second-generation men of similar class origins did (Table 5).

As for sons born into working-class homes, the evidence available seems consistent with our earlier generalizations made on the basis of tables lacking a control for the

Table 5. *Class Origins, Ethnicity, and Entry into High Nonmanual Posts,*
1850-79 Cohort

Generation	Starting High White Collar in %	Ending High White Collar in %	N
	Sons of Blue-Collar Fathers		
2nd generation	1	5	375
WASP	5	14	112
	Sons of White-Collar Fathers		
2nd generation	13	31	95
WASP	23	46	174

father's occupation. Even when their lowly class origins are taken into account, first-generation immigrants
started badly and were less mobile upwardly and more
mobile downwardly than any other group. The number
of cases in the 1880–89 cohort upon which this judgment
is based is pathetically small, but the percentage differences are very large, especially when we recall that the
point of comparison given is not WASPs but a group that
included both WASPs and second-generation newcomers.

The second generation, however, was in a more favorable position. We noted earlier that after a poor initial
start the second generation moved upward into the white-
collar class at about the same rate as WASPs; confining
our gaze to men of working-class origins makes plain that
the upward mobility of the second generation during the
course of their careers was considerably more impressive
than that of old-stock American youths; 21% climbed,
but only 8% of the WASPs did. Two important qualifications must be added, however. First, the upward mobility of second-generation immigrants was typically
movement into minor white-collar positions; only one in
twenty, as opposed to three in twenty WASPs from labor-

ing homes, ended their careers as professionals, proprietors, or officials of large enterprises (Table 5). Second, men of the second generation were unusually prone to downward as well as to upward mobility. Holding the father's occupation constant does not alter our previous conclusion on this point.

All in all, then, men of foreign birth and even of native birth but foreign parentage were handicapped vis-à-vis old-stock Americans of similar class origins. Their lowly origins, at least to the extent that the father's occupation is a proper index, do not suffice to explain their failure to obtain a larger fraction of jobs that ranked high in income, security, prestige, and power over others.

Some Hints of Differences Between Specific Ethnic Groups

It is not illegitimate to attempt to generalize about immigrants and the children of immigrants. But it is true, of couse, that painting with such a broad brush may obscure important variations in the ways in which men of varying national background coped with the American environment. Regrettably, the samples on which this study is based quickly become too small to yield reliable findings when we attempt refined comparisons of the career patterns of several different immigrant groups. Only in certain instances were the individual national groups themselves represented in sufficient numbers in the samples to permit detailed analysis. But in at least these few cases it is possible to ask whether our observation about a broad group—the foreign-born of the 1880–89 cohort, or the second-generation immigrants in the 1860–79 group, for instance—applies equally well to the specific nationalities that comprise that group.

Table 6. Career Mobility Between First and Last Jobs for Particular Immigrant Groups, Late Nineteenth Century

Birth Cohort, Generation, and Group	Starting White Collar in %	Ending White Collar in %	Blue-Collar Starters Climbing in %	White-Collar Starters Skidding in %	N
1850-59					
1st Generation	18	24	13	25	68
2nd Generation	25	44	34	25	98
Irish	15	33	35	33	61
Non-Irish	41	51	32	20	37
WASP	69	74	32	7	141
1860-79					
1st Generation	49	59	33	15	41
2nd Generation	45	47	21	22	401
Irish	35	38	13	27	214
British	59	55	16	18	76
West European	49	61	31	18	83
WASP	75	74	26	10	210

In Table 6 we have the information about generational differences in career-mobility patterns for the 1850–59 and 1860–79 cohorts originally presented in Table 2, with figures indicating how much particular immigrant groups conformed to or deviated from the general pattern. A number of deviations of interest are visible. In both cohorts the distinctiveness of the Irish is glaringly apparent. There are too few cases to ascertain if men actually born in Ireland were in a notably worse position than immigrants from Germany, Scandinavia, England, Canada, and such countries; all we can note is that the foreign-born in general were handicapped. But the disabilities of American-born youths whose fathers were Irish rather than some other European nationality, stand out dramatically. Of the young men born in the 1850s, during the first wave of massive Irish immigration to Boston and other Eastern cities, only 15% of the second-generation Irish began work in the upper reaches of the occupational structure, as opposed to 41% of all other second-generation immigrant youths. And although those Irish beginning their careers in a manual job had relatively good prospects of reaching a middle-class calling later—their rate of upward mobility was as high as that of both other second-generation immigrants and WASPs—the select 15% of them who did enter the white-collar world at the outset were much more likely to fall back into the working class, about 50% more likely than non-Irish second-generation men, nearly seven times as likely as WASPs.

The troubles of the second-generation Irish are similarly, if less dramatically, evident in the 1860–79 cohort, consisting of men who first entered the labor market in the last two decades of the century, at the time the Irish were obtaining political supremacy in Boston. About a third of these Irish-American youths began work in white-

collar posts, a great advance over the record of men a decade or two earlier. But this entire age cohort started out
better, because it had lived in the community longer, so
that there remained a large gap between the Irish-American and other second-generation men. One in three second-generation Irish youths, but six in ten lads of British
origins and five in ten of other West European stock,
began their careers in the middle class. Not only was there
an initial gap between the Irish and other second-generation immigrants; there was a widening gap. The Irish rose
to nonmanual jobs after a manual start less often than
second-generation West Europeans, though slightly more
often than the British. And the Irish who did start in the
white-collar class again had a distinctively strong propensity to fall back into blue-collar work as their careers unfolded. The end result was that in both cohorts something
under four in ten of the second-generation Irish held middle-class jobs at the end of their careers, whereas more
than half of the second-generation youths of non-Irish
stock did so.

This closer look at the career patterns of specific groups
suggests certain qualifications to the generalizations offered earlier about the mobility of different ethnic generations. None of the second-generation groups started
their careers at such a high level as WASPs, but some were
much closer to it than others. The range went from the
second-generation Irish of the 1850–59 cohort, who were
more heavily proletarian in their first jobs than even the
initial immigrant generation, to the second-generation
British of the 1860–79 cohort, who were midway between
the second-generation median and the third-generation
American figure. After their initial more-or-less poor
start, the second-generation groups tended to rise at a rate
roughly comparable to that of WASPs and notably faster

than first-generation immigrants. But men of foreign birth or parentage who started out wearing white collars were in every group much less likely to retain their position than were third-generation Americans. Again the Irish were far to one end of the scale, displaying a distinctively strong propensity for downward mobility, as well as distinctively heavy initial concentration in blue-collar occupations.

Before we speak too freely about the failures of the second-generation Irish, however, or the impressive attainments of men of British stock, we must consider the possibility that these differences are misleading, stemming from nothing more than the fact that the fathers of the relatively unsuccessful Irish were more often lowly blue-collar workers than the fathers of the more successful British. Does holding constant the occupational rank of the fathers of these men make these differences disappear, or was it the case that Irish-American youths fared badly compared to other second-generation immigrants whose fathers were similarly located in the occupational structure? Table 7 bears on this issue. There were too few middle-class fathers of second-generation immigrants in the sample to permit a detailed breakdown of their sons' mobility patterns, and we must likewise drop the 1850–59 cohort from consideration because of the small number of cases remaining, but the pattern for sons from working-class homes in the larger 1860–79 cohort is at least suggestive. Employing an occupational control does largely remove the initial advantages of the West Europeans vis-à-vis the Irish. Table 6 had indicated that 49% of them began in white-collar jobs, but little more than a third of the Irish. But this was apparently due primarily to the fact that more of these youths of West European stock came from middle-class homes. Among sons of blue-

Table 7. Career Mobility Between First and Last Jobs in the 1860-79 Cohort by Immigrant Group, Working-Class Sons Only

Group	Starting White Collar in %	Ending White Collar in %	Blue-Collar Starters Climbing in %	White-Collar Starters Skidding in %	N
2nd Generation	38	39	17	26	317
Irish	31	34	19	31	189
British	55	48	11	21	60
West European	34	40	18	18	50
WASP	59	56	22	21	90

collar workers, the West Europeans started out with only a shade more nonmanual positions than the Irish. The earlier finding that West European men rose more rapidly than the Irish after their first job also appears spurious, the result of their higher class origins. Working-class sons of both stocks had the same chance of being upwardly mobile after their first jobs. The Irish, however, remained distinctive in their propensity to fall back into the blue-collar class after a white-collar first job; 31% skidded, as opposed to 18% of the second-generation immigrants of West European origins. By the end of their careers the Irish were accordingly more heavily concentrated in the working class than any other second-generation group.

The contrast between the experience of the Irish and of men of British stock is not at all blurred by introducing an occupational control. It cannot be attributed to the higher occupational rank of the fathers of British-Americans. Irish working-class sons were far more likely to start their careers working with their hands, and, although they were upwardly mobile between first and last job somemore frequently than the British, they were also more prone to skid after holding a white-collar job initially. Only a third were on the upper side of the manual/nonmanual divide at the time of their last job, as opposed to nearly half of the British-American youths from laboring homes. Controlling for the father's occupation makes clear that the second-generation British not only fared better than men of other immigrant stocks; they closely approximated the pattern for third-generation Americans of similar class origins. Of the British, 55% began work wearing white collars, compared to 59% of the WASP youths; and although the British were slightly less successful in the course of their subsequent careers, nearly half of them ended as white-collar workers as compared to 11 out of 20 WASP youths. (It should be noted, how-ever, that British-American men found the highest white-collar stratum much more difficult to penetrate. Only 4% of them reached the high nonmanual category, whereas the figure for WASPs of comparable origins was three times as high.) Much, though by no means all, of the advantage of native-born sons of native-born parents over native-born sons of British-born parents stemmed from the simple fact that the fathers of the former were dis-proportionately concentrated in the upper reaches of the occupational structure.

Neither "the immigrants" nor the "second-generation immigrants" of Boston, then, were an undifferentiated mass. In many ways the differences between particular ethnic groups were as important as those between immi-grants, the children of immigrants, and WASPs in gen-eral. Men whose families originated in Great Britain or Canada had one kind of experience; those of Irish descent had quite another.

Some further insight into differences between the ex-periences of different nationalities in adjusting to the American scene may be gleaned from Table 8, which dis-plays the career mobility patterns of men in two later cohorts, those born in the 1880s and the first decade of the twentieth century. In neither case, unfortunately, is it possible to distinguish second-generation immigrants from other native-born Americans; these figures refer to men actually born abroad, and it is important to recall that the native-born group against which they are com-pared included large numbers of second-generation youths. Nor is it possible to control for the father's occu-pational rank here; in the later group the sources pro-vided no information about the father's occupation, whereas in the former it was known in too few cases to

Table 8. Career Mobility Between First and Last Jobs for Particular Immigrant Groups in the Twentieth Century

Birth Cohort and Group	Starting White Collar in %	Ending White Collar in %	Blue-Collar Starters Climbing in %	White-Collar Starters Skidding in %	N
1880-89					
1st Generation	23	39	28	33	206
Irish	33	33	25	50	33
Italian	10	33	28	20	48
West European	9	26	19	0	35
East European	34	49	38	29	61
2nd Generation or More	51	61	32	13	215
1900-09					
1st Generation	23	31	14	14	95
British	10	20	11	0	20
Italian	5	15	14	50	39
East European	72	68	14	11	25
2nd Generation or More	40	47	23	17	146

permit a detailed breakdown. With these glaring gaps in the evidence, a lengthy analysis of the table does not seem called for, but there is at least some further reinforcement here for our emphasis upon differences between particular immigrant groups.

The record of the Irish was rather less dismal, in the one cohort in which there were enough Irish-born to compute their distribution separately. But what is perhaps most notable about the Irish is that despite their initial gains in the white-collar category, they still displayed unusually high rates of downward mobility, and thus ended their careers with no greater representation in the middle class than the Italians, and little more than the West Europeans. There is also a suggestion that at least by the 1930s, when the 1900–09 cohort was in mid-career, the Italians of Boston were faring especially poorly, with 95% of them beginning work in blue-collar jobs and 85% of them remaining in such jobs at the end of their careers. There is an indication that, whatever the successes of the second-generation British in the earlier period, men born in Britain or British Canada in the first decade of the century and migrating to Boston subsequently were another breed; 90% of them held manual posts at the outset, 80% still wore blue collars at the time of their final jobs.

Most striking of all were the dramatic successes of men born in East Europe, most of them East European Jews. By World War I many Americans were coming to believe that the "new immigrants" from Eastern and Southern Europe were much less capable of entering the American mainstream than earlier groups like the Irish, the English, the Germans, etc.[9] The far from successful experience of the Irish in Boston does not square with this model; the record of the East Europeans contradicts it ever more. Half of the East European immigrants in the cohort born in the 1880s obtained nonmanual positions by the end of their careers, a much higher proportion than in a classic "old immigrant" group like the Irish. And in the 1900–09 cohort more than two-thirds of the East Europeans reached the middle class, a figure well above that for native-born Americans. (If the data permitted a separate tabulation for second-generation immigrants and WASPs, we may surmise, the East European and WASP figures would probably be much the same.)

Concluding Observations

At least two propositions of interest have emerged from this long and possibly tiresome foray into the dense underbrush of urban social history. In one major American city in the classic period of heavy immigration there were dramatic differences in the occupational opportunities open to immigrants, the children of immigrants, and Americans of native stock, with the second generation in a particularly critical and uncertain position vis-à-vis both their parents and their more-established WASP rivals. These differences were largely independent of the social class origins of the newcomers, to the extent that it has been possible to hold these constant in the analysis. Second, there were important differences in the experiences of newcomers of various national backgrounds. Some groups were exceptionally well suited to flourish in the American marketplace; others adjusted much more slowly and painfully.

A host of questions about these findings spring all too quickly to mind. Some of them concern the validity of the description offered here, and the extent to which it may be generalized to other communities; others have to do with what underlying *causes* explain the patterns observed. I draw some comfort from Joseph Schumpeter's remark that "we need statistics not only for explaining things but in order to know precisely what there is to be explained." In an area like this one, where very little is known, a description that at least clarifies what precisely there is to be explained is a necessary first step. But it is only a first step, and the next is to discover *why* the mobility patterns of second-generation Americans differed in the way that they did from those of their parents and of their better-established WASP rivals, and why particular nationalities fared so much better than others. Was there something in the characteristic life styles and values of some groups that impeded their adaptation to American society—or, if you like, that inoculated them against the competitive virus that infected most of the population? Was it, rather, that the receiving society treated men differently according to their ethnicity, welcoming some, placing obstacles in the way of others? Are the rough national differences under scrutiny here best understood in terms of national cultures, or might they not stem from another variable—i.e. religion—which happens to be correlated with national origins? That two of the groups conspicuously toward the rear of the procession—the Irish and the Italians—happen to have been Roman Catholic suggests the need to reconsider the hypothesis suggested by Max Weber. How stable were these patterns over time, and when and why did they begin to fade away? Yet another unanswered question, and one of the utmost relevance, is how the mobility of late nineteenth- and early twentieth-century immigrant groups compared to that of black Americans in the past and present.

Some of these matters will be further explored in the larger study from which this paper is drawn; the influence of religion upon mobility patterns, for instance, will be the subject of an entire chapter, and a lengthy attempt at isolating underlying causes will be offered.[10] But there is abundant room for inquiry by other scholars. Boston is but a single city; other communities will have to be examined to provide a solid basis for generalizations about American society. There were, in addition, deficiencies in the sources and sample design employed here that sorely limit the findings. The size of my samples was severely restricted by pocketbook considerations; larger samples will be required to say anything very persuasive about differences between particular immigrant groups, and I believe that if nothing else this paper has demonstrated that differences between particular groups were important enough to demand attention. I was unable to separate out second-generation immigrants from other native-born Americans except in the sample taken from the manuscript schedules of the U.S. Census of 1880; that difficulty can be partly overcome by others once the 1900 census is open to investigators, as it presumably soon will be. My initial hope of estimating Negro social mobility in Boston was frustrated, because Negroes were a small fraction of the population. Although I deliberately oversampled in order to have an adequate number of Negroes in the samples, the exceptionally high out-migration rates of the group reduced to a mere handful the number of cases in which career lines were clear. This again points to the necessity of large samples. It might be added that the cheapest way of doing this—drawing a large random sample of Negroes and a similarly sized random sample of whites—will not be satisfactory, for "white society" is not a monolith but a mosaic of groups with different experiences. Meaningful comparisons cannot be made between blacks and whites, but must instead be between blacks and other impoverished newcomers to the city, which will require substantial representation in the sample of the major ethnic groups of the community under scrutiny. The question is not whether blacks rank below whites, but how Southern-born black migrants compare to European-born migrants, and how "second-generation" black city dwellers compare to second-generation immigrants. Indeed, as this paper suggests, the key question is more specific still: not whether blacks have moved at the rate of "the typical immigrant," but whether their experience fits anywhere on the immigrant spectrum that runs from the Irish and Italians at the low end to the British and Jews on the high end, or whether they fall so far below even the Irish and Italians that the immigrant-group analogy is entirely inapplicable. The answer to this question is not at all clear.[11]

*I am grateful to the American Council of Learned Societies, the American Philosophical Society, the Mathematical Social Science Board, and the M.I.T.–Harvard Joint Center for Urban Studies for the financial support which made this research possible.

1. E. P. Hutchinson, *Immigrants and Their Children, 1850–1950* (New York, 1956) treats the United States as a whole. Local studies based on similar methods include W. Lloyd Warner and Leo Srole, *The Social Systems of American Ethnic Groups* (New Haven, 1945); Jerome K. Myers, "Assimilation to the Ecological and Social Systems of a Community," *American Sociological Review, 15* (1950), 367–72; Francis A. J. Ianni, "Residential and Occupational Mobility as Indices of the Acculturation of an Ethnic Group," *Social Forces, 36* (1957), 65–72; and many of the studies cited in Fred L. Strodtbeck, "Jewish and Italian Immigration and Subsequent Status Mobility," in David McClelland *et al., Talent and Society* (Princeton, N.J., 1958), pp. 259–68.

2. Yet another serious flaw in the Hutchinson book and similar studies employing data applying to the United States as a whole is that immigrants and their children are typically concentrated in cities more heavily than the general population, and some immigrant groups more so than others. Access to the opportunities provided by the urban labor market is an important variable that must be controlled to make meaningful comparisons between immigrants and natives or between particular immigrant groups.

3. The terms "first job" and "last job" are not strictly accurate. It would require a questionnaire administered to men at retirement to identify these with precision. Those who attempt to reconstruct career patterns of individuals by tracing them through historical records must settle for far less satisfactory data, data pertaining to the date at which the census taker or some other record keeper happened to gather information. In this study "first job" was arbitrarily defined as the first job known to have been held by a sample member, so long as he held it prior to age thirty. In many instances an individual was caught at what probably was his first actual job, at the age of sixteen or seventeen perhaps. But in some cases men were already in their twenties before they could be located occupationally, so the concept really pertains to some job held while still a relatively young man. Likewise, "last job" means the last job held in Boston as revealed by the tracing method, so long as it was held at the age of thirty or older. The "last job" of some sample members was held when the individuals in question were in their fifties or sixties, but some died or migrated out of Boston at an earlier point. If there was information to rank them occupationally after they had reached the point of settling down that usually takes place around the age of thirty, it was deemed sufficient. The choice of thirty as the watershed was dictated not by the assumptions of today's rebels in the war between the generations but rather by the data of the study itself, which disclosed a marked slowing of occupational mobility for men thirty and above.

4. For a thorough analysis of this, see Peter Blau and Otis Dudley Duncan, *The American Occupational Structure* (New York, 1967), pp. 227–41.

5. The most important break in the occupational hierarchy of Boston in the years treated here, it is assumed, was between white-collar and blue-collar jobs, though both of these broad classes had important subdivisions. Within the nonmanual category we can distinguish two strata: professionals and proprietors or officials of large businesses constituted the higher of these, with clerks, salesmen, and petty proprietors ranking in the "low nonmanual" stratum. The manual class was in turn divided into skilled, semiskilled and service, and unskilled workers. Proof that this division into two occupational classes and five strata accurately reflected the distribution of income, security, prestige, and power in the community will appear in the full report of the study, but an illustrative piece of evidence on the matter of job security may be offered here. The 1900 census revealed that 17% of the adult males of Boston had been unemployed for a month or more in the preceding twelve months. The rate for lawyers and physicians, however, was a mere 1%, for merchants and bankers 3%, for white-collar workers only 6%. The rate for all blue-collar workers, by contrast, was a striking 24%, and for unskilled blue-collar workers an appalling 41%. Calculated from detailed data on 129 occupations in U.S. Bureau of the Census, *U.S. Census of 1900, Special Reports—Occupations* (Washington, D.C., 1901), pp. 495–98. For evidence of similar class differences in income, see Robert K. Burn, "The Comparative Economic Position of Manual and White Collar Employees," *Journal of Business*, 27 (1954), 257–67.

6. The term "WASP" is used here as a convenient label for native-born Americans of native-born parentage. Strictly speaking it refers to white Americans of Anglo-Saxon Protestant background. A few of the youths so designated here may in fact have been Roman Catholic. My usage, furthermore, leaves outside the WASP category American-born sons of British Protestant origins, who are placed with other second-generation immigrants. As will become clear later, the mobility patterns of these youths closely approximated those of old-stock American WASPs; the economic and social assimilation of the second-generation British was very rapid. The term seems more suitable as a synonym for old-stock Americans than any other, however, and it is so used here.

7. Readers unfamiliar with gamma, a simple measure of association especially well-suited to the relatively straightforward questions historians are likely to put to statistical data, should consult the lucid exposition in Leo A. Goodman and William Kruskal, "Measures of Association for Cross Classifications," *Journal of the American Statistical Association*, 49 (1954), 732–64.

8. Most of them were too young to be at work at the time of the Census of 1880. Since individuals were traced at ten-year intervals, the

"first job" recorded for these youths was in 1890. One of the chief findings of the study is that there was a strong positive correlation between length of residence in the city and occupational rank; migration from the community was occupationally selective. That many of these youths had lived in Boston for a minimum of a full decade before holding what is designated their "first job" here probably accounts for the high proportion holding white-collar jobs at that point.

9. For an incisive critique of the "new immigrant–old immigrant" dichotomy, see Oscar Handlin, *Race and Nationality in American Life* (Boston, 1957), ch. 5.

10. On this, see my essay "Religion and Occupational Mobility in Boston, 1880–1963" in a forthcoming volume on quantitative methods of historical analysis, Robert W. Fogel, ed.

11. I am somewhat less inclined that I once was—see "Up From Slavery," *Perspectives in American History, 1* (1967), 434–40—to emphasize the similarities between Negroes and European immigrants to American cities, but I am still convinced that simple black-white comparisons are extremely misleading, and that the method of comparative ethnic-group analysis urged in that essay is essential. We still know very little about what was distinctive about the socioeconomic position of black Americans in our cities of the past or present. It is not even clear that Irish policemen in Italian ghettos forty years ago behaved any better than Italian or Irish policemen do in black ghettos today. Research now under way by Herbert Gutman of the University of Rochester and Laurence Glasco of the State University of New York at Buffalo, dealing with Negro family structure and occupational position, is yielding some fascinating results, and it is to be hoped that their lead will be followed by others. For a tantalizing fragment of evidence, based unfortunately upon tiny samples, see Richard J. Hopkins' article on the occupational mobility of Negroes, immigrants, and native whites in late nineteenth-century Atlanta in the May 1968, *Journal of Southern History*. Hopkins is currently at work on a fuller study of the topic.

MOBILITY AND CHANGE IN ANTE-BELLUM PHILADELPHIA

Stuart Blumin

The measurement of the magnitude of vertical mobility is a particularly important consideration for the student of the Amercan city. For in America, more than in most other countries, this particular measure coincides with one of the central ingredients of the prevailing ideology. "This is a country of self-made men," boasted Calvin Colton in 1844, "than which nothing better could be said of any state of society."[1] More specifically:

> Money and property, we know, among us, are constantly changing hands. A man has only to work on, and wait patiently, and with industry and enterprise, he is sure to get both. The wheel of American fortune is perpetually and steadily turning, and those at the bottom today, will be moving up tomorrow, and will ere long be at the top.[2]

Colton's is certainly not a minority view of American culture, nor is it the exclusive property of pre-Civil War propagandists. Rather, it is one of our most durable and widely shared propositions, concerning not only what America is, but also what it should be. In the 1960s we know that for large numbers of individuals the American Dream is an illusion. Yet we have never surrendered the idea that the best society is a fluid society, and the characteristic response to the problems of poverty and racism, among those who admit their existence, is to restore equality of opportunity.

This paper is an attempt to study vertical mobility in a major American city, Philadelphia, during the period 1820 to 1860, when Calvin Colton and others were elevat-

ing the concept of wordly success to its eminent place in
American social thought. But, sensitive both to the tentative nature of my results and to the methodological temper of this volume, I have tried to focus here not simply
on substantive rates and patterns of mobility. I have
sought as well to extend the relevance of this type of study
to the general problems of urban historical research. The
study of mobility is a complicated operation involving
numerous procedures which, when viewed together, may
reveal more about the city than simply the fluidity of its
social structure. Further on, I shall explore the relevance
of the observed mobility patterns to difficult questions of
economic change in the ante-bellum city.

Technical Considerations

The study of mobility may be examined in a number of
different ways. Typically, it is the study of intergenerational occupational mobility—that is, the study of the
relationships between the occupations of a group of men
and those of their sons. These relationships are used to
infer the magnitude and pattern of social mobility in the
period and place of the son's youth or adult life, depend-
ing on whether the son's original or ultimate occupation
is recorded. Since social mobility is inferred, occupations
are ranked or grouped according to an assumed or em-
pirically derived prestige scale, an example of which is
the well-known NORC scale.[3]

It is important to point out, however, that the validity
of inferring social mobility from occupational mobility is
virtually never examined. Leaving aside the question of
whether the inference of social mobility from occupational mobility is valid even in contemporary research,
we must recognize the inappropriateness of applying a

mid-twentieth-century prestige ranking of occupations to early nineteenth-century conditions. The economy and the occupational structure have changed too much to support such a procedure. Furthermore, the creation of an accurate ranking system based on pre-Civil War opinion is made especially difficult in light of the amorphous character of surviving historical documents.

A possible solution may emerge, however, from a simple redefinition of the problem. Although recent studies of the concept of success in America claim for it a certain amount of complexity,[4] the straightforward matter of making money has always been its most basic ingredient. In the effusive words of Calvin Colton, success is conceived of entirely in term of "money and property." Accordingly, we may reinterpret the scale of social mobility as the measurement of economic mobility. We probably lose little information in doing so, for the magnitude of one would no doubt closely resemble the magnitude of the other, and it permits us validly to base our ranking or classification of occupations on the more workable basis of the wealth or incomes of the men who worked within each occupation.[5]

Other problems inherent in the application of this method to the past are not as easily overcome. They often arise from the absence or incompleteness of appropriate data, for we must bear in mind that we are attempting to apply a method oriented toward survey research to a society that is no longer susceptible to personal interview. I have discussed these problems in another place,[6] and will return later to the question of validity.

The first step of any occupational mobility study is to define the vertical dimension of the occupational structure—to rank or classify occupations. As the above discussion implies, this was achieved through the use of whatever data were available for determining the average wealth of the members of each occupation.[7] For the closing year of the period, 1860, manuscript federal census schedules were used to rank fifty-one occupations, from import-export merchant to boatman (see Table 1). To assure that the occupational structure was sufficiently stable thoughout the period, a similar ranking was created for 1820, on the basis of local tax records. These rankings were compared statistically, resulting in the following rank-order correlation coefficients; Spearmans r=.759, Kendall's Tau=.625.

Table 1. Rank Order of Occupations According to Mean Wealth, 1860 ("Journeymen" Excluded)

Rank	Occupation	Mean Wealth
1	Merchant	$50,357[a]
2	Attorney	34,948
3	M.D.	23,879
4	Watchmaker	20,972[b]
5	Broker	16,961
6	Manufacturer	16,910[c]
7	Druggist	12,281[d]
8	Agent	10,369
9	Saddler	9,980
10	Tanner and Currier	8,950
11	Brickmaker	8,433
12	Cabinetmaker	7,272
13	Grocer	5,767
14	Bricklayer	4,308
15	Storekeeper	4,062[e]
16	Carpenter	3,755
17	Teacher	3,746
18	Machinist	3,627
19	Tobacconist	3,512
20	Printer	3,510
21	Baker	3,507
22	Victualler (Butcher)	3,414
23	Coachmaker	3,371
24	Plasterer	3,243
25	Hatter	3,175

Rank	Occupation	Mean Wealth
26	Cooper	3,020
27	Shipwright	2,935
28	Confectioner	2,662
29	Stonecutter	2,425
30.5	Innkeeper	2,324[f]
30.5	Gardener	2,324
32	Tailor	2,317
33	Bookbinder	2,300
34	Shoemaker	2,114
35	Blacksmith	2,089
36	Painter	1,788
37	Carter	1,727
38	Tinsmith	1,625
39	Clerk	1,410
40	Stonemason	1,150
41	Salesman	546
42	Watchman	457
43	Conductor	454
44	Domestic Servant	328
45	Carpet Weaver	186
46	Laborer	180
47	Coachman	170
48	Mariner	113
49	Weaver	106
50	Ironworker	88
51	Boatman	50

Source: *Eighth Census of the United States*, microfilmed manuscript schedules, County of Philadelphia.

a. Includes only those listed as "merchant," with no further specifications. As a rule, the term "merchant," when unaccompanied by the name of a product, indicates a large-scale, general importer-exporter.

b. Includes jewelers and silversmiths.

c. Includes all manufacturers, whether or not a product is specified. The mean for unspecified manufacturers is $1 lower.

d. Excludes one extreme case, George W. Carpenter, whose wealth was listed at $2,120,000. The mean for druggists, including Carpenter, is $136,147.

e. Includes those specified simply as "storekeeper."

f. Includes innkeepers, tavern keepers, and hotelkeepers. These terms appear to be interchangeable, in spite of the fact that a few large hotels existed in Philadelphia in 1860.

These occupational rankings produced few surprises. At the top of Table 1 are the merchants, often merchant-manufacturers, followed by the professionals, manufacturers, and one group of craftsmen specializing in highly esteemed and expensive products. Lower, but still above the middle range, are several craftsmen, such as tanners and brickmakers, who are more properly considered small manufacturers, as well as such nonmanual businessmen as druggists, agents, and grocers. Storekeepers, innkeepers, and a host of craftsmen form the middle range of the rank order, with clerks and carters intermingled with the lower end of this group. Finally, the last ten ranks consist of unskilled workers, domestic servants, and weavers. Weavers in this period were not master craftsmen, but wage-earning machine operatives. Their wages were little higher than those of unskilled workers.

Missing from the rank order is an army of journeymen craftsmen. Journeymen, as wage-earning and usually propertyless individuals, would logically fall near the bottom of the rank order. Unfortunately, city directories do not include journeymen. Proprietors are regularly reported, and unskilled workers less reliably so, but journeymen craftsmen are almost invariably excluded from the Philadelphia directories because the stated purpose of the early directories was to report the names, occupations, and addresses of heads of household and those who were "in business."[8] Journeymen craftsmen represent the only adult male group that is systematically excluded by these terms.

Thus, we have arrived at a major qualification of our attempt to calculate rates of occupational mobility—namely, that we cannot directly observe the mobility experience of one of the most interesting groups in the occupational structure. We will refer later to the question of the journeyman's opportunity. Here we must simply declare that our mobility rates will apply primarily to the city's proprietors, a much larger range of individuals than we might at first expect, and, with a great deal of hesitation, to its unskilled workers. With regard to this latter group, we will see that we have generated rates of mobility that are frankly unrealistic. This phenomenon, which might appear at first to be a striking affirmation of the American Dream, is actually a product of incomplete directories. The directories were likely to include only those unskilled workers who were upwardly mobile.

A second important limitation concerns the type of mobility that proved accessible for study. We have mentioned thus far only the method of intergenerational mobility, the study of occupational change from father to son. Equally important, however, is the study of intragenerational mobility, the study of the occupational history of individual men. In this Philadelphia study both kinds of mobility measures were made; the intragenerational measure provided the more fruitful results.

Intragenerational mobility of course introduces problems of its own. The tracing of an individual career requires not two but many observations in the sequential editions of the Philadelphia city directory. With each attempted observation there arises the possibility of loss of trace due to death, out-migration, incomplete data, or the spiritual debilitation of the researcher. To minimize these pitfalls, the tracing process in this study was restricted to a single decade for each of four separate samples drawn from the city directories of 1820, 1830, 1840, and 1850. A sample of names drawn from the 1820 directory was traced to the 1830 directory. An entirely new sample was drawn from the 1830 directory and traced through 1840, and so on until four decades of observations were available. No attempt was made to exclude individuals from more than one sample, since the samples are sequential, and such an exclusion would have interfered with the comparability of their "age mix."

What follows, then, is a series of matrices measuring the intragenerational occupational mobility of a particular (but rather extensive) subset of the adult male working population of ante-bellum Philadelphia. It should be noted that these matrices apply not to individual careers in their entirety, but to the magnitude of mobility observed within a given decade. It is the decades that are being measured and compared.

Thus far I have emphasized the factors shaping the study of socioeconomic mobility. The city directories include material on the residential addresses as well as the occupations of the men listed. This means that a second variable, residence, can be used to illuminate further the nature of mobility in the ante-bellum city. We will consider this point in due course.

Occupational Patterns

Table 2 presents the occupational mobility matrix for the first decade, the 1820s. The fact that it is a five by five matrix requires some explanation, for we have thus far spoken only of a ranking of a large number of individual occupations. To make a mobility matrix serviceable, it was necessary to collapse the rank order to a limited number of categories. In order to retain as much descriptive power as possible, however, and to avoid the influence of an artificial classification scheme, occupations were coded both to retain their individual identities and to produce a number of alternative classification schema. Thus, matrices were produced to reflect five oc-

Table 2. Occupational Mobility, 1820-30

	1820 Occupational Category					Total	% of Sample
	1	2	3	4	5		
1830 Occupational Category							
1	160 (88.9%)	15 (7.5%)	9 (2.0%)	2 (4.3%)	—	186	19.6
2	8 (4.4%)	160 (80.0%)	26 (5.8%)	5 (10.9%)	3 (4.1%)	202	21.3
3	9 (5.0%)	19 (9.5%)	408 (90.5%)	3 (6.5%)	13 (17.8%)	452	47.6
4	3 (1.7%)	2 (1.0%)	2 (.4%)	35 (76.1%)	1 (1.4%)	43	4.5
5	—	4 (2.0%)	6 (1.3%)	1 (2.2%)	56 (76.7%)	67	7.0
Total	180 (100.0%)	200 (100.0%)	451 (100.0%)	46 (100.0%)	73 (100.0%)	950	100.0
% of Sample	19.0	21.0	47.5	4.8	7.7		

cupational categories, two different sets of four categories, three categories, and the "functional" categories of "non-manual proprietors," "manual proprietors," "nonmanual employees" and "manual employees." Each of these schema produced results consistent with the others. Accordingly, it was decided to present the results in the form of the most descriptive interpretation of the occupational rank order, the five by five matrix. The first category, the highest, consists mainly of merchants, professionals, and manufacturers, were merchants comprising over half of the category in each sample. In terms of Table 1, it represents those occupations with a mean of wealth of $16,000 or higher. The second category, representing the range in means of approximately $5,000 to $12,000, consists mainly of druggists, grocers, agents, and high-ranking craftsmen. The third category is best described as "craftsmen," although it also includes tavern keepers, minor public officials, dealers, tobacconists, and most teachers. In terms of the rank order it is the "middle class," with means ranging from approximately $1,500 to $4,000. The fourth category represents something of a departure from Table 1, as its few occupations—carter, clerk, accountant, and salesman—are pieced together out of the lower range of the middle category. The final category, representing occupational means under $500, are mostly semiskilled and unskilled laborers and domestic servants.

The most striking feature of Table 2 is the magnitude of upward mobility from the fourth and fifth categories, 21.7% and 23.3% respectively. Of course, we have already seen that abnormally high rates from these categories were to be expected, and that these rates reflect, to a large degree, the incompleteness of the directories rather than the actual mobility of manual and nonmanual workers. Upward mobility from the other categories is quite a bit lower, with 7.5% of the second category and 7.8% of the third category moving into higher categories by 1830.

More interesting, perhaps, than these purely quantitative expressions are the specific patterns of occupational change that Table 2 does not reveal. With regard to upward mobility, the most prominent pattern is the tendency for change to occur within situs, that is, between closely related occupations. For example, of the fifteen members of the second category who were upwardly mobile, all but one had become merchants by 1830. Seven of these fifteen had been storekeepers, three were grocers, and the others were sea captains, auctioneers, and agents. Not one had been a craftsman in 1820. Six craftsmen from the third category did move into the first by 1830, but the pattern is not destroyed. Two of the six became manufacturers of products closely related to their skills, and, interestingly, three became high-ranking government officials, a term that applies here to such positions as judge, alderman, and mayor. (As only two members of the 1820 sample were high-ranking public officials in 1820, these three cases hint that politics may have been an important avenue of mobility.)

The pattern of movement between related occupations is preserved in the largest cell of upward mobility, that which represents movement from the third to the second category. Of the twenty-six changes, twenty-two involved closely related occupations. Thus of five men who became retail clothiers, four had been tailors.[9] Both of those who became shoe retailers had been shoemakers. Of the six who became grocers, three had been innkeepers, one was a baker, and one was a butcher. Four cabinetmakers had all come from lower-ranked woodworking crafts. The editor had been a teacher. The pattern is retained even in the badly distorted bottom categories, with "white-collar" employees becoming merchants, storekeepers, and bank cashiers, and manual workers moving into higher manual positions.

Downward mobility presents a somewhat different pattern. Although the rather large movement from the first category (11.1%) presents almost a mirror image of movement into that category, the 12.5% downward mobility from the second category does not tend to occur between related occupations. Rather, there are two occupations, tavern keeper and minor public officer, neither of which required much investment or skill, that seem to have served as recourse for those who either failed at, or perhaps simply retired from higher-ranked occupations. Just under half of all those who were downwardly mobile into the third category became tavern keepers or officials, and yet these two occupations together accounted for only 5% of the third category in 1820.

In both its magnitude and its underlying pattern, then, occupational mobility in Philadelphia in the 1820s suggests a rather stable economic and social order. In subsequent decades this stability appears to break down. Space does not permit a detailed discussion of each of the matrices, but we can at least note that Table 3 and Table 4, representing the 1830s and 1840s respectively, depart from the patterns of Table 2. Specifically, the pattern of movement within situs is considerably weakened. In the most important cell in Table 2, representing mobility from the third to the second category, 85% of the cases moved into closely related occupations. In the 1830s this figure is reduced to 56%, and in the matrix representing the 1840s it is 37%. In the 1820s, as we have seen, none of the high-ranking craftsmen of the second category had

Table 3. Occupational Mobility, 1830-40

1840 Occupational Category	1830 Occupational Category					Total	% of Sample
	1	2	3	4	5		
1	192 (94.0%)	28 (12.3%)	29 (5.6%)	10 (20.8%)	7 (7.5%)	266	24.4
2	5 (2.5%)	162 (71.4%)	25 (4.8%)	2 (4.2%)	6 (6.5%)	200	18.3
3	4 (2.0%)	31 (13.7%)	452 (87.1%)	7 (14.6%)	14 (15.1%)	508	46.6
4	1 (.5%)	4 (1.8%)	6 (1.2%)	22 (45.8%)	5 (5.4%)	38	3.5
5	2 (1.0%)	2 (.9%)	7 (1.3%)	7 (14.6%)	61 (65.5%)	79	7.2
Total	204 (100.0%)	227 (100.1%)	519 (100.0%)	48 (100.0%)	93 (100.0%)	1091	100.0
% of Sample	18.7	20.8	47.6	4.4	8.5		

Table 4. Occupational Mobility, 1840-50

		1840 Occupational Category					Total	% of Sample
		1	*2*	*3*	*4*	*5*		
1850 Occupational Category	1	337 (92.1%)	10 (3.7%)	29 (3.3%)	10 (12.3%)	7 (3.1%)	393	21.4
	2	10 (2.7%)	228 (84.4%)	33 (3.7%)	4 (4.9%)	18 (8.0%)	293	16.0
	3	8 (2.2%)	21 (7.8%)	785 (88.0%)	8 (9.9%)	38 (16.8%)	860	46.9
	4	2 (.5%)	5 (1.9%)	5 (.6%)	47 (58.0%)	4 (1.8%)	63	3.4
	5	9 (2.5%)	6 (2.2%)	40 (4.5%)	12 (14.8%)	159 (70.4%)	226	12.3
	Total	366 (100.0%)	270 (100.0%)	892 (100.1%)	81 (100.0%)	226 (100.1%)	1835	100.0
	% of Sample	20.0	14.7	48.6	4.4	12.3		

moved into the "white-collar" occupations of the first. In
the 1830s, these craftsmen comprised one-third of the
upward mobility from the second category, and in the
1840s they constituted 60%.

Downward mobility reveals a similar change. The tendency for the downwardly mobile to become tavern keepers and public officials is overshadowed in the 1830s by
an increase in the number who are downwardly mobile
into low-ranking crafts and other manual positions. By
the 1840s, even the downward mobility of merchants is
affected. In the 1820 sample, fourteen merchants were
downwardly mobile, all to other "white-collar" occupations. But in the 1840 sample, fifteen of twenty-three
downwardly mobile merchants had assumed manual positions, seven as craftsmen and eight as laborers!

These and numerous other examples seem to indicate
a fundamental change in the pattern of occupational
mobility in the two decades following 1830. Occupational
mobility seems to have lost the orderliness that prevailed
in the 1820s. In that decade, mobility was largely a "white-
collar" phenomenon, a reshuffling of merchants, grocers,
and clerks. Those craftsmen who did advance tended to
remain within the general area in which they were
trained, usually to become retail merchants of goods they
formerly made themselves, or perhaps larger-scale manufacturers of these goods. In the 1830s and 1840s, however,
craftsmen comprised a larger and larger proportion of
those who were both upwardly and downwardly mobile,
and began moving into trades quite different from their
own. Merchants and storekeepers, for their part, also began moving into unexpected fields. All of this seems to
imply that some kind of basic change in the urban economy may have occurred in the period following 1830.
We are not lacking in theories that tend to support this

proposition, most notably the "merchant capitalism" theory of John R. Commons.[10] But this is a question to which we must return later. Perhaps it will be interesting to note, however, that in the 1830s downward mobility from the fourth category increased from 2.2% to 14.6%. The latter figure consists of seven cases, all of whom had been carters. It was in this decade that the streetcar and the railroad first appeared on the streets of Philadelphia.

Strangely, mobility in the 1850s, represented by Table 5, seems to have reverted somewhat to the pattern of the 1820s. Fewer craftsmen participated in occupational change, and larger numbers of them restricted their movements to related trades. Mobility from low-ranking to high-ranking crafts still shows a strong tendency toward unrelated areas, but of eleven changes from craftsmen to shopkeepers, ten were within situs. Approximately 46% of the changes from the third to the second category involved closely related occupations, which is a moderate reversal from the rapid downward trend of this percentage in the previous decades.

Thus far, I have discussed only the underlying patterns of mobility that do not appear in the matrices themselves. But what of the overall trend in the magnitude of mobility, as measured in the preceding tables? For the sake of simplicity, Table 6 summarizes all four mobility matrices, and is itself summarized on the bottom row, which presents an average upward and downward mobility rate for each decade. Average upward mobility, according to Table 6, follows no stable progression, but rather rises and falls with each decade. Its range lies between 10% and 15% for each decade, although we have already seen that this average is inflated by the artificially high percentages of the bottom two categories. Downward mobility, on the other hand, increases in magnitude each dec-

Table 5. Occupational Mobility, 1850-60

| | | 1850 Occupational Category | | | | | | |
		1	2	3	4	5	Total	% of Sample
1860 Occupational Category	1	181 (90.0%)	13 (8.9%)	17 (3.2%)	9 (20.5%)	4 (2.3%)	224	20.6
	2	7 (3.5%)	109 (74.7%)	28 (5.3%)	4 (9.1%)	9 (5.2%)	157	14.4
	3	6 (3.0%)	12 (8.2%)	439 (83.8%)	2 (4.5%)	31 (17.9%)	490	45.1
	4	7 (3.5%)	4 (2.7%)	13 (2.5%)	25 (56.8%)	8 (4.6%)	57	5.2
	5	—	8 (5.5%)	27 (5.2%)	4 (9.1%)	121 (69.9%)	160	14.7
	Total	201 (100.0%)	146 (100.0%)	524 (100.0%)	44 (100.0%)	173 (99.9%)	1088	100.0
	% of Sample	18.5	13.4	48.2	4.0	15.9		

Table 6. Summary of Occupational Mobility, 1820-60, in Five Occupational Categories Expressed as Percentages

Occupational Category	Upward Mobility				Downward Mobility			
	1820-30	1830-40	1840-50	1850-60	1820-30	1830-40	1840-50	1850-60
1	–	–	–	–	11.1	6.0	7.9	10.0
2	7.5	12.3	3.7	8.9	12.5	16.4	11.9	16.4
3	7.8	10.4	7.0	8.5	1.7	2.5	5.1	7.7
4	21.7	39.6	27.1	34.1	2.2	14.6	14.8	9.1
5	23.3	34.5	29.6	30.1	–	–	–	–
Average Mobility	10.0	15.0	11.0	14.1	6.2	6.9	7.3	9.6

ade. Actually, the progression is not consistent within each category, but seems to derive from the steady and rather large increase from the third category. This is by far the largest group in each sample, and includes most of the master craftsmen. It may be of some importance to note that downward mobility from this category increased from an unimportant 1.7% in the 1820s to 7.7% in the 1850s. At the same time, upward mobility from the middle category remained essentially constant. By the final decade the upward and downward mobility experiences of this critical group were about equal in magnitude.

In purely quantitive terms, then, upward occupational mobility appears to have been fairly stable in the four decades immediately preceding the Civil War, whereas downward mobility seems to have gradually increased. This overall pattern holds true whether occupational classifications are derived from our empirical rank order, or whether they are defined functionally, as in Table 7. Must we conclude, then, that the American city failed to generate increasing opportunities for economic advancement in the age of the "self-made man"? Not necessarily. Such a conclusion assumes the validity of inferring economic mobility from occupational mobility, and, as we have seen, this inference may well be invalid. The only statistical procedure that could be brought to bear on this problem in the present study was an indirect one, the analysis of variance relating the static variables of occupation and wealth. Its results are inconclusive. Specifically, occupation (regardless of how that term is defined) accounts for approximately one-sixth of the variation in the wealth of the members of the sample drawn from the 1860 census schedules.

Such a relationship does not appear to justify the inference of economic mobility from occupational mobility.

Table 7. Summary of Occupational Mobility, 1820-60, in Functional Categories, Expressed as Percentages

Occupational Category	Upward Mobility				Downward Mobility			
	1820-30	1830-40	1840-50	1850-60	1820-30	1830-40	1840-50	1850-60
Nonmanual Proprietors	—	—	—	—	8.4	10.5	11.5	11.0
Craftsmen	5.4	10.4	7.2	9.2	2.6	3.5	4.5	7.2
Clerks, etc.	25.0	37.8	30.0	26.4	—	—	3.7	5.7
Unskilled Workers	21.7	32.1	28.1	28.3	—	—	—	—
Average Mobility	9.1	15.3	12.8	14.9	4.6	6.2	7.1	8.6

Neither does it necessarily invalidate it. What it does suggest is that economic mobility, like social mobility, is a complex phenomenon that is best approached through complex, rather than unidimensional procedures. It is precisely this consideration that leads us to consider a second variable for observing mobility. Perhaps it will prove to be a more valid index of economic mobility. Perhaps it can be combined with occupational mobility to provide a better inference than either variable acting alone.

Residential Mobility

That residence should be that second variable was dictated by the format of the city directories. It is a variable that we would probably have turned to in any event, for residence is a workhorse in the literature of stratification. W. Lloyd Warner's famous (and, admittedly, controversial) Index of Status Characteristics, for example, consists of four variables: occupation, source of income, and two variations of the concept of residence, house type and dwelling area.[11] This, of course, does not mean that we should not be just as skeptical of residence as we were of occupation, and we will subject it to the same examination. It does indicate, however, that we have expanded our methodology in a very important direction.

Since our information extends only to the address of each sample member, "residence" will refer not to the type, size, or value of each house but to its location. Before this concept acquires meaning, therefore, we must discover some means of differentiating one location from another. That is, we must define the neighborhoods of the city, just as we prepared our ranking of occupations. In the present study this was achieved through two methods.

First, local tax records were used to define "neighborhoods" in strictly quantitative terms. A preliminary scan-
ning of the tax register indicated that neighborhoods did
in fact exist (that houses in a given area of the city had
very similar assessments), and that these neighborhoods
were much larger than the city's political wards. This
means that a Philadelphia ward map, containing average
residential assessments within each ward, can be used as
a fairly reliable guide to the boundaries of the city's
neighborhoods.

Figure 1 presents just such a map, based on the wards
and tax records of 1820. The area presented is not merely
the City of Philadelphia (the rectangle of fourteen wards
stretching between the Delaware and Schuylkill rivers),
but also includes those semiautonomous districts ("liberties") that had grown up along the Delaware long before
the city itself filled up from river to river. In 1820, population was of urban density throughout each of the eastern city wards and throughout the adjoining districts, but
tapered sharply in the western portions of the long wards
to the west of 4th Street. Thus, Philadelphia in 1820 was
a city of approximately 120,000 inhabitants, extending
some three miles along the Delaware River, with a maximum width of about a mile.[12] In its northern and southern extensions, the distance from the edge of the city to
the river was perhaps no more than a half-mile.

The average assessments in Figure 1 reveal a very interesting pattern. Specifically, there is a direct and very
pronounced relationship between high average assessment and centrality. The highest averages are in the heart
of the city, in four wards comprising a small square of
perhaps one quarter of a square mile. Immediately to the
west of this square are wards with somewhat lower
averages, and immediately north and south of it are wards

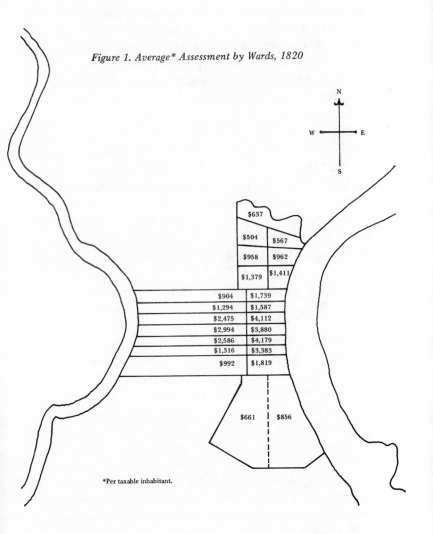

Figure 1. Average* Assessment by Wards, 1820

*Per taxable inhabitant.

with averages that are appreciably lower. These averages, in turn, are significantly higher than those on the perimeter of the city. The fact that the average assessment in each eastern ward is higher than in the ward immediately to its west represents an enlargement of this basic pattern, once the "center" of the city is located—not at its geographic center, but a few blocks west of the Delaware, midway between the northern and southern extremes of dense population.

If we were to rely solely on Figure 1, we would describe the city as a series of radiating zones of affluence, much like the classic theory of Park and Burgess. According to this theory, the central zone is an affluent one, but the first concentric ring is the poorest. Thereafter, the quality of the neighborhood increases, all the way out to the suburbs.[13] The pre-Civil War city, however, seems to present a partial reversal of this pattern. The interior zone is the most affluent, the surrounding ring is middle class, and the urban poor are located on the periphery.

In light of the absence of urban transportation systems in the early nineteenth-century city, this reversal of the classic pattern should be no surprise. The major institutions of the city—the port, the banks, the Merchants' Coffee House, the State House, the fashionable and important shops—were all located in its center. Before the omnibus and the streetcar, proximity to these institutions was the first requisite of urban life and, accordingly, the major criterion for judging the desirability of a neighborhood. Yet, to define the city's neighborhoods solely in terms of average ward assessments is clearly to oversimplify a complex matter. Accordingly, Figure 1 (and subsequent maps that were prepared for each decade) was examined in the light of qualitative data, usually in the form of descriptions of the city. Interestingly, the results of these two basic methods coincide quite closely. The following, for example, is from a description of Philadelphia in 1820 by its greatest historian:

> the smart quarter of the city was that in the vicinity of Third and Spruce streets. In the circle of a few blocks, around the spot where Thomas Willing had fixed his home, there were now a number of fine houses. Many substantial Quaker families were settled in Arch street, and some had gone out to Spring Garden and the Northern Liberties where they had built themselves large and comfortable residences. This neighborhood, however, was identified in most minds with butchers, drovers, and market people. The negro and poor white quarters were already in and south of Cedar or South street. Chestnut street was early spoken of as the city's fashionable promenade ground.[14]

Third and Spruce streets ("the smart quarter"), Chestnut ("the city's fashionable promenade ground"), and Arch Street (the home of "many substantial Quaker families") all lay within the small, inner zone as defined by Figure 1. Spring Garden does not appear on our map because it was not yet taxed by the city, but Northern Liberties, just to the north of the city's political boundary and just east of Spring Garden, does. It is largely a "middle class" region, except for its northern extremes, and in the above description it is "identified in most minds with butchers, drovers, and market people." As the public markets of Northern Liberties were located in its southern wards, Oberholtzer's description obviously applies to these wards; in other words, to those with middle-class averages. Finally, the "negro and poor white quarters," south of Cedar Street, are the low-average wards at the bottom of Figure 1. Indeed, only one item in Oberholt-

zer's description fails to coincide with Figure 1. The
"comfortable residences" of Northern Liberties and
Spring Garden seem to intrude on our middle-class
neighborhood. Actually, subsequent maps indicate that
this was merely the advance guard of a northward expansion of the wealthy community.

Thus, it is with some confidence that we have identified three areas, or zones, of Philadelphia, each associated
with a particular level of residential life. These zones
were defined for 1820 by Figure 1, and then adjusted
slightly on the basis of descriptive data. This procedure
was repeated for each decade, retaining the three-zone
system but changing its boundaries to reflect the growth
and history of the city. Within this system, each member
of the four directory samples was traced from residence to
residence, just as he was traced from occupation to occupation.

*Relations between Occupational and
Residential Mobility*

Table 8 summarizes the residential mobility of each
sample. Interestingly, its results are strikingly similar to
the overall pattern of occupational mobility in both magnitude and trend. Average upward mobility remained
stable for each group through the first three decades, and
decreased somewhat during the fourth. Actually, this decline probably reflects an error of judgment in defining
the zonal boundaries of 1860. Relative to the previous
decades, the proportion of the final sample in the outer
zone was quite large, indicating that the inner zones
should perhaps have been expanded more than they
were. If this had been done, the decline in upward residential mobility would probably have been erased, and

Table 8. Summary of Residential Mobility, 1820-60, Expressed as Percentages

	Upward (Converging) Mobility				Downward (Radiating) Mobility			
	1820-30	1830-40	1840-50	1850-60	1820-30	1830-40	1840-50	1850-60
Zone 1								
To Zone 2					14.3	19.0	19.4	24.1
To Zone 3					4.2	9.2	9.7	11.8
Total					18.5	28.2	29.1	35.9
Zone 2								
To Zone 3					10.3	14.4	21.7	28.3
Average Downward Mobility					14.2	21.4	24.7	31.8
Zone 2								
To Zone 1	11.0	11.3	11.1	9.6				
Zone 3								
To Zone 2	12.4	11.0	12.3	7.8				
To Zone 1	3.7	5.5	3.2	3.8				
Total	16.1	16.5	15.5	11.6				
Average Upward Mobility	13.7	13.9	13.4	10.9				

mobility would have been stable throughout the forty-year period.

Downward residential mobility also resembles occupational mobility, in that it increased through each decade for all groups. Its magnitude relative to upward mobility, however, was much greater than was the case with the first variable. In the 1820s, upward and downward residential mobility were about equal in magnitude. Thereafter, the latter became increasingly more common. Although the 3:1 ratio indicated in Table 8 is probably inflated, downward residential mobility (as defined here) was perhaps twice as high as upward mobility in the 1850s.

Thus, with both of our measurements we have obtained similar results: stable upward and increasing downward mobility. What, then, do we make of these results? Aside from their intrinsic interest, what do they tell us about the fluidity of the urban economic class system? The appropriate statistical analysis of this question (correlating economic mobility with occupational and residential mobility) is not possible with the data that are available, and the "indirect" analysis (of the static variables of wealth, occupation, and residence) is again inconclusive. Specifically, when both nominal variables are combined into a two-way analysis of the variation in wealth, the amount of variation accounted for is not appreciably different from the amount explained by each nominal variable acting alone.[15] This peculiar fact is explained by the correlation between occupation and residence, that is, by the tendency of members of high-ranking occupations to reside in the inner zone, and for members of low-ranking occupations to reside in the outer zone (see Table 9). Thus, for purposes of analyzing variation in wealth, we may use either variable, or we may use both. The same variation is explained in each case.

Table 9. *Residential Distribution of Occupational Categories, 1820-60, Expressed as Percentages*

Occupational Category

	1	2	3	4	5	Average
1820 Sample						
Zone 1	60.2	33.0	21.5	23.9	5.5	30.2
Zone 2	26.0	35.5	34.8	45.5	30.1	33.4
Zone 3	13.8	31.5	43.7	30.4	64.4	36.4
1830 Sample						
Zone 1	57.3	37.5	27.3	27.1	22.6	34.7
Zone 2	29.0	32.5	35.4	47.9	32.4	34.0
Zone 3	13.7	29.9	37.3	25.1	45.2	31.3
1840 Sample						
Zone 1	51.4	26.3	17.2	13.6	13.7	24.7
Zone 2	34.7	35.6	37.5	43.1	25.7	35.5
Zone 3	13.9	38.2	45.2	43.2	60.6	39.8
1850 Sample						
Zone 1	51.8	24.7	16.8	9.1	7.5	22.5
Zone 2	26.5	26.7	26.3	34.0	28.4	26.9
Zone 3	22.0	48.7	57.0	56.7	64.2	50.6

Have we added nothing, then, with our second variable? Again, we must remember that it is the dynamic variables of economic, occupational, and residential mobility that we are interested in. We have neither proved nor disproved our basic inference, and we cannot do so until we can find a direct measurement of economic mobility. In this connection, it is interesting to note that we are able to correlate occupational and residential mobility, and that the relationship between them is actually quite weak. As Table 10 indicates, none of our samples reveal a strong direct or inverse relationship between occupational and residential mobility. Perhaps they are essentially unrelated phenomena, each, in turn, unrelated

Table 10. Cross-Classification of Occupational and Residential Mobility,
1820-60

1820 Sample
Occupational Mobility

		Downward	Static	Upward	Total
Residential	Downward	8	69	9	86
Mobility	Static	39	674	63	776
	Upward	9	74	8	91
	Total	56	817	80	953
		G = −.041			

1830 Sample
Occupational Mobility

		Downward	Static	Upward	Total
Residential	Downward	10	123	27	160
Mobility	Static	59	685	88	832
	Upward	6	69	24	99
	Total	75	877	139	1091
		G = .042			

1840 Sample
Occupational Mobility

		Downward	Static	Upward	Total
Residential	Downward	36	209	28	273
Mobility	Static	73	1200	104	1377
	Upward	13	140	32	185
	Total	122	1549	164	1835
		G = .194			

1850 Sample
Occupational Mobility

		Downward	Static	Upward	Total
Residential	Downward	22	131	18	171
Mobility	Static	61	672	92	825
	Upward	8	68	16	92
	Total	91	871	126	1088
		G = .157			

to economic mobility. Or, perhaps they are significant and *additive* components of economic mobility, providing between them a reliable estimate of its magnitude and trend.

If occupational and residential mobility are additive components of economic mobility, we may come closer to a valid inference by combining both nominal variables into a new set of matrices that would represent mobility within both dimensions simultaneously. In the preceding matrices, the inference of each particular sample member's economic mobility depended almost entirely on which variable was being observed. As we have seen in Table 10, those who represented upward and downward mobility in our occupational matrices were not those who were mobile in our residential matrices. The coincidence of overall results has perhaps served to distract our attention from this problem, but it is a significant one nonetheless. What would we be thinking now if mobility rates on each dimension had contradicted the other?

By combining the two variables, we establish what would seem to be more realistic criteria for inferring economic (and probably social) mobility. For example, in the combined matrices, upward occupational mobility that is accompanied by movement to a wealthier neighborhood would be regarded as a clear indication of upward economic mobility. But if the same upward occupational change had been accompanied by movement to a poorer neighborhood, the individual's status could well be regarded as unchanged. In all probability, he achieved the upward occupational mobility only while moving to a neighborhood where the rents were lower and the incomes smaller.

Table 11 summarizes the results of four new five by five matrices representing the combination of the two

Table 11. Summary of Two-Dimensional Mobility, 1820-60, Expressed as Percentages

	Upward Mobility				Downward Mobility			
	1820	1830	1840	1850	1820	1830	1840	1850
Category 1	–	–	–	–	10.3	9.7	11.7	19.1
2	9.3	13.6	6.9	12.6	14.2	18.5	18.8	16.0
3	10.1	12.9	7.3	9.8	11.9	15.3	19.6	26.0
4	20.9	22.7	18.6	15.4	2.6	4.8	7.8	8.8
5	23.0	32.4	30.3	31.3	–	–	–	–
Average	14.4	17.7	14.5	16.6	9.6	12.5	14.5	17.2

nominal variables. In the first category of these matrices are those members of the first occupational category who lived in Zone 1 and Zone 2. The second category consists of the remainder of the first occupational category (those who lived in Zone 3) as well as the members of the second category who lived in Zones 1 and 2. Each occupational category and residential zone is divided in this manner except the lowest occupational category, which is placed entirely in the fifth combined category. The results generated by these matrices are, unsurprisingly, quite similar to those we have observed within each separate dimension. Average upward mobility remained rather stable throughout the period, and average downward mobility gradually increased until it approximated the magnitude of the former. It is doubtful that any other method of classifying and combining occupations and residence, or even the elimination of the built-in errors that we have noted, would have produced results that would contradict this basic generalization.

The question of whether or not these patterns validly indicate the magnitude of economic or social mobility remains largely a matter of conjecture. On the other hand, they do seem to point to a significant alternation of the urban social structure that is itself relevant to the question of fluidity. Specifically, the steady expansion of the magnitude of downward occupational and residential mobility strongly suggests that the lower-ranked occupations and neighborhoods were themselves expanding— that is, the city's lower classes were growing significantly faster than the rest of its population. In addition, the specific patterns of occupational change, in the 1830s and 1840s especially, indicate that this shift in the class pyramid may have been related to a critical change in the city's economic life.

Table 12. *Proportion of Occupational Groups to the Adult Male Working Force, 1820 and 1860, Expressed as Percentages*

	1820^a	1860^b
Merchants and Professionals	21.5	24.2
Manufacturers	1.0	2.3
Total Nonmanual Proprietors	22.5	26.5
Clerical Workers	4.6	2.9
Total Nonmanual	27.1	29.4
Master Craftsmen	34.3	c
Journeymen Craftsmen	21.9	c
Total Craftsmen	56.2	47.0
Day Laborers	5.8	13.9
Other Unskilled and Service Workers	10.9	9.7
Total Unskilled Workers	16.7	23.6
Total, Manual	72.9	70.6
Total	100.0	100.0

a. **Edward Whitely**, *The Philadelphia Directory and Register for 1820* (Philadelphia, McCarty & Davis, 1820); manuscript tax assessors' lists, County of Philadelphia, 1820.

b. Manuscript schedules of inhabitants of the County of Philadelphia, Eighth United States Census, 1860.

c. Not specified.

Table 12 sheds a small amount of light on this matter by comparing the relative sizes of occupational groups in 1820 and again in 1860. In this comparison, one significant shift is evident. Although the ratio between nonmanual and manual positions remained about the same, the latter group reveals a significant expansion of unskilled positions and contraction of skilled positions. Thus, the proportion of craftsmen to the adult male working force declined from 56.2% to 47%, whereas the proportion of unskilled workers increased from 16.7% to 23.6%. The growth of the unskilled category, furthermore, is more than accounted for by increases in day laborers from 5.8% to 13.9%.

But the most significant shift in the occupational structure is the one that Table 12 cannot measure, the increase in the number and proportion of journeymen craftsmen. We have already seen that the 1860 census schedules do not generally make the distinction between masters and journeymen. Other data, on the other hand, indicate that the number of journeymen in Philadelphia in 1860 was at least 40,000, and was possibly as high as 50,000.[16] From our sample from the census schedules we may project a total craftsman population of approximately 60,000. From these figures, therefore, we may derive a conservative ratio of journeymen to masters of 2:1. This compares to the 1820 ratio of approximately 2:3, indicating a tripling of the proportion of journeymen, relative to masters, in the forty years before the Civil War. When this assumed 2:1 ratio is applied to Table 12, the previously noted changes are enormously heightened. The proportion of master craftsmen to the total work force is reduced by more than one-half, from over 34% to approximately 16%. The total manual wage-earning class increases from a minority of 38.6% to a majority of some 55%. In 1820, in other words, there was a skilled, proprietary position for almost every skilled and unskilled wage-earning position. By 1860 the manual, wage-earning jobs outnumbered the manual proprietorship by more than three to one.

It would be difficult to exaggerate the importance of this shift. In 1820, Philadelphia was dominated, numerically and physically, by small shops and shopkeepers. The demand for master craftsmen was great enough to provide any ambitious and competent journeyman with the opportunity to set up his own shop. During the next forty years, the number of shops remained substantially the same. But at the same time the population had quadrupled, and in this new city of a half-million people, a

few thousand could no longer dominate the landscape.
Nor could a few thousand proprietorships give much
hope to forty or fifty thousand journeymen. Never again
would this American city be described, as John Fanning
Watson once described it, as a place where,

> almost every apprentice, when of age, ran his equal
> chance for his share of business in his neighborhood, by
> setting up for himself, and, with an apprentice or two,
> getting into a cheap location, and by dint of applica-
> tion and good work, recommending himself to his
> neighborhood.[17]

A Theory and the Data

What had happened to Philadelphia since the days when,
as Watson continues, "every shoemaker or tailor was a
man for himself"?[18] One important event, no doubt, was
the massive immigration of Irish in the 1840s—poor,
rural Irish, absolutely unequipped for urban life.[19] The
significant increase in day laborers, noted in Table 12,
consisted largely of Irish (and to a lesser extent German)
immigrants. But a more fundamental answer is suggested
by John R. Commons' theory of "merchant capitalism"
as the intervening stage between craft and factory production in American history. This theory, first explored by
Commons a half-century ago in a study of American (and
usually Philadelphia) shoemakers, has gradually become
the most widely respected interpretation of economic
change in the immediate pre-Civil War period.[20] In
essence, it states that the rapid expansion of markets,
created by the revolutionary developments in transportation, eroded the craft system by giving large merchants
increasing control over the production of goods. In the

days before the canal and the railroad, indeed before the
Jeffersonian embargo and the War of 1812, the large,
urban merchants interested themselves but little in
American manufacturing. In the 1820s, however, and
especially in the 1830s, it was becoming evident to the
organizers of trade that the greatest opportunities lay not
to the east but to the west and south. This was a trade of
an entirely different type—indeed, the reverse of that
trade which had occupied urban merchants for generations. Now, instead of importing manufactured goods
from Europe and exporting American raw materials,
merchants would turn increasingly to the westward and
southward shipment of Eastern manufactures, in exchange for grain, meat and cotton. In the exploitation of
these new markets, the merchant had numerous advantages over the master craftsman. Only the merchant could
afford to invest in a stock of merchandise large enough to
make shipments on a profitable basis to Illinois or Alabama. Only the merchant could afford to wait six months
for payment, or pay the rent on a large warehouse. Only
the merchant had the skill, the credit, and the personal
contacts to organize such a trade. As a consequence, the
merchant increasingly dominated the craftsman. At first,
he merely bought his product. But the advantages of
large-scale production, of control over the supply of
goods, indeed, of the elimination of the profits of the
independent craftsmen, were too obvious. Increasingly
the merchant organized production himself, bringing
large numbers of journeymen under one roof, training
new journeymen in brief periods for specialized tasks,
and hiring former masters to serve as foremen. By the
mid-1830s, according to Commons, the merchant-manu-
facturer had emerged into full view in the Philadelphia
shoe industry. By the 1840s he dominated it.[21]

The value of Commons' theory in the present context
is that it helps to explain the emergence of a large, "blue-
collar" working force in a period that precedes, in all but
a few industries, the emergence of the mechanized factory. Historians have long recognized the significance of
industrialization in shaping the career expectations of the
working man, but in doing so they have tended to miss
the significance of the ante-bellum period. The reason,
no doubt, rests in the customary association of industrialization with the mechanization of production, and in
the further association of mechanization with the latter
decades of the nineteenth century. In the shoemaking
industry, for example, mechanization was not fully accomplished until the 1880s.[22] Yet, from the standpoint
of the master and journeyman shoemaker, the industry
experienced its most critical changes a full fifty years
earlier.

An extensive report on manufacturing in Philadelphia,
published in 1858, indicates that the same sequence held
true for most other industries as well. The clothing industry seems to confirm Commons' theory in detail.[23] In
other industries, such as furniture, carriages, bricks, rope,
cigars, brushes, barrels, candy, and hats, it is not clear
just who the manufacturer was—whether he had previously been an import-export merchant, or whether he
had risen from the ranks of the craftsmen. But in each of
these industries it is evident that the growth of a small
number of large producers was accomplished with little
mechanization of the manufacturing process. In each of
these industries the mechanized factory may have come
much later. But the working force that is usually associated with this factory preceded the Civil War.

A number of industries, of course, were mechanized
before the Civil War. In most of these—metals, machine-

ry, paper, beer and ale, liquor—production had been
organized into a few large shops even before the beginning of our period. The mechanization of the textile
industry before the Civil War is classic, and needs no
elaboration for the nation's third largest area of textile
production. Yet, perhaps ironically, the textile industry
is not primarily responsible for the restructuring of the
working population that this paper has explored. Most of
the operatives in the cotton and woolen mills of Philadelphia were women and children. In this study, we have
concerned ourselves only with their husbands and fathers.

Thus, even though the adult male factory operative
was primarily a phenomenon of the latter nineteenth century, the emergence of a large wage-earning class was evident around mid-century. The numerical domination of
this class in Philadelphia was probably achieved in the
1850s, the product of forces that had become visible in
the 1830s and 1840s. It is here that our mobility matrices
become especially revealing. For our proposition of critical change and our observed patterns of mobility are
mutually reinforcing. The expansion of the lower classes
tends to explain the observed growth of downward mobility. In turn, the disruption in the 1830s and 1840s of
stable patterns of occupational mobility seems to reflect
the impact of "merchant capitalism" on the economic
life of the city.

In one very important sense, then, economic change in
ante-bellum Philadelphia seems to have lessened opportunity for worldly advancement. But a decline in the extensiveness of opportunity does not necessarily make the
success ideology less potent. The American Dream is fed,
not by such mundane matters as mobility matrices, but
by isolated cases of spectacular success. And in Philadelphia, the very forces that seem to have threatened the

extensiveness of upward mobility also seem to have made the stakes a great deal more interesting. The schedules of the 1860 census may give us an interesting perspective on this matter by permitting a tabulation of the distribution of wealth at the end of our period. Figure 2, a Lorenz Curve, reveals that distribution to be one of remarkable inequality. One-third of the sample of male family is described as propertyless.[24] When the curve begins it rises very slowly until it reaches the upper 20% of the sample, the bottom 80% owning a mere 3% of the sample's reported wealth. Even the next to highest 10% owned less than their "equal share" of the wealth. Thus, it is only in describing the wealth of the richest 10% of the sample that the curve begins to soar. The wealthiest 10% owned 89% of the sample's wealth. The wealthiest 1% owned one half!

The slope of this curve may be interpreted statistically by calculating the Schutz Coefficient of Inequality, a measure defining absolute equality as 0 and values approaching 1.0 as reflecting increasing degrees of inequality.[25] The Schutz Coefficient for Figure 2 is an understandably high .79. Unfortunately, we cannot compare this measure to earlier points in time, as our earlier data are not comparable to the schedules of the Eighth Census. One item, however, may be of some use. Tabular tax assessment data for the city of Boston seems to provide at least a rough basis for assessing change in the distribution of wealth.[26] If we accept these data on faith, they yield Coefficients of .537 for 1820, .637 for 1830, and .694 for 1845. Comparing these figures to .79 for Philadelphia in 1860 reveals a picture of increasing inequality.

In any case, the inequality of the distribution of wealth in 1860 speaks for itself. Philadelphia, on the eve of the Civil War, was a society of extreme economic stratifica-

Figure 2. The Distribution of Wealth: Philadelphia, 1860

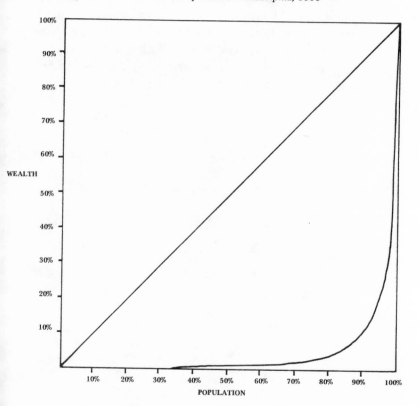

tion. Many of its inhabitants were poor, and most were entirely dependent on the continued wages of one or two persons. Opportunities for establishing some other basis of economic support were seemingly on the decline. On the other hand, for those who did dream of economic success, the drama of that dream must have been considerably heightened by the appearance of individual fortunes of unprecedented proportions. Indeed, in these two statements we come to the very heart of both opportunity and change in the ante-bellum American city. For never before were the rich so rich. And never before were the poor so plentiful.

1. *Junius Tracts* (New York, 1844), p. 15.

2. Ibid., p. 6.

3. National Opinion Research Center, "Jobs and Occupations: A Popular Evaluation," *Opinion News* September 1, 1947, pp. 3–13.

4. See Irwin G. Wyllie, *The Self-Made Man in America* (New Brunswick, 1954), and John G. Cawelti, *Apostles of the Self-Made Man* (Chicago, 1965).

5. Or, we may dispense with the inference altogether by observing, not changes in occupation, but changes in levels of wealth or income. This would constitute a direct study of economic mobility. Unfortunately, the incompleteness of data in Philadelphia made such a procedure impossible in the present study.

6. "The Historical Study of Vertical Mobility," *Historical Methods Newsletter, 1* (September 1968), 1–13.

7. The average employed here is the mean, since it is less susceptible to variation caused by sampling error than is the median. No workable data were discovered in Philadelphia for averaging incomes.

8. See, for example, *The Philadelphia Directory and Register . . .* (Philadelphia, 1820).

9. The problem of understanding the meanings (and especially the possible interchangeability) of occupational terms is a highly critical and difficult one to resolve. Clothiers and tailors, for example, were distinguished more by the type of shop each maintained than by the functions of selling or sewing.

10. Probably the earliest articulation of merchant capitalism as a specific stage of American economic development is John R. Commons' "American Shoemakers, 1648–1895," *Quarterly Journal of Economics, 24* (1909), 39–84.

11. W. Lloyd Warner, *Social Class in America*, paperback edition (New York, 1960). See especially, pp. 131–85.

12. The Fourth U.S. Census reports the population of the city at 63,802, and the remainder of Philadelphia County at 73,295. A portion of the latter lived outside the area of density, on farms and in other towns. United States Census Office, *Census for 1820* (Washington, 1821), p. 17.

13. Robert Park and Ernest W. Burgess, *The City* (Chicago, 1925).

14. Ellis Paxson Oberholtzer, *Philadelphia: A History of the City and Its People* (Philadelphia, n.d.), 2, 102.

15. See Blumin, "The Historical Study of Vertical Mobility," for a detailed explanation of this analysis.

16. The two most important sources of this estimate are, United States Census Office, *Manufactures of the United States in 1860* (Washington, 1864), pp. 522–27, and Edwin T. Freedley, *Philadelphia and its Manufactures* (Philadelphia, 1858).

17. John F. Watson, *Annals of Philadelphia, and Pennsylvania, in the Olden Time* (Philadelphia, 1900), *1*, 220–21. Watson wrote these words in 1844, the same year that Colton wrote of the "self-made man," to lament the passing of a simpler and nobler era.

18. Ibid.

19. In three of our four decades, Philadelphia grew at a rate of approximately 38% per decade. In the 1840s, the city's rate of growth was approximately 58%.

20. Commons, "American Shoemakers," particularly pp. 59–72. The most significant adoptions of this theory are George R. Taylor, *The Transportation Revolution, 1815–1860* (New York, 1951), and Louis M. Hacker, *The Triumph of American Capitalism* (New York, 1940). Yet it spent more than a few years in obscurity. In 1926, Harvey A. Wooster wrote of it as, "A Forgotten Factor in American Industrial History," in the *American Economic Review, 16* (March 1926), 14–27.

21. Commons, "American Shoemakers," pp. 63–64.

22. Ibid., p. 73. A study of the boot and shoe industry conducted by the state a few years before Commons' article appeared concurs in this timetable: Secretary of Internal Affairs of the Commonwealth of Pennsylvania, *Annual Report, 29*, Part 3 (Harrisburg, 1902).

23. Freedley, *Philadelphia and its Manufactures*, p. 220.

24. The enumerators' instructions called for no entry in the property columns if the individual reported less than $100, although there were in fact many entries below $100. In addition, pride and suspicion undoubtedly caused some respondents to report higher equities and some to report lower equities. Thus, the proportion who were truly propertyless may have been somewhat higher or lower than one-third.

25. Robert R. Schutz, "On the Measurement of Income Inequality," *American Economic Review, 41* (1951), 107–22.

26. Lemuel Shattuck, *Report of the Committee of the City Council Appointed to Obtain the Census of Boston for the Year 1845* . . . (Boston, 1846), p. 95.

SOCIAL STRUCTURE IN HAMILTON, ONTARIO

Michael B. Katz

Consider three men who lived in Hamilton, Ontario, in the early 1850s:

E. McGarry, a thirty-year-old Roman Catholic laborer born in Ireland lived in a two-story frame house on Merrick Street, which he rented for £11 a year. With him lived his wife, two sons, aged seven and five, and his two-year-old daughter. Sharing the house were McGarry's twenty-five-year-old laborer brother, his young wife and infant daughter. Aside from his rent, McGarry reported £3 of personal property and his earnings averaged less than £1 a week. Although he must have lived always on the edge of economic disaster, McGarry was a bit more well-off than three-quarters of the laborers in Hamilton.

J. McFatradge, a forty-year-old Presbyterian shoemaker also born in Ireland, owned his own house, a two-story frame dwelling on Vine Street assessed at £9 annual value; his income was £50 per year. McFatradge's family consisted of his thirty-five-year-old wife, also born in Ireland, and his five children, two sons aged twelve and six and three daughters aged fifteen, four, and two; the McFatradges kept one boarder but no servants.

J. D. Pringle, prosperous young Canadian-born lawyer and member of the Church of Scotland, rented a house on Merrick Street for which he paid the enormous sum of £45; he earned a solid £150 per year. Pringle, aged thirty-two, had a twenty-three-year-old wife and a two-year-old daughter. Naturally enough, the well-off Pringles kept a servant.

Messrs. McGarry, McFatradge, and Pringle did nothing in particular that justifies their rescue from historical oblivion. They were perfectly ordinary and unremarkable citizens of a mid-nineteenth-century city. Yet their very lack of historical importance gives them a significance from one point of view, for these were, in fact, men "representative" of the Hamilton population in certain ways. In just what sense were they representative? How do we know that they were representative? What is the significance of their representativeness? The answers to these questions require placing Messrs. McGarry, McFatradge, and Pringle back into the social context from which they have been abstracted and plotting the complex series of relationships that will reveal its recurring patterns. In short, our three obscure gentlemen pose the problem of the nature of nineteenth-century urban social structure.

This paper reports our experience to date in an ongoing examination of the impact of industrialization on nineteenth-century social structure and social mobility.[1] For these purposes we chose to study the city of Hamilton, Ontario, from 1850 to 1880. A lakeport about forty miles west of Toronto, Hamilton expanded and changed from a prosperous commercial city of 14,112 people, very few of whom worked in settings larger than a shop in 1851, to a burgeoning industrial center with a population of 35,961 and fifty-two factories in 1881. The sample for this study is the entire population of the city in each of four census years. For each year we shall code, in their entirety, the manuscript census and assessment rolls. To date we have coded and partly analyzed the assessment roll of

1852 together with some census data. The discussion that follows reports, first, on the relations between wealth, occupation, and age in mid-nineteenth-century Hamilton and then reflects on the bearing of these relationships on problems of social stability and social class.[2]

When we complete our study, we expect to find that an increase in social and economic stratification accompanied industrialization and urbanization, which had contradictory effects upon social mobility. On the one hand, new white-collar and managerial positions came into existence in large numbers; yet the increased social distance brought about by industrialization and the formation of an industrial working class increased the odds against lower-class children or adults improving their position. Promoting or retarding chances of individuals in this period were cultural patterns (such as family size and school attendance) associated with their social, ethnic, or religious affiliation; religious and ethnic affiliations themselves enhanced or diminished an individual's chances in a way that cut across economic lines.[3]

Such is the hypothesis of the study. Still it must be emphasized that we are more interested in being able to arrive at some reasonable suggestion that it is true, false, or somewhere in the middle than we are in just which one of the three it happens to be. But we are a long way from that point. At the moment we have partly analyzed three variables—wealth, occupation, and age—in 1851 and 1852.

Wealth, Occupation, and Age

To begin we shall consider *general* patterns relating to wealth, occupation, and age. When wealth is used here it refers to the total assessed value of an individual's property. In all a figure representing wealth exists for 2,555 individuals in 1852. Of these all but 130 were men.[4] Table 1 shows the distribution of wealth within this group, and two observations of considerable importance emerge from a study of it. First, we can safely conclude that at least nine-tenths of the poorest 40% of the work force were disenfranchised for economic reasons because the 40% line corresponds roughly to the suffrage qualification: £11.2 for urban tenants and £5.5 for urban home-owners. If the purpose of suffrage legislation was to keep the vote from those too poor to have a stake in society, then we may define the group below the fortieth economic percentile as the poor.[5]

The relationship between home ownership and wealth was perfectly linear, as revealed in Table 2. As a whole, people in Hamilton were over two and one-half times as likely to rent as to own their home. In fact, except for people in the top economic tenth of the work force, everyone was more likely to rent than to own, although the proportion of home owners to renters increased at each higher economic level.

The second observation relating to Table 1 concerns the inequality in the distribution of wealth. Nearly half

Table 1. Total Assessed Population of Hamilton According to the Assessment Roll of 1852 Divided into Eight Major Economic Groups

Income Percentile	Range in Pounds	Percentage of Total Assessed Wealth	
0–20	1–5	1.6	
20–40	6–11	4.3	
40–60	12–18	7.3	
60–80	19–37	13.2	
80–90	38–78	13.7	
90–95	79–143	13.1	
95–99	144–488	25.5	
99–100	489–2159	21.3	100%

Table 2. *Relationship Between Homeownership and Wealth Among Total Assessed Population in Hamilton, 1852*

Income Percentile	Home Owners	Non-Home Owners	Total
0– 20	24	494	518
	4.6%	95.4%	
20– 40	100	382	482
	20.7%	79.3%	
40– 60	155	389	544
	28.5%	71.5%	
60– 80	175	320	493
	35.4%	64.6%	
80– 90	99	158	257
	38.6%	61.4%	
90– 95	72	54	126
	57.1%	42.9%	
95– 99	63	40	103
	61.2%	38.8%	
99–100	20	4	24
	83.3%	16.7%	
	708	1841	

the assessed wealth in the city was in the hands of a mere 5% of the work force, or about 125 people. At the other end of the spectrum, the bottom 20%, or roughly the poorest 500 persons, controlled only 1.6% of the wealth. One way to examine the significance of the distribution of wealth is to compare it to that in contemporary society. Has there been a steady trend toward greater equality for over a century? Or, alternatively and consistently with the hypothesis advanced earlier, did inequality increase with the onset of industrialism and continue until checked in the twentieth century by the intervention of government? Or is the division of wealth today even less equitable? We do not yet know the answers to these questions, but analysis of future assessment rolls should help us begin to find them.[6] For now it is important to note that the distribution of wealth is significant not only in itself but in relation to other aspects of the social structure as well: most notably, occupation.

Over two hundred distinct occupations existed in Hamilton in 1852. With a few minor exceptions we have coded occupation from both assessment and census exactly as it appears on the manuscript. This does not indicate insensitivity to the problem of classification; indeed, it has been a major concern to date. However, there are many possible ways of classifying occupations, and it is important to retain the flexibility to experiment with several.

Aside from the question of classification, it is important to know how men viewed themselves. As J. R. Vincent has argued, it is of major significance that in the mid-nineteenth century men deliberately blurred distinctions between masters and journeymen, owners and employers. The impossibility of differentiating master and journeyman "over a wide variety of crafts" does not imply a lack of economic distinction and even "technical function"; rather it signifies "a feeling that people engaged in making the same kind of thing were the same kind of people . . . if in the nineteenth century the pattern of self-description implies that the social distance a shoemaker might move above and below the normal shoemaker was not important to them, then probably it was not objectively important either." The preservation of this sort of fuzziness, itself a key clue to the nature of social structure, demands that coding schemes be constructed with scrupulous attention to the language of the manuscript.[7]

In some instances it will be desirable to study individual occupations, but the forming of generalizations makes mandatory a reasonably small number of fairly inclusive categories. Thus, we had to devise a means of reducing the number of occupations listed. Our task would have been immensely lightened had we chosen one of the well-established occupational scales; but an occupational scale based on mid-twentieth-century conditions is inappropriate for a study of the nineteenth century because the occupational structure has changed in fundamental ways.[8] Thus, we found it necessary to devise our own occupational scale, the first requisite of which is that the occupations grouped be similar according to defensible criteria. We asked, as well, if it was possible to encompass economic status and to rank groups of similar occupations by the wealth of their members. For a scale reflecting two dimensions will have more analytic utility and predictive power than a scale based on only one factor. We therefore grouped occupations according to function, with skill cross-cutting where relevant. The major groups we derived in this way were: the *Artisans,* 40% of the work force; the *Businessmen,* 20%; the *Professionals,* 4%; the *Laborers,* 17%; the *Public Employees,* 3%; the *Gentlemen,* 4%; and the *Unemployed,* 3%. Each major group is subdivided into minor groupings, and we can thus easily analyze our data at three levels of generality: major groups, minor groups, or individual occupations.

An important question regarding this scale is its relationship to wealth. The second column of Table 3 indicates the percentage of the group in the top 20% (£38 and over) of those assessed in 1852. The third column indicates the percentage of the group in the bottom 40% (£0–11). For reasons discussed earlier, it is assumed that those in the bottom 40% are poor, whereas those in the

Table 3. Major Occupational Groups in Total Assessed Population, Hamilton, Ontario, 1852: Ranked by Wealth

Group	N	% in Top 20%	% in Bottom 40%
Gentlemen	107	52.4	12.1
Professionals	104	48.0	15.4
Businessmen	508	41.5	19.7
Public Employees	76	36.0	20.3
Artisans	994	13.7	36.0
Laborers	486	3.9	67.5
Unemployed	73	0.0	98.7

top 20% must be considered at least comfortable. It will be noticed that the ranking of the groups varies inversely in each column in exactly the same order.

Two observations suggested by Table 3 are relevant at this point. First, as one might have predicted, business offered a surer route to economic comfort than the trades. How long this situation remained unchanged will be of particular interest, to anticipate the argument, because of the extremely large numbers of young men who were entering business occupations. Did the early and evident linkage between business and success lure many impatient young men who found their dreams of success progressively harder to realize?[9] The second observation is the extent to which the occupation-wealth ranking corresponds to a historian's intuitive sense of status hierarchy. If this should turn out to be the case and the scale has validity for ranking by prestige as well as occupation and income, then we shall have devised a powerful analytic tool indeed.

We must not forget, certainly, that each occupational category, except the Unemployed, runs the gamut from poverty to undisputed comfort. Why the variation? Were some men more skilled than others, some more lucky? That, undoubtedly, is part of the answer. We also wondered to what extent age played a role, for could not variation be explained in part by the different rewards that came to novices and experienced practitioners? This question led us to code the ages from the census onto the assessment cards before we proceeded further; no analysis of occupation and wealth, we felt, could be adequate without the consideration of age.

Hamilton's work force was young. Its mean age was thirty-seven years; its median age thirty-five; the thirty- to thirty-five-year-olds were the modal group. Over three-fifths of the entire work force was under the age of forty, and nearly one-quarter was between twenty and thirty. On the other hand only 17% was fifty or over and 5% in the sixties. These aggregate statistics do not reveal some of the interesting vital statistics for the city. For instance, consider the distribution of age at death shown on Table 4.

Overwhelmingly, the first months of life were the most difficult to survive. In fact the early years of childhood

Table 4. Age at Death, Hamilton, Ontario, 1851

Age	N	%
Under 1	43	21
1	36	17
2—5	27	13
6—10	12	6
11—19	8	4
20—29	25	12
30—39	15	7
40—49	17	8
50—59	10	5
60—69	9	4
Over 69	2	1
Unknown	5	2
Stillborn	1	—
Total	210	100

were a period in which death frequently occurred; 51%
of the people in Hamilton who died in 1851 were under
the age of five. To what extent these infant and childhood
deaths were related to social or economic status is an important question we have not yet answered. Comparisons
are very difficult to make, but insofar as they are possible
it appears that Hamilton had a low death rate in general
but an exceptionally high incidence of deaths among
children under the age of five.[10]

The tables that follow show the relationships between
wealth and age. The first, Table 5, provides raw data and
percentages. Two of the next tables, Tables 6A and 7A,
are expressed in terms of rounded percentages grouped
for more easy scrutiny; the other two, Tables 6B and 7B
are indexes derived from dividing the percentage in a
particular category (for instance, the young and the poor)
by the relevant percentage for the entire population (for
instance, the percentage of young people in the entire
population). The reasoning here is that if the distribution were "perfect" the percentage of the young who
were poor would be the same as the percentage of the
young in the entire population. Thus a score of 1.00 on
the index indicates the expected or normal relationship.
A score of less than 1.00 indicates that the presence of the
group in a particular category is smaller than expected; a
score of more than 1.00, that it is greater. Each of the
index tables is derived from the preceding table of percentages.

The data suggest a number of generalizations concerning the relationships between age and income. First of
all, for every age-group the chances of being poor were
much greater than the chances of being well-to-do. Bearing this in mind, however, a number of interesting varia-

Table 5. 1852 Assessment Roll, City of Hamilton: Age vs. Total Assessment for 1,863 Individuals (of 2,555 Total for Which Age Data Was Available

Total Assessment: Eight Percentile Groups

Age-Range		0–19	20–39	40–59	60–79	80–89	90–94	95–99	99–100	Row Total N	Row Grand Total
Less than 20	N	11 30.6	12 33.6	6 16.7	4 11.1	2 5.5	0 0	1 2.8	0 0	36	2.0
	%	4.2	3.5	1.4	1.0	1.0	0	1.3	0		
20–29	N	114 25.4	79 17.6	110 24.5	80 17.8	35 7.9	16 3.6	12 2.7	3 0.7	449	24.9
	%	43.5	23.2	25.2	20.7	17.1	15.8	16.0	15.0		
30–39	N	69 10.9	112 17.6	146 23.3	153 24.4	74 11.6	44 6.9	31 4.8	4 0.6	635	34.6
	%	26.3	32.8	33.5	40.2	36.1	43.6	41.3	20.0		
40–49	N	38 9.4	79 12.1	102 25.2	79 9.4	55 11.1	23 5.7	21 5.2	7 1.7	404	21.9
	%	14.5	23.2	23.4	20.5	26.8	22.8	28.0	35.0		
50–59	N	18 9.4	38 19.8	42 21.8	48 25.0	29 15.2	9 4.7	5 2.6	3 1.6	192	10.5
	%	6.9	11.1	9.6	12.4	14.1	8.9	6.7	15.0		
60–69	N	11 12.3	17 19.1	24 26.9	16 17.9	8 8.9	7 7.9	4 4.4	2 2.2	89	5.0
	%	4.2	5.0	5.5	4.1	3.9	6.9	5.3	10.0		
69 & over	N	1 4.8	4 1.9	6 28.5	4 19.0	2 9.5	2 9.5	1 4.7	1 5.0	21	1.3
	%	0.4	1.2	1.4	1.0	1.0	2.0	1.3	4.7		
Column Total		262	341	436	384	205	101	75	20	1863 Grand Total	
Column % of Grand Total		14.5	18.8	23.8	21.1	11.2	5.5	4.0	1.07	100 Grand Total	

Table 6. Age-groups in Total Assessed Population, Hamilton, Ontario, 1852, by Economic Status

A. Age-Range	% of Age-Range in Entire Population	% of Poor (0—40th percentiles)	% of Very Well-to-Do (Top 10th Economically)
Under 30	27	45	6
30—39	35	29	12
40—49	22	22	13
50—59	11	29	9
Over 60	6	30	15

B. Index of Age-Group in Relation to Economic Status

Under 30		1.67	0.22
30—39		0.83	0.34
40—49		1.00	0.59
50—59		2.64	0.82
Over 60		5.00	2.50

Table 7. Economic Status of Total Assessed Population, Hamilton, Ontario, 1852, by Age-Groups

A. Poor	Under 30	30—39	40—49	50—59	Over 60	% in Entire Population
(0—40)	36	30	19	9	6	33
Well-to-Do (Top 10th)	7	12	26	9	9	11

B. Index of Economic Status in Relation to Age Categories

	Under 30	30—39	40—49	50—59	Over 60	
Poor	1.08	0.81	0.58	0.27	0.18	
Well-to-Do	0.64	1.09	2.36	0.82	0.82	

tions did occur. The poor were most likely to be under forty years of age, and the well-to-do were more likely to be in their forties than in any other age-group. The young (men under thirty) were more likely to be poor than men of any other age whereas the old were more likely to be well-to-do than other groups. However, in relation to their percentage of the work force, people aged sixty and over were both the wealthiest and poorest of any economic group. The foregoing should not obscure the fact that neither young nor old were excluded from top or bottom income categories. As might be expected, the middle aged bunched in the middle economic ranges.

Relationships between age and wealth correspond in a rough way to relationships between occupation and age. For the major groups the relationships are shown in Tables 8 and 9.

In terms of the total population Gentlemen were grossly underrepresented among the young and overrepresented among the old. At the other extreme the Unemployed were grossly overrepresented among the young and underrepresented in all other categories. Among the middle aged the Professionals and Businessmen were substantially overrepresented. The Professionals, as one would expect, made up a disproportionately small percentage of the young and, more surprisingly, of the old as well. The Businessmen were found in very small numbers among the very young and, like the Professionals, among the old. Considering the population as a whole, the Artisans and Laborers were the most normally distributed occupational groups. The Artisans did figure rather prominently among the twenty-year-olds and among the very old as well, whereas the Laborers, who in terms of their percentage of the entire population made up a disproportionate share of the young, were not to be

Table 8. Major Occupational Groups, Total Assessed Population, Hamilton, Ontario, 1852, by Age Categories

Occupation	Young (under 30) in %	Middle Aged (30 to 49) in %	Late Middle Aged (50 to 59) in %	Old (60 and over) in %
Gentlemen	6.0	49.2	26.5	19.2 100%
Professionals	21.1	63.4	12.7	2.8
Businessmen	27.0	61.3	8.6	3.1
Public Employees	22.6	54.8	11.3	11.3
Artisans	29.7	56.4	8.2	5.6
Laborers	25.1	57.8	12.6	4.5
Unemployed	59.6	36.2	4.3	0.0
% Pop. in Cat.	26.8	51.8	10.5	6.1

Table 9. Age Categories, Total Assessed Population, Hamilton, Ontario, 1852, by Major Occupational Groups

Age-Group	Gentlemen in %	Professionals in %	Businessmen in %	Public Employees in %	Artisans in %	Laborers in %	Unemployed in %	Other in %
Under 20	–	–	13.9	5.6	38.9	27.8	5.6	8.4 100%
20–29	1.1	3.2	19.9	2.6	44.6	17.3	5.6	5.6
30–39	3.7	4.8	22.4	2.8	40.8	17.9	2.0	5.6
40–49	3.9	3.4	18.7	3.9	38.3	22.6	1.0	8.1
50–59	11.2	4.6	15.8	3.6	31.1	23.0	1.0	9.7
60–69	10.8	2.2	11.8	6.5	34.4	17.2	–	17.2
Over 69	28.6	–	–	4.8	47.6	–	–	19.0
% of Pop.	4.5	3.8	19.3	3.3	39.9	19.3	2.5	7.4

found among the very old. The disproportionately large share of the elderly in the "Other" category (Table 9) is explained by the fact that this group contained a large number of widows, who for the moment are not being treated separately.

Given what we have already learned, these distributions are not surprising. The bifurcation of wealth and poverty among the old is reflected in the increasing dominance of a wealthy group, Gentlemen, and a poor group, Artisans, and the progressive disappearance of the solidly upper-middle rank, Professionals and Businessmen, in the older age categories. The prosperity associated with the years thirty to fifty was largely that of Professionals and Businessmen at the peak of their careers. The poverty of youth was the poverty of age-groups dominated by poor occupations, Laborers, the Unemployed, and Artisans.

Perhaps the most interesting problem left for speculation concerns the bifurcation of the old into rich and poor. Did the earning power of some men decline as they passed a certain age? If so, in which occupations was this true? Were there two different life patterns among people of similar occupations, some men starting at low levels in their twenties, increasing throughout their thirties and forties and spurting ahead to wealth in their sixties, whereas others after their mid-forties began to drop back into poverty? We can answer these fascinating questions only through time, as we study the fate of individuals from decade to decade.

Earlier we noted that a general analysis using gross occupational categories sometimes obscures as much as it reveals. Now that the overall picture has been presented it will be instructive to examine refinements and note the variations within major categories. First to be examined are variations according to the minor occupational categories, and of special interest here are the hierarchies within the general categories of Businessmen, Artisans, and Laborers, presented in Table 10. Within the business group the men who owned establishments that sold food and lodging, the innkeepers and hotelkeepers, as well as the owners of stores and other mercantile operations, were clearly the best-off economically. The men who worked for them, especially the young clerks, were the poorer members of the business community.

Clear distinctions emerge within the Artisan group, and these underscore the importance of using extreme caution in treating this category as a single unit in historical or sociological analysis. Four main groupings can be identified: the prosperous luxury and metalworking trades; the less prosperous but still primarily comfortable

Table 10. *Economic Status of Selected Minor Occupational Categories, Total Assessed Population, Hamilton, Ontario, 1852*

	Poor (0–40%)	Well-to-Do (80–100%)
Businessmen		
Sellers of Food and Lodging	0	56.0
Merchant-Shopkeepers	12.1	53.6
Business employees	41.6	13.7
Artisans (excluding "other trades" and agriculture)		
Luxury trades	12.6	29.1
Metalworking trades	19.2	28.8
Construction trades	30.5	10.9
Food trades	33.4	29.1
Transportation service trades	42.5	13.8
Clothing trades	42.6	9.0
Homefurnishing trades	52.3	7.7
Laborers		
Semiskilled	48.6	7.7
Unskilled	75.5	2.4

construction and food trades; the economically marginal transportation servicing and clothing trades; and, finally, the generally poor homefurnishing trades. The problem of accounting for the differential prosperity of the trades is intriguing. Certainly the prosperity of those who dealt in luxuries and metals is not surprising; they made and sold products requiring much skill and, more important, products for which people were willing to pay a high price. The differences among the remaining groups, however, are more puzzling. Why, for instance, were the cabinetmakers, who dominated the homefurnishing trades, so often poor? Why were tailors, the largest group in the clothing trade, generally poorer than carpenters, the dominant group in the construction trades? These are questions for which we have as yet no definite answers, but the relationship between age and occupation suggests useful lines of approach.

The substantial difference between the skilled and semiskilled laborers reveals the importance of a specific occupational identity. Even if the job required little skill or training, for instance stevedore or waiter, the fact that it was identified with a specific industry apparently served to increase its rewards. Among the employed workers the unskilled whose laboring jobs were defined by lack of a specific function were by far the poorest.

The relationships between the minor occupational groupings and age categories suggest some reasons for the differential economic returns of the trades. Those relationships are shown on Table 11, which reveals the age structure of the occupations whose economic status was portrayed in Table 10. Comparing Tables 10 and 11 will show how the age structure of a category corresponded to its economic status.

Within both the Business and Artisan groups a relation

Table 11. Age-Range of Selected Minor Occupational Categories, Total Assessed Population, Hamilton, Ontario, 1852

Occupation	Young (under 30) in %	Middle Aged (30 to 49) in %	Late Middle Aged (50 to 59) in %	Old (60 and over) in %
Businessmen				
Sellers of Food and Lodging	9.0	79.1	6.0	6.0
Merchant-Shopkeeper	25.2	63.2	8.4	3.4
Business employee	41.9	46.6	10.5	1.0
Artisans (excluding "other trades" and agriculture)				
Luxury trades	11.1	72.2	5.6	11.2
Metalworking trades	35.9	48.7	12.8	2.6
Construction trades	23.0	62.1	8.9	6.0
Food trades	25.0	59.4	9.4	6.2
Transport service trades	30.0	60.0	8.6	1.4
Clothing trades	31.3	55.4	6.0	7.2
Homefurnishing trades	46.0	44.9	5.6	3.4
Laborers				
Semiskilled	33.6	55.1	8.2	3.1
Unskilled	21.9	58.8	14.2	5.0

seems clear. The proportion of young men in an occupation and the proportion of the occupation in the poorest two-fifths of the work force rise together. This is true for the three groups in Business. With the exception of the clearly anomalous and numerically small (39) group in the metalworking trades, it is true for the categories of Artisan. Thus the explanation for the differential rewards of the various trades is the age of the men who followed them. The more young men in a trade the greater the proportion who were poor. Therefore, a large part of the problem of explaining the variation in rewards associated with the different trades becomes translated into the task of explaining their different age structures.

At times it may be important to be even more detailed and precise in the process of analysis. Although the minor occupational groupings offer a considerably more refined picture than the earlier scheme, they are still composite categories. However, it is a herculean task to pay detailed attention to each one of hundreds of distinct occupations; further, it is not possible to follow a composite group with no real existence beyond its creation by the authors. A middle ground exists in the determination of representative occupations. When we examine the minor occupational groupings it becomes apparent that each is usually dominated by one particular occupation. It is therefore possible to choose a distinct occupation to represent each of the most significant occupational categories. This procedure yields a group of seventeen representative occupations.

An inspection of the relationships between these groups and wealth shows that they do indeed closely, though not exactly, represent the category from which they have been chosen. This is shown by Table 12. By comparing Table 12 with Table 11, the representative-

Table 12. Economic Status of Representative Occupations, Total Assessed Population, Hamilton, Ontario, 1852

	Poor (0—40%)	Well-to-Do (80—100%)
Gentlemen		
Gentlemen	11.7	52.4
Professions		
Free Professions, Barristers, and Attorneys	7.6	69.2
Other Professions: engineers	16.6	24.9
Businessmen		
Sellers of Food and Lodging: Innkeepers	0.0	50.8
Merchant-Shopkeepers: merchants	2.5	69.4
Business employees: clerks	45.2	11.1
Public Employees		
Upper: male teachers	10.0	10.0
Lower: constables	18.2	9.1
Artisans		
Luxury Trades: watchmakers	0.0	50.0
Metalworking Trades: tinsmiths	14.3	25.1
Construction Trades: carpenters	38.7	7.7
Food Trades: bakers	44.0	32.0
Transport Service Trades: blacksmiths	45.8	4.2
Clothing Trades: shoemakers	40.0	8.7
Clothing Trades: tailors	47.0	9.4
Homefurnishing Trades: cabinetmakers	59.2	6.6
Laborers		
Laborers (unskilled)	75.5	2.4

ness of the seventeen occupations becomes evident. Should we choose to confine the rest of our study merely to these seventeen, our results would differ little statistically from an analysis of the entire work force subdivided into the major and minor categories we have devised.

Stratification, Stability, and Class

The data on relationships between wealth, occupation, and age demonstrate clearly that Hamilton in the early 1850s was a highly stratified society characterized by enormous inequality in wealth. What then were the mechanisms that preserved the stability and tranquility of such an unequal society? Two alternative positions must be considered: the poor were too dispersed, too illiterate, too apathetic and mired in the problems of everyday life to seek a reordering of society. The leadership for basic change then would have had to come from the affluent and especially the educated. But the main currents of educated social thought stressed the dire consequences of overreliance on governmental welfare measures, and so did nothing to energize the forces that could have inspired the poor to participate in a campaign for greater social justice. On the other hand, there could have existed mechanisms *within* the society that eased the misery of the poor and thus blunted the edge of their discontent. These mechanisms might have emerged from family and neighborhood groupings that provided the individual with a sense of community and shared experience. We might also include the ministrations of evangelical religion in focusing the expectations of the poor on a world to come.

It is probable, however, that the ever-bright hope of

economic or occupational mobility, if not for oneself
then for one's children, could have alleviated discontent
and so helped to stabilize society. Horatio Alger was an
unlikely figure in mid-nineteenth-century Hamilton, and
even less extreme instances of mobility were unlikely on
a large scale. It seems scarcely possible that people living
as near the margin of existence as most of Hamilton's
population could sufficiently utilize the rudimentary
means of education to permit their children entry to the
professions, or accumulate the capital necessary for a successful business career. But what we must examine with
great care is the extent to which limited instances of mobility occurred. We must find out how common it was for
people to advance to home and land ownership, and how
common it was for individuals to move from unskilled or
semiskilled work to higher pursuits. The presence of upward mobility, no matter how undramatic, would have
been of the greatest importance in preserving social peace,
for, from the vantage point of a poor man living in mid-
nineteenth-century Hamilton, even such a small incre-
ment could have seemed enormous and its prospect
enough to provide a steadying aim for his existence.[11]

Speculation about mechanisms of social stability leave
us once again with a series of important questions to
answer. At this juncture, one of the crucial issues is the
problem of class, as it relates to the question of age,
wealth, and work in Hamilton. The resolution of this
important question depends on the definition of class, a
complex, often confusing issue about which social scientists hold widely varying positions.

The strict Marxian point of view that stresses the objective existence of classes based on the different relationships of men to the means of production is of little
use in a city like Hamilton. As we noted earlier, the men

engaged in production deliberately described themselves in ways that blurred distinctions between owner and worker, master and journeymen. This reflects economic and social conditions that make it absurd to break the society into groups based solely on their relationship to the means of production. However, rejection of a crude Marxian formulation should not obscure the importance of the economic component of any definition of class. The problem is defining that component in a broad and suitable fashion. An expanded conception of nineteenth-century economic interest must look beyond the moment to an individual's likelihood of increasing his wealth and to the impact that technological progress would have upon his prospects. It should encompass not only the steadiness with which an individual could expect to work but also the settings and social relationships that differentiate kinds of work as much as income.[12]

Through the application of a broad notion of economic interest we can reduce the seven major occupational groups within Hamilton to four, which we term Gentlemen, Entrepreneurs, Artisans, and Laborers. To explain this division we start by noting the critical distinction between manual and nonmanual work within nineteenth-century society. If social values in Canada were similar to those in Britain, then this was the principal dividing line in contemporary opinion. Applied to the seven occupational groups it separates the Artisans and the Laborers from the rest. Within the nonmanual group all workers could expect to attain a better than average income and to work steadily. Technological innovation and the development of an industrial society obviously offered them increased economic opportunity. Although the nineteenth-century countinghouse offered a more personal and far less bureaucratic work setting than the twentieth-century office, occupational designations recognized distinctions between employers and employees as well as a rudimentary hierarchy in a fashion still alien to the trades. For these reasons the business, the professionals, and the public employees form one group broadly similar in economic situation and interest.[13]

The Gentlemen form a discrete group because their relationship to technological progress is more ambiguous; industrialization had a corrosive impact on the position of the gentry in Britain, and this is reason for suspecting that it may have had a similar impact in Canada. Besides, the fact that gentlemen deliberately gave to themselves a nonentrepreneurial and nonprofessional designation signifies that they saw themselves as a group apart from the rest of the nonmanual workers. Analysis still in progress of economic variables underlines the distinctiveness of the Gentlemen, whose sources of wealth lay in real property that generally enabled them to forgo undertaking any sort of remunerative employment.[14]

The Artisans differed from the other manual workers in a variety of ways. They could expect to work more steadily and within one shop. Laborers worked casually and often drifted from employer to employer. Artisans worked in a relatively nonhierarchical setting in which common skills bound master and men in an identification that transcended other social or economic distinctions; Laborers were strictly employees and subordinates. Technological innovations, such as sewing machines, frequently threatened skilled Artisans; Laborers would find more work than ever in the first stages of industrial development.[15] In fact, our analysis of income as differentiated from total wealth reveals even more than do the figures in this paper that as a class the Laborers were far poorer than Artisans.

Before deciding whether these four economic groups are classes, we must consider other conceptualizations, especially the one that rejects the objective existence of social class and defines it as a subjective phenomenon that results from the pooled evaluations people make about each other's prestige. This notion will not do for the historian. Were it possible to make precise ratings of prestige he would still distrust this approach to social class, for its subordination of objective social forces rests upon glaring theoretical and methodological weaknesses. These weaknesses are thoroughly discussed in contemporary sociological literature and need not detain us here.

Although we may reject a formulation of social class resting entirely upon prestige, status is one important kind of social ranking. Max Weber differentiated it from class, which he defined in economic terms, whereas others consider it an essential component of class. Fortunately we can avoid the theoretical complexities that surround this issue. In contrast to the situation in the twentieth century, in the nineteenth century a man usually occupied a similar economic and status rank, which was signified by his occupation. David Lockwood has emphasized this point:

Working with one's hand was associated with other attributes—lack of authority, illiteracy, lowly social origin, insecurity of livelihood—which together spelt social depreciation. The dominant values underlying differences in social worth were those of the entrepreneurial and professional middle classes. The most widely influential criteria of prestige therefore were those which expressed the occupational achievement of the individual. The education required for the job, the rewards and responsibilities it offered, the fact that it was clean and non-manual, and therefore "respectable," gradually established themselves as the key determinants of a person's social standing over a wide range of the society. . . . In a word, status consciousness inflamed class consciousness, and social distinctions.[16]

Thus, we suggest that the four groups already identified shared similarities in both economic interest and social status or prestige.[17]

Similarity in economic interest and prestige may not provide adequate grounds for claiming the existence of a class because it fails to encompass power and consciousness; and to some theorists it is shared consciousness of kind that transforms aggregates into classes discernable by their deliberate activity aimed at the promotion of class interests. Peter Laslett's exposition of the one-class nature of preindustrial English society in *The World We Have Lost* offers a particularly successful example of this position. Only those of gentry status and above, a small minority of the whole population, consciously shared common interests that transcended their village and had access to both the geographical and intellectual sources of mobility necessary for crystallization into a self-conscious national class force determined to advance its own interest. The rest of the population shared a narrow and circumscribed existence in country villages. Hence they lived in conditions that militated against the formation of broad common interests and the taking of common action. They were poor; that was their status, but, in this interpretation, they did not form a class.[18]

The strength of this conception rests primarily on the existence of attitudes and activities that spanned economic and status divisions. To take but one example from mid-nineteenth-century Ontario: increasing urbanization and commercial prospects spawned what has been termed an "urban outlook," an attitude combining entrepreneurial ambitions and values that are distinctly urban in nature and point of reference. But this outlook was not confined to the city. As metropolitan areas increased their influence, an urban outlook spread even among the rural population. It undoubtedly cut as well across status and occupational lines to encompass a broad slice of the population, whose political and social activities it stimulated in particular directions. This may be the group we shall eventually wish to call middle-class. Were there still groups who identified themselves with older values characteristic of landed aristocracy? Had any groups expressed serious reservations about the spread of the entrepreneurial spirit and its technological counterparts? When did there emerge enough consciousness of collective identity to define a working class? Which groups coalesced into effective political forces? These examples are not intended as arguments for the existence of particular attitudes in mid-nineteenth-century Hamilton. Rather, they indicate the line of thought and questioning that the investigation of class might take if we define the notion in terms of mutual consciousness.[19]

Two serious problems arise from the stress on a combination of power and consciousness as the defining elements in class. One involves the source or origins of the consciousness. Is it economic? Does it lie in status? Or in the power itself? These questions lead us in a circular fashion back to the problems with which we began. The second problem stems from the fact that insistence that group members be conscious of broadly shared interests in their everyday transactions or participate in political action creates enormous difficulties in labeling any col-

lectivity a class. The way out of the second problem lies
in a combination of the notion of potential consciousness
or the potential exercise of power with an emphasis on
shared aspirations and values. A group need not be conscious always of its similar interests but the potential for
that consciousness to be triggered by a stimulus, such as a
threatening event, must be present. Likewise, a group
which bears the label of class must manifest common
values and attitudes, shared hopes, fears, and tensions. We
might look for the *manifestation* of consciousness not in
everyday events but rather in special occurrences, like the
formation of a trade union, or in times of economic crisis.
Yet the existence of shared values, should be traceable to
ordinary transactions within the society. The theoretical
issue involved in the first problem, the specification of
the source of group cohesiveness, we shall avoid for now;
it is our contention that it existed in potential or actual
form within the four groups we have defined as similar in
economic interest and social status. The Gentlemen were
probably most explicitly class conscious, the Laborers
least. The potential consciousness of the Artisans would
become explicit in reactions to technology and later in
the beginnings of the trade-union movement. The "urban
outlook" and perhaps most of Canadian political activity
in the mid-nineteenth century were manifestations of
class consciousness and class power by the Entrepreneurial group.

Our hypothesis is that by starting with occupational
function we have identified four groups broadly similar
in economic interest, social status, power, and outlook.
Consequently we suggest that four classes existed in mid-
nineteenth-century Hamilton: the *Gentlemen Class,* the
Entrepreneurial Class, the *Artisan Class,* and the *Laboring Class.* It should be observed that this division could

be defended according to any leading current conception
of class. For purposes of refined analysis we should note
distinctions of degree, rather than of kind, within classes.
For instance, the *Entrepreneurial Class* includes wealthy
merchants, small shopkeepers, and clerks; we shall call
each such subgroup a stratum. Exactly where within a
class the line separating strata begins is a difficult question to answer, and the exact specification of the relationship between stratum and class is another intricate theoretical problem we need not consider at the moment.
However, we can now return to the specific problem of
defining class in terms appropriate to mid-nineteenth-
century Hamilton.

Let us begin by assuming the validity of the arguments about the correlation between different criteria of
stratification. We signify the group or class that shares a
similar rank on these scales by an occupational title.
Thus, occupational designation provides an index of
class position because it reflects the elements that define
class, namely, shared attitudes and prestige based on the
possession of objective and socially desired attributes
such as income, education, and the "cleanliness" of work.
In this definition the origins of class lie in objective circumstances, the conditions and rewards associated with
different categories of occupations. Nevertheless, the historian of class may begin his search for distinctions in
either objective indexes or in the realm of attitudes,
which as in the case of the "urban outlook" provide insight into groupings whose empirical boundaries may
then be traced.[20]

We have labeled our classes by occupational function.
This has been a matter of convenience, for these designa-
tions fit both the data and the discussions within this essay.
We could as easily have chosen other labels, such as work-

ing and middle, white collar and blue collar, and the like. The choice of class designation is almost arbitrary; the substance of class definition is not.

It is possible now to return to Messrs. McGarry, McFatradge, and Pringle, the three men with whom this paper began. In what sense were they representative? Each came from a different class: the *Laboring Class,* the *Artisan Class,* and the *Entrepreneurial Class;* each was of an age and possessed a degree of wealth common to that class.

Knowledge of the place of these men within Hamilton society represents insight into the way that society was constructed. The significance of Messrs. McGarry, McFatradge, and Pringle thus rests partly on the case for the study of social structure in history. That case may be stated briefly, for much of it should be obvious. Conceptions of social structure underlie most historical interpretations. Whether or not the historian makes them explicit, his assumptions about the characteristics that define a society enter inescapably into his writing. The resulting images of society are ubiquitous in historical topics and problems. Consider the following as examples: the basis of political appeal, the nature of economic interest, religious controversy, the role of formal education, responses to social issues such as poverty and immigration, or the emergence of nationalism and the nature of national character. A discussion of any of these must presuppose and at least imply definite notions of the contours of society at different points in time. The historian can escape the social structures that impinge upon his characters no more than we can escape the social structures in which we live, and act completely autonomously as if networks of institutions, systems of stratification, and methods of control just did not exist.[21]

Accurate, precise knowledge of social structure thus

may help in the testing of existing historical interpretations, or in the generation of new explanations. Its absence may even have profound consequences for the development of social and political thought, as Asa Briggs
has strikingly pointed out:

> The comparative history of the economic and social
> structures and political movements of Manchester and
> Birmingham shows just how different two individual
> cities could be. If Engels had lived not in Manchester
> but in Birmingham, his conception of "class" and his
> theories of the role of class in history might have been
> very different. In this case Marx might have been not
> a communist but a currency reformer. The fact that
> Manchester was taken to be the symbol of the age in
> the 1840's and not Birmingham . . . was of central po-
> litical importance in modern world history.

Briggs reminds us here that the relationship between the
historian and social structure is reciprocal. As much as
the participants in history about whom he writes, the historian himself is shaped by the social structure in which
he lives, and through his work his images of society may
modify that structure itself. The analysis of social structure, it must be emphasized, is the study of the context of
life. Herein lies its greatest importance for the historian.
Once we grant that men are at least partly the product
of their environment, we have granted the case for the
historical study of social structure.[22]

It is already clear from even this limited analysis that
the city of Hamilton in the mid-nineteenth century represented a world different from both the society of Tudor
and Stuart England—the premodern society delineated
by Laslett—and the modern industrial world with which
we are familiar. In a sense the world of Hamilton was

poised delicately and ephemerally in the interstices between the two. The complexity of the economy, the division of labor, the early introduction of machinery: all
were harbingers beckoned by the entrepreneurial spirit
and echoed in the ongoing construction of the railroad.
But the shade of the older society was there too, especially
in the lack of distinction between master and journeyman
and in the identification in the trades of man and craft
rather than man and position. Although Hamilton was
the fourth port in Canada, the lines between retail and
wholesale and between production, distribution, and
sales were still indistinct enough to differentiate the Hamilton of 1852 from the modern industrial age. It was then
a prosperous, an expanding, and a commercial city, but
the scale of life had not yet reached those gargantuan and
impersonal proportions that have marked the industrial
city. Productive enterprises were typically small; a master
worked alone or with a few journeymen. Aside from some
large mercantile houses, small shops sold the goods that
were not produced in Hamilton. Transportation remained rudimentary and life had to center predominantly around the neighborhood where one lived, worked,
and shopped. The administration of the city could hardly
be called a bureaucracy, and the handful of officers were
not yet a remote officialdom. Still we must remember that
this was a highly stratified society in which life for the
many poor people was precarious, a constant struggle for
existence that offered only a slim chance of advancement
into the relatively small middle ranks of society and more
likely than not an old age of increasing poverty for those
who managed to survive. It was a small and sufficiently
tightly knit society for the older men of wealth and the
"gentlemen" to exert their influence over its actions and
define its social tone; it was a world in which it remained

possible to define a man's place with some precision and ease. Yet its balance was unstable and its transformation imminent. As much as seventeenth-century England, mid-nineteenth-century Hamilton is a "world we have lost." To watch and trace the process through which Hamilton acquired the lineaments of modernity will be an exercise filled at once with challenge, excitement, and nostalgia.

1. The use of the term "we" in this paper has special significance, for it is the result of the labor and thought of a number of individuals who have formed with the author a somewhat amorphous project group, which includes Ian Winchester, John Tiller, Peter Ross, Anne Marie Hodes, and Susan Houston.

2. Thus far this project has been entirely supported by funds from the Department of History and Philosophy of The Ontario Institute for Studies in Education.

3. This hypothesis is similar to the conclusions of Douglas Miller in *Jacksonian Aristocracy Class and Democracy in New York, 1850–1860* (New York, 1967).

4. A good recent historical study of distribution of wealth that grapples intelligently with these issues is James T. Lemon and Gary B. Nash, "The Distribution of Wealth in Eighteenth Century America: A Century of Changes in Chester County, Pennsylvania, 1693–1802," *Journal of Social History*, 2, (Fall 1968), 1–24. For suffrage qualifications see 12 Vic. Cap. 27 (1849). The figure for wealth represents basically either his total annual rent if he was a tenant or, if an owner, roughly 6% of the total actual value of all real property (lands and buildings). Sometimes both rent and property are included, for a number of individuals were simultaneously tenants and owners. Added to this figure are 6% of income when an individual earned more than £50 per year or 6% of certain categories of personal property. Generally those individuals assessed were heads of households or independent adults. Thus the assessment roll does not include children who worked and lived at home nor does it include, with one exception, female servants.

5. The calculation of eligible votes is the subject of a forthcoming paper.

6. On contemporary income distribution and its relation to stratification, see Melvin M. Tumin, *Social Stratification: The Forms and Functions of Inequality* (Englewood Cliffs, N.J., 1967), and John Porter, *The Vertical Mosaic: An Analysis of Social Class and Power in Canada* (Toronto, 1965).

7. J. R. Vincent, *Pollbooks: How Victorians Voted* (Cambridge, England, 1967), pp. 52–53. Unless otherwise specified all numerical data in this paper are derived from census and assessment rolls. The system of assessment was based on the Assessment Act of 1850, 13 and 14 Vic. Cap. 67 (1850), and the Amendment to it, 14 and 15 Vic. Cap. 110 (1851). The former took effect January 1, 1851, and called for the asessment year to coincide with the calendar year. This means that the figures best matching those on the Census of 1851 are those on the assessment taken in the early months of 1852. Moreover, the completed forms for the Census of 1851 were actually collected in January 1852.

8. For examples of contemporary scales see the one used by Porter in *Vertical Mosaic*, derived from the census of Canada, 1961, and in his useful volume, *Canadian Social Structure: A Statistical Profile* (Toronto, 1967). The problem of occupational classification is usefully handled in A. M. Carr-Saunders and P. A. Wilson, *The Professions* (London, 1933). It would seem that we attribute more importance to this problem than most historians dealing with the subject. For instance, see W. A. Armstrong, "Social Structure from Early Census Returns," in D. E. C. Eversley, Peter Laslett, and E. A. Wrigley, *An Introduction to English Historical Demography* (London, 1966), pp. 209–37, which uses the Registrar-General's scheme.

9. Late nineteenth-century American commentators pointed to an overabundance of young men seeking clerkship and white-collar positions.

10. For comparative death rates see Porter, *Canadian Social Structure*, p. 46, and Adna Ferrin Weber, *The Growth of Cities in the Nineteenth Century, A Study in Statistics* (New York, 1899).

11. Stephan Thernstrom, *Poverty and Progress: Social Mobility in a Nineteenth Century City* (Cambridge, Mass., 1964), reveals the prevalence and importance of very small increments of financial or occupational mobility.

12. There are many adequate reviews of theories of stratification. For the general issue we have found useful Tumin, *Social Stratification;* Leonard Reissman, *Class in American Society* (New York, 1959), esp. Chap. 11; Seymour Martin Lipset, *Revolution and Counter-revolution: Change and Persistence in Social Structures* (New York, 1968), Chap. 4; and Ralf Dahrendorf, *Class and Class Conflict in Industrial Society* (Stanford, 1959), which is especially illuminating on Marx. The emphasis here on expectations derives from Max Weber's stress on life-chances rather than actual conditions as a criterion of stratification on different dimensions; see "Class Status and Power," in H. H. Gerth and C. Wright Mills, eds., from *Max Weber: Essays in Sociology* (Oxford, 1958). The notion of the importance of the work setting derives from David Lockwood, whose explication of this concept in *The Blackcoated Worker* (London, 1958) is an important contribution to stratification theory.

13. On British opinion regarding manual, nonmanual distinctions see Lockwood, *The Blackcoated Worker*, p. 210. My own previous work suggests that nineteenth-century professionals shared an entrepreneurial point of view: see Michael B. Katz, *The Irony of Early School Reform Educational Innovation in Mid-Nineteenth Century Massachusetts* (Cambridge, Mass., 1968), pp. 23–27 and 31–35.

14. See Lockwood, *The Blackcoated Worker*, pp. 30–37, on "Gentlemen."

15. On the relation of artisans to technological innovation, see Katz, *Irony of Early School Reform*, pp. 80–86.

16. Lockwood, *The Blackcoated Worker*, p. 99.

17. I refer here of course primarily to Lloyd Warner's conception of class; for excellent critiques of this idea, the first as a contemporary theory, the latter historical, see Reissman, *American Class Structure*, pp. 94–102, and Thernstrom, *Poverty and Progress*, pp. 225–39.

18. Peter Laslett, *The World We Have Lost* (New York, 1965), Chap. 2. See also Dahrendorf, *Class and Class Conflict*, for an argument of this sort.

19. The concept of an "urban outlook" has been formulated by Susan Houston in her essay, "Politics, Schools and Social Change in Upper Canada Between 1836 and 1846" (unpublished M.A. thesis, University of Toronto, 1967). See also J. M. S. Careless, "Frontierism, Metropolitanism, and Canadian History," *Canadian Historical Review*, *5:35* (1954), 1–21.

20. For an illuminating discussion of nineteenth-century class distinctions that begins with the latter sort of evidence, see Asa Briggs, "The Language of 'Class' in Early Nineteenth Century England," in Asa Briggs and John Saville, eds., *Essays in Labour History* (London, 1960), pp. 43–73.

21. Assumptions concerning social structure in Canadian history are considered in an important paper, S. R. Mealing, "The Concept of Social Class and the Interpretation of Canadian History," *Canadian Historical Review*, *46:3* (1965), 201–18.

22. Briggs, *Victorian Cities* (London, 1963; paperback edition, Pelican Books, 1968), p. 116.

PART TWO: URBAN RESIDENTIAL PATTERNS

RESIDENCE AND SOCIAL STRUCTURE:
Boston in the Ante-Bellum Period

Leo F. Schnore and Peter R. Knights

Contemporary sociological interest in the city includes considerable emphasis upon such subjects as suburbanization, the spatial distribution of ethnic groups (including, most prominently, the segregation of Negroes), and the ecology of socioeconomic status groups. In all of these instances, there is a lack of historical perspective on the problems under consideration. Some preliminary data from a full-scale study of Boston in the nineteenth century shed historical light on some of these topics.

Suburbanization

Most social scientists today tend to regard suburbanization as a product of the 1920s. With the coming of mass ownership of the automobile, and the development of the all-weather road, it is assumed, population growth around the periphery of our large cities began to exceed that of the central areas themselves. In the aggregate, of course, this may be a fair characterization. One of the most thoroughgoing studies of the suburban phenomenon, for example, was subtitled "Decentralization Since 1920."[1] But close examination reveals that this inference was based on data for all metropolitan areas taken together, and there is reason to believe that at least some of the older and larger places experienced suburbanization well in advance of the coming of the automobile.[2]

Consider the case of Boston. If one examines the population growth of the city from the first to the most recent

federal census, together with comparable data for the
surrounding counties within the same State Economic
Area, the findings are intriguing. Table 1 shows the results. Boston contained a mounting proportion of the
area's total population only until 1880; since that date it
has shown a progressive decline. In other words, the outlying counties have exceeded the city in rates of growth
since the 1880s. Much of this outlying growth, at least

Table 1. The Suburbanization of Boston (County-Based)

Date	Boston City	Five-County Total *	Boston as % of the Five-County Total
1790	18,320	175,060	10.5
1800	24,937	193,428	12.9
1810	33,787	225,472	15.0
1820	43,298	254,674	17.0
1830	61,392	307,999	19.9
1840	93,383	397,884	23.5
1850	136,881	571,789	23.9
1860	177,840	749,383	23.7
1870	250,526	900,806	27.8
1880	362,839	1,120,817	32.4
1890	448,477	1,427,592	31.4
1900	560,892	1,799,667	31.2
1910	670,585	2,169,623	30.9
1920	748,060	2,472,079	30.3
1930	781,188	2,774,237	28.2
1940	770,816	2,824,955	27.3
1950	801,444	3,065,344	26.2
1960	697,197	3,357,607	20.8

* The counties included are Essex, Middlesex, Norfolk, Plymouth, and
Suffolk.

initially, must be attributed to the influence of the street railroad in the late nineteenth century.[3]

Table 2 presents a similar picture. This tabulation is based on a retrojection of the 1960 delineation of the Standard Metropolitan Statistical Area, formed of cities and towns rather than counties. The different basis of calculation does not alter the main findings. Again, as in Table 1, suburbanization is found to have started in the

Table 2. The Suburbanization of Boston (Town-Based)

Date	Boston City	Total SMSA*	Boston as % of the SMSA
1790	18,320	93,214	19.4
1800	24,937	109,742	22.7
1810	33,787	134,274	24.8
1820	43,298	155,882	27.8
1830	61,392	191,585	32.0
1840	93,383	256,140	36.5
1850	136,881	382,712	35.8
1860	177,840	518,648	34.3
1870	250,526	635,535	39.4
1880	362,839	797,610	45.5
1890	448,477	1,029,453	43.6
1900	560,892	1,312,784	42.7
1910	670,585	1,602,023	41.9
1920	748,060	1,868,859	40.0
1930	781,188	2,168,566	36.0
1940	770,816	2,209,608	34.9
1950	801,444	2,410,572	33.3
1960	697,197	2,589,301	26.9

* The 1960 town- and city-based Standard Metropolitan Statistical Area retrojected to 1790.

Table 3. Intercensal Growth Rates in Boston and Surrounding Rings, 1790—1960

Decade	Boston	First Ring	Second Ring	Third Ring	Fourth Ring
1790—1800	*36.1**	27.0	10.3	9.9	10.5
1800—1810	*35.5*	7.4	13.4	21.8	8.8
1810—1820	*28.2*	17.3	17.9	6.6	6.5
1820—1830	*41.8*	34.9	17.9	9.5	7.3
1830—1840	*52.1*	35.8	25.3	19.7	14.4
1840—1850	46.6	*81.3*	42.0	38.1	31.4
1850—1860	29.9	*67.6*	32.4	27.7	18.2
1860—1870	40.9	*44.7*	23.8	19.9	11.3
1870—1880	*44.8*†	33.1	24.3	29.3	18.4
1880—1890	23.6	41.3	*46.6*	26.0	17.5
1890—1900	25.1	*42.6*	36.8	20.1	16.2
1900—1910	19.6	21.8	*26.9*	23.6	17.2
1910—1920	11.6	22.5	*31.6*	9.5	16.7
1920—1930	4.4	22.6	*39.4*	12.9	20.1
1930—1940	− 1.3	0.8	7.1	3.3	*7.8*
1940—1950	4.0	8.4	14.6	11.1	*19.0*
1950—1960	−13.0	0.6	20.4	22.8	*55.9*

* The highest value for each decade is italicized.

† Boston annexed Dorchester in 1870, and three towns in 1874; these towns, together with their 1870 populations, were:

Brighton (1874)	4,967
Charlestown (1874)	28,323
West Roxbury (1874)	8,683

Assume that these three areas did not grow between 1870 and 1880. Subtracting their *1870* total population (41,973) from the recorded *1880* Boston total (362,839), and computing the Boston growth between 1870 and 1880 in the area unaffected by annexation, yields an adjusted growth rate over the decade of 28.1%.

1880s, well before the advent of the automobile. Whether our areal unit is based on a combination of counties or on a combination of cities and towns, the inference is the same.

But we have even more detailed data at our disposal. Table 3 arranges the cities and towns around Boston in a series of concentric rings or distance zones extending outward from the core. Growth rates are shown for each decade since 1790. It will be seen that Boston city's growth, which was highest in the early part of the nineteenth century, has been the lowest in the series for the past four intercensal decades. In general, zones of rapid growth have shifted outward as time has passed. For example, the second ring registered highest rates of growth during the early decades of the twentieth century, but has now been surpassed by the more distant zones. Indeed, by 1950–60, there was a perfect direct relationship between rate of growth and distance from the center. While Boston was losing population (–13.0%) and the first ring registered virtual stability (0.6%), the most rapid growth (55.9%) was being recorded in the fourth, or most distant, ring.

Racial and Ethnic Segregation

Another topic of great interest to contemporary social science is that of residential segregation according to racial and ethnic background. But most of our detailed knowledge of this subject comes from examination of twentieth-century data. The focus of the larger study from which this chapter is drawn is the ante-bellum period, 1830–60. What was the situation in Boston at that time?

Let us first consider the subject of Negro-white segregation. The proportion of Negroes in Boston was quite low throughout the ante-bellum period. Negroes constituted only 3% of the total population of the city in 1830, and by 1860 this proportion had been cut in half. Yet, at the same time, Boston's Negro population—small as it was—became even more segregated as time passed. In 1830, about 44% of Boston's Negro population would have had to shift to another ward of residence in order for the two racial groups—white and Negroes—to be evenly distributed. By 1860, the index of segregation[4] had mounted to 62.3, signifying the fact that over six out of every ten Negroes would have had to be moved to another ward of residence in order for perfect lack of segregation to prevail. This suggests that it was neither the absolute nor relative number of Negroes in the city that made for greater segregation. The impact of color differences alone was sufficient to account for mounting segregation.

What about other ethnic groups? We have some ward-based data for ten ethnic groups in Boston in 1855. Table 5 presents the results of computing "deltas" (indexes of

Table 4. Racial Segregation in Boston, 1830–60

Census Date	Negroes in the city in %	Negro-White Index of Segregation (Based on Wards)
1830	3.1	44.4
1840	2.3	52.4
1850	1.5	59.1
1860	1.3	62.3

Table 5. Indexes of Segregation (by Wards) between Residential Distributions of Native U.S. Population and Those of Selected Foreign Groups, City of Boston, 1855

England and Wales	11.9
Scotland	15.0
Ireland	18.9
Canada	18.7
France	20.4
Germany and Holland	33.0
Norway and Sweden	41.1
Denmark	47.4
Italy	56.5
Portugal	76.2

Source: Massachusetts Secretary of the Commonwealth, *Abstract of the Census of the Commonwealth of Massachusetts . . . June 1855* (Boston, 1857), Table III, pp. 124-25.

segregation) between each individual group and the distribution of the native-born U.S. population, used here as a reference point. It will be seen that the groups that are most similar in cultural terms have the most similar residential distributions. Those groups originating in the United Kingdom exhibit the four lowest indexes, all ranging below 20 in value. Four other groups with Western and Central European origins (France, Germany and Holland, Denmark, Norway and Sweden) reveal values between 20 and 50. The most distinctly segregated groups are those from Southern and Eastern Europe—Italy and Portugal—whose indexes are roughly at the same level as that for the Negroes. It is regrettable that we do not have comparable data for other dates, so that trends could be established. However, we do have trend data for the foreign-born, taken as a whole, compared with the native-born.

Table 6 shows the indexes of segregation for native- and foreign-born for the period 1830–65. In general, it will be seen that the indexes declined in value by about one-half during this period. This decline occurred in the face of considerable foreign immigration.

Table 6. *Indexes of Segregation (by Wards) for Native- and Foreign-born Populations, City of Boston, 1830–65*

Census Date	Foreign-born in %	Indexes of Segregation (by Wards)
1830	5.7	28.6
1845	23.7	21.0
1850 (old wards)	45.7	24.4
1850 (new wards)	45.7	18.8
1855	53.0	22.6
1865	34.2	14.8

Conclusions

We have shown that Boston has gone through two quite distinctive phases as far as population redistribution is concerned. The first, which lasted until about 1880, can be characterized as a period of "centralization," in which the city's population grew more rapidly than did the surrounding territory, and in which the city contained a mounting fraction of the total area's population. The second, which has lasted from 1880 to the present, has been one of "decentralization," wherein outlying suburban growth has outstripped that of the city, and in which the city's proportion of the total area's population has diminished rather regularly.

These massive population shifts must be considered as the *context* within which more specific changes in residence and social structure are observed. The entire ante-bellum period, for example, was one in which centralization was occurring, and the other trends discussed in this chapter must be viewed in that light. In contrast, Stephan Thernstrom's chapter in this volume, which deals with late nineteenth-century and twentieth-century Boston, must be read with the understanding that his observations refer to a period in which massive decentralization was taking place.

The other trends observed in this chapter, where the focus is the period from 1830 to 1860, are as clearly etched. Whereas the proportion of Negroes fell during the entire ante-bellum period, the degree of Negro segregation mounted substantially. In contrast, the degree of segregation between other native- and foreign-born elements of the population was drastically reduced.

What is now needed is a whole series of observations of nineteenth-century cities, so that some broadly based generalizations might become possible. The value of such case studies as this one must remain limited, providing only examples of important topics to be pursued on a truly *comparative* basis.

1. Amos H. Hawley, *The Changing Shape of Metropolitan Areas: Decentralization Since 1920* (Glencoe, Ill., 1956).

2. Leo F. Schnore, "The Timing of Metropolitan Decentralization: A Contribution to the Debate," *Journal of the American Institute of Planners, 25* (November 1959), 200–06.

3. Sam Bass Warner, Jr., *Streetcar Suburbs: The Process of Growth in Boston, 1870–1900* (Cambridge, Mass., 1962).

4. The index is "delta," or the sum of positive or negative percentage-point differences between groups arrayed according to the same spatial units (in this case, political wards). A value of zero indicates perfect lack of segregation, or identical residential distributions. A value of 100 signifies complete segregation. The technical qualities of this index are most fully discussed in Karl E. Taeuber and Alma F. Taeuber, *Negroes in Cities* (Chicago, 1965), Appendix A, pp. 195–245.

POPULATION TURNOVER, PERSISTENCE, AND RESIDENTIAL MOBILITY IN BOSTON, 1830–60[1]

Peter R. Knights

Although many researchers have focused their attention on gross population movement, few have studied the ante-bellum period in the United States. Fewer still have examined the ante-bellum urban scene, and these have neglected the question of population movements *within* cities and the links between the various kinds of movements. Yet it has been nearly a decade since a leading theoretician of urban history recommended that "an autonomous social history ought to begin with a study of population: its changing composition and distribution in time and space."[2] Of the several topics possible within those limits, this paper concentrates upon three: gross turnover of households, persistence of heads of household, and their residential mobility. Limited space precludes analysis of Boston's massive internal ante-bellum population redistribution.[3]

The terms *movement, persistence, mobility,* and *turnover* will be used as follows: *movement* will refer to all population shifts; *persistence* is the proportion (usually expressed in a percentage) of a population remaining in a delimited area after a given time interval (usually a decade).[4] *Turnover,* strictly speaking, is the sum of all population movements *into* an area (including births) and all *outward* movements (including deaths). It has been defined loosely as $(100\% - p)$, where p is the persistence. The strict definition will hold here. *Mobility* will refer to the time rate of change of residence among the population. To avoid confusion, the term will often appear as "residential mobility."

Our grasp of the urbanization process in nineteenth-century America will be feeble indeed if we have little notion of conditions encountered by urbanizing individuals. Of these conditions one of the most prominent was residence. What kinds of population movements did ante-bellum Bostonians experience?

Two information sources serve to answer this question. The first, a 1,540-member random sample of heads of household drawn from the 1830, 1840, 1850, and 1860 federal censuses of Boston, is basic.[5] The second consists of Boston's city directories, which appeared annually during the 1830–60 period (there were two directories in 1846).[6]

Between 1830 and 1857 the compilers of Boston's city directories claimed to have included a total of 596,124 names in their volumes (including continuations from year to year). During those years, the compilers made 509,866 changes in directory listings, equal to 85.5% of the total number of listings. Yearly the compilers particularized "names dropped," "names added," "removals, &c.," and "total alterations."[7] These statistics do not measure *absolute* population movements, yet by assuming their *relative* accuracy one may use their *ratios* to help gauge population turnover. A basic, probably unverifiable, assumption is that errors in "names added" (the sum of household heads entering Boston plus local residents reaching age twenty-one) were about as prevalent as those in "names dropped" (the sum of household heads quitting the city and those dying).

Restricting the inquiry to heads of household bypasses the problem of determining "net natural increase," the (usual) excess of births over deaths. The units of study, adult heads of household, were much more likely to enter the records, either by reaching age twenty-one or by dying, than were multitudes of children in a city where life expectancy was about twenty-two years.[8] Age distribution profiles of the population permit crude decadal estimates of the number of persons reaching age twenty-one, and fragmentary death records provide data for approximating the totals of deaths of persons aged twenty and over (the assumption being that all such males and one-sixth of such females were household heads).[9] The estimates appear in Table 1.

Table 1. *Estimated Numbers of Males Reaching Age Twenty-one, and of Deaths of Household Heads (Age Twenty and Over), by Decade, Boston, 1830–60*

Group	Decade		
	1830–40	*1840–50*	*1850–60*
Estimated number of males reaching age 21[a]	9,825	14,275	15,800
Estimated number of deaths of household heads[b]	4,600	6,350	10,246

Sources: Lemuel Shattuck, *Report to the Committee of the City Council . . .* , Appendixes 14, 15, 17–19; *Abstract of the Census of the Commonwealth of Massachusetts . . . 1855 . . .* , pp. 89–90; *Abstract of the Census of Massachusetts, 1860 . . .* , pp. 46–49; Shattuck, *The Vital Statistics of Boston . . . for the Last Twenty-Nine Years . . .* (Philadelphia, 1841), p. 13; *Boston City Documents Nos. 4* (1850), p. 20; *10* (1851), pp. 19, 24; *7* (1852), p. 13; *10* (1853), p. 12; *12* (1854), p. 16; *10* (1855), p. 22; *10* (1856), p. 30; *14* (1857), p. 27; *9* (1858), p. 24; *13* (1859), pp. 39–40; *85* (1860), pp. 44–45.

a. Estimated by taking five times the sum (number of males aged twenty at end of decade) plus (number of males aged twenty at start of decade).

b. Estimated by taking the total number of deaths of males aged twenty-one and over, plus one-sixth the total number of deaths of females aged twenty-one and over (to allow for female heads of household).

A comparison of the number of city directory listings with the number of households in Boston reveals that ordinarily there were from 1.22 to 1.69 times as many listings as households.[10] Dividing the directories' "names added" and "names dropped" figures by the appropriate ratios, and calling the results "households added" and "households dropped," we obtain Table 2. Then, sub-

Table 2. Estimates of "Households Added" and "Households Dropped" in Boston City Directories, 1830–60

Group	Decade		
	1830–40	1840–50	1850–60
Initial number of households (census)	9,518	14,047	24,667
Estimated "households added"	+26,230	+53,720	+83,190
Estimated "households dropped"	−21,760	−38,860	−71,540
Surplus of "households added"	(+ 4,470)	(+14,860)	(+11,650)
Estimated final number of households	13,988	28,907	36,317
Actual final number of households (census)	14,047	24,667	33,633

Sources: Number of households from manuscript federal censuses of Boston, 1830, 1840, 1850, and 1860 (microfilm from National Archives); estimates from data in Boston city directories, 1831–57, as explained in accompanying text.

tracting from "households added" the estimated number of males reaching age twenty-one in each decade,[11] and subtracting from "households dropped" the estimated number of deaths of household heads, both as given in Table 1, there remains the estimated in- and out-migration of households shown in Table 3. At least twice as many households passed through Boston in each decade as lived there at the start of any decade.

Table 3. Estimated In- and Out-Migration of Households, Boston, 1830—60

Migration Group	Decade		
	1830—40	*1840—50*	*1850—60*
Estimated in-migration (households)	16,405	39,445	67,390
Estimated out-migration (households)	17,160	32,510	61,294
Surplus (or deficit) of in-migration (households)	(-- 655)	(6,935)	(6,096)

Sources: Derived from Tables 1 and 2 as explained in accompanying text.

Table 4. Percentage of Sample Members Present in Boston at Start of Selected Years, 1830—60 (N = 385 in Each Sample)

	Per Cent Present in Sample of			
Year	*1830*	*1840*	*1850*	*1860*
1830	100.0	40.8	20.5	11.4
1831	84.4	42.4	20.8	12.0
1835	63.2	56.4	24.9	15.1
1839	49.1	80.8	30.4	17.7
1840	43.9	100.0	32.7	18.5
1841	42.4	89.6	35.1	19.2
1845	34.0	68.3	46.2	24.7
1849	27.8	50.9	72.4	33.5
1850	25.7	48.6	100.0	38.4
1851	24.4	44.4	88.0	39.7
1855	17.2	33.0	61.0	52.7
1859	13.3	27.8	42.1	77.1
1860	12.2	27.6	39.0	100.0

Source: Sample data.

These figures show the vast increase in the importance of migration as a factor in Boston's population growth. During the '30s, net in-migration was less than net out-migration; the city's net growth came from "net natural increase." But by the '40s, net in-migration supplied just under one-half the net increase of Boston's households, with the remainder coming from the surplus, above deaths, of local residents reaching age twenty-one. In the '50s, the proportion accounted for by net in-migration rose slightly, to just over one-half.

These indicated population turnover figures may seem incredible, for census data, which show only net changes, do not suggest such findings. Other evidence, however, corroborates high turnover among Boston's ante-bellum residents. Table 4 shows, for selected years, the persistence of sample members. Between 1830 and 1831, for example, 15.6% of the 1830 sample left Boston. The corresponding figures for the 1840 and 1850 samples, in 1840–41 and 1850–51 respectively, were 10.4% and 12.0%. Again, between 1839 and 1804, 19.2% of the 1840 sample arrived in Boston. The corresponding percentages for the 1850 sample in 1849–50 and the 1860 sample in 1859–60 were, respectively, 27.6 and 22.9. These figures suggest an annual turnover circa 1830 and 1840 of about 30%, increasing to about 40% circa 1850 and 1860. Taking as an example a group of 1,000 persons who live in an area, imagine that 30% of the group leaves yearly, and that there are no replacements. At the end of ten years, only twenty-eight persons will remain. Yet, if we analogize the 1,000-member group to a city, replacement enters the picture. Over a ten-year period in the "city" of 1,000 persons, not only has the departure of 972 persons not reduced the population; net in-migration and net natural increase have raised the population above the original 1,000 mark. Thus, for the original group, there has been a turnover of at least 1,944 (= 2 x 972) persons. Extending the example yet further, we might represent the population each year by the 1,000 figure, reducing it yearly by 30% and simultaneously increasing it by slightly more than 30%. Many such series would operate all at once in a real population, and total turnover for a decade could easily reach several times the initial 1,000.[12]

An alternative approach is to derive from Table 4 the percentage rates of growth and decay for the sample groups (see Table 5). These samples show their highest rates of change in the years just before and just after the samples' census years, gradually falling off until the rate of gain or loss stabilizes at about 7 or 8% per year twenty years on either "side" of the samples' census years. It is worth noting that with an annual growth or decay rate of 7%, one-half of a population will enter or leave an area in 9.6 years. But if the rate is raised to 8%, the time decreases to 8.3 years; if to 10%, then 6.6 years; 15%, 4.3 years; 20%, 3.1 years; 30%, 1.94 years; and 40%, 1.36 years. Assuming that the turnover rates on either "side" of the sample's census years were in fact typical of the entire ante-bellum period, rates for the whole era would have averaged about 30 to 40%, implying that one-half of Boston's population would have disappeared and have been replaced every one to two years. Thus, this method indicates that total turnover during a decade could reach several times the city's total population. It is important to stress this point, since census returns, which report only net population changes, completely neglect the matter of turnover.[13]

It would seem, then, that overall population mobility in ante-bellum Boston was at least as great as the oft-

Table 5. Annual Growth or Decay Rates of the Samples

	Sample Group			
Decay: Number of Years After Sample Year	1830 (%)	1840 (%)	1850 (%)	1860 (%)
1	15.60	10.40	12.00	n. a.[a]
5	10.84	9.09	11.62	n. a.
10	8.74	7.70	9.93	n. a.
20	6.90	6.55	n. a.	n. a.
30	7.00	n. a.	n. a.	n. a.
Growth: Number of Years Before Sample Year				
1	n. a.	19.20	27.60	22.90
5	n. a.	13.34	17.56	14.80
10	n. a.	9.48	11.68	10.09
20	n. a.	n. a.	8.00	8.50
30	n. a.	n. a.	n. a.	7.21

Source: Calculated from data in Table 4, using the formulas $G/DR = 100\%$ x $(1-r)$ and $r = p^{\left(\frac{1}{n-1}\right)}$, where G/DR represents the growth or decay rate in percent, p represents the proportion of persons (a figure between 0 and 1) present in Boston after n years, and r stands for the annual ratio of growth or decay (analogous to r in geometric series).

a. n. a. = not available. Since the study gathered no data outside the thirty years of its concern, it is not possible to calculate growth or decay of the samples outside those limits.

quoted modern figure for the United States: 20% per year, or "one family in five moves every year." The actual turnover rate for ante-bellum Boston was higher yet. Having established the plausibility of an annual rate of at least 30%, let us examine that population mobility, particularizing portions of it.

Generally speaking, residential mobility varied during the period from 1830 to 1860, remaining nearly constant until the mid-1840s, then finding a newer, higher level. The city directories' "total alterations" classification provides a measure of this phenomenon, for the proportion of "total alterations" to total listings rose sharply after 1842, reaching a figure of over 90% by 1845 (see Table 6).

The samples also provide residential measurements, but these are longitudinal rather than cross-sectional like the city directories. That is, knowing about the residential mobility, say, in 1831 of the 1830 sample members reveals little about total mobility in Boston during 1831, for by 1831 the 1830 sample was "losing touch," or representativeness, with the population. To gauge the 1831 situation would require an 1831 sample, which is impossible since no 1831 census was taken. But if both the samples nearest in time to the year for which we desire information agree generally on the trend of activity for that year, it would seem safe to assume their indications to be not too far from the "real" situation. This is about as near as

Table 6. "Total Alterations"[a] as Percentage of Total Listings in Boston City Directories, 1831–56[b]

Period	Total Listings	"Total Alterations"[a]	"Total Alterations" as % of Total Listings
1831–34	51,658	37,169	71.9
1835–39	77,737	59,542	76.6
1840–44	100,225	76,064	75.9
1845, 1848–49[b]	87,988	83,310	94.7
1850–54	189,792	172,466	90.9
1855–56[b]	88,724	81,325	91.7

Source: Boston city directories, 1831–56, with exceptions (see [b]).

a. "Total alterations" is the sum of "names added," "names dropped," and "removals, &c."

b. No figures are available for the years 1830, 1846 (Adams' directory), 1847, 1857, 1858, 1859, and 1860.

we can approach the problem in the absence of yearly censuses and samples.

How, then, to measure residential mobility? Clearly any such measure must derive the rate of change of residence per unit of time. Changes of residence appear from a comparison, for each sample member, of his addresses in consecutive city directories. But how can one compute averages for a group whose members stay in Boston for varying periods? A solution is to denominate one year's residence in Boston by a sample member as one "residence-year," a measure analogous to man-hours. One then computes the ratio $\dfrac{\text{total moves}}{\text{total residence-years}}$ to obtain an expression of residential mobility for a group. In analyzing population movements in ante-bellum Boston, the 1830–59 period was divided into six inclusive quinquennia, 1830–34, 1835–39, 1840–44, etc. Table 7 shows how, as each sample group approached its census year, it achieved its maximum mobility. The values for the cen-

Table 7. *Mobility Ratios (Total Moves/Residence-Years) for the Sample Groups, 1830–59*

| Period | Sample Group | | | |
	1830	1840	1850	1860
1830–34	0.342	0.275	0.156	0.147
1835–39	0.266	0.377	0.259	0.188
1840–44	0.229	0.306	0.278	0.240
1845–49	0.213	0.288	0.464	0.355
1850–54	0.209	0.241	0.321	0.285
1855–59	0.205	0.175	0.349	0.417

Source: Sample data. Maximums are underlined.

sus years were 0.358 in 1830, 0.307 in 1840, 0.338 in 1850, and 0.496 in 1860. (Averages for the sample years may be lower than those for the five-year period on either side because the number of sample members falls off sharply on either "side" of the census years, reducing the base from which ratios are calculated, and possibly inflating the ratios.)

In practice, these ratios mean that about one household in three moved during each of the four sample years, and presumably in the nonsample years as well, assuming the sample years typical of their times. Even this ratio, nearly twice that of today, is an underestimate, for since city directories appeared annually, an individual household head could be credited with at most one move in any year. Then too, Boston's directories discriminated against the lowest economic orders, who were among the most mobile of the population.[14] There exists indirect evidence, from a few duplicated directory listings and from dual appearances in the manuscript census, that some persons, particularly those of lowest socioeconomic status, moved several times yearly. All in all, then, the "true" overall residential mobility ratio for the ante-bellum era in Boston was probably over 0.4 and perhaps as high as 0.5 if we take into account the large transient or "floating" population, the instability of the lowest socioeconomic groups, and their omission from city directories.[15] A rule of thumb would be that ante-bellum Bostonians were at least twice as mobile residentially as are Americans of today.

Without forcing the longitudinal sample measures of residential mobility into a situation they were not designed for, we may nevertheless note that the 1850 sample group, during 1845–49, achieved the highest mobility ratio of the ante-bellum era, 0.464 (see Table 7). It was just then, in the late '40s, that residential mobility, as measured by changes in the city directories, registered a sharp upswing (see Table 6). The samples indicate that residential mobility dropped slightly during the '50s; the city directory changes dipped somewhat then also, but the difference may be insignificant. At least there is substantial agreement.

But, as we shall see, mobility was not evenly distributed throughout all groups in society; neither was persistence. Taken as a whole, the most mobile members of the population were the least persistent, whereas the least mobile were the most persistent. This was not a necessary situation, for one might imagine a city in which residential mobility for all groups was high, although persistence varied greatly, e.g., a company town whose owners housed all employees, yet did not renew one-year leases on individual dwellings. But in Boston the inverse relationship held; it was marked along ethnic lines. For example, Table 8 shows the persistence, during 1830–60, of various city population components. The disparity between native-born and foreign-born residents increased during the period. Whereas the native-born in the three earliest samples stayed about twice as long during the period 1830 to 1860 as did the foreign-born, the margin grew to three to one in the case of the 1860 sample. The average persistence of all groups decreased during the thirty years. Declining persistence tends to corroborate the increasing mobility and turnover noted earlier: "churning" of the population was on the rise.

Foreign-born Bostonians, in addition to being less persistent than native-born residents, were more mobile (see Table 9). The results in the case of the foreign-born suggest why the 1845–49 period manifested such high mobility rates, for not only did the 1850 sample then achieve

Table 8. Persistence of Residence in Boston During 1830–60 of Various
Sample Components, 1830–60

Area of Birth	Average Length of Stay (Years) in Boston During 1830–60, by Sample							
	1830	N	1840	N	1850	N	1860	N
Outstate Mass.[a]	20.3	72	22.9	100	15.5	85	13.4	49
Mass. (entire)	20.4	100	21.9	142	19.4	125	19.4	88
Other U.S. States Outside Massachusetts	22.4	28	19.4	46	14.1	77	9.2	82
Total United States	20.9	128	21.3	188	17.4	202	14.5	170
Total Foreign	9.7	42	8.1	68	8.3	183	5.2	215
Total Sample	11.3	385[b]	15.7	385[b]	13.1	385	9.3	385

Source: Sample data.
   a. This includes all places in Massachusetts outside Boston.
   b. In the 1830 and 1840 samples, the sum of United States and Foreign
categories does not equal 385 because of the presence in those samples of
persons of unknown origin (215 and 129, respectively).

Table 9. Mobility Ratios (Total Moves/Residence-Years) for Foreign-Born
Members of the Sample Groups, 1830–60

Period	Sample Group			
	1830	1840	1850	1860
1830–34	0.414	0.532	0.333	0.529
1835–39	0.285	0.590	0.614	0.512
1840–44	0.264	0.294	0.348	0.450
1845–49	0.326	0.293	0.786	0.567
1850–54	0.207	0.223	0.357	0.363
1855–59	0.250	0.220	0.393	0.561

Source: Sample data. Maximums are underlined.

its highest value, but the 1860 sample did too. Census results show this period as one of considerable net decentralization of Boston's foreign-born residents. Comparing residential mobility ratios of foreign-born sample members with those of native-born sample members, shown in Table 10, demonstrates that mobility ratios

Table 10. Mobility Ratios (Total Moves/Residence-Years) for Native-Born Members of the Sample Groups, 1830–60

| | Sample Group | | | |
Period	1830	1840	1850	1860
1830–34	0.274	0.219	0.150	0.118
1835–39	0.207	0.300	0.216	0.142
1840–44	0.176	0.235	0.262	0.187
1845–49	0.167	0.230	0.337	0.287
1850–54	0.193	0.239	0.292	0.245
1855–59	0.192	0.155	0.315	0.296

Source: Sample data. Maximums are underlined.

for the foreign-born were usually nearly twice as large as those for native-born. Since city directories included proportionately more native-born than foreign-born, the "true" ratio was probably higher than two to one.

Turnover and persistence were not necessarily related in ante-bellum Boston, as Table 11 shows. Turnover continued rising whereas persistence peaked and fell off. But that table also suggests some other relationships. In it, net population growth and persistence appear to vary directly with one another,[16] as do net population growth and residential mobility (and of course persistence and mobility). Subject, as all of these conjectures are, to verification by studies of other cities, we may also note that persistence seems to decrease with increasing city size, at

Table 11. Summary: Turnover, Persistence, Mobility, and Net Population Growth, Boston, 1830—60

	Decade		
Population Characteristic	*1830—40*	*1840—50*	*1850—60*
Estimated turnover of households (sum of "households added" and "households dropped")	33,565	71,955	128,684
Persistence of household heads (%)	43.9	48.6	39.0
Mobility ratios of total samples (maximums are underlined)			
1830 Sample	<u>0.324</u>	0.220	0.207
1840 Sample	<u>0.336</u>	0.298	0.213
1850 Sample	0.214	<u>0.390</u>	0.332
1860 Sample	0.170	0.307	<u>0.365</u>
Net population growth (%)	38	63	28

Sources: Table 2; sample data; population figures used for Boston are 1830: 61,392; 1840: 84,401; 1850: 138,788; 1860: 177,840.

least in the 1850s.[17] Certainly the question of the relationships among these four population characteristics—turnover, persistence, residential mobility, and net population growth—deserves much more, and much more detailed, attention than we have been able to give it here if we are to understand the nineteenth-century urbanization process.

1. The research underlying this paper was carried on when the author was a research assistant in the project "Ecological Patterns in American Cities: Some Quantitative Studies in Urban History," supported by National Science Foundation grant GS-921 and by the University of Wisconsin Graduate School. Leo F. Schnore (Sociology) directs the project. For criticism of earlier drafts of this paper I am indebted to him and to Eric E. Lampard and Walter Glazer. They are not responsible of course, for its errors or omissions.

2. Eric E. Lampard, "Urbanization and Social Change: on Broadening the Scope and Relevance of Urban History," in Oscar Handlin and John Burchard, eds., *The Historian and the City* (Cambridge, Mass., 1963), p. 236.

3. It is hoped that this more technical matter will be published elsewhere.

4. *Persistence* seems to have been used first by James C. Malin in "The Turnover of Farm Population in Kansas," *The Kansas Historical Quarterly, 4* (November 1935), 339–72; at least, Malin is unaware of a prior use. (Conversation, January 13, 1969, Lawrence, Kansas.)

5. The sample drew 385 heads of household, stratified by ward, from each federal census. For further information, see the Introduction to the author's "The Plain People of Boston, 1830–1860: A Demographic and Social Study" (unpublished dissertation, University of Wisconsin, 1969).

6. For information on Boston's city directories, see Dorothea N. Spear, comp., *Bibliography of American Directories Through 1860* (Worcester, 1961), pp. 51–57.

7. No such listings appeared covering the years 1830, 1846, 1847, 1858, 1859, and 1860.

8. Lemuel Shattuck, *Report to the Committee of the City Council Appointed to Obtain the Census of Boston for the Year 1845 . . . .* (Boston, 1846), p. 162; *Boston City Documents Nos. 10* (1851), p. 11; 7 (1852), p. 14; *10* (1855), p. 12.

9. This method was devised independently of that reported in Sidney Goldstein, "City Directories as Sources of Migration Data," *American Journal of Sociology, 60* (September 1954), 169–76, but is essentially similar to it.

10. The "surplus" listings presumably were accounted for by business firms, second listings for households having sons over twenty-one, and persons living in hotels and boarding houses (which counted, regardless of the number of inmates, as single households).

11. This assumes that the number of female household heads aged twenty-one is negligible.

12. For instance, in Norristown, Penn., during 1910–20, a net gain of 1,570 adult males (from 7,030 to 8,600) involved in-migration of 3,830 and out-migration of 2,140 adult males, a turnover of 5,970, according to Sidney Goldstein, *Patterns of Mobility 1910–1950: The Norristown Study* (Philadelphia, 1958), pp. 100, 126.

13. To calculate these "half-life" periods, use $\dfrac{\log 2}{\operatorname{colog} r} = n$ years, where r and n are defined as in Table 5.

14. Boston city directory inclusiveness is assessed in my "City Directories as Aids to Ante-Bellum Urban Studies: A Research Note," *Historical Methods Newsletter, 2* (forthcoming, September 1969).

15. The results tend to support the suggestion by Sidney Goldstein in "Migration: Dynamic of the American City," *American Quarterly, 6* (Winter 1954), 337–48, that there were two kinds of population in American cities, "migrants" and "continuous residents."

16. This is also true for Philadelphia during 1830 to 1860; cf. Stuart M. Blumin, "Mobility in a Nineteenth-Century American City: Philadelphia, 1820–1860" (unpublished dissertation, University of Pennsylvania, 1968), p. 107. (The decadal growth rates for Philadelphia County were 36.7%, 58.6% and 38.4%, whereas the persistence rates were 30.4%, 38.1%, and 31.6%.)

17. Blumin's study of Philadelphia (see note 16 supra), a larger city than Boston, finds lower persistence than is reported here.

PART THREE: URBAN ELITES AND POLITICAL CONTROL

THE COMMUNITY ELITE AND THE
EMERGENCE OF URBAN POLITICS:
Springfield, Massachusetts, 1840–1880

Michael H. Frisch

Analysis of an urban elite, however the group is defined, implies consideration of its community function as well as its internal structure. Both these aspects have received ample attention in the sociological studies responsible for so much contemporary interest in the elite concept. Historians, however, have recently tended to concentrate on the latter dimension—on the composition and social background of elites—and on the overall social structure of the community. Behavior has often been seen as a function of this structure, and there has been less systematic attention to the actual role played by elites as something important on its own terms. The current interest in urban history may right this imbalance; we now take more seriously the details and processes of local development, often finding in the history of individual cities clues to the more general implications of urbanization and social change. In this paper, I would like to explore some of the possibilities of this approach.

This essay grows out of a larger study of Springfield, Massachusetts, and its transition, between 1840 and 1880, from small town to sophisticated city.[1] I would like to focus here on the relation of the local establishment, such as it was, to these overall changes. In particular, I shall be concerned with the expansion of local government and with the politicization of local affairs. I shall try to show that these institutional processes are crucial to understanding the meaning of the elite in a transitional community. That one must know the history of a community in order to understand the history and nature of its elite is, I recognize, something of a truism. Yet, if so, I think it is one historians still have great need to explore.

Just as we have a readily accessible image of the stable, deferential, old New England town, there is an equally familiar image of the political life cycle of the growing city. Robert Dahl provides one of the most well-known models in the long historical introduction to his study of modern New Haven. He pictures three successive dynasties in local affairs: the oligarchic Patricians rule first, until they are pushed aside by the ambitious new Entrepreneurs, who are replaced in turn by the rising immigrant and lower classes—the largely Irish "Ex-Plebes," as he calls them.[2] Such schematization has obvious validity in depicting very broad and long-term changes. But my research has indicated that in order to understand what really was going on in a nineteenth-century city like Springfield, our framework needs considerable refinement. This is particularly true of developments within Dahl's second stage—before the rise and triumph of the Irish.

The first thing one must consider is that in nineteenth-century Springfield there was virtually no distinction, much less conflict, between the patrician aristocracy and the business elite; the former was defined more or less by the latter. In fact, I doubt to what extent the patriciate was exclusive even in the eighteenth century, when Springfield's imposing town elders were known throughout New England as the "River Gods." The town had been established in 1636 to be a trading post; its founder, William Pynchon, was thus Springfield's first businessman before he was its first citizen and founded its first family. Through the years, the ranks of these families always included great merchants and manufacturers, like the prestigious Dwights, along with the expected complement of ministers, lawyers, and gentlemen farmers. And during the nineteenth century, in any event, wealth generally continued to bring influence, respectability, and, after a decent interval, a good measure of social recognition. I suspect that what separated the two centuries was more a difference of pace and scale than a new process of elite recruitment. The creation of opportunities for wealth and business success, and the rate at which new men were rising, accelerated so rapidly that the broadened community leadership inevitably took on a quite different tone.[3]

In this inflation of honors, perhaps just as important as the multiplying opportunity was the extraordinary degree of geographic mobility characterizing New England society at the time. This was true not only for the laborers Stephan Thernstrom found drifting in and out of Newburyport, but also—perhaps especially—for ambitious businessmen, professionals, and skilled craftsmen. Many of these young fortune seekers would arrive in town, become successful, well known, involved in community life, and in all senses established. Within a decade or two, they were often indistinguishable from the most prominent of the "old citizens."

By mid-century, the local establishment was overwhelmingly composed of people like this. Springfield became a city in 1852, but it would be twenty years before a native son was chosen as mayor, and this in a time when the office was still more a social honor than political prize. More impressive is the evidence of an 1893 volume of local biographies, one of those nostalgic tributes to a fast-fading nineteenth-century aristocracy. It was compiled by Charles Chapin, scion of a noble family that had been in Springfield since the beginning, two hundred and fifty years earlier. Predictably, his selection was

weighted toward the blue bloods and toward those community leaders who flourished in the first half of the nineteenth century. Nevertheless, of the almost three hundred
Respectables honored by full biographical sketches, only
ninety—well under one third—had been born in Springfield, the city they had come to epitomize. So much for the
iron grip of the old families.[4]

These facts are important, because they suggest that
the character of the elite group had been well established
before the onset of more rapid late nineteenth-century
growth. As Springfield became a bustling young city, it
had neither patrician elite nor closed local aristocracy to
be overthrown by rising new businessmen. Throughout
the following decades, though there certainly was no lack
of conflict, I could detect no *consistent* patterns of division between old and new wealth, between established
locals and aggressive newcomers, between the clean
money from trade and finance and the grimier profits of
the mills, factories, and railroads. The man villified in
the 1870s as Springfield's Boss Tweed, for instance, had
been brought to town as a young child half a century
earlier; he had served frequently and effectively in honorific town government posts since the 1840s. At the same
time, the man who opposed him, a man who represented
the acme of civic virtue, public service, and community
pride, had arrived in Springfield that same decade as an
unknown journeyman engineer. The absence of all the
often-posited conflict patterns in the community's busi-
ness/social elite, then, makes all the more dramatic the
significant changes that *did* occur.

In the 1850s, just before and indeed after it formally
became a city in 1852, Springfield's 12,000 people still
made up a relatively informal and intimate community,

much closer to the small town of fifty or even a hundred years earlier than to the city it would be in the next twenty-five years. Local government reflected the nature of the community in several ways. Functionally, government was quite limited. It was asked to do little that had not been done for decades; it did little; and it was generally reluctant to do very much more. It was concerned, for the most part, with the interests of the tax-paying property holders and, in this regard, there was not much real distinction between private and public matters. The town, and later the city government was simply the place where overlapping and conflicting private purposes were adjusted. Because of this focus, the community continued to accept the ancient principle that those with the greatest stake in society should have the loudest voice in its affairs. The institutions of town-meeting democracy were qualified by this traditional and natural deference—or, often, just indifference—to the leadership of the propertied "best people." In any event, local affairs rarely occasioned formal political conflict; it seemed neither appropriate nor necessary.

This is significant, because in other ways politics was quite important, even fundamental, to the life of towns like Springfield—not least as a primary form of public recreation. National and state politics, especially in the turbulent ante-bellum decades, called forth frantic activity on the local level. Party organization and partisan conflict had long pervaded the town meeting itself, extending at times down to the choosing of fence-viewers and hogreeves. But all the turmoil was generally limited to the nomination and election of officials, not to the actual process of government; local parties existed largely for the purpose of organizing county and state conventions, and for getting out the vote. Although there was

thus a surfeit of politics in local life, it is still true that
local affairs themselves were not yet politicized to any
significant degree.

This apolitical, deferential community of taxpayers
had, however, another side to its character. Just as much
as local government was a means for realizing the limited
purposes of the propertied, it was also an expression of
the general sense of community identity that still tied
Springfield's people. There was the common responsibility for the poor and for the education of children, to
give the best functional examples. Perhaps more representative of the attitude toward government was the tradition of amateur volunteer service, from all levels of
society. A glance at the occupational backgrounds of
those serving in the most important elective offices illustrates this point.

Springfield's Board of Aldermen was the source of virtually all power in the government; it consisted of eight
men, elected annually by the city at large but with one
nominally standing from each of the eight wards. For
analytical purposes, I divided them into categories representing broad levels of status as it is usually conceived. I
found that in the 1850s, the slow period before the dramatic surge of the Civil War years, Springfield's aldermen
came, as expected, mostly from three groups: 11% were
lawyers, bankers, insurance executives, and leisured
gentlemen; 28% were merchants and businessmen; and
20% were manufacturers and builders. Surprisingly
enough, however, 32%—almost a full third—were artisans and workingmen. Fragmentary evidence for leadership under the old town meeting indicates similar levels
of participation extending back to the early nineteenth
century.[5]

The large workingman presence at a time when the

elite dominated the community can be explained, in part, by the respect and visibility traditionally enjoyed by Springfield's craftsmen, especially those at the U.S. Armory, where the famous Springfield rifle was made. But nevertheless, this presence is impressive in its own right. It reflected the informality of city affairs and roles in them; it reflected the degree to which government still expressed the community's sense of inclusiveness and cohesion. In the 1850s, then, the conduct of city government, as opposed to just its election, had these two dimensions: government was at once a symbolic public institution and a narrow, functionally limited, private-oriented, deferential, taxpayers' association. It is important, I think, to see how both these dimensions were combined in the older idea of community. Especially for the elite, neither in fact nor in concept was there any clear distinction between the public and the private sectors.[6]

By 1880, all this had changed dramatically, though the steps in the process had been gradual. The Civil War made Springfield into a nationally famous boom town virtually overnight, which didn't surprise anyone as much as did the continuation of this growth after the war's end. The city population almost tripled between 1850 and 1875, and despite the inhibiting effects of the long depression in the 1870s, Springfield was established by that decade's end as one of New England's most dynamic rail, industrial, and commercial centers. Just as significantly, it took on in these years all of what seemed then to be the trappings of modern urbanity, from imposing business blocks, stone churches and public buildings, to squalid slums and aggravated social problems. And as Springfield grew, the city government, inevitably, became involved in community life in many new ways and

on a vastly different scale. It evolved rapidly from a simple representative body to a complex of executive, administrative, and political structures, usually overlapping and confused. In this context, the many local
problems and issues generated by rapid growth became,
for the first time, sources of frequently bitter political
conflict.[7]

These changes all deeply affected the old elite's view of
government. Another look at the Board of Aldermen
suggests the dimensions of this impact. The merchants
and businessmen, 25% of the aldermen through the
1850s, rose steadily to 42% in the 1870s. A similar rise is
seen for the manufacturers; the two groups together,
which earlier had accounted for less than half the seats on
the board, were now an overwhelming 75%. And to these
businessmen, public service was becoming less cere-
monial and more serious: the length of the average stay
among them was now two and one-half annual terms, a
doubling of the normal period of service in the first years
of city government.

It is interesting to note, remembering the three-dy-
nasty cycle described by Dahl, that in all this there was
no conflict with the supposedly distinct professional,
social, and financial establishment. Far from being driven
out as the businessmen moved in, the lawyers, bankers,
and insurance men also increased their representation
from 12% to 18%. Proportionally, they stood in almost
exactly the same relation to the business categories
throughout the thirty years considered. This would seem
to confirm, as was suggested earlier, that the *structure* of
what may broadly be considered the elite in government
hardly changed at all, whereas the *level* of its participation increased strikingly. The big losers, of course, were
the workingmen. By the 1870s, their 32% had evapo-

rated: only two of the thirty-three aldermen in that decade, holding only six of the eighty terms, were artisans or workingmen. This seems to have resulted more from the businessmen's awakened interest in serving than from any conscious effort to eliminate working-class participation, but the result was the same: the virtual elimination of this traditional presence. It is an ironic paradox that the fading of the informal old deference politics, reputedly marked by homogeneous leadership, was thus accompanied in fact by a marked decrease in the social diversity of officeholding.

The politicization of the elite can be understood in several ways, some of them more obvious than others. In the first place, as it became more active, government was of course becoming much more important to substantial businessmen and property owners. They feared the rising taxes and the soaring public debt, on the one hand, and on the other they were attracted by the government's new role in promoting prosperity, in building the city, and in increasing the value of their property through improvements. Because of this, because so much money and power had come to be at stake in public decisions, local affairs now required the more active participation of businessmen—as businessmen—to protect and further their own interests.

But this is only part of the story, and perhaps not the most important part at that. To picture the elite as suddenly acting out of purely particularistic motives would be to forget their earlier combination of public and private roles, and the sense of leadership that was so important to them. As the city grew, the public meaning of government increased just as significantly as did the implications of its action for private property. Step by step, the association of taxpayers was becoming an interdepen-

dent body of citizens, relying on the community for vital
life services that individuals could no longer provide for
themselves—for water and public sanitation and street
planning, and for the basic conditions of continued economic growth.

The expanded role of the elite, or so it seemed from
their vantage point, was needed as much to meet these
increased burdens of public responsibility as it was to
protect their own interests. Or rather, the two concerns
remained for them almost indistinguishable. Public and
private interest, public and private responsibility—to the
old elite, given their understanding of community, there
was little difference. Changes in these ideas would have
much to do with the more general breakdown, in later
years, of the elite's position in society. But such disinte-
gration would not really be a product of challenge from
below. Rather it is important to see it as beginning here,
while the group still firmly held power. Indeed, it was in
an important sense a function of the very factors that
were increasing this power.

This is because the growth of the city placed increasing
pressure on old assumptions. As the community became
deeply involved in meeting basic needs through government action, I found that the concepts of the public and
private sectors became differentiated. The taking on of
each new municipal responsibility, whether water or
sewers or secondary schools or street improvements; the
crossing of each new threshold in levels of debt and taxation—every step involved a conscious rethinking of what
public needs were, a redefinition of what the government
obligation was and should be, and a reevaluation of how
private interests were related to public needs. The gradual expansion of the public role was thus not a mere
response to the pressure of increased density and manifest

needs. Rather, the process was a much more complex interaction between conditions and the framework that determined how they were perceived and understood.

There is not the space here to examine the dynamics of this process in detail, but the result can be stated clearly: the idea of a public interest came to be articulated as the supposed touchstone of public policy, an undefined but general standard that subsumed the entire community, taxpayers and nontaxpayers as well. It was invoked, whether sincerely or as rationalization, or both, as something transcending private purposes, something far more than the resultant of particularistic forces, however calculated. The articulation of this guiding concept could, I found, become a source of confusion and conflict for the elite, particularly because of its essentially abstract nature. Like any large abstraction, the concept of public interest had great power and reach. But it also had all the inherent weaknesses: however potent a symbol, by itself it was cold and empty. It needed to be defined and interpreted in real terms; it had to be embodied in real institutions and policies; above all, it had to be realized through a process that touched the very real world of economic interests and political pressures. Public and private thus remained, as always, inextricable. But although the spheres in fact remained mixed, now the concepts were no longer so. Now the vastly increased importance of decisions about the public function could make the continued mixing of public and private seem inherently dangerous.

As long as growth was steady and shared, the conflict did not manifest itself. Confidence in the city's growth and in the momentum of progress overrode occasional objections that the "public interest" was merely a convenient mask behind which private power could plunder

the city. Although it was often difficult, the play of many
forces was usually able to produce general agreement on
what public policy should be. But by the 1870s, the city
had moved so quickly and so far that a sort of collective
vertigo developed. In the context of the times, these feel-
ings found a swift and natural focus. All around it,
Springfield could see other, larger cities struggling with
corruption, confusion, and selfishness; betrayal of public
trust, of course, was a major feature of national affairs as
well. The final blow was the great depression, which
afflicted Springfield from 1873 through 1878. Confidence
was virtually destroyed, and the financial pressure on the
overtaxed city government made the burden of debt that
had financed previous growth seem almost criminal.
Springfield was plunged into general crisis, and began to
ask what had happened to produce such suspicion and
despair.

On all sides, now, the public interest as any sort of
guiding concept for public action seemed cut hopelessly
adrift in a sea of particularistic currents. It was an abstraction that, in justifying almost anything, had come to
mean, so it seemed, almost nothing. Thus, investment of
public money in railroads had only a year or two earlier
been championed by most city leaders as essential to the
community's prosperity and hopes for future growth.
Now, suddenly, these same leaders saw the experiment
as a dangerous adventure. The potential indirect benefits to the city now seemed vague and distant next to the
burdens it imposed, and next to the speculative profits
reaped by real-estate interests and the railroads themselves. For the elite, especially, the fabric of ideas that had
traditionally tied public and private was, as the two sectors became more distinct, being stretched to the breaking point. In looking at this situation, the governing elite

was still in a relatively unchallenged position of leadership. But these men now were wondering whether their position meant very much, given the chaos they saw around them. They wondered whether the forces they had set in motion were proving too powerful, and running out of control. Springfield's traditional elite, in other words, looked on the face of the power they had set up in the name of the community, and it frightened them.

Their response to the crisis was fully in the spirit of the times. First, a rigid retrenchment would restore the virtues of thrift and caution to their rightful place. Second, and more important, the structure of government would be reformed to make particularism and private interests less of a threat, to make government more efficient and responsible. They felt that, above all, authority had to be consolidated and administration protected from the pressures of petty politics. In Springfield, all this took the form of a comprehensive new city charter, proposed in 1877 and similar to other reform charters adopted elsewhere at the time. The community response to this move is suggestive. Though the charter reform was backed by nearly every prestigious voice and approved in virtual unanimity by the City Council and the State Legislature, the people of Springfield rejected the entire plan by more than a two-to-one vote.

The reformers were stunned. They felt they had honestly been trying to design a way for democracy to survive the new demands of city government. "We are just discovering the difference between a town and a city," said the Springfield *Republican,* voice of the establishment. Because of the complexity of public decisions, and the welter of pressures that could obscure the public interest, it was felt, a city "requires long terms of office; it requires

unity, and intelligent system; it must subject the magis-
tracy to more clearly defined and more precisely located
responsibility, by which the public power is in reality
confirmed, rather than enervated."[8] In other words, just
as Springfield's imposing new churches and public monu-
ments made its rapidly changing cityscape more coherent
and comprehensible, so too, its leaders argued, new institutions were needed to give to the abstract concept of
the public will some substance, power, and visibility in
the cluttered life of the emerging city.

The opponents of the reform were impelled by the
same basic impulse, a deep fear of the power being generated in the urban community. But this led them in the
opposite direction. Just as the concept of public benefit
had been stretched too thin to justify, for the elite, continued high levels of public spending, for others the very
meaning of community was being stretched too thin to
sustain faith in that traditional leadership. Rather than
finding in the charter reform a confirmation of the public power, they saw it as enshrining only another, more
powerful and potentially more dangerous form of particularism.

In another sense, this impulse was leading many to
covet the same power that frightened them. The growth
of the city and the expansion of government meant, of
course, that public action was increasingly relevant to the
lives and interests of a much wider portion of the population. Appeals to the abstract standard of the public
interest, these people began to realize, could support
greater expenditures for *their* neighborhoods and property as logically as for the traditionally favored interests
of those with a greater stake in society. It all depended on
what form and substance was given to the justificatory
standard; more directly, they were coming to see, it all

depended on who was perceiving the needs and defining the terms. There was thus both reason and rationale for others to begin questioning the propriety of the older elite speaking in the name of the entire community.

The breakdown of this traditional faith was just beginning to have more general political effects. It was in these years, for instance, that Springfield's Irish took the first tentative steps on the classic trail to political dominance. In the mid-1870s, stimulated by several volatile local issues and by the temporary disorganization of state politics, they asserted their independence and fought for control of the local Democratic Party. Largely through their own efforts at naturalization and organization, the number of Irish voters in Springfield suddenly tripled between 1872 and 1875, though the Irish proportion of the population had held steady for several years.[9] As it happened, this was something of a false dawn—the real Irish move did not come until the 1880s. Similarly, the more general challenge to the dominance of the traditional elite was still more implied and potential than actual. But the Irish stirring, the charter battle, and a host of local issues related to the depression crisis suggested the new direction local affairs would take in the next decade.

By 1880, then, Springfield had a complex, widely active municipal administration, and local affairs were becoming fairly thoroughly politicized. In this process, the expanded public functions had been justified by the elite in terms of serving the community interest, but as this idea became increasingly abstract, it tended to function less as a guideline and more as a legitimizing conceptual umbrella, in the shade of which increasingly self-conscious interest groups could struggle for power. In the sense that politics is often defined as the systematic expression and management of conflict, Springfield stood on the threshold of what we would recognize as fully urban-style politics. The changing function of government had been a stimulus as well as a response to change. More importantly, perhaps, changing understandings of public affairs had provided a crucial mechanism by which general conflicts in the community could begin to find political expression.

Because so much recent research, as I noted at the start of this essay, has concentrated on social structure, these political conflicts are often seen as virtually reducible to the variations and stresses in the social fabric of the urbanizing community. For instance, in his well-known article on municipal progressivism, Samuel Hays has suggested quite necessarily that we must look past the high-minded, self-righteous rhetoric of the reformers to detect the more particularistic social meaning of their crusade, the structural determinants that shaped their perceptions and their prescriptions. Thus, the drive to rationalize, consolidate, and purify local governments was most basically the elite's way of reinforcing its own position against real or potential threats, and thus could take on more or less explicitly antidemocratic overtones.[10]

Although these points have great validity, the evidence from Springfield suggests that we limit ourselves unnecessarily by seeing the emergence of political life in such exclusively structural terms. The dynamics of political development in Springfield, I have argued here, owed perhaps as much to the elite's frustrating experience wielding power in an urban environment that was manifestly outgrowing unwieldy ideas and institutions. The unprecedented growth of American cities generated basic problems of leadership, administration, and politics in the democratic system, problems recognized at the time as the major issues of modern governmental thought. The ballyhoo about corruption, which partially concealed deeper social conflicts, was also partially concealing *these* deeper matters, which for the elite had considerable substance in their own right. Elite leaders, after all, were still making the basic city-building decisions at a time when the entire nation was becoming conscious of what an awesome dilemma the urban environment represented. They were groping for the answers to half-understood questions, searching for ways to preserve what they understood to be their democratic traditions while also serving the modern city's critical need for competent service and public responsibility. The anxieties involved in this search, I submit, were distinct from and in Springfield's case prior to the perception of conflict between old elites and new challengers. Neither dimension is reducible to the other; both were inextricably combined in the dynamics of urban growth.

More generally, by way of summary, I have suggested that the importance of the emergence of urban politics lies in its relation to broader change in the meaning of community itself. Robert Wiebe's *Search for Order* stresses that these years saw a turning from the local, immediate community to more formal and cosmopolitan loyalties—from the horizontal to the vertical orientation in society, as others put it, or from the classic Gemeinschaft to Gesellschaft.[11] This is most useful, but it is important to recognize that the local orientation could remain hugely significant. It was not that the idea of the local community was disappearing, but rather that it was changing quite basically.

Earlier, I said that Springfield in the 1840s was severely limited functionally, and that "community" had rela-

tively greater meaning as an immediate sense of association and cohesion. Over the years, I think this combination was substantially reversed. Community was in the
process of disintegrating as a feeling of association, with
contacts becoming more formalized and people seeing
themselves more fundamentally in terms of interest
groups. But, at the same time, the growing public functions of government were giving to community a new
meaning: it was becoming more important and comprehensive as an expression of interdependence, tangibly
embodied in the range of public institutions necessary to
a complex urban society. Community, in other words,
was changing from an informal, direct sensation to a
formal, perceived abstraction. And this abstract quality,
as such, enabled the institutions and roles that gave it
substance to come increasingly into question. This transformation, I think, was basic to local affairs, and must
particularly be understood when considering the meaning of the elite in the community.

It may be that in all this I romanticize and reify the
concept of community. But surely the point is that the
idea had this very reality for the people we are talking
about. It was an important part of the way they understood their own interests, their responsibility to society,
and the changes taking place all around them. Before the
power of the traditional elite could be overturned—I
close with a variation of the truism with which we began
—the idea of community legitimizing that role had to
weaken. And in this complex historical process, the developments in government which that same elite had directed and championed, played an ironically central role.

1. Michael H. Frisch, "From Town to City: Springfield, Massachusetts and the Meaning of Community, 1840–1880" (unpublished Ph.D.
Dissertation, Princeton University, 1967). Specific references in this article will be noted, but the reader is referred to the dissertation for the
detail and documentation upon which generalizations here are based.

2. Robert Dahl, *Who Governs? Democracy and Power in an American City* (New Haven, 1961), pp. 11–86.

3. The development of this aristocracy is well described in Margaret
E. Martin, *Merchants and Trade of the Connecticut River Valley, 1750–
1820* (Northampton, Mass., 1938) and to some extent in Robert J. Taylor,
Western Massachusetts in the Revolution (Providence, 1954). See also
some of the better local histories, such as Mason Green, *Springfield,
1636–1886* (Springfield, 1888) and Alfred M. Copeland, *Our County and
its People: A History of Hampden County, Massachusetts* (Boston, 1902).
A brief but interesting and sophisticated study of the town's development
is found in a recent pamphlet by Richard D. Brown, *Urbanization in
Springfield, Massachusetts, 1790–1830* (Springfield, 1962).

4. Charles Wells Chapin, *Sketches of the Old Inhabitants and Other
Citizens of Old Springfield of the Present Century, and its Historic Mansions of "Ye Olden Tyme"* (Springfield, 1893). The full tally found 90
of the 294 born in Springfield, 30 born elsewhere in the Connecticut
Valley, 80 elsewhere in Massachusetts, 77 in the rest of the nation, but
mostly from Connecticut and New Hampshire, 2 in foreign countries,
and 15 unknown. The figures are skewed somewhat by the fact that
Chapin included individual sketches of almost all the members of some
prominent families, whereas other equally important groups were
lumped in one sketch. Thus, of the 90 local-born citizens, there are 17
Chapins, 12 Blisses, 13 Dwights, and 7 Stebbins. Since this familial pad-
ding accounts for over half of the native leaders, it would appear that
their actual position was even less substantial than the overall figures
indicate.

5. The figures, compiled from Springfield City Directories, include all
of the 52 men who held the 72 annual terms on the Board of Aldermen
between 1852 and 1860. Categories are of necessity somewhat arbitrary,
and it was often difficult to assign individuals to one or another, such
as artisan-entrepreneurs or middle-level officials in a small factory; in
addition, directory descriptions themselves are often inconsistent. However, some familiarity with the community and the individuals involved
hopefully permitted a reasonably meaningful assignation in most instances.

6. Relevant here is Hans Paul Bahrdt, "Public Activity and Private
Activity as Basic Forms of City Association," in Roland Warren, *Perspectives on the American Community* (Chicago, 1966), pp. 78–85. See
also the analysis in H. H. Gerth and C. Wright Mills, *From Max Weber:*

Essays in Sociology (New York, 1946), pp. 235–39. For treatment of some related ideas in a relevant historical context, see Oscar and Mary Handlin, *Commonwealth: A Study of the Role of Government in the American Economy, Massachusetts, 1771–1861* (New York, 1947), pp. 53–72, 147–66, 195–205.

7. The city grew from 12,000 at its 1852 incorporation to 15,000 in 1860; 22,000 in 1865; 27,000 in 1870; 31,000 in 1875; and 33,000 in 1880. Some indication of the changing scale of government is seen in the growth of annual expenditures from $23,000 in 1850 to a peak of $782,000 in 1874, and by the growth of the municipal debt from only $18,000 in 1850 to over $2,000,000 by 1875. For these and other helpful official figures, see "Table showing the Growth of Expenditure in the Various Departments of the Public Service, the Resulting Increase of Taxation, and the Accumulation of the Municipal Debt, of Springfield, Massachusetts, from 1845 to 1876, inclusive, Compiled from Official Sources," in *Municipal Register of the City of Springfield for 1877* (Springfield, 1877); follows p. 203.

8. *Springfield Republican,* January 25, 1877. For a fascinating and perceptive portrait of this newspaper and its editor, who was one of the nation's leading journalists as well as a hugely influential and prestigious local figure, see George S. Merriam, *The Life and Times of Samuel Bowles* (two volumes, New York, 1885).

9. Between 1865 and 1875, official statistics show, with all other contemporary sources indicating the real change after 1872, the foreign-born electorate in Springfield grew by 200%, from 441 to 1,307, or from 9% to 19% of the total electorate, not far below the foreigners' 25% of the city population. There was, in this, little question about which groups were politically aggressive, even statistically: in Springfield, as throughout the state, the Irish were the only nationality to have more voting-age males naturalized than not, surpassing even the English and the Scots in this respect. Only 60% of Springfield's eligible immigrants, the Irish were by 1875 over 70% of its naturalized voters. See the *Census of Massachusetts: 1875* (Boston, 1876), *1*, Tables II, VIII, and X.

10. Samuel P. Hays, "The Politics of Reform in Municipal Government in the Progressive Era," *Pacific Northwest Quarterly, 55* (October 1964), 157–69.

11. Robert Wiebe, *The Search for Order* (New York, 1967).

SOCIAL STRUCTURE, SOCIAL STATUS, AND CIVIL-MILITARY CONFLICT IN URBAN COLOMBIA, 1810–1858[1]

Anthony P. Maingot

That warfare is a major agent of social change needs no elaboration; the recruiting of armies displaces men from standing occupations, their mobility exposes them to new experiences; those who remain behind tighten their belts to provide the supplies and pay the taxes necessary for the war effort. The best and the worst aspects of man and society are often brought out under these circumstances. Some of these vanish after the hostilities; others remain as permanent legacies embedded in the social structure or human consciousness.

The warfare that characterized the Spanish American Independence movements was of such intensity and duration (1810–28) that it could not help but affect the societies of the nations involved. It is not enough, however, to state that change must logically have taken place; the degree and quality of that change needs to be reconstructed and the questions asked: in what way were traditional roles and attitudes modified, and in what instances permanently so?

It would seem nearly logical that the place to start this inquiry would be in the area of the role of elites, civilian and military, and to do so within the context of the center of power of the nation, the capital city.

The patterns of civil-military relations developed in the urban centers of Latin America. It is difficult to understand the nature of early civil-military relations without some knowledge of early nineteenth-century urban social structure. On the other hand, since these were, at least until 1828, societies at war, it would be mis-

leading to attempt to discuss urban social structure and
intergroup social relationships without referring to civil-
military relations and the position of the military institutions in general.

To date, however, the body of literature on Latin
American urbanization does not lend itself to this type of
analysis. First, there is the fact that there is relatively little
cross-disciplinary research or even dialogue taking place.[2]
Second, existing research has provided little information
about the nature of the interrelationships of social classes,
and thus about social structure, in the early nineteenth-
century.[3] The whole matter is unfortunate since "it was
during this period that the role of the city in the diffusion
of culture change was established." In view of this fact, it
has been suggested that as a beginning, rather than applying Western models of class structure and dynamics, an
attempt be made to arrive at a special definition of
" 'classes' and their interaction" in the Latin American
city. Straightforward descriptions of the principal actors
(social groups) in urban society should be undertaken
with a minimum of theoretical preconceptions.[5]

The criticisms and recommendations directed to students of urban history are equally applicable to students
of civil-military relations in early nineteenth-century
Latin America. As critical for the establishment of a
given military role (and thus civilian response) as for the
development of the role of the cities, this period has been
almost completely devoid of any interdisciplinary research. What one scholar calls the "natural history" of
the armies of different states (i.e. the description and
analysis of their emegence as institutionalized groups),[6]
has been handled in two distinct ways. When it has not
been completely ignored by social scientists as an important causal factor,[7] the early history of civil-military

relations has been relegated by historians to the area of unverified historical deduction. This latter approach holds to an implicit theory of behavioral continuity and deserves fuller attention.

It is argued that conditions prevailing under Spanish colonial rule (created in the New World either by the privilege of a separate *fuero*[8] or by the introduction of the Spanish pattern of civil-military relations)[9] continued to influence the existing patterns after Independence.

Another version is that the duration and intensity of the Wars of Independence created a "military mentality" that eventually became institutionalized—something akin to a cancer that quickly spread and took control of the social body of the new nations.[10] "The Wars themselves," states a distinguished historian, "encouraged the military not the civilian virtues."[11] Edwin Lieuwen, who maintains that "the nineteenth century histories of the sixteen Spanish American nations were essentially military" in all but Chile and Costa Rica,[12] gives what amounts to a synthesis of the standard explanation for the "origins of militarism"—an explanation that is based on certain assumptions regarding the social structure:

Since eligibility for a commission was restricted to the creole elite, the officers naturally tended to identify themselves with the upper classes from which they came. This aristocratic identification continued even after independence, when the officer corps began to be drawn more and more from the middle groups in the society. Also the *fuero militar,* which exempted personnel of the armed forces from the jurisdiction of civil courts, tended to raise the army above the law, creating a privileged caste exempt from public liability and civil responsibility. Here then was the origin of the military caste system and the praetorian tradition in Latin America.[13]

This "privileged caste" explanation, however, has never been submitted to closer analysis through the case-study method. Such an analysis is intended here.

The problem on which this case study focuses is the social structure of urban Colombia in the early national period and the types of attitudes and social relationships that were both the result as well as the causes of that structure. This will be done by concentrating on civil-military relations in terms of the social status of the military vis-à-vis that of the dominant civilian sectors. It is premised that by focusing on this one aspect of urban life, something of the broader "texture" of the society of the early national period will be elucidated and brought into sharper perspective.

Basic Concepts

Since the purpose of this paper is not to build theory but rather to provide meaningful and relevant description and analysis, all one can realistically aim for as a beginning is conceptual clarity—an explicit delineation of the basic concepts guiding that description and analysis.

That evaluations of social honor and styles of life have traditionally played an important role in the stratification of Spanish and Latin American society has been a widely accepted fact. The words, or better, concepts, of *hidalguía* (literally "proper to the son of somebody") and *pundonor,* "point of honor," perhaps best embody the multiple facets of the phenomenon. Related to this concept of honor is that of *decoro,* which is more than the literal translation "decorum"; it implies dignity and honor—keeping up the necessary appearances and behavior of one's status; thus, adherence to the conventional rules that embody a status groups' style of life.[14] *Hidalguía, pundonor, decoro* all convey the importance of an honorable mode of comportment and presentation of self in the evaluation of status. Whether it is the constant striving against being what the Mexicans call *chingado,* "violated or humiliated, made a fool of,"[15] or whether it is wearing a necktie, not as decoration, but as "a badge of freedom from the social stigma of manual labor,"[16] the attitude is one and the same. These attitudes are most characteristic of a social structure such as that of Colombia during the period under discussion, i.e. one composed of strata or status groups rather than classes.[17] In such a social structure an individual's social status (the evaluation of his social position or rank within the structure) is determined largely by his claims to a position of prestige by virtue of birth and "style of life," especially the type of occupation pursued.[18] "Social esteem," "social honor," "status honor," "prestige," are all terms Max Weber uses to portray a social structure based on status groups; these are the critical factors that create the social distance between groups and generally color their relationships. "In content," says Weber, "status honor is normally expressed by the fact that above all else a specific *style of life* can be expected from all those who wish to belong to the circle."[19] The status group institutionalizes its style of life and conserves it through shared conventions and also, very importantly, by the fact that those who defy those conventions, such as by engaging in unacceptable, i.e. dishonorable, occupations, can suffer a status disqualification.[20] Considerations of racial purity, family connections, and education were all parts of the syndrome of attributes of status in Colombia.

It is good to remember, however, that behind these very real, albeit often intangible and subjective social factors there was of course the stark reality of economic power. This power in the final analysis provided the opportunities and wherewithal of a given style of life. Weber was emphatic on this point. "Stratification by status," he maintained, "goes hand in hand with a monopolization of ideal and material goods and opportunities."[21] Besides the specific status honor, which always rests upon distance and exclusiveness, all sorts of material monopolies are to be found. Such was the case in Colombia. A more or less stable distribution of economic power in favor of the Colombian upper status groups was fundamental to their continued predominance. But again, mere economic position was not sufficient for membership in the group, with its emphasis on traditional styles of life. That membership, on the other hand, would *in the long run* be empty without the economic power to sustain it.[22]

It is fundamental to understand that while the Colombian upper or high status groups claimed a monopoly of prestige and honor, and secured that claim through economic power, their claim was largely sustained by value judgments that were part of the conventions of the society. In a sense all groups strove to occupy this high status.

The social status the Colombian military occupied between 1810 and 1858 must be analyzed in terms of the existing social structure, and, as the preceding discussion indicates, that status depended largely on their style of life.

The First Army

The officer corps of the first Colombian army was a direct legacy of the Spanish military structure and tradition.

With the exception of the garrison at the port of Cartagena, the Spanish military presence in the Viceroyalty of New Granada at the turn of the eighteenth century was negligible.[23] Yet in New Granada, as everywhere else, the Spanish army was highly status-conscious. Troops were separated into white and colored (pardo) regiments, and even in the latter, positions in the officer corps were filled by "selecting the men [who were] believed to have the best breeding and social positions." This was in line with the Crown's great concern with the public image of the militia, a concern that "even influenced matrimony."[24] Two-thirds of the officer corps of the regular army was recruited from the young men, in the majority higaldos, who volunteered for the army and served in expectation of a commission (cadetes); the other third was recruited from "worthy" sergeants.[25]

The role of the military in the politics of the new nation can be said to have begun in 1810 when Creole patriots won over the allegiance of key officers of one of the units of the Spanish military establishment in the capital. Don Antonio Baraya, commander of one of the companies of the auxiliary batallion in the Bogotá garrison, was the key military contact of the socially distinguished group of Creoles who, having gained the alliance of that critical institution, took the first steps toward nationhood on July 20. The fact that Baraya was linked through strong family ties[26] to the highest Creole status group might explain the particular way in which he proceeded, and with him so many of those who formed Colombia's first army.

The bulk of the officer corps of the first Colombian army was composed of Creole military hidalgos, some Spaniards, and enthusiastic civilians of the upper status group. This group, which had formed the Creole social

elite under the colony, now monopolized political power.
It became Bogotá's, if not Colombia's, power-prestige seg-
ment. Some of the family names represented in the first
army are described by a military biographer as follows:

> *González* (Francisco Javier): He enjoyed the double
> prestige of the honorableness of the family to which he
> belonged and of a well-earned fortune.
> *Cabal:* . . . from one of the wealthiest and most illus-
> trious families of Popayán.
> *Ricaurte:* . . . from the most illustrious and extended
> [families] of the capital.
> *Jirardot:* . . . illustrious because of his education, his in-
> telligence . . . he seemed to belong, because of his
> physiognomy, to the teutonic race.
> *Santander:* . . . parents [belonged] to families of high
> social position.
> *Fortoul:* . . . of illustrious family originating in
> France.[27]

Colonel Vicente Vanegas, who also joined the first
army in 1810, had many relatives who "upon submitting
proof of *limpieza y nobleza de sangre*" were admitted to
one of the exclusive schools of the capital.[28] A Colombian
historian doing research on two officers of this period
states that he used their families' own *Genealogía y limpieza de sangre*.[29] A typical statement in one of these
genealogies read that the members of that family, "eran y
son hijos de algo, notorios de casa y solar conocidos, de
armas poner y pinter."[30]

This was a group of people who took pride in their
heritage, their intellectual pursuits, their elegance and
aristocratic nature. It might even be possible to speak of
a Colombian high-status-group "type" as represented in

this description of the nation's first President, Antonio Nariño:

> he was the finished model, and perhaps the first example of what later on was to known as the *cachaco santafereño:* elegant, courteous, talkative, witty, mocking hospitable, . . . habitually superficial to an extreme, but serious and heroic when life challenged him in truth. A dandy, thus, of high caste, and spoiled by society.[31]

Abstract as this description of the Colombian gentleman or *cachaco* is, it was an unmistakable fact. His economic position based on landownership, his dress, language, bearing, and convictions, were the hallmarks of a style of life invested with power and prestige. This identity he shared with the rest of the members of his status group. They were the bearers of convention; all "stylization" of life originated and was conserved by them, and that style was urbane to the extreme.

Both the source of recruitment, largely from these Creole "types," and the military regulations, which continued to be Spanish, tended to make the officer corps of the first army a highly status-conscious institution despite the prevalence of enlightened ideas among some leaders. Something of this status-consciousness is reflected in the following exchange of orders:

> *Order of the 27th of May, 1813:* Since there has been an enquiry as to whether sergeants and corporals of the unit can become actors in the theater, the President [Nariño] lets it be known that since actors are of no less social status *(condición)* than cobblers, tailors, carpenters and other mechanics which form the greatest part of the army . . . even though the [Spanish] *orden-*

anzas are still in effect, such a prohibition would go against the provisions of our constitutions as regards the Rights of Man.

Order of the 28th of May, 1813: In order to avoid any "dissenting interpretations which disturb the peace," let it be known that the Commander will be in charge of establishing the distinctions in occupations since mechanics cannot become officers.[32]

This status-consciousness is only one of the indications of the survival of the pre-Independence social structure; the role of kinship ties in politics is another. Just as family links had provided part of the reason for the behavior of some of the officers who joined the patriots in 1810, so those same kinship links strongly influenced the behavior of some officers throughout Colombian history. During the period of the Patria Boba (the first period of Independence, 1810–16), the ruling stratum was split into two antagonistic parties. In the course of the nation's first civil war, the first president, Nariño—a centralist—was betrayed to the federalists by a few of his most trusted military commanders who were in part responding to kinship loyalties.[33]

The emerging political groups continued to recruit members from this high status group, and traditional rules of conduct continued to exercise a strong influence to their behavior.

If the social structure and its corresponding attitudes remained unchanged, the same was not true of the military institution after 1816. The Secretary of War informed Congress in 1823 that although there were a few members of the army who had been recruited in the years between 1817 and 1819, "the majority" had entered service since 1820.[34] One reason for this was the fact that

many of the original patriots who had formed the civil
and military backbone of that first movement were killed
either during the civil war or during the "pacification"
and destruction of the Patria Boba by the reconquering
Spanish General Pablo Morillo. Although some did survive to join Bolívar, it is noteworthy that the roster of
fallen granadinos reads the roll call of the elder sons of
Nueva Granada's first families.[35] The initial military en-
thusiasm of this generation was not repeated. The Constitution of 1811 had provided Congress with the power
to raise and organize an army for the common defense of
the State; members of high status groups enthusiastically
answered Congress' call to make a weekly drill a matter
of "religious" duty.[36] They even attempted to regularize
military instruction by the establishment of a military
academy which would produce "military gentlemen."[37]
But all this was to change in important ways—for the
worse as far as the respectability of the military institution was concerned. The elimination of this generation
of gentlemen-soldiers contributed to the changes in the
recruitment of officers, a trend that was further impelled
by the dramatic change then occurring in the nature of
the war.

Bolívar's Army

During the years 1816–19 Nueva Granada was occupied
by the Spanish, but in Venezuela Simón Bolívar, after
some serious setbacks, had declared a "war to the death"
—a guerrilla war with none of the niceties of traditional
fighting.[38] This type of war required a different type of
army. Both that new army and that kind of warfare were
introduced into Colombia with the entry of Bolívar in
1819, and both became unpopular in a very short time.

The changes that occurred in the Wars of Independence with Bolívar's call for a "war to death" introduced
a whole system of styles and behavior patterns quite alien
to the elegant world of Colombia's high status groups, at
least to those who were left after the bloodletting. With
the generation of Spanish-trained officers reduced to a
minimum, it was becoming increasingly clear that what
was needed was not a group of men with some military
skill acquired in Sunday afternoon drills after church,
but men whose whole life and outlook contained the ingredients and spirit of the warrior. The Spanish infantry,
though certainly no longer the best in Europe, could
nevertheless be defeated only by a warrior people led by
men who understood and even admired those pugnacious
qualities that were repugnant to men who adhered to
certain standards of urbane behavior.

That warrior people and those leaders were provided
by Venezuela—which is not to say that the granadinos
did not contribute their share to the new independence
armies.[39] There is more truth than poetry in the Colombian assertion that, of the three regions forming the
state of Gran Colombia, in Venezuela the soldier was
important; in Colombia, the university; and in Ecuador,
the monastery. In a sense this assertion is a reflection of
a historical reality. Historically, it was in Venezuela that
Bolívar inaugurated his "guerra a muerte" in answer to
Spanish atrocities, and it was then and there that the experience of warfare became so intense and so all-encom-
passing that there could not but emerge a certain "type"
—one that stood in sharp contrast to the urban Bogotano
as exemplified by Nariño. Of this "type," José Antonio
Páez was representative; his behavior and attitudes, including a social gruffness, a distrust of urban intellectuals,
and an enormous political suspicion and drive, have been

explained by his mixed racial origin[40] and the socializing influence of his *llano* (plain) environment.[41] In Colombia, on the other hand, the avant garde had been intellectual, the pen rather than the sword serving as principal weapon. Though no less damaging to Spanish armor in the long run, it brought to the top a different group, a group that in a sense was already at the top—the high-status civilian intellectual elite of the capital city, Bogotá.

By 1820 the majority of the officer corps, including seventy-four Venezuelan generals and colonels, eighteen Colombians, eighteen "foreign," and four Ecuadoreans,[42] was recruited from what one high-status Colombian contemporary called "the lower orders of society."[43] Changes were brought about by the destruction of a generation of soldiers, the sheer size of the army, and the desperate need for men, preferably those who knew the terrain and were natural warriors, but realistically any man who was willing or could be forced to put up with the hardships of the kind of war being fought.[44] It was this fact that opened the door of the military to all, if not completely on a basis of achievement, at least on the basis of immediate need. In a sense, thus, the army was, at the time, a "democratic" institution in comparison with the other social institutions. Even so, José María Samper, remarking on the mixed composition of the officer corps, noted how the differences between the "eminent men of pure Spanish blood" and those of the "inferior classes of the society" formed two great social groups within the military. "While some *criollos* rose to very high ranks and dignities by virtue of their genius and patriotism," he recalls, "the promotions of the men of color were due exclusively to their heroism."[45] The figure of Bolívar and that of Páez most closely represent each major group, the latter

typifying the large number of mestizos and mulattoes
who rose to the top through rigorous stages of promotion.

The nexus between a status-conscious society, the base
of recruitment, and the attitudes of literate sectors toward the military profession at the time is described by
Tomás Rueda Vargas:

> With the promotion to the highest ranks or with the
> deaths of members of the first group of officers re-
> cruited from the first families of the capital and prov-
> inces, the initial contingent of officers was exhausted
> *(se agotó)*. . . [recruitment came from different sectors
> now] so that at the end of the war one found in posi-
> tions of high rank not a few men who could hardly
> sign their names or could only crudely draw the initials
> of their names at the bottom of the proclamations
> which others drew up for them. This system [of recruit-
> ment] continued after the peace and even more so than
> during the war; to the extent that upper class youth
> turned, with the creation of *colegios* and universities,
> to the liberal professions.

The result of that changing attitude and recruitment,
states Vargas, was that, "There began to be formed a
garrison officer corps *(oficialidad de cuartel)* which was
lazy, uncouth, and which slowly but surely destroyed the
prestige of the army and created problems of different
solutions."[46]

Although it is true that there was an institutional continuity in terms of constitutional provisions for an armed
force and in terms of its representation in the governmental structure, it would be tenuous at best to argue that
the mere presence of such institutional continuity is a
guarantee of continuity in behavior. No longer fulfilling
the dominant group's social expectations in terms of a

style of life, the military's former status as a privileged caste attractive to sons of the high status groups ended. Multiple consequences flowed from this change in the institution's recruitment pattern. Dating from approximately 1820, "military" behavior was contrasted in the Colombian's mind with "urbane" behavior—a clash between the cultured urban type *(persona culta)* and the plainsman *(campesinote, inculto)*.[47]

The clash between these two "types" was not long in coming and is reflected in the llanero's hostility toward General Santander. This, according to the Venezuelan historian Baralt, stemmed from their belief that Santander "did not possess instruction in his field [war] or a natural disposition for making war: he belonged to that group of officers whom the llaneros called *de pluma* in a deprecatory fashion."[48] Their hostility was also based on the feeling that he was anti-Venezuelan, a feeling of which Santander himself was aware.[49]

It is in the encounter of these two intrinsically distinct groups—distinct in their traditional styles of life as well as in their immediate personal experience and political frames of reference—that civil-military relations of lasting import began. It was not long before there developed between the urban writers and lawyers of Colombia and the officers and llaneros of Venezuela what one student correctly described as an "open and declared antagonism."[50] This mutual antipathy did not remain limited to the civilian elite in Bogotá, nor was it a matter of party loyalties; it was rather a general urban phenomenon.[51] And no one better understood the nature of the clash between these intrinsically different status groups than did Bolívar. "If it is not the llaneros who will bring about ruin," he wrote Santander, "then it will be the gentle philosophers of Colombia."[52]

The ingredients of this clash, the elements composing the different "styles of life" were many. In a major sense it was the clash between the city and the frontier, a clash as important in Colombia as in the rest of Latin America.[53] Santander must have had this in mind when he wrote Bolívar, who was returning from Perú, not to bring his army to Bogotá; their presence in the city would be "both scandalous and superfluous"[54]—although certainly Santander must also have had political and economic reasons for his admonition.

An ethnic distinction between the Venezuelan and the Colombian further accentuated the difference in the two styles of life, and thus added to the tension and conflict. The following approximate figures provide an idea of the ethnic distribution at the beginning of the Wars of Independence.

Table 1. *Ethnic Distribution at the Beginning of the Wars of Independence*

	Whites	Indians	Colored (pardos)	Negro slaves
Nueva Granada (Colombia)	877,000	313,000	140,000	70,000
Venezuela	200,000	207,000	433,000	60,000

Source: José María Samper, *Ensayo sobre las Revoluciones Políticas*, p. 75.

Urban Colombia was predominantly white and, it can be safely argued, quite conscious of this fact. It was in Bogotá that the issues giving shape to the pattern of civil-military relations were critical. Bogotá, with a population of some 20,000 in 1827, was a city in which the top families *(familias raizales)* continued to demonstrate the strongest aristocratic spirit, emphasizing their purity of blood *(limpieza de sangre)*, family links, and "pure" *(puras)* occupations. Whether out of virtue or hypocrisy, they adhered to a very circumspect style of public behavior that stressed reserved and conservative personal conduct.[55] *Decoro* was of the utmost importance. The behavior of the llaneros, for the most part *pardos* or mestizos, was anything but circumspect and reserved. Even the life of their leader, Simón Bolívar, himself of aristocratic birth, was a source of shock and gossip to the delicate inhabitants of the highland city. "A mistress in the palace and soldiers in the street," was the indignant utterance repeated over dinner from house to house.[56]

A further distinction was made between those who had additional sources of income and those who did not. This was a critical distinction for, as Weber has noted, if it was the social norm of the gentleman *(cachaco)* that surmounted the structure, it was monopoly or near monopoly of political power and its deep roots in economic power that gave it its base. Social status, being broader and more inclusive than status within an institution, depended on attributes that did not include being a military man. An officer could have a higher social status in Colombia—despite the fact that he was a military man—only if he possessed other attributes such as land or political status independent of the military. The military enjoyed in Bogotá little social status and much less "social esteem."[57] It is not surprising therefore that the death of a military member of the Colombian upper status group, General Juan José Neira, elicited this comment from one of his peers: "It is necessary to understand that Neira should not be confused with the mass of military men with whom we are commonly acquainted, those without law or restraints ... *he was very dedicated to the business of agriculture* and never meddled in public affairs."[58] And in Colombia, contrary to the case in Vene-

zuela and Perú, there is no evidence to indicate that military men were provided with the opportunity to acquire
attributes of status such as land or marriage into a prominent family—at least not on any significant scale. Although individual leaders such as Santander did receive
substantial grants of land, the practice was certainly not
widespread; no new group of landholders emerged in
Colombia as in Venezuela. This of course reflected the
relative power of the military as a pressure group in each
region. Competition for the scarce resources of these nations was intense, and each group resented the gains made
by the other.

It is doubtful whether the military were being over-
compensated for their duties, to judge from the salary
scales (see Table 2), even if these salaries were actually
paid, which was not always the case. What did seem to
be occurring was that prior to 1830 military men occupied many of the political and administrative positions. A contemporary, José Manuel Restrepo, claimed
that the majority of municipal-level posts, *prefecturas*
and *comandancias,* were occupied by Venezuelan officers.
"In this way people consider themselves to be a colony
of the Venezuelans whom they do not love."[59]

It can fairly safely be asserted that Restrepo, a major
chronicler of this period, was expressing the strongly held
opinion of a most exclusive and powerful group of Colombian citizens.[60] This group operated as a sort of
reference group not only for the rest of the elite but also
for much of the rest of the society.

José María Samper, another influential contemporary,
in referring to the group, revealed the value system when
he noted that "it is they who guide the revolution and are
the source of its philosophy. The other races or castes . . .
do nothing more than obey the impulses of those who

Table 2. Position and Pay in Pesos per Year, 1820–30

Military Rank	1820[a]	1830[b]	Political or Administrative Position	1820[c]	1830[d]
General en Jefe	6,000	3,000	President	50,000	12,000
General de División	4,800	—	Vice-President	25,000	4,020
General de Brigada	3,600	1,680	Ministers	12,000	
Coronel	2,400	1,200	Departmental Vice-President	20,000	
Teniente Coronel	1,320	960	President, Supreme Court	5,000	
Sargento Mayor	1,080	600	Governor of Province	2,000	3,204
Capitán	840	480	Secretary (escribiente)	400	
Teniente	600	396	Official of Ministry	1,000	
Subteniente	420	192	Minor Official of Ministry	600	
Sargento 1o.		142	Government Doorman		198
Cabo 1o.		108	Government Archivist		600
Soldado			Administrator of Customs		2,400
			Editor of "Gaceta"		1,008

a. "Decreto (21 de febrero) sobre asignaciones de sueldos a los servidores de la patria 1820." República de Colombia, Codificación Nacional (Bogotá, 1926), 7, 11-13.

b. Gustavo Arboleda, Historia, 1, 142-43.

c. Decreto.

d. Arboleda.

have the prestige and intelligence, the audacity and even the superiority of the white race."[61] Of another of the members, Rufino Cuervo, it was noted that he "turned all his influence and authority to counteract the pretensions of the military who continued to consider themselves as a class superior to the civilians."[62] Vicente Azuero's already profound grudge against Bolívar and perhaps against all military men was said to have intensified from the day one of them attacked him in the street, allegedly rapping the knuckles of the hand that had written many antimilitary pieces in the openly antimilitary press.[63]

Bolívar understood the position in which the majority of the men in his army found themselves, especially the restless llaneros. Their social status was not commensurate with their constitutional obligations and governmental functions, and more importantly—from the point of view of their behavior—did not correspond with their own perception of their merits. Bolívar correctly realized that this disparity was dangerous:

> You have no idea of the spirit which animates our military leaders. They are not the same men you know. They are men you do not know, men who have fought for a long time . . . who believe that they have great merit and who are now humiliated, miserable, and hopeless of ever gathering in the fruits of their labors. They are llaneros, determined and ignorant, men who have never considered themselves the equals of others who know more and make a better appearance than they. . . . I treat them with the greatest consideration, yet even this consideration is not enough to give them the confidence and frankness which should exist among comrades and compatriots. We find ourselves at the

top of an abyss, or rather on top of a volcano that may soon erupt. I fear peace more than war.[64]

Bolívar was describing—and the facts indicated—an inconsistency between the official position (political and military responsibilities) of the military officer and the social compensations and recognitions awarded him. One of these officers, for instance, complained that the civilian lawyers "flatter the military when they are possessed with fear, and insult them in the prosperity of peace."[65] Resentful and bitter of what they perceived to be ingratitude and injustice, the "determined and ignorant" Venezuelans continued their arrogant and uncouth behavior so offensive to polite and urbane Bogotá society.[66]

That the clash between these two sectors had reached critical proportions by 1824 is illustrated by the "Colonel Infante" case. Colonel Leonardo Infante, a llanero Negro, was perhaps the prototype of the Venezuelan military man whose uncouth behavior antagonized the urbane Bogotanos. Convicted of murder and sentenced to death after a controversial trial, Infante's execution became a major contributory cause in Venezuela's secession from Gran Colombia.[67] It is not necessary to argue the merits of Infante's trial per se to see the point José Gil Fortoul attempts to make when he contends that the political situation of Gran Colombia was so critical at that moment that leniency on the part of Vice-President Santander would have been judicious.[68] But this was not to be, for as more than one scholar has noted, the Colombian civilians were bent on demonstrating through Infante's conviction and execution that civilian rule was supreme, thereby putting the military in its place.[69]

Aside from the transcendental importance this case had on subsequent events—i.e. the dissolution of Gran

Colombia into three separate nations—it also revealed a
crystallization of sentiments against Bolívar and some of
the causes of that crystallization. Several aspects of the
case throw additional light on the social structural factors involved in the erosion of Bolívar's popularity and
in the growth of antimilitarism in general. First there is
the fact that Vice-President Santander's personal honor
was involved; he was piqued because during the course
of some festivities Infante had, according to one eyewit-
ness, "in front of everybody, made some jokes about him
which were typical llanero style but which were offensive
to the military courage of the general."⁷⁰ Second, there
was the fact that the serious clash in styles of life between
the Venezuelan military and the Colombian civilians had
created a state of general hostility toward Infante in the
neighborhood (San Victorio) where he resided. Groot's
description of the situation is highly relevant to the analysis:

[His neighbors] were afraid of him because he was a
complete plainsman *(era todo un llanero)* and plains-
men have obnoxious games *(chanzas pesadas);* to which
was added his imposing presence. He was a Negro of
the purest type, a plainsman from Maturín [Vene-
zuela], a fierce cavalryman *(de lanza brava),* robust,
well shaped . . . He always wore his uniform with its
silver eqaulettes and high ribboned hat [although he
was not a drunkard nor did he ever misbehave with
anyone]. Even so, with these manners of a plainsman
he bothered those of the neighborhood, and even those
whom he knew regarded him with hostility, *because
a plainsman in a society of educated people* (gentes
cultas) *is like a bulldog which enters a hall wagging its
tail and even though its owner says that it does not bite,*

they all look at it with hostility and want it thrown out.[71]

A more appropriate metaphor to describe the clashing styles would be difficult to find. Even one as sympathetic to Infante as the priest who heard his last confession and accompanied him to the gallows describes the officer in essentially negative terms:

Although Colonel Infante was a pure Negro and was not known to have any political education, even so he was a Roman and Apostolic Catholic; and even though he could not express himself except in harsh and barbaric terms, one cannot deny that he had great talent.[72]

Infante, on his way to the gallows, is reported to have looked up at the Congress building and several civilian representatives and exclaimed, "I am the one who put you in those positions!" Again, before dying he shouted to the assembled troops, "This is the payment I am given. . . . I am the first, but others will follow me."[73]

The tensions reflected in the Infante case increased in the years after 1829 as the war against the Spanish shifted to Perú and upper Perú (Bolivia) and as demands on Colombians to finance and man the army increased. If the thirty generals and eighty colonels in Colombia in 1826 put a strain on the nation's weak finances and created considerable hostility between the civilian and the military sector, upon Bolívar's return in 1828 there were ninety generals and two hundred colonels[74] with even greater claims to wealth and honor—or so they thought. By then the overall financial demands of the war took up to two-thirds of the budget of Gran Colombia,[75] taxing the Bogotano's pocketbook as well as his tolerance and reinforcing his sense of social affront.

Threads of philosophical republicanism moved themselves into this matrix to rationalize a pattern of prejudice and hatred against Bolívar and his "military party."

Eduardo Caballero Calderón provides a neat triple explanation of the urban Colombian's reaction to the military—an explanation that gives a clear picture of the existing social and occupational status of the military:

> The reaction of the Bogotano had a three-fold cause: the civilian spirit in conflict with an arbitrary military spirit that reigned over the whole area of public administration; an incipient regional and national spirit in opposition to the retinue of Venezuelans that Bolívar took with him everywhere; and the profound displeasure at the intrusion of the mulatto and mestizo bearing swords in a society that was tranquil, prudish, and haughty in its racial prejudice . . . in his last years, when he became a dictator, Bolívar represented these three things: the arbitrariness of the sword, the insolence of the Venezuelans who were regarded as intruders, and the rebellion of the mixed bloods.[76]

This identification of the military career with what were clearly considered the worst aspects of the social order was to persist throughout the century since the social structure that entertained these ideas in 1828 and 1830 changed little during that time. At the same time the increasing deterioration of the army, due largely to the low quality of those recruited as officers, tended to confirm the worst fears of its detractors.[77] Members of the high status groups that controlled power and prestige looked down on the military and avoided military service. Men from the lower strata were recruited, rose to the top of the army, and assumed what to them must have seemed great political responsibility. But the top of the army was still very low in the Colombian social structure in terms of status.

Although the fact of the military's low social status is significant if one is to understand their continued subordination, there still remains the fact that the realities of Colombia's social structure and stratification do not by themselves explain the Colombian military's initial lack of political power. It is conceivable that the despised military men could have imposed themselves on the system (as indeed two officers, Urdaneta and Sarda, attempted to do in unsuccessful coups), acquiring the attributes of status in the short run by destroying or subjugating the upper strata and creating their own system; or in the long run for their progeny by adopting the required style of life. Why they did not is the next chapter in the story.

The Generation of 1828 and the "New" Army

Colombian historiography, in the Spanish tradition, tends to periodize the past in terms of "generations" of men whose thoughts and actions brought about fundamental changes in the course of events. In Colombia the "generation of 1828" was that group of individuals who "having their formation in the classrooms of the colegio del Rosario de Bogotá[78] had pretended to form an antimilitary republic, anti-grancolombian and democratic, even going to the extreme of an attempt against the life of the Liberator."[79] By 1828 the armed struggle against the Spaniards was won, and the internal political struggles of early nationhood, already quite intense, began to consume most of the energies of both the individual and the group. In Colombia civilian energies were expended in the struggle against the military. What makes Colombia such an atypical Latin American case is that while in other Latin American countries similar civilian groups tried also to break the power of the military, in Colombia they actually succeeded.

Social status is measured in terms of prestige, but power must also be taken into account. Prestige was an obvious monopoly of the Colombian upper strata through birth, occupations, and race. In order for them to monopolize political authority, however, it was necessary that they successfully eliminate the military as significant power contenders and then assert their control of the means of achieving power and prestige.[80] Unless they accomplished this it was still possible that the military, who were not eliminated as a group or institution and who were making strong claims to leadership, might reassert themselves. The Colombian civilian leadership established its power through two critical acts. First, it eliminated the substantial Venezuelan military challenge in the early 1830s, and two decades later (in 1854) it terminated all military pretentions of playing an important role in the system by drastic cutbacks in the military budget and standing army. The subjugation of the military was physically and socially accomplished within the lifetime of the generation of 1828.

The reknowned Swedish traveler, Carl August Gosselman, noted in 1837 that Colombia possessed two characteristics that guaranteed its political stability: one was the great number of competent civilian functionaries well versed in public administration, and the other, "a nearly total absence of the numerous military chieftains which in these recent times have been the cause of numerous internal disturbances in these countries."[81] Gosselman then related the story of the expulsion of a large number of military men, calling it "one of the most profitable exports that country could have ever made."[82] The extent of this "profitable export" is apparent from the figures in Table 3. The expulsion of the Venezuelan military caused as much happiness as the expulsion of the Spaniards. One Colombian minister put it this way when describing the entry of the Liberal Colombian troops into Bogotá:

> This day of redemption has been the most satisfactory one for Nueva Granada. No function, in twenty-one years of great events, has been as solemn; the good people of Bogotá have had no day of more satisfaction, nor another army such demonstrations of happiness; such had been the suffering, and such the desire to be free from the worst and most denigrating domination.[83]

The number of colonels in 1826 was eighty; in 1832, at the beginning of true Colombian nationhood, there were only sixteen. Along with the thirteen generals expelled from Colombia, there were also twenty-six colonels, fifteen first commanders *(Primeros Comandantes)*, ten second commanders *(Segundos Comandantes)*, sixty-one captains of different gradations, and eighty-three lieutenants of different gradations—making a total of 208 officers.[84]

Both in terms of personnel and attitudes, Colombia had a new army with the expulsion of the Venezuelans.

José María Obando, Minister of War in 1831, set the tone himself of the "new" army when he noted that the Bolivarian military structure had been totally dismantled and the new army created from a "scrupulously purified" base,[85] which should be understood to mean purified of the pro-Bolívar "military party." Two of the most important "military" caudillos of the victorious Colombian army, Obando and José Hilario López, were shortly to become champions of the liberal political cause in

Table 3. *Changes in the Military's Command Structure, 1826–32*

Top Command of Army in 1826[a]	Expelled, 1831[b]	Top Command, 1832[c]
Generales en Jefe:		
1. Juan Bautista Arismendi*	Generales en Jefe:	
2. Rafael Urdaneta*	1. Rafael Urdaneta	None
3. José Antonio Páez*		
4. José Francisco Bermúdez*	Generales de División:	
	2. Mariano Montilla	
Generales de División:	3. Laurencio Silva	None
5. Carlos Soublette*	4. Manuel Valdés	
6. José Tadeo Monagas*	5. José María Carreño	Generales Efectivos:
7. Manuel Valdés*		1. Antonio Obando†
8. Mariano Montilla*	Generales de Brigada:	2. Juan N. Moreno†
9. Francisco Esteban Gómez	6. Mauricio Encinoso	3. Ignacio Luque†
	7. Justo Briceno	4. José María Obando†
Generales de Brigada:	8. Cruz Carrillo	5. José Hilario López†
10. Miguel Guerrero*	9. Domingo J. Espinar	
11. Juan Paz del Castillo*	10. Daniel F. Oleary	
12. José Ma. Carreño*	11. Diego Ibarra	
13. Pedro Briceno Méndez*	12. Julián Infante	
14. Pedro Fortoul*	13. José F. Blanco	
15. José de Jesús Barreto		
16. Manuel Antonio Valero		

a. "Decreto (10 de junio) que determina el número de oficiales generales y coroneles efectivos del ejército," *Codificación Nacional,* Suplemento, VII, pp. 350-51.

b. "Decreto (12 de abril) sobre generales y coroneles," ibid., VII, 1832, p. 553.

c. "Relación de los generales," p. 31.

* Venezuelan origin.

† Colombian origin.

Colombia, and as presidents at mid-century, it was they who finally broke many of the colonial structures still in existence. In Colombian history, they are the re-formers. They were caudillos to be sure, but caudillos with a liberal republican world view and a strong dis-trust of any form of militarism.[86] They were, and this should come as no surprise, members of the high status group. López clearly embodied the values of the elite of that Colombian dominant status group. "My forefathers," he immediately informs the readers of his memoirs, "be-longed to the first families of the old nobility."[87] His revolutionary fervor was first aroused by the *tertulias* (private discussions) held at his uncle's home and at-tended by many members of the upper social strata of the region. He survived the years of the Patria Boba and the pacification of Morillo, and fought with Bolívar in Co-lombia. Once the war scene shifted to Perú and Vene-zuela, however, he requested his retirement from the military—something the government repeatedly refused to allow. His reasons for wanting to retire were very much in keeping with his overall set of values and were repre-sentative of those of his group in 1824:

> [My request to retire was again refused] consequently I resigned myself to the blows and travails of a career which has never flattered me during peacetime, and much less in those circumstances in which because of my low rank, I was subordinated to many commanders who, I say it with pride, did not have the well-acquired merits *(titulos)* to command me and I naturally feared an outrage which would lead to a tragic end.[88]

López never recognized the "merits" of the crude mili-tary men recruited during the second phase of the war, and a clash was not long in coming when his maternal

grandmother was insulted by some soldiers standing
guard at a meeting of socially prominent citizens.[89]
Through a newspaper he edited—another sign of his con-
formation to urban "civil" values—López propagated
"liberal" and "constitutional" Republican ideas. No
amount of military solicitation could deviate him from
his course. He recollects this conversation with the Venezuelan General Rafael Urdaneta, a close ally of Bolívar:

> You are blind, he told me; you do not know your own
> true interests. Don't you consider that in upholding
> the projects of the Liberator [Bolívar] the military are
> destined to form the first hierarchy in the new order
> and consequently will occupy the most important posi-
> tions? Don't you consider it to be a dishonor to the
> military to support those ridiculous principles of de-
> mocracy which aside from being pure theories, will
> also only result in putting us under the domination of
> the lawyers and have us lose our *fueros* and preroga-
> tives?[90]

López not only refused to join any attempt at establishing military predominance, he became a leader in the
movement to establish a civilian republican constitution.
He had been the spokesman for a group of Colombian
military officers who formally requested abrogation of
the *fuero militar,* "a step which honors us greatly."[91]
Later, when offered the Ministry of War under the civilian Presidency of Márquez, he refused on the grounds
that military men ought not to form part of the civilian
government.[92]
    Obando was Minister of War during the critical year
of 1831, and his ideas on military organization and on
the mission of the military and its role in society also
appeared to show the influence of European philoso-

phical liberalism and republicanism. His recommendations, one of which urged that young officers be deprived
of their horses so that "they may better understand the
conditions of the footsoldier,"[93] had parallels neither in
the Spanish nor in the Bolivarian system. Other aspects
indicative of a changed situation, both in terms of the
ideas they reflected and of the limitations imposed on the
power of the military as a corporate group were: (1) the
military's acceptance of the jurisdiction of Congress over
military promotions and certifications of ranks, as well as
the annual regulation of the size of the army, and (2) cur-
tailment of the *fuero de guerra* for the regular army; only
strictly military infractions would be tried in military
courts. Other measures taken included such things as the
amelioration of corporal punishment in the army's disciplinary routine, a reduction in salary of those officers
not engaged in actual command of troops, and the abolition of the *comisaria de guerra,* or quartermaster corps—
its function passed to the National Treasury.[94] This was
part of a general attitude that reflected a willingness to
submit to civilian authority.

Although the Constitution of 1830, written just before
the dissolution of Gran Colombia, specified that officers
of the army and navy had to be Colombians, the Constitution of Nueva Granada of 1832 went even further, stating
that "the officers of the army and navy shall be Granadines, and the general officers shall be Granadines by
birth."[95] Article 171 of the Constitution of 1832 noted
pointedly that "There shall not be a larger permanent
armed force than is indispensably necessary," something
the high civilian status groups managed to guarantee
throughout Colombian history. Table 4 clearly shows
that regardless of the state of the government's finances or
of the party in power, the size of the army shows a remarkable uniformity—always small.

Table 4. Size of Army (Including Officer Corps), 1831–1921

Year	Dominant Political Philosophy	Balance or Deficit in National Revenue[a]		Approximate Actual Size of the Military[b]
1831			—	2,370
1832		(+)	244,707	3,880
1834	Moderate	(+)	175,342	3,230
1835	Liberal	(+)	1,421,013	3,230
1837		(+)	76,156	3,330
1853		(−)	940,168	1,200
1855		(+)	286,515	
1856		(+)	77,432	109
1857		(+)	98,312	400
1858	Liberal	(−)	167,858	1,000
1867		(−)	519,439	2,000
1868		(−)	1,043,172	1,700
1870		(+)	264,778	1,000
1872	Radical-	(−)	1,202,969	1,246
1874	Liberal	(−)	572,375	1,200
1881				3,500
1883				3,264
1888	Núñez			6,231
1890	Conservative			6,230
1892				5,500
1910			None	5,300
1912	Conservative		None	5,585
1921		(−)	8,829,725	6,000

a. *Memorias* or *Informes* from the Ministro de Hacienda of the respective dates.
b. *Memorias* or *Informes* from the Ministro de Guerra of the respective dates.

The measures taken by the founders of Nueva Granada to demilitarize the country were very successful. The year 1830 thus represents a critical watershed in the history of Colombian civil-military relations. The consolidation of the civilians' position of power was thereafter assured through several factors.

Of great importance was depriving the military of an institutional base by abolishing offices the military traditionally held. For example, in 1832 the antimilitary gov-

ernment of José Ignacio de Márquez decreed the abolition of the old military-civilian offices of Commander
General of Departments, Provinces, and Cantons; only
those local authorities directly appointed by the Executive were retained.[96] This disposition, however, did not
eliminate the traditional *gamonal* and village *cacique;* it
did, because in this case the decree was backed by power,
tend to convert them into loyal and dependent agents of
the party that appointed them.[97] Thus early in Colombian history the regional leader, so frequently a petty
military despot in other Latin American countries, became instead an instrument of the national leadership—
not that this made him any less of a despot in his own
sphere of action. These politicized regional leaders,
rather than the standing army, became the best guaran-
tors of factional power and the most active instigators of
political violence and intolerance.

Perhaps more important was the continued divorce of
the professional military from the sources that provided
higher status, a fact that in turn had a continued adverse
effect on the recruitment pattern. With each passing year,
the Minister of War noted in 1842, "the profession of
arms appealed less" to qualified young men, and despite
its small size it was difficult to fill the vacancies in the
officer corps.[98] The army had to take what it could get. A
contemporary observer and student of the social and
political scene, José Manuel Restrepo, gave a partial explanation of why this was so, remarking that,

> The army will never be greatly improved because the
> whites and educated men will never go and form ranks
> with the ragged and negroes and mulattoes. This has
> been so, is so, and will continue to be so in the Re-
> publics of Spanish America regardless of how much

democracy is preached. This would be contrary to certain acts of private and public life and of the traditional customs and habits of a large sector of granadinos.[99]

Elsewhere Restrepo noted that the plans of the López government to create a National Guard *(Guardia Nacional)* were impracticable:

> The differences in castes that exist among us is a great obstacle to a generalized establishment of a national guard. There are very few citizens among us well enough educated and with enough "philosophy" to go and form part of a troop alongside a badly dressed and grubby Indian or Negro.[100]

As has been suggested, it is conceivable that this adverse public image of the army might have been overcome through forceful measures directed at improving the general benefits and prerogatives of the career. Nothing of the sort seems to have been forthcoming and, what is more, strictly material reasons also contributed to the low status of the career. Badly organized, administered, and regulated,[101] the military profession provided little stability and security for the officer. He did not even control the full amount of his monthly pay (see Table 5). Two additional practices persisting throughout the century helped to lower the institution's prestige and to create a negative social estimation of its honorableness. First was the fact that in the frantic search for bodies (Colombians continued to avoid the service like the plague), the old Spanish practice of drafting vagabonds for certain units during periods of crisis was reintroduced on a general basis. The *cuartel* was converted into a veritable prison for the outcasts of society. They were forcibly,

Table 5. Military Remuneration, 1842[a]

Rank	Whole Salaries	Portion to Be Paid Outright	Portion Retained. Paid only with Executive Permission
General	$206	$77	$122
Colonel	149	57	82
Lt. Colonel	100	44	55
Sergeant Major	80	37	42
Captain	55	29	25
Lieutenant	40	24	15
2nd Lieutenant	37	23	13

a. Salaries per month and in rounded figures. Adapted from "Decreto del Poder Ejecutivo" (Bogotá, June 1841), Esposición . . . Despacho de Guerra . . . 1842, Appendix No. 13.

usually violently, apprehended, roped or chained together, and marched to the cuartel; seldom thereafter did they see anything but the four inside walls of the building.[102] Second, the creation of companies of zapadores in 1845 to open roads, build bridges, and perform other public works converted the military force into something akin to a body of laborers. At least one mutiny was caused by such abuses, but the practice was not stopped until well into the twentieth century.

Given these conditions, it is hardly realistic to expect that there could have emerged any sense of corporate or institutional identity. Without this identity, on the other hand, the army was nothing but an institutional umbrella for a motley group of men who were little more than low-status members of a given political party. Since these men were not in a position to challenge the party leadership, they became useful instruments of that leadership; officers rose and fell with the party to which they belonged.

Up to the early 1840s there were no major attempts

aimed at completely abolishing the army as a part of the
system. When it did come, the challenge to the military
institution's claim to a place in the society, however subordinate, was part of the general program of change advocated by a powerful social movement late in the 1840s.
It was a logical extension of the antimilitarism of the
urban generation of 1828.

The Destruction of an Army

The political context of the critical 1848–53 period was
an urban one. It found the Liberal Party widely split into
two quite opposite social and ideological camps, the
Gólgotas or *Radicales* (radicals) and the *Draconianos*
(moderates). The Gólgotas were composed mainly of
high-status city youths (known as *cachacos*) enchanted by
European ideas, some large landowners (usually with
urban residences), and those merchants who stood to
benefit directly from the abolition of the state monopolies
on tobacco and other products and from free trade (i.e.
abolition of tariffs). The Conservative Party elite, after
their defeat in the attempted rebellion of 1851, also supported the Gólgotas, despite the fact that they were par-
tisans of centralism and that the Gólgotas sought the
framework of a federal government structure within
which to carry out their program.

The Gólgotas controlled Congress, where the sincerity
of their convictions (as expressed, for instance, in their
abolition of slavery) lent fervor to their politics. This
fervor was also reflected in the tenacity with which they
urged and fought for one of the central planks in their
program: the abolition of the standing army. To insure
this goal they pushed for a whole series of reforms. For
example, they advocated and secured complete freedom

of trade and of the use of arms by civilians. The idea of a low status institution—the army—having a monopoly of arms, thus being a potential contender for power, was obnoxious to the Gólgotas.

Ideological sincerity, however, seemed to have a limit —one set by the realities of the hierarchical social structure of Bogotá. For example, one of the objectives of the Gólgotas was the abolition of capital punishment, yet when in the heat of one of the frequent street battles between *cachacos* and *artesanos* (urban craftsmen) a member of the former group belonging to an important Bogotá family (Paris) was killed, the high status groups, regardless of party, called for the execution of the culprit. Paris' funeral "was attended by the whole upper class" and the majority of those attending the *artesanos's* execution were "dressed in jackets" (that is, they were cachacos).[103]

The same question of sincerity of belief can be asked of the Conservatives supporting the Gólgotas. Complex social, economic, and ideological factors determined political actions.

The second faction, the *Draconianos,* favored the retention of a strong executive in a centralized government and the retention of a national army to back up that authority. Their most vociferous supporters were the urban craftsmen *(artesanos)* who favored the protectionist policies inherited from the colony—policies that gave primitive manufacturers a chance to compete with the imported goods favored by the high status groups. The small army, never more than 1,500 strong during these years, sided with the Draconianos.

Although the necessary research has yet to be done to explain adequately the exact variables involved in this alignment of antagonistic forces, it is safe to say that this

period was the first real "watershed" of Colombian socio-
political history. As Robert H. Dix has noted, it was the
origin or at least the strong reinforcement of "loyalties,
hatreds, doctrines, issues and alignments which have persisted to a large extent to the present day."[104] It was during this period that the material and ideological interests
of the two traditional Colombian parties crystallized. For
a century and a half Liberals and Conservatives would
battle each other with ballots and bullets.

A cursory analysis of the role of the standing army during this critical period tends to corroborate both the
accuracy and the value of the study of civil-military relations in terms of the existing social structure, especially
that of urban Bogotá where the major political and social
battles were fought.

Just as the Venezuelan-Colombian clash had involved
and was partly caused by contrasting styles of life, so the
Gólgota-Draconiano clash was partly caused by contrasting styles of life and social statuses in an urban setting.
The very terms of identification reflected this fact. The
gentils hommes of Bogotá, *cachacos* or *los de casaca* (literally "those with jackets"), formed the backbone of the
Gólgota faction. At the other pole of the urban social
structure were the *artesanos* (artisans), also known as *los
de ruana* because of the traditional woolen poncholike
garment they wore. These artesanos were generally recognized by their locally made clothes such as the *ruana,* the
sombrero de jipijapa (broad-brimmed hat), and *alparga-
tas* (cloth sandals).[105] The wearing of foreign clothes was
a status symbol of no small dimension; the high-status-
group members thought it demeaning to wear the rough
local products, prestige rather than quality being the
criterion in their dress habits. Significantly, military uni-
forms were made from local textiles.[106] Location of resi-

dence in the city also determined status, or rather was
determined by status. In the traditional Latin American
urban pattern, the prestige residences were in the center
of the city whereas the artesanos and the military, including officers, lived in the somewhat outlying barrio
of Las Nieves.[107] These, then, were the two clearly iden-
tifiable and openly hostile status groups in the capital
city.

Were the traditional interpretations of the behavior
of the Latin American military to hold true here, we
would expect the military to side with the high status
groups, which monopolized power and prestige.[108]

The Colombian case lends itself to no such categorical
explanations, however. It was complex in one sense and
simple in another; simple in that the army supported the
Presidency, or rather the President, Obando; complex in
that the regime did not have the support of predominant
groups of the high status strata which were, in turn, the
army's worst enemy. The President had enormous charis-
matic appeal for the artesanos. As Executive he had the
loyalty of the "purified" small standing army, loyalty both
to him as a caudillo (even though he had been a major
reformer of the military in early 1830), and to him as an
ally in their social and ideological battle with the high-
status Gólgotas, who also threatened Obando.

Although it is no doubt important to take note of the
considerable European ideological influences insofar as
they relate to the antimilitary planks of the Gólgota plat-
form, these influences must be studied in the light of the
existing Colombian social structure.[109] The particular
brand of antimilitary sentiment reflected in the Gólgota
program and behavior seems to have been largely a native
phenomenon.[110] Certainly it reflected the stereotype of
the military profession which had gained predominance

during the civil-military clashes of the 1820s and 1830s.
In the 1850s the two socially and ideologically conflicting
groups prepared for political battle and, despite the fact
that the army sided with the Draconianos, it was not an
uneven contest. The very nature of the political activities
reflected the weakness of the military institution whose
very survival was at stake.

The high-status young men, although strongly against
the military as an institution and as a career, did not
shrink from political violence and the use of arms. Violence was common in the political campaigns of this hectic
period between the urban groups, the *cachacos* and *artesanos*. José María Samper recounts the way he and his
social peers, all youthful Gólgotas, organized themselves
into a regiment, converted their political meeting place
into a *cuartel,* and promoted prominent young men to the
rank of officers. He gave this description of their activities:

> This is what my first military campaign was like, with
> the rank of second lieutenant; a campaign in which
> there was no lack of oratory, since nearly every day the
> Republican society held sessions. . . . The rifle did not
> disturb the poetry or the literature, nor did militant
> politics disturb philosophical and theoretical poli-
> tics.[111]

Since the standing army hardly held a monopoly over
violence or arms, free rein was given to the different political factions to implement their goals by whatever
means they saw fit. It was a period during which young
men of fourteen and fifteen armed themselves at school
and looked forward with passion to the next "military"
encounter. Force and combat were not shunned; what
was avoided was the social stigma of being associated with
the standing army and its style of life. It was in this con-

text that the attack on the military as an institutionalized group took place. Nowhere is the nature of the attack more clearly revealed than in the records of the proceedings of the Gólgota-dominated Congress of 1854, to wit:

January 25: Project calling for the reduction of State expenditures especially towards the military. Army should be reduced from its present size of 1,772 men to 1,200.[112]

February 18: Senate passes resolution requesting the Minister of War to prohibit General Melo from living in the Bogotá garrison and keeping his horses there. [Melo, Commander General of the Army, was a cavalryman.][113]

March 4: Minister answers that by living with the garrison Melo had brought discipline, cleanliness; he paid his own expenses, and that there was no specific law prohibiting his living there.

March 4: Project in House calling for reduction of army from its present 1,080 men to 650 and for the establishment of a Commission to study the total elimination of the standing army. Project voted down by slim margin.[114]

March 6: President Obando states that because of the political strife between the parties a minimum of 1,000 men was needed in the army.[115]

March 29: Provincial legislature of Medellín petitions to have the standing army abolished and the implementation of free trade in all arms.[116]

The insults and votes of the Congress demanding the dismissal of the army commander (and sole general in the standing army), Melo, increased in intensity during the

days that followed. The encounters and street fights between groups of young officers, often joined by artesanos
and groups of cachacos, increased.

The situation in the early months of 1854 indicated
that the military were on the defensive against attacks on
the whole complex of their social, corporate, political,
and personal interests—as meager as these were. On
April 7 the House voted to allow only two full colonels
as the highest rank in the army and to fill all vacancies
from the list of *oficiales en disponibilidad*,[117] thus prohibiting promotions within the institution. Since Congress determined, by annual vote, who was put on that
list, it meant an officer corps and military structure totally
dominated by Congress.

On April 16 General Melo mobilized his troops around
the city and offered dictatorial powers to Obando. Colombian historiography has yet to answer the question
as to whether President Obando and the Draconianos
were the ones who inspired the military move, but whatever their initial role, once the step was taken Obando
and his group abandoned the military. Mechanics, tailors,
carpenters, and urban workers in general *(los de ruana),*
and the army were now masters of Bogotá, or at least of
its public buildings and streets. There groups believed
that they were fighting for their very lives. In one of the
editions of a military publication brought out during
Melo's regime it was noted that,

The whole army knows very well that if the "constitu-
tionalists" win they will be eliminated, all pensions
abolished, including the *montepío militar.* . . . They
are intimately convinced that despite [their] promises
to retain their ranks and pensions . . . these are but

words to disarm them. They also know that [they] will have four dozen jefes and officers hanged, and will deport all the democráticos [artesanos].[118]

Melo's government lasted only seven and a half months, lacking as it did the support of any important sector of Colombian society except that of the urban artisan class. The latter tried in vain to sustain the movement in urban centers throughout the country.

The fact that Bogotá itself, rather than the countryside, had become the battleground and was occupied by Melo's artisan-based army was another source of aggravation to the urban elite. They were forced to countenance *la plebe* setting up barricades, hoarding food, drilling in the streets, and even arresting them at home for aiding the enemy or failing to contribute the customary "donations" *(empréstitos forzosos)*. Since the cuarteles were not spacious enough to house the regular troops as well as the artesano irregulars, the latter housed in such places as the National Museum, earning for the military the epithet of "barbarians."[119]

The years between 1855 and 1857 were years during which the small military structure was dismantled. Between the last budget before Melo, that of 1854, and the budget of 1857, the military share was reduced by 75%. Although the Congress approved a standing army of 397 men including officers, the force actually in service in 1856 was 109-men strong, including twenty musicians. The highest rank was that of sergeant major.[120] All military pensions were abolished, and most materiel, including all the horses and cavalry equipment, was sold to private concerns.

José Manuel Restrepo, who kept a thorough daily account of events, made the following entry on November 3, 1855:

> What is called the army of Nueva Granada [Colombia] is a small contingent distributed over several provinces, which, according to what the *Gaceta Oficial* tells us, does not exceed 400 men. It seems as if the Executive power wants to destroy everything military in Bogotá. Among those buildings ordered to be auctioned off is the building called "Parque de Artillería" which was built in the time of the Spaniards at a cost of over 40,000 pesos. Nevertheless, it is said to be offered for public sale for 8,000 pesos. We do not know what our government is thinking about when it wants to do away with a building as important as the "Parque."[121]

What the government was thinking about was very clear: placing the standing military force in such a position that it would never be able to operate as an independent power contender on its own. The Radical leader, Manuel Murillo Toro, placed the civilian attitude toward the professional military on a philosophical level in 1858:

> There is no reason why the State should maintain a permanent force: it is enough that the representatives of the legal majority be authorized to appeal to the citizenry to support the administration which they have created.[122]

By 1858, then, the Colombian rejection of the military institution was complete: it had been reduced to minimal size; its functions had been limited to the performance of perfunctory police, guardian (jails and insane asylums), and mail-delivery duties; and its budget had been cut to an inconsequential sum. Philosophically it was regarded as an archaic and outdated institution by the educated youth of the cities:

> I remember that at the time there arrived a Peruvian diplomatic delegation, and we all looked with curiosity at the Secretary of the delegation because he wore a military uniform every day; not that there was any hatred against the military any more, rather they were regarded as members of an archaic and improper institution according to modern ideas.[123]

The conditions and status of the military improved little during the remaining years of the nineteenth century. One of the few impartial students of Colombian military history thus sums up the conditions of the institution, including its officer corps, in the 1890s:

> When the French mission arrived in Colombia [1896], such was the state of prostration of the army, that there were many officers who emerged from the civil wars . . . lacking the most elementary skills . . . with harmful habits of laziness and many inclined toward the national liquor. Their bearing was characterized by the heterogeneous nature of their uniforms, mixing civilian with military dress or simply totally in civilian. They were custodians of the jails like common municipal policemen and served as escort to the mail service. When they were free from these mediocre tasks, improper ones for their category as officers, they just vegetated at the entrance of the cuarteles sitting on benches put there for that purpose. They were in all manner ignorant officers, degraded through lack of legally guaranteed career and had no value at all as members of society.[124]

Far from the "privileged caste" generalization so widely given to explain Latin American "militarism," our case study indicates that the military in Colombia was more in the nature of an *"out*caste." This points to several conclusions. First and most obvious is the fact that since one deviant case brings the generalization into question, there is a clear need for reevaluating the existing explanations (historical and ahistorical ones) of Latin American civil-military relations. Second, such a reevaluation should be interdisciplinary in focus and should give special emphasis to urban social structure, since that was the stage on which social roles were played out. Studies on urban social structure and on civil-military relations have given far too little emphasis thus far to the role of styles of life, including considerations of race, in the early period of national society.

Finally, it might not be entirely out of place to suggest an alternative hypothesis to the "privileged caste" theory. Since the Colombian case indicates that much of the resentment against the military stemmed from a disparity between their perceptions of duties and responsibilities and their social rewards, it might be hypothesized that it was because they were in fact held as outcaste by the high civilian status groups that they "misbehaved" politically and socially. Intervention to "grasp" through violent, unconstitutional means that which they thought they deserved stemmed from this disparity in status. Certainly the recruitment patterns and subsequent behavior of the military in Ecuador, Venezuela, and Colombia point to the plausibility of such a hypothesis—a hypothesis firmly grounded in an important body of sociological theory.[125]

War conditions disrupted the social structure enough to permit new groups to *contend* for power and prestige in the society. One channel of mobility opened up was a career in the military; this, however, was more a channel for political mobility (in the sense that participation in decision-making at whatever level is political) than social mobility. The traditional high status groups' criteria for membership had undergone no real change. If anything, with the elimination of the colonial master their sense of power and exclusiveness, their claims to a monopoly of leadership, increased. Like the English landed gentry of the Tory party, they saw themselves as the "natural" leaders of their society. A zero-sum game resulted. Challenges to the position of the high status groups could succeed, with minor exceptions, only through displacement of the occupants. And this could not succeed through "legitimate" channels because both the machinery and the general ethos were manipulated by the elite and operated in their favor. Such were the realities of a social structure stratified on the basis of status groups, a structure left unchanged by the Wars of Independence.

It was only when disruptive social events occurred that important enough disparities in status lead to attempts to make these statuses consistent in terms of the highest one held. In Colombia the military tried and failed during the early stages of nationhood. They continue subordinate today.[126]

1. The author wishes to thank Hans-Dieter Evers, George Huaco, and Charles Faulhaber for their helpful comments.

2. One can go even further and conclude with some scholars that "researchers from the different disciplines did not know of the research and projects of their colleagues." Jorge Hardoy, et al., "Conclusions and Evaluations of the Symposium on the Process of Urbanization in America since its Origins to the Present Time," *Latin American Research Review*, 2 (Spring 1967), 87.

3. Ibid., p. 84.

4. Ibid., p. 85.

5. Richard M. Morse, "Recent Research on Latin American Urbanization: A Selective Survey with Commentary," *Latin American Research Review*, *1* (Fall 1965), 35–74.

6. Morris Janowitz, *The Military in the Political Development of New Nations* (Chicago, 1964), pp. 13–14.

7. One recent author states typically that such factors as colonial background and the nature of the struggle for independence are so nearly constant throughout the area "as to warrant ignoring their effects" on what he calls Latin American "militarism." Robert D. Putnam, "Towards Explaining Military Intervention in Latin American Politics," *World Politics* (October 1967), pp. 83, 84 n.

8. Lyle N. McAlister, *The "Fuero Militar" in New Spain, 1764–1800* (Gainesville, 1957), passim; Magnus Mörner, "Caudillos y militares en la evolución hispanoamericana," *Journal of Inter-American Studies* (July 1960), pp. 295–310.

9. Victor Alba, "The Stages of Militarism in Latin America," in J. J. Johnson, ed., *The Role of the Military in Underdeveloped Countries* (Princeton, 1962), pp. 165–68; Luis de Arasquistain, "El militarismo y la libertad," *Cuadernos*, No. 16 (January-February 1956), pp. 6 ff.; J. H. Parry, *The Spanish Seaborne Empire* (New York, 1966), p. 370.

10. J. J. Johnson, *The Military and Society in Latin America* (Stanford, Calif., 1964), p. 35. For a similar view see Robert Alexander, "The Army in Politics," in Harold Eugene Davis, ed., *Government and Politics in Latin America* (New York, 1958), p. 153.

11. R. A. Humphreys, *Tradition and Revolt in Latin America* (London, 1965), p. 11.

12. Edwin Lieuwen, *Arms and Politics in Latin America* (rev. ed. New York, 1961), p. 17.

13. Ibid., p. 18.

14. For an analysis of this see Juan Beneyto, *Historia social de España y de Hispanoamérica* (Madrid, 1961), pp. 219–20; Américo Castro, *The Structure of Spanish History*, Edmund L. King, trans. (Princeton, 1954), pp. 607 ff.

15. Octavio Paz, *The Labyrinth of Solitude* (New York, 1961), pp. 74–82.

16. William Lytle Schurz, *This New World* (London, 1956), p. 101. It should not be thought that these subjective evaluations are limited to Latin society. The same is true to *some degree* in every society, according to Talcott Parsons. See "Analytical Approach to the Theory of Social Stratification," in Talcott Parsons, *Essays in Sociological Theory* (Glencoe, Ill., 1964), p. 71. In American society, notes another student of stratification, individuals do not readily admit to being very status-conscious, yet "It influences almost every kind of decision from the choice of the car to the choice of a spouse. Fear of the loss of status, or honor, is one of the few motives that can make men lay down their lives on the field of battle." Gerhard Lenski, *Power and Privilege* (New York, 1966), p. 37.

17. See the conclusions of the many studies cited in T. Lynn Smith, *Colombia: Social Structure and the Process of Development* (Gainesville, 1967), pp. 328–72; also, Orlando Fals-Borda, *Peasant Society in the Colombian Andes* (Gainesville, 1955), pp. 154–62; Andrew H. Whiteford *Two Cities of Latin America: A Comparative Description of Social Classes* (Logan Museum of Anthropology, Monograph No. 9, Beloit College, Wisc., 1960), pp. 52–93 and passim. The first student to use Colombian status-consciousness as an independent variable in a systematic way is James L. Payne, *Patterns of Conflict in Colombia* (New Haven, 1968).

18. H. H. Gerth and C. Wright Mills, *From Max Weber: Essays in Sociology* (New York, 1958), pp. 180–95; Max Weber, *The Theory of Social and Economic Organization*, Talcott Parsons, ed. (Glencoe, Ill., 1964), pp. 424–29.

19. *From Max Weber*, p. 189.

20. Cf. "Since 1503 Castilian law allowed any subject above the rank of peasant to erect his property, real or personal, into a *mayorazgo* or entail, and thus acquire the privileges of *hidalguía* with the title of *don*, which forbade his entering any profession attached to commerce or industry on pain of loss of status." C. H. Haring, *The Spanish Empire in America* (New York, 1963), p. 198.

21. *From Max Weber*, pp. 190–91.

22. The importance of this fact, and something of the difficulty of using the concept "class," is apparent in the following description in a recent sociological study of a Colombian community: "The distinctions between the traditional upper *class* and the new upper class generally are imposed by the members of the traditional *group*. Thus the new upper *class* considers itself to be the upper class, although the traditional upper class does not identify with this *group* nor admit it to their social sphere. Therefore, it was necessary to divide it into two *strata*." The study goes on to identify the traditional group as a "stratum" that emphasizes racial purity, family lineage, education, social-club memberships, and, "Their economic position is most powerful." Owners of large estates and ranches tend at the same time to be city lawyers, doctors, and men of letters. Eugene A. Havens, Eduardo Montero, and Michel Romieux, *Cereté: un area de latifundio* (Bogotá, 1965), cited in Smith, *Colombia,* pp. 370–71. Italics added.

23. In 1803 the Viceroy of New Granada complained that the number of troops in the capital city of Santa Fé de Bogotá was too small to be considered anything other than a symbolic representation of the Crown. "Relación del Estado del Nuevo Reino de Granada, presentado por el Excmo. Sr. Virrey D. Pedro Mendinueta a su sucesor . . . Año de 1803," *Relaciones de Mando.* Compilados y Publicadas por F. Posada y P. M. Ibañez (Bogotá, 1910), pp. 536–42, passim.

24. Allan James Kuethe, "The Military Reorganization of New Granada, 1763–1803" (unpublished M.A. thesis, University of Florida, 1963), p. 40 and passim.

25. Luis Felipe Acevedo, "Bosquejo de la Organización Militar de la Nueva Granada," *Memorial del Estado Mayor General, 12* (June 1919), 164.

26. *Copiador de órdenes del Regimiento de Milicias de Infantería de Santa Fé (1800–1814),* Trascripción Indices y Comentarios de Oswaldo Díaz Díaz (Bogotá, 1963), p. 73; Capt. Camilo Riaño C., "Las milicias del 20 de Julio de 1810, origen del Ejército nacional," *Revista de las Fuerzas Armadas, 11* (October 1960), 91–106 passim.

27. José María Baraya, *Biografías militares o historia militar del pais en medio siglo* (Bogotá, 1874), passim. For further biographical data in this same vein, see M. Leonidas Scarpetta and Saturnino Vergara, *Dicionario biográfico de los campeones de la libertad* (Bogotá, 1879).

28. Alberto M. Candioti, *El benemerito Colonel Vicente Vanegas* (Bogotá, 1941), p. 54.

29. Jorge W. Price, *Biografías de dos ilustres próceres y martires de la Independencia y de un campeón de la libertad* (Bogotá, n.d.), pp. 9–12 passim.

30. Ibid., p. 18. An approximate translation would be "they were sons of Somebody, from a well-known house, entitled to bear as well as use the arms on their seal."

31. Luis López de Mesa, *Escrutinio sociológico de la historia colombiana* (2nd ed. Bogotá, 1956), p. 204. Cf. "Nariño was typical of the group of wealthy, educated, creole leaders whose careers flourished under Spanish rule and reached their summit during the revolution. . . . Like many of those with political aspirations, he was an avid journalist, owner and editor of a paper," and "through this publication vaulted into the presidency." Thomas Blossom, *Nariño: Hero of Colombian Independence* (Tucson, 1967), p. 3.

32. *Copiador de ordenes*, pp. 231–32. Paraphrased from the text.

33. Indalecio Liévano Aguirre attributes the behavior of those military men to the existing kinship and social ties with the rest of the upper strata (he uses the term class) and notes that the social pressures brought to bear included the threat of being outcast *(descastados)*. *Los grandes conflictos sociales y económicos de nuestra historia, 4* (Bogotá, n.d.), 36.

34. *Memoria del Secretario de Estado y del Despacho de la Guerra al Primer Congreso Constitucional de Colombia en el año de 1823,* p. 6.

35. Oswaldo Díaz Díaz, "Introducción," *Copiador de Ordenes,* p. 73.

36. The Constitution of 1811 in William Marion Gibson, *The Constitutions of Colombia* (Durham, N.C., 1948), p. 17.

37. The title of the following proposal is indicative of the "aristocratic" view of the war and of the military still predominant at this time: "Método que podrá seguirse para instruir a los caballeros oficiales de nueva creación en la Táctica Militar, y puntos más esenciales de su servicio, dirigido por el Teniente Coronel don José Ramon Leyva, según lo que la propuesta de la sección de Guerra ha determinado la Suprema en su Cuerpo Ejecutivo en diciembre de 1810." Reprinted in *Revista Militar de ejército, 25* (July-August 1932), 499–504.

38. It was not until November of 1820 that the Spanish General Morillo and Bolívar agreed to put their signatures to a document intended to regulate the war and remove some of its harsher aspects, especially as regards the treatment of prisoners and civilian inhabitants of occupied areas.

39. Of the 12,000 men gathered in Arequipa under General José Antonio de Sucre for a major push against the Spanish, 3,000 were Colombian. Letter, Bolívar to Santander, Quito, July 3, 1823. All of Bolívar's letters are cited from Vicente Lecuna, ed., *Cartas del Libertador* (10 vols. Caracas, 1930). It was an important fact that the major concen-

trations of Colombian troops were not in Colombia but rather in Ecuador and Perú where, after 1823, the major battles were being fought.

40. José Gil Fortoul, *Historia Constitucional de Venezuela* (Berlin, 1907), p. 397.

41. Raymond E. Crist, "Desarrollo Político y Origen del Caudillismo en Venezuela," *Revista de Geografía Americana*, 7 (1937), 253–70, provides a geographical explanation.

42. David Bushnell, *The Santander Regime in Gran Colombia* (Newark, Del., 1954), p. 250.

43. José María Samper, *Ensayo sobre las Revoluciones Políticas y la condicion social de las Repúblicas colombianas* (Hispano-Americanos). (Bogotá, n.d.), p. 186.

44. The desperate need for men and material is evidenced in the tone of this letter from Bolívar to Santander in which Bolívar again pleads for the 3000 men from Colombia he had requested more than once before: "Sweep *(arrase)* the Northern coasts taking recruits by whatever means necessary. . . . Believe me, my dear general, that these 3000 men and 3000 rifles are indispensable. . . . And, *I repeat that no matter how they are secured they will be welcome.*" Bolívar to Santander, Quito, July 3, 1823. Emphasis in original.

45. José María Samper, *Ensayo*, p. 186.

46. Tomás Rueda Vargas, *Escritos* (2 vols. Bogotá, 1963), *1*, 237. The terms "lazy" and "uncouth" of course reflect the social bias of the author.

47. The first legislative body to function in Colombia, the Junta Suprema del Reino (July 20, 1810) provided for a "Sección de Guerra." Of the three sections set up by Bolívar at Angostura in 1817, "Guerra y Marina" was one. In 1819 it became the Ministerio de Guerra y Hacienda. From then on, Secretaria de Guerra (1844–58); Secretaria de Gobierno y Guerra (1859–65); Secretaria de Guerra y Marina (1865–87); Ministerio de Guerra (1888–1965). Raimundo Rivas, "Apuntes sobre organización de las Secretarías de Estado, 1810–1914," *Boletín de Historia y Antiguedades*, Año XIV, No. 161 (February 1923), pp. 293–311. On December 22, 1965, the title was changed to "Ministerio de la Defensa Nacional." *El Espectador*, December 30, 1965, p. 1.

48. Cited in Rafael Urdaneta, *Memorias del General Rafael Urdaneta*, Prólogo de R. Blanco Fombona (Madrid, 1916), p. 104 n.

49. On January 30, 1827, he wrote Bolívar that "There are very few Venezuelans who do not detest me vehemently." Santander tended to see the attitudes of the Venezuelans as affronts to his honor and dignity.

CIVIL-MILITARY CONFLICT IN URBAN COLOMBIA   349

Letter from Santander to Bolívar, Bogotá, November 5, 1826; Santander
to A. de Sucre, Bogotá, November 8, 1826; Santander to Bolívar, Bogotá,
January 19, 1827.

50. David Bushnell, *The Santander Regime*, p. 258.

51. Ibid., Gerhard Masur, *Simón Bolívar* (Albuquerque, 1948), p.
500; José Gil Fortoul, p. 483.

52. Cited in Masur, p. 442. Masur complements Bolívar's words by
asking, "The literati of Bogotá, the men of the high-lands who wore
woolen clothing and who sat around the braziers in their houses, what
did they know of the waters of the Orinoco, of the fishermen of Mara-
caibo, of the sources of the Magdalena, or the deserts of Colombia—of
all wild and terrible contrasts so familiar to the fighting forces?" Ibid.

53. José María Samper recognizes this when he notes that there were
two categories of land, that surrounding cities, villages, and towns, and
that beyond: "The spaces between settlements, uncultivated lands, un-
civilized *(incultas)*, that is, the desert, solitude, the silence of barbarity."
Ensayo sobre las Revoluciones Políticas, p. 63. For a general treatise on
the significance of this rural-urban dichotomy in Latin American history, see Richard M. Morse, "Some Characteristics of Latin America
Urban History," *American Historical Review,* 67 (January 1962), 317–38.

54. Gerhard Masur, p. 620.

55. Gerhard Masur, p. 626.

56. Ibid. The woman in the palace was Manuela Sáenz, Bolívar's
mistress. Masur notes that "the people of Bogotá had no sympathy with
the army—especially an army whose ranking officers were in many cases
foreigners. They abhorred military dictatorship, and they detested Manuela." Ibid., p. 642.

57. That the hostility against the Venezuelan military was not restricted to Bogotá is apparent from the testimony of Gustavo Arboleda,
who tells us that the people of another aristocratically oriented city,
Santa Marta, held a deep grudge *(ojeriza)* against the "guests" and were
constantly threatening to arm themselves with sticks and throw them
out of the city. Gustavo Arboleda, *Historia Contemporánea de Colombia, 1* (Bogotá, 1928), 111.

58. José María Samper, quoted in Arboleda, ibid., p. 448. Emphasis
added.

59. José Manuel Restrepo, *Diario político* (4 vols. Bogotá, 1954), 2,
71.

60. This group, largely composed of those who formed the Academia in 1826, was beyond doubt the "power elite" in Colombia at the time: Vicente Azuero, José Manuel Restrepo, Manuel Benito Rebollo, José María del Castillo, Francisco Soto Jerónimo Torres, Santiago Arroyo, Pedro Gual, Francisco Vergara, Benedicto Domínguez, Joaquín Mosquera, Diego F. Gómez, Rufino Cuervo, Joaquín Acosta, Joaquín García, Lino de Pombo, Manuel Ma. Céspedes, General José Hilario López, José Ma. Triana *Codificación Nacional.* Suplemento VII (Bogotá, 1926), pp. 605–06).

61. José María Samper, *Ensayo,* pp. 183–84.

62. Gustavo Arboleda, *1*, 114.

63. José Antonia Páez, *2*, 14. Journalism, not always of the responsible type, was one of the favorite occupations of the urban intelligentsia and also a major source of friction with the military. Since slander suits did not have any appreciable restraining influence on these outspoken writers, direct physical attacks were a commonly used alternative, especially by the military. Cf. David Bushnell, "The Development of the Press in Great Colombia," *The Hispanic American Historical Review, 30* (November 1950), 432–52).

64. Bolívar to Dr. Pedro Gual, Guanare, May 24, 1821.

65. José Antonio Páez cited in José Gil Fortoul, p. 397. That material benefits were not enough to satisfy these officers' sense of their own worth is indicated by the fact that Páez had received an estate worth $200,000 as a bonus, as had other high-ranking officers in Venezuela. David Bushnell, *The Santander Regime,* p. 227. Personal and social esteem (status) was a strong determinant of behavior or at least of attitude. To what extent this attitude, which Bushnell claims Bolívar identified as a "sort of inferiority complex," ibid., p. 297, was shared by the rest of the military sector is an important question. It must be remembered that many of the urban-based civilians were critical of the military as an institution, not solely of the llanero.

66. For a llanero's own later admission of the numerous insults and affronts to Bogotá civilians, especially the resented intellectuals, and the violent reaction of these through the press, see José Antonio Páez, *Autobiografía del General José Antonio Páez,* 2 vols. (New York, n.d.), *2*, 14.

67. On the importance of this case see Pedro M. Ibañez, "El coronel Leonardo Infante," *Boletín de historia y antiguedades,* Año II, No. 32 (December 1905), pp. 449–66 and Año III, No. 33 (January 1906), pp. 513–32.

68. José Gil Fortoul, pp. 363–64.

69. David Bushnell, *The Santander Regime*, p. 278; José Gil Fortoul, pp. 363–64.

70. José Manuel Groot, *Historia de la Gran Colombia* (Caracas, 1941), p. 326. Groot was then an employee in the Ministry of War and Marine.

71. Ibid., p. 327. Emphasis added.

72. Fray Angel Ley, *Capilla y Suplicio del Coronel de la República de Colombia Leonardo Infante* (Bogota, n.d.), reprinted in Groot, pp. 331–36.

73. These incidents were reported by both Groot and Fray Ley.

74. José Manuel Restrepo, *Diario político y militar*, 2, 71.

75. This was the main cause of the nation's insolvency. David Bushnell, *The Santander Regime*, p. 250. For contemporary reactions to these economic demands, which seem to have been heaviest in Colombia, see Restrepo, *Diario político*, 2, 71; Gustavo Arboleda, *1*, 25.

76. Eduardo Caballero Calderón, *Historia privada de los colombianos* (Bogotá, 1960), p. 67.

77. If the military did consider themselves superior to civilians it does not seem to have been out of any pride in their professional status as military men, for they themselves showed little energy and interest in improving the organization and administration of their institution. In 1825 the acting Minister of War and Navy, Pedro Gual, named a committee to study the possible improvement of military organization. As chairman of the committee he named General Friedrich D'Eben, a German officer in the service of the Colombian army, and two Colombian colonels, Antonio Obando and Mariano Montilla. The two Colombian officers seldom turned up for the working sessions and generally showed so little interest in the project that D'Eben finally resigned from his commission and the project was never completed. Sergio Elías Ortiz, "Organización Militar projectada por el General Friedrich von D'Eben para el Ejército de Colombia en 1825," *Revista de las Fuerzas Armadas*, *8* (January-February 1964), 463–67.

78. Colegio del Rosario was the main educational center for Colombia's high status groups.

79. Eduardo Caballero Calderón, *Historia*, p. 127.

80. Cf. Reinhard Bendix and Seymour Martin Lipset: "A society is characterized not only by the facts of social stratification, but also by a system of power-relations between conflicting social groups. Hence the fact that a dominant social group possesses most of the power in a society

may be a more important reason for the apparent stability of that society than the fact that people accept privileges and burdens which are theirs by virtue of their social and economic position." "Introduction," *Class, Status and Power* (Glencoe, Ill., 1953), p. 13.

81. Carl August Gosselman, *Informes sobre los Estados Sudamericanos en los años de 1837 y 1838.* Edición, Introducción y Notas por Magnus Morner (Estocolmo, 1962), p. 117.

82. Ibid. The first student to call our attention to the importance of this event was J. Leon Helguera, "The changing role of the military in Colombia," *Journal of Inter-American Studies, 3* (July 1961), 351–57.

83. [José María Obando], *Exposición que el Ministro Secretario de Estado en el Departamento de Guerra y Marina dirige a la Convención de la Nueva Granada en 1831* (Bogotá, 1831), p. 16. This "army" was not a standing one but rather the first in a tradition of hastily recruited political armies that were as hastily disbanded.

84. "Relación de los generales, jefes y oficiales que han sido expulsados de la Nueva Granada, por traidores a la causa de la LIBERTAD, estando por consiguiente borrados de la lista militar," Documento No. 2, Obando, *Exposición*, p. 31.

85. *Esposición . . . Departamento de Guerra . . . 1831*, pp. 19–24.

86. It should be clear by now that López and Obando were "military" men only in a very loose sense. They had military titles to be sure, but their power lay not in a national professional army or military caste but rather in their membership in the upper status group and in the political armies they recruited in their home grounds. Any military structure divorced from the immediate control of these caudillos was logically a threat to their power and consequently systematically opposed. For an analysis of the distinction between this type of caudillismo and militarism see Robert L. Gilmore, *Caudillism and Militarism in Venezuela, 1810–1900* (Columbus, Ohio, 1965).

87. José Hilario López, *Memorias* (2 vols. Bogotá, 1942), *1*, 14. (Initially published in Paris in 1857.)

88. Ibid., pp. 216–17.

89. Ibid., p. 217.

90. Ibid., p. 246. There was at least a minority of Colombian officers who, while opposed to Bolívar and the Venezuelans, desired a military government, for, as one of their leaders told López, "the lawyers are no good for anything." Ibid., 2, 60.

91. Ibid., pp. 162–63.

92. Ibid., p. 223.

93. *Esposición . . . Departamento de Guerra . . . 1831,* p. 19.

94. Ibid., pp. 19–20.

95. Article 175. The Bolívar-inspired constitution of 1821 had made liberal provisions for foreigners stating that "All who have served with honor or provided other services are to be considered equal to natural born citizens" (Article 184). William Marion Gibson, *The Constitutions.*

96. Article 16 of Decree of April 12, 1832, *Codificación Nacional,* Suplemento, VII, p. 555.

97. See the account of Minister of War José Acevedo in *Esposición que hace el Secretario de Estado de Guerra y Marina sobre los negocios de su Departamento, al Congreso Constitucional de la Nueva Granada en 1842* (Bogotá, 1842), p. 13.

98. *Esposición . . . Despacho de Guerra . . . 1842,* p. 32.

99. José Manuel Restrepo, *Diario político, 4,* 276.

100. Restrepo, *Historia de la Nueva Granada* (Bogotá, 1963), 2, 144.

101. *Informe del Intendente General a la Secretaría de Guerra en Diciembre de 1846* [sic] (Bogotá, 1845), p. 3; *Informe del Intendente General a la Secretaria de Guerra en Diciembre de 1846* (Bogotá, 1846), pp. 1 ff.

102. The garrisons became known as *cuarteles de chicha* after the heady corn liquor brought to the cuartel by the *Juanas*—female relatives of the soldiers. Descriptions of the cuartel at the time carry a strong similarity to the colonial *obrajes*—workshops where the laborers were locked in. Little wonder that the Minister of War in 1874 could praise the construction of the cuarteles of Bogotá on the ground that they were "secure enough to impede the flight and desertion of the soldiers." *Informe de Guerra . . . 1874,* p. 12.

103. José María Cordovés Moure, *Reminiscencias de Santafé de Bogotá* (Bogotá, n.d.), pp. 236 and 241.

104. Robert H. Dix, *Colombia: The Political Dimensions of Change* (New Haven, 1967), p. 35.

105. José Maria Cordovés Moure provides a good account of group relationships at the time (pp. 210–22). Hostility between these two groups

apparently antedates this period. José Hilario López describes a brawl at the bullring in 1833 in his memoirs. Each group was identified by their dress and apparel, thus, those with shoes and coats against those without shoes and wearing shawls. *Memorias*, 2, 181–82.

106. Germán Colmenares, "Formas de consciencia de clase en la Nueva Granada," *Boletín Cultural y Bibliográfico*, 9, No. 3 (1966), 388–410; No. 4 (1966), 647–60.

107. José María Cordovés Moure, pp. 228–29.

108. Cf. "[The military's] social and economic conformity and political orthodoxy in effect made them the tools of those landed elements dedicated to the survival of old ideas and old formulas." J. J. Johnson, *The Military and Society*, p. 56.

109. Robert Gilmore believes that there was an element of "antiintellectual" reaction in the Draconiano attitude toward the Gólgotas. See "Nueva Granada's Socialist Mirage," *Hispanic American Historical Review*, 36 (May 1956), 202. Gilmore's main stress is on the philosophical issue then being debated. Indalecio Liévano Aguirre, on the other hand, calls the Gólgotas "pseudoliberals" and stresses the economic aspect of the conflict. This interpretation finds substantial support in David Bushnell's "Two Stages in Colombian Tariff Policy, the Radical Era and the Return to Protection, 1861–1885," in *Inter-American Economic Affairs*, 9 (Spring 1956), 3–23. José María Samper, who claims that he first used the name "Gólgota" while delivering a political speech, admits that they really knew nothing about the socialism he and his colleagues talked and lectured about. "In the name of honesty," he states, "we were really nothing more than honest and ingenuous demagogues." *Historia*, 1, 256.

110. Luis Eduardo Nieto Arteta goes so far as to disclaim any connection between the two cases, Europe and Colombia. See *Economía y Cultura en la Historia de Colombia* (Bogotá, 1941), pp. 245–46, passim. It is important to know, however, that in the English democratic and radical tradition the habit of denouncing the standing army was an old one. The barracks were regarded as made for slaves rather than free men. Could it be that the Colombians absorbed some of this along with the economic and religious ideas? Cf. Elie Helevy, *The Growth of Philosophic Radicalism* (Boston, 1955), pp. 141–42. French Enlightenment thought was also predominantly antimilitary. Cf. Alfred Vagts, *A History of Militarism. Civilian and Military* (London, 1959), pp. 75–78.

111. José María Samper, *Historia*, 1, 261.

112. *Gaceta Oficial*, No. 1664 (January 25, 1854), p. 69. (Hereafter identified as *G.O.*)

113. *G.O.*, No. 1695 (March 6, 1854), p. 200.

114. *G.O.*, No. 1697 (March 8, 1854), p. 208.

115. *G.O.,* No. 1698 (March 9, 1854), p. 216.

116. *G.O.,* No. 1714 (March 29, 1854), p. 286.

117. *G.O.,* No. 1728 (April 1854), p. 1. This category, *oficiales en disponibilidad,* was composed of civilian followers of the party who were given a military rank and kept available should the government find it necessary to request their assistance.

118. Cited in Dr. Venancio Ortiz, *Historia de la Revolutión del 17 de abril de 1854* (Bogotá, 1855), pp. 79–80.

119. This term was applied by two eyewitnesses, Angel and Rufino José Cuervo, *Vida de Rufino José Cuervo y noticias de su época, 2,* 258. Even worse things were said by the United States Consul in Bogotá who characterized the Melo government as "only an organized band of robbers, incendiaries and assassins." U.S. Consular Dispatches. John A. Bennet to Secretary of State W. L. Marcy, Bogotá, September 29, 1854. The United States never recognized the Melo government.

120. "Estado General del Personal de la Fuerza," *Informe que el Secretario de Guerra de la Nueva Granada dirige al Congreso de 1856* (Bogotá, 1856), Documento No. 1.

121. José Manuel Restrepo, *Diario político, 4,* 592.

122. Cited in Gustavo Otero Muñoz, *Wilches y su época* (Bucaramanga, 1936), p. 29.

123. Angel Cuervo, *Como se evapora un ejército* (Bogotá, 1953), p. 2. Cuervo was a member of an important Conservative family.

124. Leónidas Flórez Alvarez, *Campaña en Santander, 1899–1900* (Bogotá, 1938), pp. 18–19.

125. References is to the work of Gerhard E. Lenski on "status inconsistency" and "status crystallization," to wit: "Individuals strive to maximize their satisfactions, even, if necessary, at the expense of others. This means that an individual with inconsistent statuses or ranks has a natural tendency to think of himself in terms of that status or rank which is highest, and to expect others to do the same. Meanwhile others who come in contact with him have a vested interest in doing just the opposite, that is in treating him in terms of his lowest status or rank." *Power and Privilege,* p. 87.

126. Cf. Anthony P. Maingot, "The Gentleman and the Officer: A Case Study of Civil-Military Relations in Colombia" (unpublished manuscript, Yale University, 1969).

PART FOUR: URBAN FAMILIES

PATTERNS OF LOWER-CLASS LIFE: Irish Slum Communities in Nineteenth-Century London
Lynn H. Lees

For many of us, the nineteenth-century industrial city is brought most vividly to life not by paeans to gas-and-water progress but by the terrifying descriptions of urban slums and their inhabitants written by the few social reporters who took the time to look at back streets and alleys. Although these reporters are far removed from us in time, their descriptions of the world are familiar enough to invite instant recognition: not only do they have a strangely contemporary and controversial flavor, but the problem of interpreting them is posed for the twentieth-century reader just as for those readers of a century ago. The accepted version of Irish life in England, derived from these glimpses of a slum-dwelling population, needs to be reexamined. Although most of his work scarcely found automatic acceptance, Engels' picture of Little Ireland in Manchester, and its inhabitants, "creatures who . . . must surely have sunk to the lowest level of humanity," was essentially in agreement with notions of Celtic degradation held during the nineteenth century. In general, facts and interpretations that would have enraged observers if applied to the English working class were accepted as common knowledge when limited to the Irish poor. During most of the nineteenth century, migrants—who supposedly menaced English morals, order, and tax rates—were cast in the public mind as heathen savages caught up in a way of life that separated them from respectable sections of the community. Even relatively enlightened men, generally sympathetic to the working class and its problems, felt compelled to denounce the Irish as incorrigible wastrels fit

only for animal labor. Otherwise, the Celtic contribution
was thought to be negative:

> Debased alike by ignorance and pauperism, they have
> discovered, with the savage, what is the minimum of
> the means of life, upon which existence may be pro-
> longed. The paucity of the amount of means and com-
> forts *necessary for the mere support of life* is not known
> by a more civilized population, and this secret has been
> taught the labourers of this country by the Irish. . . .
> The contagious example of ignorance and barbarous
> disregard of forethought and economy, exhibited by
> the Irish, spread.[1]

In general, migrants were pictured as the lumpen proletariat of English society by observers of all political
persuasions. Not only were they the poorest of the poor,
but their shiftlessness and savagery removed them from
the ranks of the working class. As disreputable and quar-
relsome foreigners, they were placed both outside and
below the social organization of the communities in
which they lived:

> The Irish emigration into Britain is an example of a
> less civilized population spreading themselves, as a
> kind of substratum, beneath a more civilized com-
> munity; and, without excelling in any branch of in-
> dustry, obtaining possession of all the lowest depart-
> ments of manual labour.[2]

One cause of this social separation between English
and Irish was felt to be a qualitative distinction in the
mode of life that each followed; observers linked the
Irish to the dangerous classes, rather than to steady English artisans, whom all workers were supposed to emu-
late. For most men, the squalor of Irish slum life was
sufficient proof of degraded lives and disorderly brutal

behavior. Migrants supposedly introduced "a lawless spirit of faction" into the country, and police, in 1836, complained of their frequent brawls and predisposition to petty theft. To this reputation as a police problem must be added the claim that they had been corrupted by the poor law and turned into unscrupulous exploiters of English charity. Indeed, tales of migrants joyriding up and down the country with fares charged to the parish poor rate fed this particular stereotype, which gained currency with every additional application for poor relief. Malthusian fears of Irish fertility and lack of foresight only gave additional ammunition for the attacks.[3]

At the center of all these charges was the feeling that the Irish were corrupted: transplantation abroad, the city, their own weakness, and their "semisavage" background had somehow produced a degraded and disorganized population. Evidence to support this hypothesis was deduced from dirty homes and their lack of success in transforming themselves rapidly into sober, self-reliant artisans. Contrary evidence was ignored, as was the fact that large numbers of English laborers lived in exactly the same way as many of the Irish did. In order to avoid blaming English society for the condition of both groups, their position as a lower class in a hierarchical society where those at the bottom had neither regular jobs, rudimentary education, nor access to sanitary housing was systematically overlooked.

Although it was readily apparent that the Irish were not integrated into the communities in which they lived, the other charges leveled against them require close examination. It is clear, on the one hand, that the vast majority became unskilled laborers; in a sample of 4,000 drawn from the 1851 census schedules for five London parishes, over 54% of the total employed population held such jobs.[4] Moreover, the style of life among these people

closely resembled what Oscar Lewis has called "the culture of poverty."[5] Not only did few migrants participate
in city-wide or national institutions (such as schools, political organizations, charities, etc.), but they remained
separate on the local level from parish governments and
trade unions. They were physically isolated as well. Although not formally segregated within London, migrants
banded together in a well-established network of slum
colonies in whose centers few English families were
found. Moreover, the physical liabilities of these places
were intensified by real barriers between them and the
surrounding streets. Tucked away behind gas works, cow
sheds, and railroad tracks, these places were dead-end
streets literally as well as figuratively. Taking up the resi-
dues of a housing supply in places where there was demand for casual labor, migrants drifted into enclaves
where city life passed them by, thereby condemning their
children to the same pattern.

Although the evidence is fragmentary at best, several
of the individual and psychological characteristics identified by Lewis as part of the culture of poverty also seem
to have been present among lower-class Irish families.
Most of those who came to London in the late 1840s had
been forced out of Ireland by the famine. By the time
these people settled into the metropolis, many were physically incapable of working, and some seemed to have
become demoralized as well. At the opening of the nineteenth century, a Southwark priest described the attitudes of some of his parishioners similarly reduced by
intense misery to incapacitating despair: "In very deed
so disastrous is the condition of many whom I know, that
they seem stupified and bewildered, and hardly know
what they do."[6] Similarly, Henry Mayhew's comments
on Irish dock workers in certain trades depict men
trapped by the truck system in an abject dependence

upon publicans and other job contractors, men whose attitudes have been described as a mixture of "sullen despair and apathy" by union organizers who, at a later date, fought to arouse them.[7] Without further evidence, it is hard to judge how widespread such attitudes were, but the circumstances that bred them applied to many of the London Irish.

In addition, family structure and methods of child-rearing among migrants show striking similarities to those supposedly characteristic of the culture of poverty. Both in 1851 and 1861, over one-fifth of the London Irish families sampled were broken, most having female heads. Although the number of deserted wives was small in comparison to the figure for a middle-class section of Chicago in 1880, the percentage of single-headed households in London was high.[8] Under these conditions, children often grew up in the streets either because supervision at home was missing or because of the need to roam in search of casual jobs, factory work not being available in London. They were often drawn into the juvenile gangs of hawkers, beggars, and, sometimes, pickpockets that roamed the metropolis. Very few were sent to school in the period before 1870, although the Roman Catholic Church made determined efforts to provide places for them. Unfortunately, the combination of harsh criminal laws and street life translated into the fate of jail and transportation for many Irish children. Police commented frequently on the background of the problem, usually blaming the parents and their way of life:

There is a great deal of crime in Manchester, among Irish, both boys and girls, of very tender years. This arises from desertion; the children are forced into the streets to beg or steal, and are punished when they come home if they do not bring money. . . . This practice prevailed to a great extent among the Irish of [central London].[9]

On the surface, then, Irish migrants appear to have participated in a style of life attributed to the urban poor in many societies and time periods. But is it necessary to make another common assumption and to conclude from this evidence that the Irish were a disordered, disorganized population? By placing the Irish outside the organization of the middle and upper ranks of English society are we committed to describing their lives as lacking organization? Louis Chevalier does just this for the Parisian lower class: he asserts that conditions of urban life supposedly forced large sections of the working class into a disordered existence characterized by various forms of "pathological" behavior. The combination of demographic pressures and physical deprivation "deformed" them and also produced a group of immigrants who lived as nomads not integrated into neighborhoods or institutions. Urban life for them was a marginal existence with few ties to persons or place.[10] Without examining the parts of Chevalier's thesis that link disorder to crime and political revolution, I would like to look more closely at his basic premise concerning the disorganized character of lower-class life. This paper will present evidence of several clear patterns of organization for individuals, as well as for the London Irish as a whole. Even within those parts of the Irish community that were downwardly mobile, structural regularities and differentiated expectations brought an order into slum life usually neglected by scholars who rely on models of the lower class that stress the absence, rather than the presence, of organization.

Geographic Mobility

Neither the stereotype of a freely floating class nor the contrary one of an immobile lower class locked in the ghetto accurately describes patterns of Irish movement in London. Although migrants were geographically mobile within the city, their movements followed predictable routes that paralleled those of English residents. A network of small, densely populated colonies was established in older parts of the metropolis by the late eighteenth century; at first, these grew along with the heavy migration into London and then, after 1851, when most parts of the central city lost people to the outer zones, they declined in size. Despite a decrease of almost one-third in the number of Irish-born residing in London between 1861 and 1881, several large districts along the outside border showed continued increases in the numbers of Irish-born residents, while the old Irish colonies near the Thames were steadily shrinking. Instead of remaining within the chief working-class parishes of the period 1800 to 1850, a high percentage of both new and old migrants chose to relocate themselves in the West End and the south; nevertheless, some of the heavily Irish districts along the river continued to hold a substantial number of Irish families. This dissolution of Irish quarters was more apparent than real, however, because migrants again clustered together in newer parts of the city, establishing new centers of heavy Irish settlement.

Even though the course of internal migration within London remains obscure, a few traceable patterns link typical moves by Irish families to those made by English workers.[11] Geography and tradition divided London into three very distinct labor markets: the settled area south of the Thames, the western section, and the East End—the latter two separated by parks and the central business district. Each had focuses of working-class life where political and other communal activities developed. Even though some industries were carried on in all three divisions, the labor force was very much divided by geography. The Thames effectively stopped regular movement from north to south for all those who could not afford to travel by coach or omnibus, and the distance from east to west kept workers from crossing between the two northern divisions. Since specific job information for the unorganized and the unskilled came only from hearsay, breaking out of local labor markets was difficult. Immobile in the short run, the labor supply responded to local conditions rather than to metropolitan ones.

Not only was daily movement over long distances inhibited by ignorance and transportation difficulties, but circulation patterns in the long run were shaped by these same factors. For both English and Irish workers, the three-fold division of the city marked out the large areas in which families were most likely to move. Once Irish migrants had settled in the East End, they tended to remain; moreover, very few families arrived there after having lived in other parts of London. The south was a similarly closed area of circulation, beginning with the riverside district of Southwark, one of the oldest and most stable centers of Irish residence in London. Most migrants who moved there from other southern districts came from adjoining parishes. If they left the area, their destination was usually away from the river to the less crowded districts of Camberwell or Wandsworth. Similarly, the path of migration in the north and west also led away from the Thames. When the Irish left central London, they went into the West End or the north-central sections. But, at the same time, a current of reverse migration was set up between these suburban areas and the older Irish quarters of the inner ring, although the net movement was definitely outward. Central parishes, such as St. Giles in the Fields, continued to serve as places of first settlement for migrants moving to London from other parts of Great Britain, and they retained their attraction for those who did not succeed in establishing themselves in the West End.

Another kind of internal migration, not recorded in the census, seems to have been the major source of the notion that the poor moved constantly from place to place. Priests and local officials often claimed, around 1850, that the Irish never stayed in one area long enough to strike roots and settle into local life. This same opinion was widespread at the end of the century, when Charles Booth and his investigators systematically examined the London working class. What they seem to have been referring to, however, was a pattern of movement from place to place within a small area, because the vast majority of second-generation Irish sampled were born in the parish where their parents resided in 1851 or 1861. Although many families can be traced back and forth across the boundaries of adjoining districts, they remained within a circle of less than a mile. Except when sudden decreases in the supply of housing threatened a whole district, most moves were of short distances. One of Booth's informers described such a pattern to his investigators:

> Such people never stay very long in any place: they are constantly shifting; they get evicted, their things are put into the streets, but they manage to borrow enough to get a room somewhere near, and get along for a time.[12]

When residential stability did not characterize such people, neither did the model of a freely floating or nomadic lower class; families usually remained within relatively small working-class communities. Longer moves, which still took place within the three major geographic divisions of London, were made much more infrequently.

Although the daily instabilities of lower-class life produced a population mobile within limited areas, it required unusual pressures to force migrants out of their local district into other parts of London, pressures that were applied with increasing frequency in the period after 1830 when demolitions for "civic improvement" tore through the heart of central London. Threatened by railroads, street-widening schemes, and slum-clearance projects, few working-class parishes escaped unscathed.

Social and Occupational Mobility

One major effect of this forced movement was to speed the process of differentiation through which Irish settlements were acquiring rather different social and economic characteristics. Although the majority of migrants in the labor force worked in a very few industries—construction, transport, domestic service, general labor, and the dress trades—their distribution among these industries varied with local demands. Occupational profiles for migrants in various sections of London therefore differed considerably. Moreover, despite their undeniable concentration in low-skilled jobs, a definite movement toward greater specialization of Irish workers took place in the decade after 1851. The proportion of unskilled laborers identified with no specific industry was reduced by half, while small but noticeable changes took place in the percentages employed in a variety of skilled trades, such as metalworking and printing (see Table 1). These changes were distributed unequally among the areas of Irish settlement, but they occurred in every part of the city except central London, where movement into the least profitable, least skilled jobs continued. There, the percentage of the adult labor force engaged in general labor, in the food industry, and in other branches of

Table 1. *Distribution According to Social Class: Sample of London Irish Migrants, 1851–61**

Class		Percentage of Total Population 1851		Percentage of Total Population 1861	
I.	Owners, Managers	.05		.00	
	Rentiers	.08	.34	.23	.83
	Professionals	.18		.40	
	High Commercial	.03		.20	
II.	Subprofessionals	.08		.34	
	Lower-level managers	.28	.49	.23	.88
	Annuitant	.13		.31	
III.	Employees, clerks		.63		.94
IV.	Shopkeepers		1.06		.77
V.	Skilled labor		8.90		8.06
VI.	Semiskilled labor		9.88		11.53
VII.	Unskilled labor	20.25	26.31	18.73	25.42
	Hawkers	6.06		6.69	
VIII.	Agricultural tenants	.05	.61	.03	.14
	Agricultural laborers	.56		.11	
IX.	Outside the Labor Market:				
	Supported by family	29.88		24.08	
	Students	7.40	48.51	11.93	49.73
	Small Children	11.15		13.69	
	Retired	.08		.03	
X.	Others, unknown		3.28		1.69

* Five parishes only

street commerce rose from 1851 to 1861, these two trades becoming the largest employers of Irish residents. In four of five parishes sampled, migrants became more integrated into the local occupational structure; yet in the central parish of St. Giles in the Fields, a growing number moved into residual, nonspecialized occupations. Probably the growing differentiation among London

Irish communities began as a physical process in which those who improved their status moved out of central London and those who failed to secure regular employment drifted back into the older centers where most of the hawkers and general laborers made their homes.

The differentiation just described took place within the context of very limited social mobility, so that the vast majority of migrants remained within the working class. Because so many low-skilled jobs gave only temporary or seasonal work, the chances of men thus employed to move very far up the social ladder were slim. Very few had had more than a minimal education, and the insecurity of their lives was so great that they found it difficult to accumulate possessions or large amounts of property. (Prevailing patterns of land use and tenure blocked acquisition of the small, one-family houses in which many American workers invested, although buildings could be rented and sublet to undertenants.) Since there was little surplus in the best of times, a stock of savings could be accumulated only by forcing all members into the labor market as early as possible. For a short period, then, a family could earn collectively as long as adolescent and adult offspring remained with their parents.

Despite very real barriers to mobility, differences in status appear when the migrants sampled are divided into groups according to family status and residence. It is clear both that they were not socially homogeneous and that men at different stages in their working life constituted rather different social groups. An occupational life style appears to have existed. Although the generally disadvantaged Celtic position was widely shared, differences in social status, measured in terms of occupation, appear among household heads, sons, and lodgers (see Table 2). The few migrants who had moved into medium-level

Table 2. Distribution According to Social Class: Sample of Irish Household Heads, Employed Sons, Lodgers

	Household Heads		Employed Sons		Lodgers	
	1851 in %	1861 in %	1851 in %	1861 in %	1851 in %	1861 in %
I. Professionals, etc.	1.34	2.63	.00	.85	.28	1.27
II. Subprofessionals, etc.	1.44	1.62	.51	.42	1.07	3.83*
III. Employees (clerks)	1.18	1.71	3.58	5.95	1.13	.85
IV. Shopkeepers	4.07	2.76	.00	.85	.56	.00
V. Skilled labor	19.32	15.37	14.35	14.04	14.77	14.52
VI. Semiskilled labor	7.75	8.15	8.71	11.06	17.61	14.52
VII. Unskilled labor, Hawkers	57.29	60.32	67.17	65.09	54.68	55.12
VIII. Agricultural workers	1.48	.39	.00	.00	1.70	.00
IX. Outside the Labor Market	3.54	4.33	.00	.00	3.11	2.13
X. Other, Unknown	2.50	2.75	5.64	8.52	9.92	6.40

*2.56% are annuitants.

Source: Original data compilation by author (document source described in Table 4), 1851, 1861.

white-collar occupations were almost exclusively household heads; lodgers were virtually excluded from nonmanual work. In addition, substantially more household
heads held skilled jobs in 1851 than did either their resident sons or lodgers. Moreover, they were less likely to be
semiskilled laborers or hawkers than men who had not
established their own households. Among resident sons,
however, a significantly larger percentage worked as
clerks and low-level employees, thus placing them in a
good position for movement into better jobs as they grew
older. Therefore, even though sons as a group were most
heavily concentrated at the bottom of the occupational
ladder, they had the best chance to move upward into
jobs of higher status.

Not only did the Irish at different stages of their working lives exhibit different patterns of occupational
achievement, but contrary to the stereotype of the immobile lower class, the position of the group as a whole
improved over time. Between 1851 and 1861, when migration into London fell off sharply, every parish sampled
increased the size of its resident middle class; more individuals were found in social classes I and II, thereby
demonstrating an ability—albeit limited—on the part
of migrants to move into white-collar jobs. More striking
was the overall decrease in the percentage of unskilled
laborers and the concommitant swelling of the semiskilled group. Apparently this shift between classes VI
and VII came most easily to first- and second-generation
migrants.

At the same time, the data also reveal downward mobility: the percentage of skilled craftsmen and shopkeepers declined despite small improvements registered at the
bottom strata of the working class. Therefore, no orderly
movement by migrants into the elite of the small mer-

chants and artisans appeared at a time when these two groups accounted for about one-fourth of total metropolitan population. The decreasing Irish percentage in these two groups was most marked among household heads, whereas employed sons showed a higher ability to maintain their position. Newer migrants probably found it more difficult to establish businesses and to move into skilled trades than those who had gone to London before the heavy influx of the 1840s; as older migrants who had been proprietors and craftsmen died, they were less likely to be replaced by newcomers who had brought little capital with them and who had not lived in London long enough to acquire needed training. Sons of more recent migrants, however, had a better chance to move into higher positions. Nevertheless, a higher percentage began as semiskilled journeymen and as clerks in 1861 than had done so a decade earlier. Even if the distribution of occupations among all migrants compared unfavorably with that of the total London population, within the migrant community a second generation had begun to break through the pattern of low-skilled laboring jobs that had been characteristic of the first generation.

Not surprisingly, these gains were again distributed unevenly around London: suburban parishes attracted the upwardly mobile, whereas those who remained in the central city exhibited most clearly the continuing pattern of low-skilled work. Not only was social mobility linked to geographic mobility in this direct way, but within areas of stable Irish settlement—even those where most migrants lived in slum housing—it was possible for clusters of families to improve their position markedly. Even though the average percentage of Irish craftsmen and shopowners declined in the five parishes sampled, the percentage increased in the riverside area of St. Olave

Southwark, one of the oldest and most entrenched of the
London Irish colonies. By 1861, a few Irish-born white-
collar workeres lived in the area, and a general shift from
unskilled into semiskilled jobs had taken place.

Although these measurements of distribution do not
trace the mobility of individual families over two generations, the statistics for the group as a whole and for various sections of the total sample confirm a slow movement
by part of the migrant community into occupations of
higher social rank, while others settled into their position
at the bottom of London society. Just as Irish households
became less concentrated geographically in the decade
after 1851, they also separated into a more varied pattern
of social groups. The fact that the Irish were not integrated into the city as a whole does not imply either a
lack of mobility or a homogeneous condition of deprivation.

Family Structure

In addition to this ordering of social structure and physical mobility, uniformities of family and household
structure superimposed another set of patterns upon supposedly disordered Irish life. Although the strains produced upon families by the transition from a preindustrial to an industrial society have been amply demonstrated by various historians and sociologists, it is not
necessary for migrant families to disintegrate. A variety
of responses, including the reconstruction of kin groups
and the retention of allegiances to clans or tribes, permit
a stable integrated life to continue.[13] Such adaptations,
by reproducing in the city relationships characteristic of
preindustrial societies, allow migrants to escape extremes
of personal anonymity and disorientation. Although the

strength of these ties to clans or kinsmen has been demon-strated most clearly in the case of migrants who have left well-organized tribal units, the same kind of reordering of Irish migrants along the lines of earlier allegiances took place in London.

Households expanded to take in those who had crossed into England alone: groups of people, all from the same county or village, often occupied the same building or tiny court. For example, small colonies of Cork Irish grew up in nooks and crannies of the East End, and evidence of even tighter local allegiances shows up in census birth-place records. The basic form onto which these other at-tachments were grafted, however, was that of the nuclear family, which remained the primary residential unit for virtually all Celtic newcomers to London. But frequently incorporated into it were a varied set of people—lodgers, visitors, and, more rarely, relatives—who became part of migrants' households. This enlargement of the house-hold constituted an adaptation to the realities of lower-class urban life, carried out, however, in line with Irish rural practices.[14] Although it has been established that English preindustrial society was organized around the nuclear family,[15] a patriarchal organization with strong ties to the extended family (on the fathers' side) domi-nated Irish peasant society. A clear structure of obliga-tion and kinship linked relatives beyond the immediate family. Many households included three generations, and relatives were sometimes brought into the group to fill empty places by the death of a member: "The complete family is the complete unit of life both social and eco-nomic to the small farmer."[16]

The tie to the land, which united all members of the household in a common economic venture, also regu-lated internal relationships: control of the farm conferred control within the household and position within the village. Unless land could be provided, most adult children had, therefore, to migrate or to be married into other farming households. Although some people could find local jobs as servants or laborers, most farms were small, requiring few extra hands. Only if land was divided among children, as often happened in the earlier period, could more than one child be accommodated within the parish. When such a subdivision took place, new households, each in a separate cottage, were established. Those who neither owned nor rented a sufficiently large plot of land were often left without work and therefore placed outside productive society. However, even these people retained the family pattern of organization. In Cork, before 1850, most laborers and even beggars had their own cottages and, perhaps, a bit of potato land.[17] In the nineteenth century, as in the twentieth, society was organized into households living in one-family dwellings, whose members might span three generations or include other relatives.

Much of the stability achieved by this order late in the nineteenth century was missing from the period before the potato famine of 1846–47. Seasonal migration to England or other parts of Ireland removed for part of the year many adult laborers who left their bit of land in the charge of their wives, while they traveled to earn rent money. Other households were split either permanently or temporarily when adult members emigrated. Although society was still organized around family units, members of those units were periodically expelled in order to permit the basic pattern to continue.

But if migration began with this uprooting of individuals from a well-organized social structure, its consequence was not the creation of rootless Celtic wanderers.

Instead of joining the lumpen proletariat in London lodging houses, migrants responded to the city by quickly reorganizing themselves into family units: over three-quarters of the Irish individuals sampled in 1851 lived in households headed by Irish nuclear families. Less than 3% moved into English households, and very few unmarried migrants chose either to live alone, to set up housekeeping with friends, or to move into a lodging house. Uusually, they moved in with Irish families of their acquaintance, possibly friends from home or distant relatives. (Those who did go into lodging houses usually had either a wife or child with them and probably remained only a night or two.) Moreover, this was not merely a short-run response to city life; very little had changed by 1861 (see Table 3). Just as single Irishmen chose to live with married compatriots, heads of incomplete Irish households brought in members from the outside. Almost 60% of the widowed household heads lived with lodgers or other relatives, and only 10% lived alone. Although economic necessity undoubtedly prompted much of this banding together, working-class Englishmen were much less likely to live in nuclear families. In the area of St. Giles South, dominated by decaying courts and the colorful haunts of London's lower class, about 30% of the household heads lived alone in 1861. Similarly, in the middle-class district of Regent's Park, 20% of the households included only one person (see Table 4). But the corresponding figure among Irish household heads was only 5%. Far from destroying the Irish family, migration into London made family life all the more important as a source of an identity in a new and hostile world.

Nevertheless, the households that were established differed in several ways from the patriarchal organization

Table 3. Family Structure: Sample of Irish Households in Five London Parishes, 1851–61

Family Type	Percentage of Total Sample 1851		Percentage of Total Sample 1861	
Nuclear Only	51.29		63.37	
" Assisted	2.85		3.69	
" Dependency	24.15	79.38	15.81	83.98
" Assisted and Dependency	1.09		2.11	
Extended Nuclear Only	6.24		7.11	
" " Assisted	1.09		.40	
" " Dependency	4.48	12.35	3.03	11.07
" " Assisted and Dependency	.54		.53	
Single Member Only	5.29		2.37	
" " Assisted	.14		.13	
" " Dependency	2.85	8.28	1.32	3.95
" " Assisted and Dependency	0.00		.13	

Table 4. Family Structure: Total Population of Two London Subdistricts, 1861

Family Type	Percentage of Local Households, 1861	
	St. Giles South	St. Pancras, Regent's Park
Nuclear Only	50.87	46.81
" Assisted	3.91	9.57
" Dependency	2.97	5.88
" Assisted and Dependency	.51	2.86
	58.26	65.12
Extended Nuclear Only	7.74	7.94
" Assisted	1.23	3.81
" Dependency	.75	.92
" Assisted and Dependency	.05	.92
	9.77	13.59
Single Member Only	30.64	19.97
" Assisted	.78	2.03
" Dependency	.63	.73
" Assisted and Dependency	.00	.27
	32.05	23.00

Source: This classification is based on information extracted from Tables 34-37. Appendix to the *Report, Census of England and Wales*, 1861, P.P. 1863, 53, pt. 1, 94-95.

described by Arensberg and Kimball. The three-genera-
tion Irish household was almost nonexistent in London,
and only a minority of families included relatives from
outside the nuclear unit. Married children regularly set
up their own households; although orphaned grandchil-
dren or widowed daughters were sometimes readmitted
to the family, less than 3% of the Irish households
sampled in 1851 included either parents of the head and
his wife or their married children. If a household extended to three generations, the most likely member to
be added to the nuclear unit was the widowed mother of
the household head. A pattern followed more frequently
was the inclusion of siblings and younger relatives, neph-
ews and nieces. Since most migrants were young adults,
presumably many of them left their parents behind in
Ireland; relatives of the migrants' own generation were
more likely to make the trip to London. Apparently Irish
obligations of kinship which had bound extended families together were transferred to London, leading to the
incorporation of relatives from outside the immediate
family into migrant households. The number of these
extended families, however, was relatively small. Although Irish households were more likely to include
extra relatives than an English working-class population,
the percentage of Celtic extended families was no higher
than in a London middle-class area, St. Pancras.

Usually the extra members of Irish households were
lodgers, rather than relatives. While very few English
households in St. Giles South included lodgers or visitors,
over one-third of the Irish units sampled had taken in at
least one such person. In one case, thirteen additional
men and women lived with the household head, although
most families offered space only to a very few extra people. The description by Mayhew of several Irish families

crowding together in tiny rooms indicated the conditions under which many lived. He recorded this conversation with an old Irishman who earned a few pennies a day sweeping the footpath in front of a Protestant church:

I live, sir, in .... lane, behind St. Giles's Church, in the first flure front, sir; and I pay one and three pence a week. There are three bids in the room. In one bid, a man, his wife, his mother, and their little girl— Julia, they call her—sleep; in the other bid, there's a man and his wife and child. Yes, I am single, and have the third bid to myself. I come from County Corruk the others in the room are all Irish, and come from Corruk too.[18]

Although this household of eight was larger than average for the sample of Celtic families, about one-fourth of the total number included over six people; most of these units probably lived in one room.

Nevertheless, the complaints of contemporaries about large Irish families were more fiction than fact. Differences in size between Irish and English households were largely the result of the Irish tendency to take in members from outside the nuclear family. Statistical comparisons show little or no difference in the average number of children found among Irish and English working-class populations, and the size of nuclear families is roughly equal. Although the English census of 1861 recorded an average of 2.9 children for every household with children, London working-class families seemed to be somewhat smaller: those in St. Giles South in 1861 had only 2.5 children, a number identical to the average for the sample of Irish families. Other local surveys of the London working class confirm that most families had between two and three children. As measured around 1850, the mean family size was between 3.5 and 4.5 people.[19] (All of these figures measure the average number of living children, rather than births or the size of the completed family.) Since few Englishmen took in lodgers, and the number of servants in working-class families would have been small, their households were approximately the size of the nuclear family. But this was not the case among Irish migrants. Although the sizes of Irish and London working-class families were approximately equal, Celtic households exceeded those of their British counterparts because of the numbers of lodgers and visitors they accepted. Nevertheless, the structure of these units was far from lacking organization.

The expansion of the Irish household was only one of several signs marking Celtic migrants as a predominately lower-class population. Their distinctive occupational structure, as well as the form and the size of their households, separated them from English middle- and working-class families. At the same time, the number of households headed by women established a definite link to the structure of lower-class family life. Both the Booth survey and H. J. Dyos' studies of Camberwell show how a tendency toward matriarchal households regulary accompanied the deterioration of an area: as streets were taken over by transients, unskilled laborers, and a vast congeries of poor exotics, more and more female-headed families moved in.[20] Also, both household and family sizes became larger than the average for the surrounding district. Whereas the initial response of migrants to urban life had been to reorganize family units, the unequal incidence of death rates by occupation and social class, as well as the general instability of their economic position, worked together to undermine the continued existence of Irish families. In order to survive, it was necessary for many to expand their households by taking in other families and single individuals to share the tiny spaces that they could afford to rent. Meanwhile, most adults and adolescents were forced out of the home and into the urban labor market. As a result, the nuclear family as a working unit and as a residential unit had broken down for a substantial percentage of the Irish; yet the form retained its cohesiveness. There was virtually no movement before 1861 by individuals out of large Celtic households.

The implicit picture of chaos and disorder among the London Irish must therefore be redrawn. Not only did structural regularities appear in supposedly random wanderings from slum to slum, but the physical movements of the poor paralleled those of the population as a whole. Moreover, links between geographic and social mobility aided a slow but recognizable pattern of differentiation through which the community developed a more varied social structure. On another level, the notion of disorder was belied by the continued dominance of the nuclear family and by the absence of a separate nomadic class of individuals who remained outside organized families. Economic and biological pressures had many adverse effects upon the nuclear family. The result of these pressures, however, was not a pattern of familiar breakdown or dissolution. Instead, in a functional response to the difficulties of lower-class life, the typical family gained new strength through expansion. Neither "uprooting" nor intense poverty was followed by the chaos and social deterioration that Chevalier assumes to have occurred; the facts of deprivation are not sufficient to prove the existence of disorder. Consistent patterns of organization indicate the presence of a cohesive way of life in Irish slum communities.[21]

1. J[ames] P[hillips] Kay, *The Moral and Physical Condition of the Working Classes employed in the Cotton Manufacture in Manchester,* (2nd ed. London, 1832), p. 21.

2. *Report on the State of the Irish Poor in Great Britain,* P.P. 1836, *34,* iv.

3. Ibid., pp. xxi, xxiii.

4. This figure and all others relating to London Irish migrants have been taken from a computer analysis of census schedules drawn from the 1851 and 1861 returns for the parishes of St. Giles in the Fields, St. Olave Southwark, St. Mary Whitechapel, St. John Notting Hill, and St. George Camberwell.

5. A statement by Lewis of the elements of this life style can be found in *La Vida* (New York, 1965), pp. xlv–xlviii.

6. Quoted in Bernard Bogan, *The Great Link* (London, 1948), p. 37.

7. Henry Mayhew, *London Labour and the London Poor* (London, 1861–62), *3,* 282–85, 300; Ben Tillett, *Memories and Reflections* (London, 1931), p. 92.

8. See Richard Sennett, "Middle-Class Families and Urban Violence" in this volume.

9. *The State of the Irish Poor,* p. xvii.

10. *Classes Laborieuses et Classes Dangereuses à Paris pendant la première moitié du XIXe siècle* (Paris, 1958); the clearest statements of his thesis are on pp. 163, 258, 312, 461.

11. The following description of the London labor market is drawn from E. J. Hobsbawn, who has described its operation for English artisans in "The Nineteenth Century London Labour Market," Center of Urban Studies, *London: Aspects of Change* (London, 1964), pp. 7–9, 19–20.

12. Charles Booth, *Life and Labour of the People in London, Third Series: Religious Influences* (London, 1902), 7, 263.

13. For a discussion of possible adaptations, see Philip Mayer, *Townsmen and Tribesmen* (Oxford, 1961) and Oscar Lewis, "The Folk-Urban Ideal Types: Further Observations on the Folk-Urban Continuum and Urbanization with Special Reference to Mexico City," *The Study of Urbanization,* Philip M. Hauser and Leo F. Schnorr, eds. (New York, 1965), pp. 491–501.

14. Very little research has been done on the forms of Irish peasant society in the prefamine period, but available descriptions give evidence of great continuity; many customs and practices described by Conrad Arensberg and Solon Kimball in *County Clare: Family and Community in Ireland* (Cambridge, Mass., 1940), were reported at least a century earlier. Moreover the continued dominance of the economy by small, one-family farms and tiny villages provides additional evidence of the stability of Irish peasant society.

15. See Peter Laslett, *The World We Have Lost* (New York, 1965).

16. Arensberg and Kimball, pp. 68, 79.

17. See, for example, ibid., pp. 58–63, and D. Bullen, "Statistics of an Improved District (the Parish of Kilmurray) in the County of Cork," *Journal of the Statistical Society, 6* (1843), 352–53.

18. Mayhew, 2, 546.

19. *Census of England for 1861*, P.P. 1863, *53*, pt. 1, 11, and Table 38, p. 98. R. W. Rawson, "Result of Some Inquiries into the Condition and Education of the Poorer Classes in the Parish of Marylebone, in 1838," *Journal of the Statistical Society, 6* (1843), 44; "Report of an Investigation into the State of the Poorer Classes of St. George in the East," *Journal of the Statistical Society, 11* (1848), 204, 208.

20. H. J. Dyos, "The Slums of Victorian London," *Victorian Studies, 11* (September 1967), 32–33; Charles Booth, *Labour and Life of the People in London* (London, 1891), 2, 46–74.

21. The research upon which this paper is based was supported by the Woodrow Wilson Foundation and the Joint Center of Urban Studies of Harvard University and Massachusetts Institute of Technology.

MIDDLE-CLASS FAMILIES AND URBAN VIOLENCE: The Experience of a Chicago Community in the Nineteenth Century

Richard Sennett

Unlike the other writers in this volume, I have sought in this essay to make historical judgments that cannot be proved in a rigorous way. Historians using sociological tools find in quantitative methods and constructs the possibility of achieving great precision in describing the past; for sociologists like myself who turn to the historical frame, a rather opposite possibility exists. For us, the complexities and contradictions found in the "actual time" of human life suggest ways in which abstract concepts can be made more dense and more subtle, and so less precise, in their evocation of men's experience.

This study seeks the hidden connections between two seemingly disparate phenomena in a quiet middle-class neighborhood of Chicago in the late nineteenth century: the family patterns of the people of the community and the peculiar response made by men living there to the eruption of violence in their midst. In imagining how the structure of family life was related to the character of men's reaction to violence, I have tried to recapture some of the subtlety of what it was like to be a middle-class city dweller during this era of rapid urban growth.

In the years 1886 and 1888 an epidemic of violence broke out in this quiet neighborhood of Chicago. The striking feature of this epidemic lay not in the violent events themselves but in the reaction of shopkeepers, store clerks, accountants, and highly skilled laborers to the disorder suddenly rampant among their sedate homes. Their reaction to violence was impassioned to an extent that in retrospect seems unwarranted by events; indeed, it is the contrast between the limited character of the disorder and the sense residents had of being overwhelmingly threatened by anarchy that suggests that the response could have been a product of larger, seemingly unrelated social forces, such as the structure of family life.

The Community Setting

The scene of the disturbance, which I shall name Union Park, was an area centered on the near West Side of Chicago around a rather large park formally landscaped in the early 1850s. Like most of the middle and lower middle-class neighborhoods of American industrial cities in the later nineteenth century, the area was considered so nondescript that it was never given a special name, as were the richer and poorer sections of Chicago. Its people were the forgotten men of that era, neither poor enough to be rebels nor affluent enough to count in the affairs of the city. For a quarter century, from 1865 to 1890, Union Park epitomized that tawdry respectability of native-born, lower middle-class Americans that Dreiser was to capture in the early sections of *Sister Carrie,* or that Farrell would later rediscover in the bourgeois life of Catholic Chicago.

The beginnings of Union Park, when Chicago was a commercial town rather than a diverse manufacturing city, were much grander. For in the 1830s and 1840s it was a fashionable western suburb on the outskirts of town, separated by open land from the bustle of the business district and the noisome, unhealthy river at the heart of the city. A change in the pattern of commercial land investment, the filling in of a swamp on the edge of Lake Michigan by Potter Palmer, and the growth of a manu-

facturing district to the south of Union Park in the years
after the Civil War led fashionable people to desert the
old suburb for newer, more magnificent residences along
the lake shore of Chicago. In their place, in the 1870s,
came people of much lesser means, seeking a respectable
place to live where rents and land were becoming cheap.
Union Park for these new people was a neighborhood
where they could enjoy the prestige of a once-fashionable
address, and even pretend themselves to be a little
grander than they were. "The social Brooklyn of Chicago," Mayor Harrison called it; "a place where modest
women became immodest in their pretensions," wrote
another contemporary observer of the area. For twenty-
five years, the old holdings were gradually divided up
into little plots, and native-born Americans—who were
the bulk of the migrants to the cities of the Midwest before the 1880s—rented small brick houses or a half floor
in one of the converted mansions.

During the middle 1880s, it was in modest, cheerless
Union Park that a series of unexpected events broke out.
A bloody encounter between laborers and police took
place on its borders during the Haymarket Riot of 1886,
to be followed eighteen months later by a series of highly
expert robberies in the community, a crime wave that
culminated in the murder of a leading Union Park resident. Union Park reacted by holding a whole class—the
poor, and especially the immigrant poor—responsible for
the course of unique and rather narrow events.

The Haymarket Bombing

Certain people, mostly foreigners of brief residence
among us, whose ideas of government were derived
from their experience in despotic Germany, sought
by means of violence and murder to inaugurate a car-

nival of crime. *F. H. Head, official orator at the unveiling of the Haymarket Square Statue for policemen slain in the riot, reported in the* Chicago Daily Tribune, *May 31, 1889, p. 5.*

During the 1870s and early 1880s the warehouse district of Chicago grew in a straight line west, across the Chicago River, up to the edge of Union Park. The haymarket constituted the farthest boundary of this district; it was the dividing line between the residences and neighborhood stores of Union Park and the warehouses of Chicago's growing central city. Haymarket Square itself was enclosed by large buildings and the Des Plaines Street Police Station was just off the Square. It was hardly a place to engage in clandestine activity, but, for a peaceful meeting, the Square was an ideal forum, since it could accommodate roughly 20,000 people.[1]

The common notion of what happened on May 4, 1886, is that a group of labor unionists assembled in Haymarket Square to listen to speeches and that, when the police moved in to break up the meeting, someone in the crowd threw a bomb, killing and wounding many policemen and bystanders. This account is true as far as it goes, but explains little of what determined the event's effect on the community and city in the aftermath.

The people who came to the meeting were the elite of the working class, those who belonged to the most skilled crafts;[2] they were hardly the "dregs" of society. The crowd itself was small, although it had been supposed that events in Chicago during the preceding days would have drawn a large gathering. On May 3, demonstrations had been organized in the southwestern part of the city against the McCormick Works, where a lockout of some union members had occurred. The police had responded with brutal force to disperse the crowd. Later that same night, at a number of prescheduled union meetings, it was resolved to hold a mass meeting at some neutral place in the city.[3]

A small group of Socialist union leaders, led by August Spies and Albert Parsons, decided the time was ripe for a mass uprising of laboring men; the moment seemed perfect for an expression of labor solidarity, when large numbers of people might be expected to rally to the cause as Spies and Parsons understood it—the growth of Socialist power. Haymarket Square was the obvious choice for a neutral site. Posters were printed in the early hours of the next day and spread throughout the city.

When Parsons and Spies mounted the speakers' rostrum the next night in Haymarket Square, they must have been appalled. Instead of vast crowds of militants, there were only a thousand or so people in the Square, and, as speaker after speaker took his turn, the crowd dwindled steadily. The audience was silent and unmoved as the explanations of the workers' role in socialism were expounded, though there was respect for the speakers of the kind one would feel for a friend whose opinions grew out of a different sphere of life. Yet as the meeting was about to die out, a phalanx of policemen suddenly appeared on the scene to disperse the crowd.

Why the police intruded is the beginning of the puzzle we have to understand. Their reaction was totally inappropriate to the character of what was occurring before their eyes; they ought rather to have breathed a sigh of relief that the meeting was such a peaceful fiasco. But, as the civil riots of a later chapter in Chicago's history show, it is sometimes more difficult for the police to "cool off" than the demonstrators. In any event, just as the Haymarket meeting was falling apart, the police moved in to disperse it by force, and thus brought back to life the temporary spirit of unity and of outrage against the violence at McCormick Works that had drawn crowd and orators together.

The knots of men moved back from the lines of police advancing toward the speaker's stand, so that the police gained the area in front of the rostrum without incident. Then, suddenly, someone in the crowd threw a powerful bomb into the midst of the policemen, and pandemonium broke loose. The wounded police and people in the crowd dragged themselves or were carried into the hallways of buildings in the eastern end of Union Park, drugstores, like Ebert's at Madison and Halstead and Barker's on West Madison, suddenly became hospitals with bleeding men stretched out on the floors, while police combed the residences and grounds of Union Park looking for wounded members of the crowd who had managed to find shelter, under stoops or in sheds, from the police guns booming in the Square.[4]

Reaction of the Middle Class

As the news spread, small riots broke out in the southwestern part of the city, with aimless targets, but they were soon dispersed. By the morning of May 5, the working-class quarters were quiet, though the police were not. They, and the middle-class people of Chicago, especially those living in Union Park, were in a fever, a fever compounded of fear, a desire for vengeance, and simple bewilderment.

It is this reaction that must be explored to gauge the true impact of the Haymarket incident on the Union Park community. The first characteristic of this reaction was how swiftly an interpretation, communally shared, was formed; the middle-class people of Union Park, and elsewhere in Chicago, were moved immediately by the incident to draw a defined, clear picture of what had happened, and they held onto their interpretation tenaciously. Today it is easy to recognize, from the location of the meeting next to a police station, from the apathy of the crowd, from the sequence of events that preceded the bombing, that the Haymarket incident was not a planned sequence of disorder or a riot by an enraged mob, but rather the work of an isolated man, someone who might have thrown the bomb no matter who was there. The day after the bombing, these objective considerations were not the reality "respectable" people perceived. Middle-class people of Chicago believed instead that "the immigrant anarchists" were spilling out of the slums to kill the police, in order to destroy the security of the middle class themselves. "Respectable" people felt some kind of need to believe in the enormity of the threat, and in this way the community quickly arrived at a common interpretation.

The enormity of the perceived threat was itself the second characteristic of their reaction. The color red, which was taken as a revolutionary incitement, was "cut out of street advertisements and replaced with a less suggestive color."[5] On the day after the riot a coroner's jury returned a verdict that all prisoners in the hands of the police were guilty of murder, because Socialism as such led to murderous anarchy, and anyone who attended the meeting must have been a Socialist. Yet this same jury observed that it was "troublesome" that none of those detained could be determined to have thrown the bomb. Anarchism itself was generalized to a more sweeping level by its identification with foreign birth; the "agitators" were poor foreigners, and this fact could explain their lawlessness. For example, the *Tribune* reported that on the day after the Haymarket Riot police closed two saloons

> that were the headquarters of the foreign-speaking population, which flaunts and marches under the red flag, and heretofore they were the centers of a great throng of men who did little but drink beer and attend the meetings in the halls above.[6]

On May 5 and 6, the police were engaged in a strenuous effort to determine where the "anarchist" groups lived, so that the population as a whole might be controlled. On May 7, and this was the view to prevail henceforward, they announced that the residences of most anarchists must be in the southwestern portion of the city, the immigrant, working-class area.[7]

The assigning of the responsible parties to the general category of "foreigner" excited even more panic in Union Park. It was reported in the *Tribune* of May 7 that a fear existed in the community that lawless marauders would again erupt out of the proletarian sector of the city and terrorize people in the neighborhood of the riot.[8] These fears were sustained by two events in the next week.

First were reports of the deaths, day after day, of policemen and innocent bystanders who had been seriously wounded by the bomb on May 4, coupled with a massive newspaper campaign to raise money for the families of the victims. Second, and by far more important, fear of renewed bombing was kept alive by the phantasies of a Captain Schaack of the Chicago police who day by day discovered and foiled anarchist plots, plans to bomb churches and homes, attempts on the lives of eminent citizens. Such were the horror stories with which the middle-class people of Chicago scared themselves for weeks.

Some kind of deep communal force engendered in the people of Union Park an immediately shared interpretation of what objectively was a confused event; this same communal force led men to escalate the metaphors of threat and challenge involved in this one event. As events a year later were to show, the force that produced these two characteristics of response was also to prevent the men of Union Park from being able to deal with future violence in an effective way.

Burglaries and Murder

On Thursday, February 9, 1888, the *Chicago Tribune* gave its lead space to the following story:

> Amos J. Snell, a millionaire who lived at the corner of Washington Boulevard and Ada Street, was shot to death by two burglars who entered his house and made off with $1,600 worth of county warrants and $5,000 in checks. The murder was committed at about 2 A.M. and discovered by a servant at about 6:30 A.M.[9]

Snell had been a resident of the area since 1867, when he built a home in Union Park and bought up many blocks of desirable real estate around it.

The murder of Snell climaxed a tense situation in Union Park that had existed since the beginning of the year 1888. Since New Year's Day, "between forty and fifty burglaries have been committed within a radius of half a mile from the intersection of Adams and Ashland Avenues," the Editor of the *Tribune* wrote the day after Snell's death. The police counted half this number; it appears that the burglars had a simple and systematic scheme: to loot any household goods, such as furs, silver plate, jewelry, or bonds left in unlocked drawers. Occasionally some of the property was recovered, and occasionally a thief was arrested who seemed to have been involved, but the operation itself was remarkably smooth and successful.[10]

How did people in Union Park react to these burglaries, and what did they do to try to stop them? The reaction of the community was much like the reaction to the Haymarket bombing: they felt involved at once in a "reign of terror," as the *Tribune* said,[11] that was none of their doing—they didn't know when the danger would strike again or who would be threatened. Most of all, they didn't know how to stop it.[12] Once again, the level of fear was escalated to a general, sweeping, and impersonal level.

Before the Snell murder, the citizens of the community had tried two means of foiling the robbers, and so of quieting the fears within their families. One was to make reports to the police, reports which the Editor of the *Tribune* claimed the police did not heed. The citizens then resorted to fortifying their homes, to hiring elderly men as private night guards, but the thieves were professional enough to deal with this: "somehow or other the burglars evaded all the precautions that were taken to prevent their nocturnal visits."[13]

After the Murder: A Change in Communal Attitudes

The Snell murder brought public discussion of the robberies, and how to stop them, to a high pitch. Especially in Union Park, the vicinity of Snell's residence, the community was "so aroused that the people talked of little else than vigilance committees and frequent holdings of court . . . as a panacea for the lawless era that had come upon them."[14] Gradually, the small-town vigilante idea gave way to a new attitude toward the police, and how the police should operate in a large city. "It is no use," said one member of the Grant Club, the West Side club to which Snell himself had belonged, "to attempt to run a cosmopolitan city as you would run a New England village." He meant that the police had up to that time concentrated on closing down gambling houses and beer parlors as a major part of their effort to keep the town "respectable" and "proper." Thus they didn't deal effectively with serious crimes like robbery and murder because they spent too much time trying to clean up petty offenses; the main thing was to keep the criminal elements confined to their own quarters in the city. In all these discussions, the fact of being burgled had been forgotten. The search turned to a means of separatism, of protection against the threatening "otherness" of the populace outside the community.

Such views were striking, considering the position of Union Park. The community's own physical character, in its parks and playgrounds, was nonurban, designed in the traditions of Olmstead and Vaux; the people, as was pointed out repeatedly in the newspaper account, were themselves among the most respectable and staid in the city, if not the most fashionable. Yet here were the most respectable among the respectable arguing for abandoning the enforcement throughout the city of a common morality. The petty criminals outside the community's borders ought to be left in peace, but out of sight. Union Park existed in a milieu too cosmopolitan for every act of the lower classes to be controlled; the police ought to abandon the attempt to be the guardians of all morality and instead concentrate on assuring the basic security of the citizens against outbursts of major crime.

What Union Park wanted instead, and what it got, was a garrison of police to make the community riotproof and crimeproof. The police indeed abandoned the search for the killers, and concentrated on holding the security of Union Park, like an area under siege. In this way, the original totally suburban tone of the parks and mansions was transformed; this respectable neighborhood felt its own existence to be so threatened that only a state of rigid barriers, enforced by a semimilitary state of curfew and surveillance, would permit it to continue to function.

The effect of the riot and the train of burglaries and murder was to put the citizens in a frame of mind where only the closure of the community through constant surveillance and patrolling would reassure them. Indeed, the characteristics of their reaction to violence could only lead to such a voluntary isolation: everyone "knew" immediately what was wrong; and what was wrong was overwhelming; it was nothing less than the power of the "foreigner," the outsider who had suddenly become dominant in the city. Isolation, through garrisons and police patrols, was the only solution.

Union Park held onto its middle-class character until the middle of the 1890s; there was no immediate desertion by respectable people of the area in the wake of the violence: where else in a great city, asked one citizen, was it safe to go? Everywhere the same terror was possible.

The contrast between the limited character of civil disturbance and the immediate perception of that disturbance as the harbinger of an unnameable threat coming from a generalized enemy is a theme that binds together much research on urban disorders.

Until a few years ago, riots were taken to be the expression of irrational, and directionless, aggression. The "irrationality of crowds," and similar explanations of crowd behavior as an innate disorder, was first given a cogent interpretation in the industrial era in the writings of Le Bon,[16] for whom the irrational brutality of crowds was a sign of how the "psychology" of the individual becomes transformed when the individual acts in concert with other people. According to Le Bon, the crowd releases a man from the self-reflective, rational restraints that normally operate when a person is alone or with one or two other people. The anonymity of mass gatherings reinforces the desire each one has to cast off these rational, individual restraints, and encourages men to express more violent traits without fear of personal detection. It is the social psychology of the massive gathering to be unrestrained, Le Bon wrote, the psychology of the individual to prescribe rules for himself.[17]

This image of crowds was as congenial to many of the syndicalists on the Left (though not Sorel) as it was to the fears of bourgeois people like those in Union Park. The difficulty with the image is that, for the nineteenth century at least, it seems not to fit the facts of crowd behavior.

Thanks to the pioneering work of George Rudé and Charles Tilly,[18] it has been possible to ascertain that, in the urbanizing of English and French populations during the early nineteenth century, popular rebellions and crowd activities possessed a high degree of rationality; that is to say, the crowds acted to achieve rather well-defined ends, and used only as much force as was required to make their demands prevail. Though the work of Rudé and Tilly seems contradicted by the extensive researches of Louis Chevalier[19] on Parisian lower-class behavior during the nineteenth century, there are enough points of agreement, in looking at crowd behavior where violent coercion is involved, to rule out the "unrestrained frenzy" Le Bon saw in crowds that made them useless as a social tool to gain definite, common goals.[20] What is important in Le Bon's work, for the present purpose, was his *expectation* that this unrestrained frenzy would result from group action by the lower class.

For it is this same split between middle-class expectation of blind anarchy and the actual limitations on working-class disorder that characterized the Haymarket incidents, the same split between a reign of terror sensed during the later burglaries and the actual routine narrowness of these crimes.

The problem of the Union Park experience was the citizenry's inability to connect the facts seen to the facts as elements of what people knew was a correct interpretation. Expecting "seething passions" to erupt hysterically, the middle-class people of Chicago and their police were somehow immune to the spectacle they should have enjoyed, that of the workers becoming bored with the inflammatory talk of their supposed leaders. The expectations of a seething rabble had somehow to be fulfilled, and so the police themselves took the first step. After the shooting was over, the respectable people of Chicago became in turn inflamed. This blind passion in the name of defending the city from blind passion is the phenomenon that needs to be explained. A similar contradiction occurred in the series of robberies a half year later as well. As in the riot, the facts of the rationality of the enemy and his limited purpose, although acknowledged, were not absorbed; he was felt to be something else, a nameless, elusive terror, all-threatening. And the people reacted with a passion equal to his.

This mystifying condition, familiar now in the voices heard from the "New Right," is what I should like to explain, not through a sweeping theory that binds the past to the present, but through a theory that explains this peculiar reaction in terms of strains in the family life of the Union Park people. What I would like to explore— and I certainly do not pretend to prove it—is how, in an early industrial city, the fears of the foreign masses by a middle-class group may have reflected something other than the actual state of interaction between bourgeoisie and proletariat. These fears may have reflected instead the impact of family life on the way the people like those in Union Park understood their places in the city society.

Studies of overreaction to limited stimuli have centered, for the most part, on the idea of a "frustration-aggression syndrome." This ungainly phrase was given a clear definition in one of the early classic works of American social psychology, *Frustration and Aggression* (1939). The authors wrote that

> aggression is always a consequence of frustration. More specifically . . . the occurrence of aggressive behavior always presupposes the existence of frustration and, contrariwise, the existence of frustration always leads to some form of aggression.[21]

Applied in terms of social class, this frustration-aggression syndrome implies that when a group fails to achieve goals it desires, or when it is unable to maintain a position it covets, it becomes aggressive, and searches out objects on which it can blame its failure. This simple, clear idea Parsons[22] has applied to the formation of the Nazi party in Germany: the fall in status in the 1920s of fixed-income, middle-class groups breeding an aggressive desire to get back at their enemies, without knowing, or really caring, who they were. Lipset[23] has incorporated elements of the same idea in his essay on working-class authoritarianism in the United States after the Second World War. And of course the concept is now used to explain the hostility of lower middle-class whites toward blacks: the whites who have failed to rise high in the economic system they believe in are said to make blacks "aggression objects" of the frustration they themselves have suffered.[24]

If it is true, as this syndrome of frustration-aggression suggests, that in the character one ascribes to one's enemy lies a description of something in one's own experience, the nature of the fear of lower-class foreigners among Union Park families might tell something about the Union Park community itself. The Union Park men, during the time of the riot and robberies, accused their chosen enemies of being, first, lawless anarchists, which was transmuted, secondly, to being pushed by their base passions outside the bounds of acceptable behavior, which resolved itself, finally, to being emotionally out of control. If the poor were reasonable, if they were temperate, ran the argument, these violent things would not have come to pass.

What about the Union Park people themselves, then? Were they masters of themselves? A study I have recently completed on the family patterns of the Union Park people during the decades of the 1870s and '80s may throw some light on the question of stability and purposefulness in their lives: it is the dimension of stability in these family patterns, I believe, that shaped sources of the reaction to violence.

Intensive Family Life

In 1880, on a forty-square-block territory of Union Park, there lived 12,000 individuals in approximately 3,000 family units. These family units were of three kinship types: single-member families, where one person lived alone without any other kin; nuclear families, consisting of a husband, wife, and their unmarried children; and extended families, where to the nuclear unit was added some other relative—a brother or sister of the parents, a member of a third generation, or a son or daughter who was married and lived with his spouse in the parental home. The most common form of the extended family in Union Park was that containing "collateral kin," that is, unmarried relatives of the same generation as the husband or wife.

The dominant form of family life in Union Park was nuclear, for 80% of the population lived in such homes, with 10% of the population living alone in single-member families, and the remaining 10% living in extended family situations. A father and mother living alone with their growing children in an apartment or house was the pervasive household condition. There were few widowed parents living with their children in either nuclear or extended homes, and though the census manuscripts on which my study of the year 1880 is based were inexact at this point, there appeared to be few groups of related families living in separate dwellings but in the same neighborhood.

Is this nuclear-family dominance a special characteristic of middle-class life in this era? At the Joint Center for Urban Studies, I was fortunate in working with other researchers in this field to coordinate census measures of class and family form that could be used comparatively across different studies.[25] Comparison with these other studies, as well as within the limited range of social groups in Union Park, convinces me that this kind of family form was not a middle-class phenomenon. Within

Union Park, the 80% dominance of the nuclear families held in lower social strata (of which enough existed to measure and test statistically, since the population as a whole was so large—about 25% of the community fell into a working-class category, excluding the servants in the homes of the other 75%) and throughout the range of middle-class groups. In Lynn Lees' data on an Irish working-class district in London in 1860, it similarly appeared that about 80% of her community's population lived in nuclear family configurations, 10% in single-member families, and 10% in extended families, virtually the same distribution as was found in Chicago's Union Park in 1880.

Again, the *outer* limits on the size of families in Union Park did seem to be the product of a special class condition. Contrary to the stereotype of the sprawling families of the poor, in Union Park the size of poor families was in its contours similar to the size of the wealthier ones: few families were larger than six members, among rich or poor. Similarly, comparison of family sizes in Union Park to the poor Irish of Lynn Lee's study or to the middle-class area of St. Pancras in London reveals the limits on family size in the three areas to have been the same.

Since family studies of nineteenth-century cities are at this date in a primitive stage, the body of future research may show these present examples to be "sports" or explainable by circumstances researchers do not now understand. Yet it does now seem more fruitful to concentrate on the *function* of nuclear families or on the *function* of families of restricted size in middle-class communities in the great cities of the nineteenth century, rather than to try to locate the conditions of peculiarly middle-class life in the *structural* existence of these family types.

What I did find to be true in Union Park was the following: over the course of time internal conditions of
family structure and of family size tended to lead to similar family histories. Nuclear families had characteristic
histories similar to the experience of smaller families
having from two to four kin members in the 1870s and
'80s. Extended families, on the other hand, had histories
similar to the experience of the minority of families with
four to six kin members during these decades. What made
this process subtle was that nuclear families did not tend
to be smaller, or extended larger. Family size and family
kinship structure seemed rather to be independent structures with parallel internal differences in functioning.

Why and how this was so can be understood by assessing the patterns of the generations of the dominant group
of nuclear, small-size families during the year 1880. These
families were marked, in the relations between husbands
and wives, parents and children, by strong patterns of
family cohesion. Whether rich or poor, the young men
and women from such homes rarely broke away to live
on their own until they themselves were ready to marry
and found families, an event that usually occurred when
the man was in his early thirties. The families of Union
Park, observers of the time noted, were extremely self-
contained, did little entertaining, and rarely left the
home to enjoy even such modest pleasures as a church
social or, for the men, a beer at the local tavern. The small
family, containing only parents and their immediate
children, resisted the diverse influences of either other
kin associations or extensive community contacts. This
was the mode of family life that dominated Union Park
numerically. These families can be called "intensive
families," and their life histories contrasted to families
of larger size or more complex kinship. The intensive

families would seem to epitomize a defined order of stability among the people of Union Park. Yet, Lynn Lees and I have found some functional differences between Chicago and London in families of this general character.

Instability through Separation or Desertion

In most census collections in the United States and Britain, the official tabulations of divorce are very low, because the formal breaking of the marital tie was considered a personal disgrace to both partners. But, as Talcott Parsons has demonstrated,[26] these official figures are misleading, since a great deal of unofficial divorce through separation or desertion occurred, at a higher rate, Parsons thinks, than in our own time. One means of detecting this hidden marital disorder in the census is to locate the individuals who were officially married but living without a spouse in the family. This measurement lets in a certain number of "beachhead migrants," men who have come to the city in advance of their families to establish a job and find a house, but in Union Park such men were less common in this category than spouses who were married, living with their children, but not with their husbands (or wives).[27]

In Union Park the number of families involved in such a break was about 10%. But in London, in the middle-class district of St. Pancras, the incidence of such marital separation was one-half of this, or 5%; in the lower-class Irish district Lynn Lees studied, there were less than a third as many marital separations of this type. In all three communities, of course, the official rate of divorce was nearly zero.

The explanation for this comparatively high incidence of marital break in Union Park is obscure, since there are

now so few other comparative measures of family conditions behind the official statistics to use. In terms of
these Chicago and London communities themselves perhaps the best thing to be said is the simplest: the higher
incidence of marital break occurred in a city whose development was exclusively in the industrial era; the lower
incidence of such a break occurred in a city for whom
industrial production and large bureaucratic enterprises
were but one chapter in a very long history.

Work Mobility and Family Stability

Added to this kind of family instability in the community
as a whole, my study of intergenerational mobility in
work and residence from 1872 to 1890 revealed a complicated, but highly significant pattern of insecurity in
the dominant intensive families when compared to the
smaller group of less intensive families.[28]

In the nuclear-family homes and in the smaller families the fathers were stable in their patterns of job holding, as a group, over the course of the eighteen years
studied; roughly the same proportions of unskilled,
skilled, and white-collar workers of various kinds composed the labor force of these nuclear fathers in 1890 as
in 1872. Given the enormous growth of Chicago's industrial production, its banking and financial capital, retail
trade volume, as well as the proliferation of the population (100% increase each ten years) and the greatly increasing proportion of white-collar pursuits during this
time, such stability in job distribution is truly puzzling.
Further, this pattern of job holding among the fathers
of intensive families was not shared by the fathers in extended families or fathers of larger families living in
Union Park. They were mobile up into exclusively

bureaucratic, white-collar pursuits, so that by 1890 virtually none of these fathers worked with their hands. Within the range of white-collar occupations, the extended-family fathers and the large-family fathers gradually concentrated in executive and other lesser management pursuits and decreased their numbers in shopkeeping, toward which, stereotypically, they are supposed to gravitate.

Now the differences between fathers and sons in each of these family groups were even more striking. I found the sons in the dominant family homes to be, unlike their fathers, very unstable in their patterns of job holding, with as much movement down into manual pursuits over the course of the eighteen years as movement up within the white-collar occupations. Following the lead of Blau and Duncan,[29] we might be tempted to explain this pattern of dispersion simply as regression-toward-the-mean of higher status groups intergenerationally. But the sons of extended and large families did not move in this mixed direction. Rather, they followed in the footsteps of their fathers into good white-collar positions, with almost total elimination of manual labor in their ranks over the course of time. This pattern occurred in small-family sons versus large-family sons and in nuclear-family sons versus extended-family sons. The difference in the groups of sons was especially striking in that the starting distribution of the sons in the occupational work force was virtually the *same*, in the measure of family form and in those of family size. Thernstrom has pointed out in the conference discussions for this volume that economic aid between generations of workers ought to manifest itself more at the beginning point in the careers of the young rather than when the older generation has retired and the young have become the principal breadwinners. In

Union Park, the fact that both extended-family and nuclear-family sons, both large- and small-family sons, began to work in virtually the same pursuits as their fathers, but then became distinctively different in their patterns of achievement, strongly suggests that something *beyond* monetary help was at work in these families to produce divergences in work experience in the city.

The residence patterns of the generations of the intensive and less intensive families also bears on the issues of stability and instability in the lives of the people of Union Park. Up to the time of violence in the Union Park area, the residence patterns of the two kinds of families, in both the parents' and the sons' generations, were rather similar. In the wake of the violence it appears that, within the parents' generation, there was significant movement back into the Union Park area, whereas for the half decade preceding the disturbances there was a general movement out to other parts of Chicago. It is in the generation of the sons that differences between the two family groups appeared. In the wake of the violence, the sons of large families and of extended families continued the processes of residential break from Union Park initiated during the early years of the 1880 decade. The sons from intensive families did not; in the years following the violence they stopped migrating beyond the boundaries of the community they had known as children, and instead kept closer to their first homes.

Two Theories of Intensive Family Stability

In my study of Union Park,[30] I tried to explain these differences in work experience and in residence in terms of patterns of family life and child nurturance for bourgeois people in a new, immensely dynamic, disordered city. In so doing, my researches led me into a debate that exists between the work of the sociologist Talcott Parsons and the cultural historian Phillippe Aries.[31] For Parsons has argued that the small nuclear family is an adaptive kinship form to the industrial order; the lack of extensive kin obligations and a wide kin circle in this family type means, Parsons has contended, that the kinship unit does not serve as a binding private world of its own, but rather frees the individual to participate in "universalized" bureaucratic structures that are urban-wide and dynamic.[32] Aries has challenged this theory by amassing a body of historical evidence to show that the extended kinship relationships in large families, at least during the period he studied, were actually less sheltering, more likely to push the individual out into the world where he would have to act like a full man on his own at an early age, than the intense, intimate conditions of the nineteenth-century home. In intensive homes, the young person spent a long time in a state of independence under the protection and guidance of his elders. Consequently, argues Aries, the capacity of the young adult from small nuclear homes to deal with the world about him was blunted, for he passed from a period of total shelter to a state in which he was expected to be entirely competent on his own.[33] Aries' attack has been supported for contemporary American urban communities by a variety of studies, the most notable being those of Eugene Litwak and Marvin Sussman, and it has been supported for English cities by the work of Peter Wilmott and Elizabeth Bott.[34]

The data I have collected on Union Park during the early stages of Chicago's industrial-bureaucratic expansion clearly are in line with the argument made by Aries. The young from homes of small scale or from homes

where the structure of the family was nuclear and "privatistic," in Aries' phrase, had an ineptness in the work
world, and a rootedness to the place of their childhood
not found to the same degree among the more complex,
or larger-family situations. (I have no desire to argue the
moral virtues of this rootedness to community or failure
to "make it" in the city; these simply happened to be the
conditions that existed.) But the context of these Union
Park families as new urbanites, in a new kind of city
form, alters the meaning of stability and shelter leading
to instability in the next generation among the intense
family households. For it is clear that the nineteenth-
century, privatistic, sheltering homes Aries depicts,
homes Frank Lloyd Wright describes in his *Autobiog-
raphy* for his early years in Chicago, homes that observers of the time pointed to as a basic element in
the composition of the "dull respectability" of Union
Park, could easily have served as a refuge themselves
from the confusing, dynamic city that was taking shape
all around the confines of Union Park. It indeed seems
natural that middle-class people should try to hold onto
the status position they had in such a disrupting, growing milieu, make little entrepreneurial ventures outside their established jobs, and withdraw themselves into
the comfort and intimacy of their families. Here is the
source of that job "freeze" to be seen in the mobility patterns of fathers in intense-family situations; the bourgeois intensive family in this way became a shelter from
the work pressures of the industrial city, a place where
men tried to institute some control and establish some
comforting intimacies in the shape of their lives, while
withdrawing to the sidelines as the new opportunities of
the city industries opened up. Such an interpretation of
these middle-class families complements, on the side of

the home, the interpretation Richard Hofstadter has made of the middle classes politically, in the latter part of the nineteenth century. He characterizes them as feeling that the new industrial order was not theirs, but had passed them by and left them powerless.[35] It is this peculiar feeling of social helplessness on the part of the fathers that explains what use they made of their family lives.

Confusion in the Desire for Stability

What makes this complex pattern of family stability–instability significant for wider social orientations are the values about work to be found in the middle classes of this era. For here the idea of seizing opportunities, the idea of instability of job tenure for the sake of rising higher and higher, constituted, as John Cawelti has described it,[36] the commonly agreed-upon notion of how sure success could be achieved at this time among respectable people; in the same way, this chance-taking path was presented, in the Horatio Alger novels and the like, as the road into the middle class itself. One should have been mobile in work, then, for this was the meaning of "opportunity" and "free enterprise," but in fact the overwhelming dislocations of the giant cities seem to have urged many men to retreat into the circle of their own families, to try simply to hold onto what they knew they could perform as tasks to support themselves, in the midst of the upheaval of urban expansion.

This is deduction, to be sure, and perhaps it is characteristic of sociologists dealing with history that they speculate where historians would prefer to remain silent and let the ambiguities stand. Yet the body not only of Union Park data, but the memoirs, fictional portraits, and secondary studies of this period seem to me to indicate that such an internally contradictory response to urbanization among the heads of middle-class families is the means by which the differences in social mobility between kinds of families can be explained. Conditions of privacy and comfort in the home weakened the desire to get ahead in the world, to conquer it; since the fathers of the intensive families were retreating from the confusions of city life, their preparation of their sons for work in Chicago became ambiguous, in that they wanted, surely, success for their sons, yet shielded the young, and did not themselves serve as models of successful adaptation. The result of these ambiguities can be seen directly in the work experience of the sons, when contrasted to the group of sons from families which, by virtue either of family form or size, were more complex or less intense. Overlaid on these family patterns was a relatively high rate of hidden marital breakdown in Union Park—one in every ten homes—while the expectation was, again, that such breakdown must not occur, that it was a disgrace morally.

These contradictions in family process gave rise, I believe, to the characteristics of Union Park's reaction to violence during the years 1886 to 1888.

The Feeling of Threat Generated by the Family Experience

In the older version of the "frustration-aggression" syndrome it was assumed that if a social group failed to achieve a certain goal, it searched for an enemy to punish. But the goals of these middle-class people in Union Park were themselves self-contradictory: they wanted success in the work of the city and yet they didn't want it, given the definition of success at that time as an entrepreneurial grasping of opportunities rather than the fruit of plodding and routine service. The goals for the home were also contradictory: they wanted a stable shelter from the confusion and terror of the city, yet somehow they expected their sons, growing up sheltered, to be able to make it in that city world, and the sons of the dominant family groups seemed unable to do so. Divorce was a disgrace, yet there is evidence that one out of every ten of the neighborhood families were involved in a marital separation or desertion, a voluntary condition as opposed to the involuntary break of widowhood. Thus, because the goals of these middle-class people were bred of an equal desire to escape from and succeed in the city, the possibility of a wholly satisfying pattern of achievement for them was denied. The contradictory nature of the family purpose and products was innately frustrating so that a family impulse in one direction inevitably defeated another image of what was wanted. This meant that the sources of defeat were nameless for the families involved; surely these families were not aware of the web of self-contradictions in which in retrospect they seem to have been enmeshed; they knew only that things never seemed to work out to the end planned, that they suffered defeats in a systematic way. It is this specific kind of frustration that would lead to a sense of being overwhelmed, which, in this community's family system, led easily to a hysterical belief in hidden, unknown threats ready to strike at a man at almost any time.

Feeling of Threat and Perceptions of Violence

What I would like to suggest is that this complex pattern of self-defeat explains the character of the Union Park reaction to violence. For the dread of the unknown that the middle classes projected onto their supposed enemies among the poor expressed exactly the condition of self-instituted defeat that was the central feature of the family system in Union Park. And this dread was overwhelming precisely because men's own contradictory responses to living in such a city were overwhelming. They had defined a set of conditions for their lives that inevitably left them out of control. The fact that there was in Union Park a desire to destroy the "immigrant anarchists" or to garrison the neighborhood against them, as a result of the incidents of violence, was important in that it offered an outlet for personal defeats, not just for anger against lawbreakers. This response to violence refused to center on particular people, but rather followed the "path of hysterical reaction," in Freud's phrase, and centered on an abstract class of evildoers. For the fear of being suddenly overwhelmed from the outside was really a sign that one was in fact in one's own life being continually overwhelmed by the unintended consequences, or "latent consequences" as Merton calls them, of what one did.[37] By blaming the urban poor for their lawlessness, these middle-class people were expressing a passion for retribution that had little to do with riots or thefts. The retribution was rather in the nature of what Erikson calls a "cover object" for hostility, an expression of inability to deal with the issues of one's own life, of mobility and stability in the city: the fear in these middle-class people was that if they were to act entrepreneurially in the work world they might be destroyed, yet their desire was to make it big suddenly. The desire to escape to the safety of the simple home of father, mother, and children became, unexpectedly, a crippling shield when the sons went out into the world.

This dilemma, expressed in the terrible fear of attack from the unbridled masses, was also related to the fear of falling into deep poverty that grew up in urban middle-class families of this time. To judge from a wide range of novels in the latter half of the nineteenth century there was a dread among respectable people of suddenly and uncontrollably falling into abject poverty; the Sidwells in Thackeray's *Vanity Fair* plummet from wealth to disorganized penury in a short space of time; Lily Bart's father, in Edith Wharton's *Age of Innocence,* is similarly struck down by the symbol of entrepreneurial chance in the industrial city, the stock market. This feeling of threat from the impersonal, unpredictable workings of the city economy was much like the sense of threat that existed in the Union Park families, because the dangers encountered in both cases were not a person or persons one could grapple with, but an abstract condition, poverty, or family disorder that was unintended, impersonal, and swift to come if the family should once falter. Yet what one *should* do was framed in such a self-contradictory way that it seemed oneself and one's family were always on the edge of survival. In this way, the growth of the new industrial city, with its uncertainties and immense wastes of human poverty not all to be dismissed as personal failures, could surely produce in the minds of middle-class citizens, uneasy about their own class position, living out from the center of town, the feeling that some terrible force from below symbolized by the poor, the foreigner, was about to strike out and destroy them unless they did something drastic.

The demographic reaction among most of the families to the eruption of violence bears out this interpretation of events. With the exception of the upwardly mobile, extended-family sons, most family members did not try to flee the community as a response to the threats of riot and the organized wave of crime. The demographic movement mirrored a renewed feeling of community solidarity in the face of violence, a solidarity created by fear and a common dread of those below. Again, it is significant that the group that did not show this pattern of "sticking out the trouble" is the generation of young family members who lived in more complex family circumstances than the majority, and who achieved, on the whole, greater occupational gains than the majority.

The relations between family life and the perception of violence in this Chicago community could be formed into the following general propositions. These were middle-class families enormously confused in what they wanted for themselves in the city, considered in terms of their achievements in the society at large and in terms of their emotional needs for shelter and intimacy; their schema of values and life goals was in fact formed around the issues of stability and instability as goals in a self-contradictory way. The result of this inner contradiction was a feeling of frustration, of not really being satisfied, in the activities of family members to achieve *either* patterns of stability or mobility for themselves. The self-defeat involved in this process led these families naturally to feel themselves threatened by overwhelming, nameless forces they could not control, no matter what they did. The outbreak of violence was a catalyst for them, giving them in the figure of the "other," the stranger, the foreigner, a generalized agent of disorder and disruption.

It is this process that explains logically why the people of Union Park so quickly found a communally acceptable villain responsible for violence, despite all the ambiguities perceived in the actual outbreaks of the disorders themselves; this is why the villain so quickly identified

was a generalized, nonspecific human force, the embodi-
ment of the unknown, the outside, the foreign. This is
why the people of Union Park clung so tenaciously to
their interpretation, seemed so willing to be terrorized
and distraught.

If the complex processes of family and social mobility
in Union Park are of any use in understanding the great
fear of disorder among respectable, middle-class urbanites of our own time, their import is surely disturbing.
For the nature of the disease that produced this reaction
to violence among the industrial middle classes was not
simply a matter of "ignorance" or failure to understand
the problems of the poor; the fear was the consequence,
rather, of structural processes in the lives of the Union
Park families themselves. Thus for attitudes of people
like the Union Park dwellers to change, and a more
tolerant view of those below to be achieved, nothing so
simple as more education about poor people, or to put
the matter in contemporary terms, more knowledge
about Negroes, would have sufficed. The whole fabric of
the city, in its impact on staid white-collar workers, would
have to have been changed. The complexity and the diversity of the city itself would need to have been stilled
for events to take another course. But were the disorder
of the city absent, the principal characteristic of the industrial city as we know it would also have been absent.
These cities were powerful agents of change, precisely
because they replaced the controlled social space of village and farm life with a kind of human settlement too
dense and too various to be controlled.

And it comes to mind that the New Right fears of the
present time are as deeply endemic to the structure of
complex city life as was the violent reaction to violence
in Union Park. Perhaps, out of patterns of self-defeat in

the modern middle classes, it is bootless to expect right-wing, middle-class repression to abate simply through resolves of goodwill, "education about Negroes," or a change of heart. The experience of these bourgeois people of Chicago one hundred years ago may finally serve to make us a great deal more pessimistic about the chances for reason and tolerance to survive in a complex and pluralistic urban society.

1. Henry David, *The Haymarket Affair* (New York, 1936), p. 198.

2. See Foster Rhea Dulles, *A History of American Labor* (New York, 1949), passim.

3. *Chicago Daily Tribune*, May 4, 1886, pp. 1, 2.

4. See the full account in the *Chicago Daily Tribune*, May 5, 1886, p. 1.

5. David, p. 226.

6. *Chicago Daily Tribune*, May 6, 1886, p. 3.

7. *Chicago Daily Tribune*, May 7, 1886, p. 8.

8. Ibid.

9. *Chicago Daily Tribune*, February 9, 1888, pp. 1–2.

10. Ibid., p. 4.

11. Ibid., pp. 1–2.

12. See the statements of the Union Park fathers in *Chicago Daily Tribune*, February 9, 1888, p. 2.

13. *Chicago Daily Tribune*, February 9, 1888, pp. 1–2.

14. Ibid.

15. Ibid.

16. G. Le Bon, *The Crowd: A Study of the Popular Mind* (London, 1909).

17. It is interesting that Le Bon was led by this route into looking later in his life for a different set of psychological "instincts" in crowds than in individuals.

18. George Rudé, *The Crowd in History, 1730–1840* (New York, 1954) and Charles Tilly, *The Vendée* (Cambridge, Mass., 1964).

19. L. Chevalier, *Classes Laborieuses et Classes Danguereuses* (Paris, 1958).

20. I understand Chevalier is now more convinced of the "rationality" hypothesis. See, as one indication of this, the writings on Belleville in L. Chevalier, *Les Parisiens* (Paris, 1967).

21. J. Dollard, L. Boob, J. Miller, E. Mower, J. Sears, et al., *Frustration and Aggression* (New Haven, 1939), p. 1.

22. See "Democracy and Social Structure in Pre-Nazi Germany" in Parsons, *Essays in Sociological Theory* (rev. ed., Glencoe, Ill., 1954).

23. See Seymour Martin Lipset, *Political Man*, Pt. I, Chap. 4 (New York, 1960).

24. This theory, widely expressed in the press by amateur sociologists, explains the phenomenon neatly as a whole, but explains nothing of the particulars of class jealousy or fear.

25. Stephan Thernstrom and Lynn Lees, work in progress (description to be found in Joint Center *Bulletin* of 1968). The measures are also relatable to the social class categories used by D. V. Glass in his study of intergenerational social mobility in Britain; Part III of *Social Mobility in Britain*, D. V. Glass, ed. (London, 1954).

26. Talcott Parsons and Robert Bales, *Family*, Chap. 1 (Glencoe, Ill., 1955).

27. See Charles Tilly, *"Migration to an American City"* (unpublished manuscript on file at Joint Center for Urban Studies) for an excellent discussion of migration patterns.

28. There were, of course, no two-generation households in the single-member families.

29. P. Blau and O. D. Duncan, *The American Occupational Structure* (New York, 1967).

30. *Families Against the City* (Cambridge, Mass., 1970).

31. Phillipe Aries, *Centuries of Childhood* (New York, 1965).

32. Parsons and Bales, Chap. 1.

33. Bernard Wishy, in *The Child and the Republic* (Philadelphia, 1967), has material relevant to this idea for America in the late nineteenth century.

34. See Sennett, *Families Against the City*, Chap. 9, for a review of this literature.

35. Richard Hofstadter, *The Age of Reform* (New York, 1958).

36. John Cawelti, *Apostles of the Self-Made Man* (Chicago, 1965).

37. The Union Park situation was, in fact, a classic case of Merton's theory of latent consequences.

AFTERWORD
Norman Birnbaum

It might be helpful to close this volume with some thoughts on the intellectual dimensions of these essays. I can begin by discussing their effect on a sociologist like myself whose interests have a somewhat different focus. As a political sociologist (in the sense that my work has been an attempt to develop a critical understanding of the conflicts of industrial society), I often have had recourse to the inquiries of social historians and historical sociologists. Indeed, I have developed a certain skepticism as to whether these categories are in fact separable. For instance, in the historical sketch that is a large part of my recent *The Crisis of Industrial Society,* I discussed the differential development of the class systems of the Western nations, their distinctive internal components, and the political traditions that shaped the relations of the classes, the selective assimilation of industrial technology and urbanism. In an attempt, neither desperate nor quite serene, to save what could be saved of the Marxist legacy, I treated the destruction of the peasant and artisan communities of Europe, the rise of a working class with its own internal schisms but also with its own cohesiveness, the displacement of the older bourgeoisie by entrepreneurs and then by managers, the rise of the new classes. My focus was global: the essays represented in this anthology are correctives, administered by concrete and painstaking scholarship, to my kind of intellectual endeavor.

My reference has been to social classes, but the studies in this volume deal with the city. Precisely, the industrial city has been the *via regis* for the historical ascent of the class system, not alone in the West but in those parts of the Third World in which traditional societies are being dislocated and destroyed. The cultural dynamism and moral fluidity of the city, its concentration of economic activities, the political antagonism of the economic groups, their spatial and social interdependence and interpenetration, make of urban history our best means for visualizing the crystallization of class relations, their concretization in routine. The volume's studies in urban history, then, are contributions to our understanding of the armature as well as of the texture of industrial society as a whole.

Three major points emerge from the extremely varied (and often complex and dense) papers in the collection. (1) The United States, insofar as major aspects of its past are concerned, remains an unknown country. Many of the essays deal with critical aspects of our past which hitherto have been but cursorily explored. We are at the beginning of a voyage of self-discovery that may yet revise some of our notions of our social provenance. (2) The insertion of the dimension of time in the analysis of urban social structures illuminates the limitations, indeed, the fragilities, of many of our conceptions of urban social organization under industrialization. (3) The combination of historical analysis and quantitative social research technique, as employed in these papers, is often highly productive; however, it can obscure as many problems as it solves. Let us consider these matters in turn.

The debate on the different political consequences of industrialization and urbanization in Western Europe and the United States has not been resolved by these contributions, but they have added a new sharpness to our formulations of the problem. It has been a commonplace that the very openness of American society, which permitted the relatively limitless development of the pro-

ductive forces, also inhibited the reactions against un-
restricted capitalism so evident in Europe. The American
working class, ever renewed by immigration, profited not
alone from the expanding wealth of the economy but
from its expansion of opportunities. It did not, therefore,
develop an anticapitalist movement of a European type.
Some of the recent work on mobility (by Bendix and Lipset, Blau and Duncan, S. M. Miller, and Rogoff) has made
the comparison between the two continents more difficult of explanation: the burden of these findings is that
there was no appreciable difference in rates of mobility
between American and European variants of industrial
society in the nineteenth and twentieth centuries. This
volume offers, at the very least, a refinement of our perspectives.

The essays by Blumin, Griffen, and Thernstrom,
among others, show that the mobility of different groups
within the American working class was very variable.
Ethnic and religious context, the structure of opportunities (including, of course, changes in the distribution
of occupations and in the organization of production and
exchange), stages in the development of nineteenth-century American capitalism, the particular character of
city and neighborhood, separately influenced the specific
mobility rates of the groups scrutinized by the authors.
With the advance of the nineteenth century, industrialization resulted in a contraction in the number of independent artisans and craftsmen, but large-scale immigration
enabled the native-born American—or, more precisely,
important numbers of them—to better their positions.
They became skilled workers or foremen, moved into the
clerical middle class, or even struck out as entrepreneurs
(Gutman has some evidence on this last point, and his
work again constitutes an addition of surprising detail to

a landscape we thought we knew). If Blumin's paper, for
instance, offers telling data on the larger size of even
small-scale production units and on the declining numbers of independent craftsmen, Thernstrom's tells us that
the native-born and their offsrping were better placed
to profit from the new situation. The disparity of experience within the American working class, then, might
serve as an alternative explanation for the absence of a
socialist consciousness. In Europe, the labor aristocracy
often assumed the leadership of a (relatively) ethnically
homogeneous working class. In America, the labor aristocracy preferred to exploit its favored position.

The authors, let it be said, offer little or no data on the
self-consciousness of the nineteenth-century urban working class (or of urban groups). Instead, they extrapolate
from their findings concerning external indexes of social
position to hypothesized states of political and social consciousness. Surely, qualitative materials (contemporary
observations, letters, political discourse of one or another
kind) are available which would make this extrapolation
something other than hypothetical. And we could have
been spared (with all respect for the many merits of the
author's contribution) the demonstration by Katz that,
contrary to orthodox Marxism, a class is not a class until
it attains consciousness of itself. Marx himself drew the
distinction between a class in and of itself *(an sich)* and
a class consciously acting on its own behalf *(für sich)*. Further, as Marx's own writings and his *Enquête Ouvrière* of
1880 (reproduced in Bottomore and Rubel, *Karl Marx,
Selected Writings in Sociology and Social Philosophy*)
show, the old sage had a high degree of appreciation of the
necessity of obtaining empirical data on working-class
consciousness. For historians, some of our authors have
proceeded in a curiously ahistoric manner.

One factor is adduced by the authors, in general, as a cause of the political acceptance by the new working class of the American socioeconomic system: the visibility of those who were mobile and prosperous. Gutman, in his description of the accession to entrepreneurship by (Anglo-Saxon) artisans, poses the problem as a question. The question remains—the more so as much of the data (Blumin's and Griffen's are very persuasive on this score) suggests that nineteenth-century cities manifested a very considerable degree of residential segregation by occupation and income, as well as by ethnic grouping. This very finding makes tenuous the assertion of the visibility of the opportunity for mobility. What was visible were the tangible signs of social superordination and subordination. The new pattern of the industrial city destroyed the curious combination of social heterogeneity and spatial homogeneity that constituted the preindustrial city. The findings of these studies suggest, without quite intending to do so, that the class society in its modern urban form is incompatible with that mixing of the classes so commended to us by some contemporary social planners.

Some of the volume's studies have the merit of analyzing the internal structure of the social groups occupying the city's space. In particular, the inquiries on family structure show how the social relationships of production and the larger processes of urban life were in some cases reinforced, in others attenuated, by familial organization. Lees' work on the continuity of Irish family ties in the emigration to England is striking. Here, the substitution of countrymen for kinsmen allowed an equivalent of the original extended household system to maintain itself as a source of support and moral cohesion in new and disturbing circumstances. Scott's work on the glassblowers in Provence is a demonstration of the indispensability of familial tightness to a migrant community. Further, the group's very patterns of occupational succession were familial: it was a generational unit that accomplished the move into the middle class. The very strength of familial organization in this artisan group may have enabled these families to move from a preindustrial style of life to bourgeois occupations without passing through the stage of industrial work itself. (The autonomy expressed in the glassblowers' cooperative in Albi was, presumably, a reflection of as well as a contribution to this singular independence of the usual condition of the industrial workers.)

Sennett's study, by contrast, suggests that a tight-knit familial system can lead to refusal of or inadaptation to the possibilities of mobility. His depiction of an angry and privatized group, using home and neighborhood as retreats from a world become incomprehensible and threatening, employs psychological hypotheses to interpret the external indexes of family size, occupational pattern, residential propinquity, and political action. Sennett was rather vigorously criticized for this at the conference, but implicit (and often ad hoc) psychological hypotheses were used in their own work by many of his critics. Nevertheless, one would wish to see in the future a precise treatment, possibly by way of content analysis with psychological categories, of the attitudinal materials mentioned by Sennett: diaries, letters, memoirs.

The persuasiveness of the inquiries into the family contrast with a singular omission in the collection: there is very little discussion of neighborhood organization. The point is important: neighborhood presumably served as a link between family (where status as well as cultural and and material possibility was given by the occupation of the household head) and community. Indeed we also suffer from too little attention to the communal aspects of urban social structure in the nineteenth century. To what extent were these cities societies in which a minimal set of common beliefs, of solidarities, and reciprocities, defined or established a mode of living together for their inhabitants? To what extent, conversely, were they ecological aggregations, systems for facilitating exchanges between groups sharing a physical and social space but doing so mechanically? Classical social theory (we think, of course, of Toennies on the distinction between Gemeinschaft and Gesellschaft) had a definite answer to the question. A new generation, however, might well take as its task the reexamination of the actual state of affairs in the nineteenth century.

Lees, for the London Irish, does tell us much about the distribution of this group in London—but, again, the discussion of life in London Irish neighborhoods in the nineteenth century is sparse. Others (Schnore and Knights, Griffen) deal with residential differentiation and segregation, but tell us little about the content of neighborhood relationships. Frisch writes of a change in the conception of urban community in Springfield, attendant upon the decline in artisan participation in city government and a certain change in the balance of political participation by elite groups. His observations are highly suggestive, but a detailed analysis of the structure of perceptions and conceptions of community—as manifested by different groups in Springfield—would have been welcome. Maingot magnifies the scale of inquiry, in his contrast between an urbanized and nonurban nation, to probe the issue of community consciousness. But the magnification has problems of its own: there is more social matter to be seen, but its clarity is not therefore sharper. Scott confronts the issue more precisely, with an analysis that demonstrates a reciprocal relationship between the growth of a distinctive working-class politics and working-class

settlement in an urban community. The reformist socialism that grew out of the original anarchosyndicalism of
the French working-class movement may indeed, like German Social Democracy and British Labourism, owe much
of its eventual reformist temper to local victories in those
urban milieus where the working class could affect politics.

Briefly, we are led by these papers to suppose that a
form of consciousness of community must have been a
major element in the emergence of a distinctive urban
consciousness in the nineteenth century. It surely affected
perceptions of the permeability and sharpness—as well as
of the durability—of class distinctions originating in the
process of production. Ideas of community conceivably
could have modified the impact of deprivation—or
heightened it by collision with notions of local social
unity. The papers point in the direction of new inquiries.
To what extent was the nineteenth-century city a unified
social entity in the minds of its inhabitants, and to what
extent did its spatial elongation and class segregation reflect and strengthen a conviction of the decomposition
of previous social bonds, the failure of anything else to
replace them?

The papers, then, point to as many problems as they
solve—indeed, to more. What methodological reflections
do they evoke? The editors, in their Introduction, seem
to think that a rapprochement of sociological and historical method is under way. Perhaps—but is this necessarily a desideratum? The sociological method in question, upon examination, consists of certain notions of
quantification and therewith of comparability of observations which depend upon (as Katz sees) high degrees of
continuity and standardization in the observed milieus.
The application of categories designed to elicit quantified

data from given historical sequences presupposes no discontinuity in the units to be compared through the duration of the sequence. The authors have been remarkably careful to specify the limits of their techniques (for instance, in noting the changes in the content and context of craftsmanship over time in the nineteenth century). We may ask, however, whether the availability of these techniques has not dictated the questions asked. Public opinion polling of the dead is not likely to prove very fruitful: the ascertainment of community sentiment cannot be accomplished by quantitative means in this case, and yet its ascertainment would have enabled us to assess some of the authors' extrapolations from phenomena of a more quantitative kind, like mobility rates, the accumulation of property, and residential and social segregation. The study of the urban phenomenon as a social totality would have been much enhanced.

A second methodological issue, no less troubling, arises. The assumption of the comparability of units rests on some notion of the rightness of fit of certain categories. It is generally agreed that categories arbitrarily taken from one set of historical circumstances and applied to another will not work, or (worse than an obvious failure) will distort the results of historical inquiry. The reconstruction of urban realities in the nineteenth century with the aid of units of measurement and conceptions of a social-psychological kind (ideas of the effects of mobility, notions of communal ties, hypotheses on social motivation generally) derived from contemporary social research entails the danger of circularity. We may assume precisely that which is to be proven: the extent to which the constituent elements of twentieth-century social life were present in the nineteenth.

When all is said, these papers represent a contribution

to the solution of a problem as troubling to sociology as it is fundamental to it: the insertion of the dimension of time in systematic analysis. This obviously entails something more than the study of the past (however welcome that may be). It requires the development of conceptions and techniques for the study of change in social structures over time. The authors of these papers have proceeded cautiously, in the first instance by calling our attention to qualitative changes in the objects of their inquiries over time (as in the notion of "gentleman" or the associated socially accepted categories of status placement), and secondly by specifying the precise dimensions of their samplings from history: time, place, and the elements of the situations under scrutiny. No amount of methodological refinement can substitute, in the last analysis, for the disciplined imagination necessary for the reconstruction of the past and for the seizure of the inner processes and patterns of change. It can aid, however, in the disciplining of the imagination. The present studies have enlarged our vision and disciplined it at the same time: their very difficulties and lacunae point forward.